The Abingdon Creative Preaching Annual 2014

The Abingdon Creative Preaching Annual

Jenee Woodard
Editor of textweek.com

Abingdon Press
Nashville

To Jaie, who knows the value of a good story;
and to Phil, the wisdom, opportunity, and light of my life

CONTENTS

July

August

September

October

November

December

Introduction

What is "creative preaching"? And why would one be interested in a print-based journal for creative preaching in 2014?

Creativity has become identified with new forms, whether they are new forms of music, presentation, information gathering, or expression. When we think about being "creative preachers," we automatically tend to think toward a method of expression with which we may be familiar outside the church, or which may be "common with the young," as if by using these forms, we are automatically being creative. Creativity seems to mean using the media-of-the-minute to express the gospel so we can reach a "new generation" or "meet people where they are." We step down from the pulpit, encourage tweeting during the sermon, turn up the volume on the rock band's speakers, welcome those dressed most casually, serve coffee, and pull down a large screen from the ceiling. Is this the heart of creativity in preaching? Or does this sometimes become yet another "formula" and the opposite of an honest encounter with scriptural text that is then communicated, in whatever form, honestly to hearers who come from various places, cultures, and lifestyles? Do we sometimes put so much energy into the form of our presentation that we forget that creativity lies, first, in our own honest encounter with Scripture, one that often is anything *but* creative because we jump so quickly to media which expresses...what? Do we take the time to think creatively about what it is we're trying to express?

This volume is about this "forgotten" part of the process. Here you will find diverse paths *into* Scripture. You will find new ways to think about Scripture, written by people with whom you will not always agree. You will find short ideas with which you can converse as you "live" Scripture each week—as you dive in and wrestle with the ideas in Scripture and ways other Christians understand them today and have understood them throughout the centuries. You will be invited to wrestle with what these scriptures have meant to others in their own situations and times, and then to think about what the Scriptures are saying to you and to your own congregations.

This is the heart of creative preaching. It is not in finding the newest manner of expression, but rather in placing oneself deeply in conversation with those with whom one may not automatically converse. It's about understanding diverse expression of Scripture through poetry, through exegesis, through hymn, through liturgy, through honest wrestling with what a passage means and has meant within specific places and times. This volume contains short, "digestible" approaches to this part of the preaching process—the part that sometimes gets lost in our rush to be "relevant."

As I read these contributions, I think about the people who have written them, the places they have been, the reasons they have expressed their understanding of Scripture in the ways they have expressed them. I enter into conversation with all of them and imagine them in conversation with one another. And then, I think about my own communities of faith and faithfulness. How are they or we approaching these texts this week? What is God saying to *us* through these words—not necessarily what has God said to others, though that is part of it. But what is God saying to *us* this week? How are the examples in this journal part of the discussion among God, Scripture, and our own congregation this week?

This volume is not necessarily a place to "grab a sermon." It's a place to be in conversation with some very interesting people as they have wrestled with Scripture in their own contexts, in their own ways, within their own congregations and communities. It's a place to find different sorts of expression which may spark ideas about communicating the gospel through your own strengths of communication as well as the kinds of communication in which folks in your communities can hear the Word of God most clearly. It is a weekly community in which you can live as you seek to hear God's Word for your own community, and then to create what that communication will become each week.

Some of these ideas may seem challenging to you or may not be right for your congregation. If we have clearly represented some of the diversity in today's church, this will almost necessarily be the case. But all of our congregations include folks who struggle with these ideas—if not with these words, then in thoughts much like these. How do we speak to them each week? How do we create an atmosphere where these people, too, hear God's Word for them each and every week? It is our hope that this journal will help you wrestle with these ideas each week—with the diversity within your own communities and how your own deep encounters with the texts can help you be a truly creative preacher—one who speaks to many and brings the Word to life within your own community, no matter what media does it best.

The Table of Contents (pp. 7–11) lists not only the date of each week's entry but also the liturgical season, the proper number, where appropriate (from the Revised Common Lectionary), and the Scripture texts, acting as Scripture index as well. The Conversation Partner Index includes brief biographies of the wonderful contributors to this volume and indicates where in the book you can find their writings.

Finally, the Online Media and Other Helpful Resources list at the end of the book offers some Internet links to possibilities for finding expression of themes through music, film, art, and other media. These can be very helpful for presentations of the texts each week. But, I would not start there. I would begin with reading and thinking through the ideas presented in these pages for each week. Before deciding how to express the gospel creatively, I invite you to immerse yourself in deeper expressions of how differently diverse folks have understood these texts each week. From this, I believe strongly, comes truly creative preaching.

Jenee Woodard
Editor, *Abingdon Creative Preaching Annual 2014*
Curator, textweek.com

January 5
Epiphany (Year A)

Isaiah 60:1-6; Psalm 72:1-7, 10-14; Ephesians 3:1-12; Matthew 2:1-12

Rick Morley

Matthew 2

In contrast to the lowly and rugged shepherds who are bidden to come to the newborn Christ in Luke's Gospel, Matthew tells the familiar tale of the magi who follow the wandering star. Matthew doesn't tell us exactly what nation they come from or even how many of them there are, but the picture Matthew paints is quite clear that these are some strange people to be walking around Judea.

They are certainly Gentiles, most probably pagan, and quite possibly practitioners of the ancient magical art of astrology. In any event, they aren't in danger of being identified as poster-boys for faith and righteousness in ancient Israel.

And yet…it is they, not the temple priests and teachers of the law, who know that the Messiah has come. It is they, not King Herod, who want to go and actually pay homage to the newborn Savior.

When the wandering star stands still in the sky, signaling that they are at their destination, they are "overwhelmed with joy," and, when they are brought into the home of the holy family and the Lord Jesus, they fall on their knees.

The Magi may have been seen as a strange lot walking through the ancient Holy Land, but they stand early in the Gospel of Matthew as a testament to the fact that no one is beyond the reach of the Good News. No one is so strange and foreign that he or she can't make a way to Christ, or so blind that he or she cannot be drawn in by his most wondrous light.

And for that, the presence and astounding acts of faithfulness of the magi in the second chapter of Matthew brings me much comfort and relief. For, if they can make it, then so can I.

Teri Peterson
http://clevertitlehere.blogspot.com

Matthew 2

Each night they looked at the sky, gazing at stars, hoping for a sign. Why would they be looking? Why do any of us look? During these darkest days of the year, light is fleeting. During dark times in our lives, light can be almost painful. Sometimes dark is comfortable because light shows the unknown, something we fear. But then again, on a dark and stormy night or a foggy morning, a light can be a life-saver, hope made visible. And light is always stronger than darkness—no matter how small the light, it can't be made darker just because of surrounding darkness. A dark room doesn't put the candle out—in fact, the darker the room, the brighter the candle appears. The same with stars—the darker it is, the brighter the stars appear.

One night, there was a new light. What makes the wise men wise is that they knew this new light was not the thing they were looking for—it was a map, a guidepost, a beacon. Following the star would guide them to perfect light, and so they went. The candles on the Advent wreath are not the light of the world, they are a symbol of that light. The star the wise men followed was not the light, it was the guide to the light. The true splendor and glory were to be found in a child, a helpless wonder in a crib who was joy and peace and light for all the world.

Couldn't we use a star? Where is our guide to the light? Where is the beacon shining in the night? How will we know our way to the manger when we look for the true light of the world, the deeper meaning of God's words "let there be light"?

I suspect each of us could answer this question differently. Some might say we no longer need a star, now that the revelation of God's light has been given to us. Some might say the symbols of our faith—the cross, the table, the baptismal font—are the sign that points the way. Some might say the story of God's work in the world, of God's interaction with people, the story of Scripture, is the guiding star. And all of those are true and good and right.

And yet I wonder...if *we* might be the star? We, the community of God's people, the body of Christ, the gathering of those who have heard the calling. Could we be the star, the candle that gives off even a feeble light, a sign that shows the way? I know the church has often gotten things wrong, done horrible deeds, perpetuated hate and darkness rather than love and light. But I still wonder—are we the beacon that points to the light of the world? And is that where our beacon points? Are we a symbol of hope, a guide to the perfect light? Is it possible that we are the ones we have been waiting and looking for?

Natalie Sims
http://lectionarysong.blogspot.com

General Songs for Epiphany beyond "We Three Kings"...

"Arise Your Light Is Come!" (Ruth Duck)—Good general words of Christ coming to bring justice. I love the idea of mountains bursting in song. A good song for the start of the worship service as it fits many different tunes; I like it sung to ST. THOMAS.

"Every Nation Sees the Glory" (Francis Patrick O'Brien)—Beautiful words and very familiar tune (BEACH SPRING); "...Star sent forth from highest heaven, / dancing light of God's design." Highly recommended! Lyrics, sample sheet music, and nice sound sample (http://www.hymnprint.net/).

"When God Almighty Came to Be One of Us" (Michael Hewlett)—This is a great Christmas and Epiphany song. It's also set to a very easy (and fun!) tune to sing (URQUHART). I especially love verse 3. Lyrics (http://barefootand laughing.blogspot.com/2005/12/merry-christmas.html).

"Will You Come and See the Light?" (Brian Wren)—Excellent Christmas/Epiphany words to the tune KELVIN-GROVE (The Summons) "Will you hide, or decide to meet the light?"

"From a Distant Home / De Tierra Lejana Venimos" (Traditional Puerto Rican carol, translated by Walter Ehret and George K. Evans)—Simple folk tune and pretty standard words of the gifts that the wise men brought. Would be a good change from "We Three Kings."

Recorded Music

"Heavenly Child" (Peter Mayer)—This is a great song from the viewpoint of one of the wise men, particularly for those who have traveled far in their spiritual journey but hold on to the image of the heavenly child. Lyrics and sound sample (http://petermayer.net/music/?id=7).

John Petty
http://progressiveinvolvement.com

Matthew 2:1-12

Matthew introduces us to Herod. Herod became "king of the Jews" in 37 BCE. Thoroughly pro-Roman, Herod couldn't do enough for Caesar Augustus. The "magi" originated in the Persian priestly class. They were sorcerers, fortune-tellers, astrologers. They represent the "wisdom of the east."

The magi tell Herod about the birth of a "king of the Jews"—a title that technically belongs to Herod. (Note that Herod refers to the child as "messiah," not—pointedly—as "king of the Jews.")

The magi have seen his star "at its rising"—*en te anatole*. In response, Herod is *etaraxthe*—agitated, troubled, disquieted, filled with inner turmoil—"and all Jerusalem with him."

Jerusalem is a "company town," dominated by the temple bureaucracy and their overseers, the Romans. A "king of the Jews" other than Herod could be upsetting for business. To paraphrase a popular saying, "Better the devil you know than the messiah you don't."

Herod quizzes the magi on the time the star appeared. This establishes a range of age that will set the stage for Herod's slaughter of the innocents, which follows immediately upon this lection. All born within two years of this "exact time" will be killed.

The word for time here is *chronon*—chronological "business as usual" time, and not *kairos,* which is God's time. In *chronos* time—"business as usual" time—extreme brutality and arbitrary violence is the way.

Chronos time is attended by lies. Herod sends the magi to Bethlehem on a covert mission to supply him information about the child. He wants to "worship" him, he says, but, of course, he really wants to eliminate this rival "king of the Jews." Lying and violence go together. They are "business as usual."

The magi seem to go along with this. They "hear" Herod and do what he says. As they go out, however, the star reappears and guides them to the child. Literally, verse 10 reads: "Seeing the star, they rejoiced exceedingly great joy greatly"—four words in Greek, which pile superlative upon superlative. Contrast this with the defensive and fearful reaction of Herod, whose system is wracked by agitation and inner turmoil.

Gifts were always presented to kings. The gifts of the magi include myrrh, a very expensive perfume used by the Romans to mask the smell of burning corpses. Nero had reportedly burned a massive amount at the funeral of his wife Poppaea. What is Matthew saying with this inclusion of myrrh? Is it a signal that Jesus will be done in by the Romans?

The magi receive a dream from God that tells them to avoid Herod, and they go home "by a different way"—*di' allys idou*. The magi are led and instructed by God onto a new path, not the "business as usual" path of lying and violence, but the different "way"—as Christianity was known in the time of Matthew's writing—of Christ the Lord.

Julia Seymour
http://lutheranjulia.blogspot.com

Matthew 2:1-12

There are names for the wise men. Much ink has been used to talk about the gifts they brought and the significance of those gifts. There are maps of their journey. There has been speculation as to their ethnicity and race. Historical astronomical charts have been consulted, so that we might know the signs they saw and interpreted to know about Jesus' birth.

Whither the writing about Jesus' drawing Gentiles to himself, even from birth? Who will step forward and speak to strangers who are able to (1) discern the birth of a king who will change the world and (2) heed their dreams and the voice of the Spirit? Whence the commentaries and articles on not only the *ability* of God to use all kinds of people but also the *intention* of God to do precisely that?

For many years, Epiphany's "Wise men still seek Him" was the response to Christmas's "Jesus is the reason for the season." Yet, bumper-stickering Epiphany cuts short the meaning of this season of light. How can our hearts "be radiant" or "thrill and rejoice" if we are not willing to open to the reality of what God is revealing to us in this time of growth through revelation (see Isaiah 60:5)?

Let the epiphany of this winter be that Jesus came for all people. Let the understanding thaw our frozen lines of categories of election, perfection, and rejection. Let the light that shines in the darkness illumine the barriers that the church has put around the understanding of salvation, so that they might be torn down and abandoned. Let the inspiration of the Spirit reveal the gifts that we can bring to honor the King of all.

In a season of history, we can review what has been written about the wise men. Or we can truly look at their story, at the gift of the simply written word, and realize the gift of faithful action into which God drew them. And we can pray that we might receive the grace to be used in the same way.

Thom Shuman
http://lectionaryliturgies.blogspot.com

Call to Worship
We gather wondering, "Where will we find the Bethlehem baby?"
We will find him in the laughter of children, in the wisdom of grandparents.
We gather asking, "where will we find the Child of Christmas?"
We will find the Child where the needy are blessed, where the oppressed are set free.
We gather wanting to know, "where will we find the Christ who has come for us?"
We will find hope where grace overwhelms fear,
where love shatters hatred, where joy fills all people.

Prayer of the Day
We have heard
of your grace,
Star Shaper;
from those set free
from injustice;
from children
who whisper of your joy;
from greeters
of dawn's fresh start;
from late risers
listening to the stories
of the needy.

We have heard
of your Light,
Bright Star of the morning:
which can illumine
the shadows of our lives;

which can show
the path to God's heart;
which can point the way
to where we become
servants of the gospel.

We have heard
of your promised peace,
Wisdom's Radiance:
which can end war,
as well as heal our hearts;
which can conquer our fears,
and flood us with faith;
which can enter our lives
and overwhelm us with hope.

We have heard of you, God in Community, Holy in One, and will proclaim your glory to all, even as we pray, saying, **Our Father...**

Call to Reconciliation
Why do we huddle in the shadowed corners of life, rather than running to the Light of life? Why do we love the wrong we do rather than grasping the good news offered to us? As we struggle with such questions, let us speak to God of all we have failed to do, seeking hope and grace as we pray together,

Unison Prayer of Confession
We search for your light, Star Caster, but too often end up settling for the dimness of temptation. Our motives for seeking to find Christ are not always pure, for we expect him to fulfill our desires, rather than your hopes for us. We want the gifts of wealth, health, success, fulfillment, rather than those of servanthood, of compassion, of peace.

Forgive us, Shaper of our lives, that we are so foolish to put our needs ahead of your grace. Help us to be like those wise people of so long ago, who found hope, instead of a destination; who found grace, instead of gratitude; who found salvation, instead of a sign. As we journey with your Son, our Lord and Savior, Jesus Christ, fill us with the light of your joy and love. *Silence is kept.*

Assurance of Pardon
Up, on your feet! Grace has been poured into our hearts, love has flooded our souls,
the light of hope shines in us.

This is the light which has come to all, the light we will carry and give to everyone we meet. Thanks be to God. Amen.

John Wesley's Notes on the Bible
http://www.ccel.org/ccel/wesley/notes.txt

Matthew 2:1

The title given (the magi) in the original was anciently given to all philosophers, or men of learning; those particularly who were curious in examining the works of nature, and observing the motions of the heavenly bodies. "From the east"—So Arabia is frequently called in Scripture. It lay to the east of Judea, and was famous for gold, frankincense, and myrrh. "We have seen his star"—Undoubtedly they had before heard Balaam's prophecy. And probably when they saw this unusual star, it was revealed to them that this prophecy was fulfilled. "In the east"—That is, while we were in the east.

Karoline Lewis

Matthew 2

So, just what is Herod afraid of? While not a Roman ruler, he was still given a position of power, King Herod, a mighty military leader and building project coordinator extraordinaire. Granted, his reign was over Judea, which was likely not the most desirable or influential regional assignment for a king in the service of Rome, but still, his role and successes are well documented. Can Herod really be that insecure about the rumor of a baby being born who will be king of the Jews? Scared of a child? And all of Jerusalem with him? The answer to these questions is probably a resounding no. Herod is almost certainly not that afraid, unless he has a massive insecurity complex, and it's hard to imagine that *all* of Jerusalem would blink an eye at the prospect of a potential king somewhere down the line. The exaggeration is perhaps best understood as theological hyperbole. And yet, it is a sobering claim on the nature of power.

Threatened by persons or events that might usurp our position or security, our first inclination is to squelch the threat. What does such an indictment of our human propensity for self-preservation have to do with the birth of Jesus and the presence of God? Everything. The story of the wise men from the East, sent to find Jesus at the behest of Herod's fear, reminds us that behind and in the midst of every moment of struggle for power and authority is humanity's fear that power could be shared. This will be one of the reasons for the resistance to Jesus' authority and the eventual removal of it. God's power, however, reveals itself not as "over and against," but as "for the sake of."

January 12
Baptism of the Lord

Isaiah 42:1-9; Psalm 29; Acts 10:34-43; Matthew 3:13-17

Beth Quick
http://bethquick.blogspot.com

Isaiah 42

• "I have put my spirit upon him; / he will bring forth justice to the nations" (v. 1b NRSV). This reminds me of another Isaiah passage (61:1): "The spirit of the Lord is upon me . . . " Both are marking the identity of Jesus, the task to which Jesus is called—at least that is how we (and, to an extent, Jesus) interpret them. This is the role he seeks to fulfill.

• "A bruised reed he will not break" (v. 3). Remember Jesus asking about John the Baptist (Matthew 11:7 NRSV): "What did you go out...to look at? A reed shaken by the wind?"

• "I have taken you by the hand and kept you" (v. 6b). This is no God who sits back and watches from a distance, but an up-close-and-personal God. We are God's, and God wants us to make no mistake about it.

• "To open the eyes that are blind, / to bring out the prisoners" (v. 7). Again, compare this to Luke 4/Isaiah 61.

Psalm 29

• This psalm speaks about God's voice, and visualizes God creating or in relation to a strong and powerful thunderstorm. We see God over the waters, God's glory thundering, breaking the cedars, flashing forth flames, God's voice shaking the wilderness. The psalmist makes God's voice come alive for us.

• What imagery would describe God's voice in your life? I like the process theology metaphor of God's lure, God slowly luring me, calling, until slowly, I follow.

Acts 10

• Peter is speaking to Cornelius and his friends and relatives in Caesarea. Cornelius had been visited by a messenger from God telling him to invite Peter to his home and hear him speak.

• "God shows no partiality" (v. 34 NRSV). Do we get that? Believe it? Preach it? Live and practice it?

• "Preaching peace by Jesus Christ" (v. 36). Ah, the gospel message is a message of peace! Too much of our Christian history seems to counter that claim, but we strive nonetheless to convey the gospel of peace.

• Peter preaches a mini-sermon, all the facts needed to share the good news packed into one blurb. He won't waste this opportunity.

Matthew 3

• "John would have prevented him" (v. 14 NRSV). When and for whom do we play John's role? Assisting others in their ministry journey is extremely important—"proper" as Jesus says, and necessary. If we decline our role, we're preventing others from fulfilling their roles.

• We might all wish for the heavens to part and for a dove to descend and for God to declare in front of all that we are pleasing and beloved in God's sight, but it doesn't usually work quite that way for us. So, how does it work for us? How can we know God loves us? What are the markers and milestones in our lives and ministries?

Melissa Bane Sevier
http://melissabanesevier.wordpress.com

Bruised Reeds He Will Not Break (Isaiah 42)

Here in Kentucky, January 2012 has come beautiful and bright. But December was another story. It certainly wasn't our snowiest on record, but you couldn't have convinced us of that. Every few days, it seemed, we had some kind of frozen precipitation that had to be shoveled, salted, and swept. Days were mostly gray, and the temps were well below normal. Most people will tell you they can put up with the snow, but the freezing rain is a different story. Lovely though it is, ice is scary, heavy, and dangerous. It breaks trees and power lines and makes even a short walk to the mailbox either outright funny or downright frightening.

Gardeners start to pay attention this time of year to winter weather, wondering how it will play out in the spring. A blanket of snow can actually protect roots from super cold nights, but ice can permanently damage shrubs, tender trees, perennials. The problem is, there is no way to know for sure now what sort of lasting problems, if any, will result. One must just wait.

I know a lot of people who felt roughly treated by life at the end of last year, and are entering a new year with some mixture of hope and trepidation. Bruised by the economy, chilled by frozen relationships, weighed down by anxiety, these bright days of sunshine at the cusp of a new year may lift their spirits. What they hope, more than anything, is that they will come out on the other side of winter with some promise of better tomorrows. Change, for the better.

Isaiah wrote about hope in one who would come to bring justice and change, but not in the expected manner. This one would not come in a show of warfare and power, wielding sword to crush whatever and whoever was in the way. No, change would come in gentleness, so that already bruised reeds would not be broken and the dimly burning wick of nearly dead hope would not be extinguished. Isaiah spoke of justice to his own readers, but Christians through the ages have read these words and also seen how Jesus lived them out hundreds of years later.

This morning the weather has turned gray again, and there is a light dusting of snow on the ground. The long-range forecast is a mixture of light snow and cloudy days. Certainly, we'll have more bad weather, perhaps even damaging ice storms. But spring, distant as it now seems, will finally arrive and bring with it the regeneration of earth and plant life.

No matter how long our winter of bad mood, sickness, trouble, depression, and anxiety, there is one who treats us with gentleness even as change is coming, who will not extinguish the dimly burning wicks of our hope and faith, who will not break the bruised reeds of our spirits. In the meantime, we have hope to keep us warm.

Martha Spong
http://marthaspong.com

Psalm 29; Matthew 3

When we go to church, we hope maybe, just maybe, God will have something to say to us, that God will put something we need to hear into words we can understand. Psalm 29 tells us God speaks in things we can see and hear and feel, but does not promise words. The Gospel gives us a God who speaks, but it's not clear if anyone but Jesus hears the Voice.

John is there, baptizing him, perhaps a little warily. He knows the relationship ought to be the other way around, that Jesus has something to give him that he cannot give back in equal measure. So even though it's not clear whether John saw the heavens open up around Jesus or heard the voice of God proclaiming Jesus as a beloved child, John's hesitation tells us he knew this wasn't some ordinary guy coming out to the River Jordan for a cleansing dose of repentance.

It's a funny little conversation they have, an awkward acknowledgment that they stand at the edge of more than a river. They stand at the edge of incarnation, of God's knowing habitation in human flesh.

When you put it into words, it's pretty amazing. And I wonder, did Jesus know what he was getting into when he went to John? If he was God, surely he knew, we might say. But he was human, too, and maybe he had a sense that something was up, and maybe he didn't really know it all the way for sure until he heard the Voice put it into words. "You are dearly loved," said the Voice, on his baptism day.

We may not remember the details of the event. Perhaps we were babies, gently held while a kind hand cupped full of water touched our sweet heads. Perhaps we were older, guided by a strong arm as the water rushed over us. Each baptized Christian has been acknowledged as a member of the same loving family in which Jesus is a dearly loved son. Promises were made, whether for us or by us, to renounce evil and oppression and to follow in the way he laid out for us.

At baptism, we put it into words. We name each baptized person as a child of God. As members of God's family, we have work to do in this life we live. It is a work of faith, a belief in the Christ who came among us and lived a human life, in the Spirit that lights the way we are to follow, and that even in the darkest times, there is a God—there IS a God!—whose Voice calls out that we are dearly loved, too.

Carolyn Winfrey Gillette
http://www.carolynshymns.com/

Down by the Jordan

Down by the Jordan, a prophet named John was baptizing,
Preaching a message the people found bold and surprising:
"God will forgive! Show that you'll change how you live!
Surely God's new day is rising!"

There by the river, the crowd came with great expectation:
"Are you God's Chosen One, sent here to rescue our nation?"
"No!" John replied. "He who is mightier than I
Judges and offers salvation."

Jesus, you went to be baptized along with the others,
Taking your place among sinners, God's lost sons and daughters.
Then with great love, God's Spirit came as a dove!
Your work began in those waters.

Here in the Church, we are baptized and filled with God's Spirit.
Freed and forgiven, we're welcomed with joy! Can you hear it?
This is God's sign! This is how God says, "You're mine!"
Let's take the good news and share it!

NOTES
Scripture Texts: Matthew 3:1-17; Mark 1:1-11; Luke 3:1-22; and John 1:6-8, 14-34.
Tune: LOBE DEN HERREN 14.14.4.7.8 ("Praise Ye the Lord, the Almighty"), *Straisund Ernewerten Gesangbuch,* 1665. Harm. *The Chorale Book for England,* 1863
Text: © 2000 by Carolyn Winfrey Gillette. All rights reserved. Originally published in *Songs of Grace: New Hymns for God and Neighbor* by Carolyn Winfrey Gillette (Nashville: Upper Room Books, 2009), 12.

Rick Morley

Matthew 3

Nearly 1,500 years before Jesus made his way to the Jordan River to be baptized by John, the children of Israel approached Jordan from the east. It was the moment, forty years in the making, when they crossed from the wilderness into the land that God had promised them. When they made their way to the other side of the river they were finally a people who were not only free from Pharaoh's hand; they had a land of their own.

In this dramatic moment, Joshua, who had taken over for Moses, instructed the priests bearing the Ark of the Covenant to step into Jordan's flowing water, and when they did, the water stopped flowing. Just as the Red Sea had been split to allow Israel to cross over, so it was with Jordan's waters.

The momentous nature of this event can't be overstated. Crossing Jordan ended the forty-year sojourn in the wilderness, but even more it marked a new beginning for God's chosen people. One chapter was closing, and another one was about to be written.

John the Baptist could have chosen most anywhere to begin his baptismal ministry, and Jesus could have gone to countless different places to be baptized. But it happened at the River Jordan, the same place where those priestly feet bearing the Ark had once waded into the waters.

At that very spot where the identity of God's People was forged over a thousand years before, and where God was proven once again to be a God who kept his sacred promises, Jesus forged for his faithful people a new identity—in him. And, promises that God had made to generations long gone were beginning to be fulfilled in new and wondrous ways, there in Jordan's waters.

Lowell Grisham
http://lowellsblog.blogspot.com/

Prayers of the People

Presider: Let us pray to our God who gives breath to all people upon earth and spirit to those who walk upon it, that through baptism we may be empowered as God's beloved children to share in the healing and reconciling work of Christ, saying: God shall give strength to the people; God shall give us the blessing of peace.

Litanist: Uphold your chosen servant the Church, O Blessed One, and put your spirit upon her, that she may not grow faint or be crushed until all have known the power of Christ's resurrection. God shall give strength to the people;
God shall give us the blessing of peace.

Let your gentle spirit be upon this nation and upon all in authority throughout the world, that they may share in your work to bring forth justice upon the earth. God shall give strength to the people;
God shall give us the blessing of peace.

Look upon all humanity with your divine compassion, and bring your light to the nations to open the eyes that are blind and to bring from the prison those who sit in darkness. God shall give strength to the people;
God shall give us the blessing of peace.

Visit this community with your indwelling Spirit to declare new things that speak of justice and peace, that we may go about doing good and healing all who are broken or oppressed. God shall give strength to the people;
God shall give us the blessing of peace.

May the heavens open and your Spirit descend upon this congregation, bringing your love and grace to all for whom we pray, especially _____ . Hear our grateful thanks and praise for your manifestation of presence and love in our lives and in the lives of others, giving thanks especially for _____. Welcome with your divine pleasure all who have died, especially _____ , that they may have a place in your eternal domains. God shall give strength to the people;
God shall give us the blessing of peace.

Presider: Gracious and loving God, you have anointed your people with the waters of Baptism and have made us your beloved children: Let your Spirit spread mightily through us, that we may share in the work of your Son, bringing reconciliation and light to all the world in the power of the Holy Spirit, through Jesus Christ our Lord. **Amen.**

John Wesley's Notes on the Bible
http://www.ccel.org/ccel/wesley/notes.txt

Matthew 3:16

Let our Lord's submitting to baptism teach us a holy exactness in the observance of those institutions which owe their obligation merely to a Divine command. Surely thus it becometh all his followers to fulfil all righteousness. Jesus had no sin to wash away. And yet he was baptized. And God owned his ordinance, so as to make it the season of pouring forth the Holy Spirit upon him. And where can we expect this sacred effusion, but in an humble attendance on Divine appointments? "Lo, the heavens were opened, and he saw the Spirit of God"—St. Luke adds, in a bodily form—Probably in a glorious appearance of fire, perhaps in the shape of a dove, descending with a hovering motion, till it rested upon him. This was a visible token of those secret operations of the blessed Spirit, by which he was anointed in a peculiar manner; and abundantly fitted for his public work.

Karoline Lewis

Matthew 3

On this Baptism of our Lord Sunday, congregations most likely expect a sermon on the baptism of Jesus or a general message on the meaning and significance of baptism for the life of a Christian. The problem with these preaching options in the year of Matthew is that the actual baptism of Jesus does not seem to be the point. Rather, the narrative space, at least for Matthew, is given to the exchange between John and Jesus on John's worthiness (or perceived unworthiness) to baptize Jesus. John's question to Jesus, "Who? Me?" encapsulates the irony of the entire good news of Jesus.

If we are honest, our response to God wanting to be with us, to be Immanuel, is the same as John's. That God would choose to be us elicits the same question, "Who? Us?" The radical promise of the incarnation should not wear off this close to Christmas, yet we easily leave it behind and replace it with our doubts, our questions, and even our denial. "God with us" can be tolerated for only so long before we convince ourselves that God's decision can't really be true. John's question to Jesus reminds us that we move too quickly away from the claim of Christmas and risk forgetting why Christmas occurred in the first place. Could a sermon on this text create a new experience of the meaning of *Immanuel* through the lens of baptism? How can baptism be another expression of "God with us"?

January 19

2nd Sunday after Epiphany

Isaiah 49:1-7; Psalm 40:1-11; 1 Corinthians 1:1-9; John 1:29-42

John Wesley's Notes on the Bible
http://www.ccel.org/ccel/wesley/notes.txt

Isaiah 49:3

"O Israel"—As the name of David is sometimes given to his successors, so here the name of Israel may not unfitly be given to Christ, not only because he descended from his loins; but also because he was the true and the great Israel, who, in a more eminent manner, prevailed with God, as that name signifies, of whom Jacob, who was first called Israel, was but a type.

Ann Scull
http://seedstuff.blogspot.com

A Useful Image

• A photo of my boot on a rock that, of course, goes well with Psalm 40:2 and the Gospel reading. You can find the image at http://seedstuff.blogspot.com.au/2011/01/epiphany-2-january-16-following-with.html (accessed March 22, 2012).

Listening Songs

• Iona, **"Dancing on the Wall"** on *Iona* (Various locations: What Records, UK, 1990), CD Edition. This song is about Jesus calling us to be his disciples and the benefits to us when we respond to his call.

• U2, **"40"** on *War* (Dublin: Island Records, UK, 1983), CD edition, or on *Under a Blood Red Sky* (various locations: Island Records, UK, 1983), CD edition. This song is a rather famous version of Psalm 40 sung as the psalmist would never have imagined it could be sung! U2 often close their concerts with this song and the audience sings along with them. The song is pre-recorded on the *War* album and live on the *Under a Blood Red Sky* album.

• Winans Phase2, **"It's Alright (Send Me)"** on *We Got Next* (USA: Myrrh Records, 1999). This is a song about responding to Jesus' call to ministry. *Discussion Questions:*

1. What is the one thing you would need to know about somebody before you followed them?

2. Have you ever followed somebody (other than Jesus)?

3. What is it about Jesus that made you want to follow him? (This would also make a good interview question for one or two [three or four?] members of your congregation—their answers could take the place of the sermon for the week—you would have to give them prior warning in order for this to work well.)

4. Define *disciple.*

Drama

• **"For Me"** by Keith Stiller, *Drama Resources 2* (Adelaide: Lutheran Publishing House, 1986), 29–30. This is a drama about discipleship.

Stories

- **"The Journey Thus Far"** by Athol Gill, *Life on the Road* (Scottsdale, Pa.: Herald Press, 1989), 11–22. This introductory chapter of a book on discipleship and the messianic lifestyle has some very useful illustrations for introducing or explaining the Gospel reading.
- **"Uncompromising Determination"** by Wayne Rice, *Hot Illustrations for Youth Talks* (El Cajon, Calif.: Youth Specialties, 1994), 214–15. This is a very funny illustration when told well. I matched this story with the Isaiah reading because it talks about how we are valued and how much we matter. It is also a good illustration of how we should stick with God without being distracted.

Prayer/Poem

- **"Deny Self and Imitate Christ"** by Thomas A'Kempis, *Of the Imitation of Christ* (Springdale, Pa.: Whitaker House, 1981), 207. These are very famous words repeated in an old chorus we often sing but worth hearing again—and well matched to the Gospel reading.

Dan Clendenin
http://journeywithjesus.net

1 Corinthians

When I was in high school, my father stopped going to church. He never went back. Whatever else that was, it was an act of bravery, for at our small church in a small town he still dropped us off and picked us up every Sunday (my mother didn't drive). I still remember how awkward that felt, seeing Dad waiting at the curb in his car, seeing and being seen by the neighbors with whom he used to worship. I like to think that my father lost his faith in the church as an institution but not his faith in God or the gospel.

There are good reasons to quit the church. Tops on most people's lists are gross hypocrisy, violence, and intolerance. Other people leave church because they find it irrelevant, mediocre, boring, or perfunctory.

One response to the church's failures is to long for a return to the "golden age" of the earliest believers. Unfortunately, the epistle for this week (1 Corinthians 1:1-9) disabuses us of this romantic fallacy. Paul taught at Corinth for eighteen months (Acts 18:11), and he knew those people well. In his letters to the believers at Corinth Paul addressed numerous ugly issues—sectarian divisions in which each side claimed to be more spiritual than the other, boasting about incest ("and of a kind that does not occur even among pagans," 1 Corinthians 5:1 NIV 1984), lawsuits between fellow Christians, eating food that had been sacrificed to pagan idols, disarray in worship services, and predatory pseudo-preachers who masqueraded as super-apostles.

We should never ignore the church's faults and failures. Rather, we should name them, own up to them, repent of them, and do what we can to correct them. Losing our illusions about church (disillusionment) is necessary and good.

One of our earliest Christian creeds is the Old Roman Creed, dated to the late second century. One of the fragments that predates it simply reads, "I believe in God the Father Almighty, and in Jesus Christ His only Son, our Lord. And in the Holy Spirit, the holy Church, the resurrection of the flesh" (Walter A. Elwell, *Evangelical Dictionary of Theology* [Grand Rapids: Baker, 2001], 87). Such early creeds served as baptismal confessions, as the basic instructional material used for teaching, as a summary of our faith, and as affirmations used in public worship. The centrality of the church in such a succinct expression of faith serves as an important reminder. And so with the Benedictine nun Joan Chittister, I aspire to be what she calls "a loyal member of a dysfunctional family" (*Called to Question: A Spiritual Memoir* [Lanham, Md.: Sheed & Ward, 2004], 135).

Suzanne Guthrie
http://www.edgeofenclosure.org

"Come and See" (John 1)

Love at first sight. What else can account for the disciples' eagerness? "Where are you staying?" "Where do you abide?" "Where are you going?"

The enigmatic answer is, "Come and see." No simple answer suffices for the complex, beautiful, and terrifying transformation awaiting the questioner. "If you come with me you will see the dwelling place prepared for you" (John 14:3 RSV). Nothing else is revealed. And there's nothing to do but follow the mystery.

When I fall in love my old values, smaller goals, dreams, ideas, interpretations of reality fade in light of the allure of the unknown drawing me toward the fulfillment of my spiritual destiny.

Darest Thou Now O Soul

Walt Whitman

Darest thou now, O Soul,
Walk out with me toward the Unknown Region,
Where neither ground is for the feet, nor any path
   to follow?

No map, there, nor guide,
Nor voice sounding, nor touch of human hand,
Nor face with blooming flesh, nor lips, nor eyes,
   are in that land.

I know it not, O Soul;
Nor dost thou—all is a blank before us;
All waits, undream'd of, in that region—
   that inaccessible land.

Till, when the ties loosen,
All but the ties eternal, Time and Space,
Nor darkness, gravitation, sense, nor any bounds,
   bound us.

Then we burst forth—we float,
In Time and Space, O Soul—prepared for them;
Equal, equipt at last—(O joy! O fruit of all!) them
   to fulfill, O Soul.

Leaves of Grass (Philadelphia: David McKay, 1891–92), 338.

Rick Morley

John 1

In the prologue to John, the Word of God was not *comprehended* by the darkness (v. 5), was not *known* by the world (v. 10), and wasn't even *accepted* by God's own people (v. 12). But, when the Light, the Word, became flesh, his glory was evident (v.14). The Incarnation makes all the difference.

Of course, that's the very center of faith in John's Gospel: We receive the One who has come among us, the Incarnation of God. In John 1:29-42 that responsive, receptive brand of faith is demonstrated by John the Baptist. Unlike the elemental forces of the universe and the vast expanse of humanity, John the Baptist sees Jesus and immediately identifies him. He is the Lamb of God. He is the one who takes away the sin of the world.

John is usually identified as the one chosen by God to make way for the Messiah to come, and here he clearly fulfills that role. But John the Baptist also provides an example of what faithfulness looks like: he sees Jesus, he identifies Jesus as Messiah, and he proclaims Jesus to those around him. We also see how infectious this kind of faith can be; because of John's witness Andrew approached his brother Peter with the good news that the Messiah had come.

The kind of faith we see extolled in the prologue, and the kind of faith we see lived out in the life of John the Baptist, isn't an exercise in navel-gazing. It's an active faith. Just as God's love for us is active in creation and in the giving of his own Son.

Paul Nuechterlein
http://girardianlectionary.net/

John 1:29-42

"Look, the Lamb of God, who takes away the sin of the world!" (John 1:29b NIV). How we understand "Lamb of God" makes all the difference in the world. If we understand Jesus as God's Lamb sacrificed in our place to appease God's retributive justice, then we remain trapped in the sacrificial logic of Anselm's doctrine of atonement.

But if we hear "Lamb of God" as Jesus inviting us to *invert* sacrificial logic, when he quotes Hosea 6:6, "Go and learn what this means: 'I desire mercy, not sacrifice'" (Matt 9:13a NIV), we must look for a deeper understanding of such an inversion—which is now available through the anthropological work of Stanford scholar René Girard. Girard locates the sacrificial logic deep within the origins of *homo sapiens*, where it constitutes an "original sin" that continues to dictate the power structures of human community. From the very beginnings as a species, humans learned the power of a "scapegoating mechanism" that allows the community to cohere together by being over against the Other. This mechanism, which became ritualized in the blood sacrificial rituals at the foundations of all cultures, then developed into religions of the Sacred, whose gods demand blood sacrifice.

At the time of Jesus there is an overlap between cultures still relying on ritual blood sacrifice as the basis for societal order and cultures that were developing an updated form of sacrifice, namely, a law-based society that keeps the peace on the basis of retributive justice in the form of punishment that, at the extreme, takes a life through state execution. Jesus brings both of these ordering mechanisms together on the cross. He dies at Passover (especially in John's Gospel, which ensures the timing is precise) as the Lamb of God, revealing the sin behind both ritual sacrifice and state-sanctioned sacrifice—execution. In John's Gospel, the "Lamb of God" comes before Pilate, who represents human justice, "to testify to the truth" (John 18:37 NIV). As Pilate condemns Jesus to execution, our human social ordering mechanisms are explicitly revealed.

But if the Lamb of God truly came to take away those mechanisms of social ordering that have helped us survive as a species, then the crucial question involves how we can continue to survive. In John the answer comes as *abiding*. The Jesus of John's Gospel invites us to "come and see" (1:39) where he is *abiding* ("staying," 1:38; Greek *meno*). Ultimately, that *abiding* is in Jesus himself, like branches in a vine (John 15; *meno* is featured), and who himself abides in God the true Father by virtue of the coming of the Holy Spirit descending upon Jesus in baptism and "abiding" (*meno*; "resting," 1:33). When we are reborn from above in the Spirit (John 3:3), we come to abide in the true God of Love, not the wrathful gods who demand sacrifice. The true God of Jesus invites us to abide in him and shows us the new way of restorative justice. This is how we might survive.

John van de Laar
http://www.sacredise.com/

John 1

A few years ago a beggar approached my car. I tried to ignore him, but he leaned over, placed his smiling face directly in my line of sight, and waved. I could do nothing but smile and wave back. Satisfied that I had acknowledged him, he moved on.

There is something powerful about really *seeing* someone, which is why the writer of John's Gospel invites us to truly *see* the incarnate Word. The entire book, but most especially the first four chapters, demonstrates how *seeing*, *recognizing*, and *understanding* who Jesus is changes everything. The pericope for this week is just one small representative section of this journey.

It begins with John the Baptizer, who moves from failing to recognize Jesus (see vv. 31,33) to confidently proclaiming who he is: the "Lamb of God" and "God's Chosen One" (vv. 29, 34 NIV). The lamb reference is enigmatic, but expresses John's faith that Jesus would bring forgiveness and liberation. The title of "Chosen One" relates back to the called and anointed servant of Yahweh in Isaiah 42:1. Indeed, it is witnessing the anointing of Jesus by God's Spirit that finally opens John's eyes. The result is that he readily encourages his disciples to follow this "Chosen One."

Two of John's disciples decide to follow Jesus at a distance, until he turns and addresses them. When they ask where Jesus is staying, he invites them to "come and see" (v. 39). The afternoon they spend with Jesus is enough for them to be completely convinced that John was right, and so they invite their friends to come and see, too. Andrew calls his brother Simon, boldly declaring that he has found the Messiah. Throughout this narrative the Gospel writer invites us to journey with the disciples into true sight—seeing Jesus for who he is—and into faith.

But those who *see* Jesus are also *seen*, and are changed as a result. The Baptizer now knows that his time is ended, and he happily retreats from the scene. Andrew becomes someone who regularly leads others to Jesus (6:8-9; 12:22). But Simon gives the clearest picture of transformation. When they meet, Jesus looks at him *intently*. It's a deep, searching gaze, and the result is that Jesus immediately proclaims who Simon can and will become. By giving him a new name Jesus calls Simon to live into his best self, his God-called and God-empowered self. It will take years, and some traumatic experiences, before Peter embodies his new name, but he can never avoid the knowledge that Jesus saw something significant in him.

The invitation that Andrew offered Peter is the same invitation that John's Gospel offers us: "Come and see"—discover that Jesus really is God's "Chosen One" and believe! But, never forget that you will yourself be *seen*—receiving a new insight into who God has made and called you to be. Never underestimate the power of this moment when we receive the gift of true sight.

Karoline Lewis

John 1

The Gospel lesson for this Sunday holds two stories together. One possible avenue to explore in preaching this week is to juxtapose last week's account of Jesus' baptism and this week's narration of the same event. While Matthew's story of Jesus' baptism clearly focuses on John's sense of unfitness for his task, the Gospel of John narrates no such angst. John's Gospel has no interest in John's sensitivities to his calling, because his role is profoundly different for the Fourth Evangelist. He is not John the Baptist, but John the witness. In fact, he is never called "the Baptist" in the Fourth Gospel. A careful reading of this Gospel's baptism story reveals that John is not the baptizer. That's the role of the Father with the Spirit. John is the one who witnesses, who points and says, "Behold! The Lamb of God who takes away the sin of the world" (v. 29 NKJV), where sin is unbelief or the absence of a relationship with God. The other story is the calling of the first disciples who will also be witnesses to God's presence in Jesus. When the disciples ask Jesus, "where are You staying?" (v. 38), they are asking for the experience of abiding in Jesus. This abiding is fiercely intimate, another way to express believing in or having a relationship with Jesus. The invitation to "come and see" (v. 39) is a primary component of witness and discipleship. The Samaritan woman will say the same words to her townspeople, inviting them to have their own experience of Jesus (see John 4). The theme of finding is also rich ground for preaching. Jesus is in the habit of finding disciples (9:35), and his own disciples will need to be about finding more believers (10:16).

January 26
3rd Sunday after Epiphany

Isaiah 9:1-4; Psalm 27:1, 4-9; 1 Corinthians 1:10-18; Matthew 4:12-23

Peter Woods

Isaiah 9; Psalm 27; 1 Corinthians 1; Matthew 4

There is a lot of name referencing in the readings this week. Jesus heads to Galilee after the beheading of John the Baptiser. Matthew, telling this story, quotes Isaiah, referencing the prophecy relating to Zebulun and Naphtali, obscure tribes of Israel. Paul confronts the Corinthians, who are in conflict for having aligned themselves behind some "big names": his own, Cephas, or Apollos. What to make of all these names? It's rather overwhelming.

The naming continues. Jesus calls disciples, Simon and Andrew, James and John, and he not only changes their profession to fishers of people, but some time later, he also changes the name of Simon to Peter.

As a preacher, I suppose the worst thing I could do is try to introduce my hearers to each of the names. It would certainly fill the "seventeen minutes" of sermon time, but it would be unbelievably boring. What to do?

One of the best introductions I have ever been given as a visiting preacher was, "This morning we are privileged to have as our preacher the person of whom Billy Graham said, (long pause) . . . 'Who?'" Not only was it a lovely roast, it was a reminder that people come to church for no other name than the name of Jesus. Truth be told, all the names in our passages today would have been lost in time and memory were it not for their association with Jesus.

The greatest fear of the Jew was to be forgotten. "Who will say Kaddish for me?" (Kaddish is the prayer for the dead.) Can you sense the fear in the question? We want to be remembered.

"Do not cast me off, do not forsake me, O God of my salvation!" cries the psalmist. "Follow me, (forget yourself) and fish for others," says Jesus.

Todd Weir
http://bloomingcactus.typepad.com/

Isaiah 9

The best thing about mornings is the new light. I love the feeling of moving from darkness to light. Early morning light is soft and gentle, it is happy and hopeful. One morning I was catching a flight, and we reached the top of a mountain pass right at dawn. Rose-colored streaks suddenly crept into the darkness and drove it away. I suddenly remembered reading the *Iliad* in high school and Homer's phrase, "the rosy fingered dawn." I felt a kinship with other early risers stretching over the millennia.

Epiphany calls us to move from darkness into light. The lectionary first pulls us into morning dawn with Isaiah 9:2 (NRSV), "The people who walked in darkness / have seen a great light; / those who lived in a land of deep darkness— / on them light has shined." I wonder what happened to those people of Naphtali and Zebulon that moved them from darkness? These were lands of battle and conflict, because of their location at the crossroads between Asia and Africa. These tribes always experienced warfare because they controlled the mountain passes and trade routes into northern Israel. In Isaiah's day, they were ruled by Assyria, so Isaiah 9 is referring to breaking the power of foreign domination. If we look at the map of modern Israel, we can quickly see how little has changed. These lands contain the Golan Heights, Israel's border with Syria to the east, which was captured by Israel in the Six Day War in 1967. To the north is Lebanon, where the Druze militias have historically launched rocket attacks on Israeli towns.

In Jesus' day, this was called Galilee, heavily Roman lands where retired centurions and other seekers of wealth went to live on the fruits of the trade routes and rich soil. Jews were at the bottom of the social heap. Many were poor fishermen living off their catch and selling to the wealthy Romans. This is where Jesus made his home and where he launched his ministry, among poor Jews and Gentiles who were not counted as important to Empire or Temple. Matthew says it was much like the times of Isaiah, where people living in darkness saw a great light. Jesus' ministry there was not an unfortunate choice of venue, but a fulfillment of a prophecy centuries old.

Naphtali and Zebulon endured and saw a great light of freedom. Fishermen left their boats when they saw light in Jesus and hope for their future. Let us resolve this year to keep focused on the light rather than on the darkness. When I worry, I don't act like a person who has seen a great light. Rather than shining Christ's light on others, I become a source of gloom myself. I find it is not enough that I saw the light in the past; I need to keep seeing it every day. I stand in need of new morning light, the rosy-fingered dawn, each day.

Liz Crumlish
http://somethingtostandon.blogspot.co.uk/

1 Corinthians 1

Driving through rural Scotland, bridges often appear seemingly out of nowhere and sometimes with very little obvious purpose. Perhaps to link farmland that has become separated through sprawling urbanization. Or to allow the passage of livestock across a busy road that has materialized in a formerly rural landscape. It often seems that a lot of effort and expense has been incurred for correspondingly little benefit. Except history would decree a different story and place in context the need for a gap to be bridged and a new pathway to be created. And the many, creative, picturesque styles of bridges do make the scenery even more beautiful and varied.

Divisions in the church are nothing new—as old as the church itself. We become quite tolerant and even, at times, indulgent of these divisions. But St. Paul places in context the need for bridges to be built—or chasms dispensed with. The divisions and our pandering to them, claims Paul, distract us from the mission to which we are called—preaching the gospel.

This makes me uncomfortable. I would rather chip away at finding similarities in our differences, common ground over which we can agree than work at a real solution that would bring about unity. I am more content with living with the differences than with dismantling a system that, in the end, still excludes. I cling to the arguments, rationalizing that they lend some spice to life, even, on occasion, beauty. Cozying up with division means that all the while, the gospel remains unpreached, far less lived out in the life of the church. Once again, Paul presents us with the unpalatable facts that we'd rather simply ignore, just as we try to ignore the erosion of our open spaces and the deterioration of our rural culture, threatened by inappropriate land use, even if that does result in some pretty bridging structures.

John Wesley's Notes on the Bible
http://www.ccel.org/ccel/wesley/notes.txt

1 Corinthians 1:13

"Is Christ divided"—Are not all the members still under one head? Was not he alone crucified for you all; and were ye not all baptized in his name? The glory of Christ then is not to be divided between him and his servants; neither is the unity of the body to be torn asunder, seeing Christ is one still.

Kathryn Schifferdecker

1 Corinthians 1

There is a deep longing for community in our fragmented and mobile society. Witness the astounding growth of Facebook and other social networking sites. But building community is hard work, even (or especially) in the church, where we have to deal with people face-to-face, people with whom we may not otherwise choose to associate. We know we should love our neighbor as ourselves, but sometimes our neighbor makes that really difficult to do.

For better or for worse, church conflict is nothing new. Even in the early Christian church, congregational members did not always love and care for one another as brothers and sisters in Christ. In the church at Corinth, for instance, disagreements arose over many matters, including who had the best spiritual gifts, and the church became divided into factions.

Paul writes to this conflicted congregation to provide direction and encouragement. He quotes the Corinthians themselves: "[E]ach of you says, 'I belong to Paul,' or 'I belong to Apollos,' or 'I belong to Cephas,' or 'I belong to Christ.' Has Christ been divided? Was Paul crucified for you? Or were you baptized in the name of Paul?" (vv. 12-13 NRSV).

Paul planted the church at Corinth. It would have been understandable had he taken pride in the fact that some of the believers there remained loyal to him. Who doesn't like to be remembered and honored? But Paul demonstrates in his own life what he calls for from the Corinthians: a certain measure of humility and a desire for unity in Christ. That unity subverts human pride because it is based neither on eloquent wisdom nor on any other human ability but on the foolishness of the cross, the power of God for those who are being saved. On that solid foundation, the Spirit builds true community.

Julie Craig
http://winsomelearnsome.com

Matthew 4

I've been thinking a lot about Zebedee this week. Imagine sitting in the boat, and watching your two sons—who are more to you than just your flesh and blood, but also your business partners—just up and leave when somebody comes by with a better offer. And a cryptic offer it was at that. "Fish for people." What does that *mean*?

On one hand, maybe I'm thinking about Zebedee because I am now at the age when my children are moving on with their lives, making decisions of their own. On the other hand, I am aware that in my family of origin I am the person who left. It's not so easy being the one who moved away, hearing the updates on how my aging parents are getting along from my siblings, who still live near them.

I guess this is what they mean by "sandwich generation"—caught between the need to make sure my children are thriving and the need to take care of my parents. Sometimes I feel pulled between two equally compelling forces, both worthy and good reasons to be somewhere or do something.

It was much more clear-cut in Matthew's day. Children—even adult children, and especially sons—stayed to help the parents. Especially if they had learned a family trade from their fathers, as James and John had. Adults did not leave family unless it was for the good of the family for them to do so. People stayed close to home, and stayed on in whatever enterprise in which the family had been established for years and years. If your father was a shepherd, you were a shepherd. If your father was a potter, you were a potter…and so on.

I wonder sometimes if the Church is experiencing its own sandwich generation. Having thrived in a culture and a community that once upon a time supported the status quo, the pull to keep on doing what has always worked in the past is strong. At the same time, the Church is expected to thrive in a very new environment, where potential members, leaders, and disciples have many other options available to them. And so denominations and local churches alike find themselves—ourselves—in a very perplexing place. Do we maintain our loyalty to the heritage that brought us here, or do we try to reach out and meet the spiritual needs of a world that is rapidly changing?

God meets us where we are, not where God wishes us to be. God calls us to a life of discipleship based on what plans God has for us, and how we are to grow—not based on our weaknesses or where we've been, or the failures we've made of ourselves. God calls us to risk, and to calm fears, reshape the world, bring about the Reign of God…but never alone. Never alone. Thanks be to God.

Marci Auld Glass
www.marciglass.com

Matthew 4

When did you decide to follow Jesus? Some of you have a clear answer to that question and could tell me the minute, hour, day, month, and year that Jesus told you to leave your nets and follow him.

It isn't as clear for all of us. I couldn't tell you the day I followed Jesus. I grew up going to church. So I don't remember *the* moment. But I remember a lot of moments.

• My Sunday school teachers who taught me that Jesus loved us, even when one of us was a young boy who liked to cut my hair during the Bible lesson.

• I remember being Wise Man Number 2 in the Christmas pageant one year, and having to say Wise Man Number 1's lines as well when he got sick in the middle of the pageant.

• I remember my pastor in college who spoke the very word of God to me at the moment I most needed to hear it.

So I can look back at a lot of moments on my road to discipleship. And I am thankful for all of those people who played a role—for my family, my Sunday school teachers, youth group leaders, pastors—the list is long.

I wonder about the disciples. Their moment is written in Scripture. I wonder if they wondered why Jesus would have chosen them. Because we wonder. Why would you pick your disciples from random fishermen you found on a beach when you could select the best students from the rabbi schools?

But Jesus tells them to leave behind their nets, their boats, the giant haul of fish they just caught, and to also leave behind their fears of their own inadequacy, their fears that they have nothing to offer to God because they are just fishermen, and their fears that Jesus has made a bad decision that he will regret in a few days. Because it isn't about us. It is about Jesus.

Even the selection of the disciples is an illustration of Grace and a reminder of the mysterious mind of God that is beyond our comprehension.

So, do not be afraid. Have no fear. From now on, you will be fishing for people. Leave your nets, leave your boats, leave your distractions, leave your fears, and get ready to follow Jesus. There may have been lots of moments that led to this day. But the moment is now. Jesus is calling you. Yes, you.

NOTE: Adapted from "Disciples R Us," a sermon preached by Marci Auld Glass (http://marciglass.com/2011/07/23/disciples-r-us/).

February 2
4th Sunday after Epiphany

Micah 6:1-8; Psalm 15; 1 Corinthians 1:18-31; Matthew 5:1-12

Beth Quick
http://bethquick.blogspot.com

Micah 6

• I'm stuck on the word "require" in verse 8. *Require* is a strong word. We're not *advised* to do these things. We're *required*. What else are you required to do? How do you treat these requirements, as opposed to those God sets for us?

• Another good word: the "*controversy* of the LORD"—what a label! (v. 2, NRSV). Who wants to be called God's controversy?

• Another passage (like Psalm 51, among others) where the author recognizes that it is not the acts of sacrifice and ritual themselves God desires, but the devoted hearts that bring such offerings to God. God wants *us*.

• Do justice, love kindness, walk humbly (v. 8). What would happen if everything we did as a church was based on or could be tied to one of these three things? Anything that doesn't fall into one of those commands is something we should examine carefully!

Psalm 15

• Who may dwell with God? The blameless. If those are the only ones who can dwell with God, we're in trouble!

• The psalmist gives us a list to which to aspire: Do what is right. Speak the truth. Do not slander. Do not do evil. Do not reproach.

• On the other hand, as much as we think it is quite a list, why is it so hard to measure up to those requirements? Is it so hard to love? We so desire to be loved. Why is it so hard to love others?

1 Corinthians 1

• "For the message about the cross is foolishness to those who are perishing" (v. 18, NRSV). This verse is repeated from last week's reading. An instrument of weakness is made into an instrument of power. That is what God does to things: gives them a whole new life and meaning.

• God doesn't just change meanings of things around, but meanings of people. We're flipped inside out by this "foolishness" of Jesus Christ.

Matthew 5

• Compare Matthew's and Luke's recording of the Beatitudes. In Luke 6, Jesus gives the "blessings and woes," which are very tangible. "Blessed are you who are hungry now, for you will be filled" (v. 21 NRSV); the implication is of physical hunger. Matthew gives a spiritual spin to everything Jesus says: Blessed are the "poor in spirit," and those who hunger for righteousness (5:3, 6 NRSV). Personally, I'm glad they are recorded in two different ways. We need both!

• Most of these make sense to me: the one who is making peace is God's child. The meek inherit, those seeking righteousness are filled. But what about the poor-in-spirit part? What do you think is meant by being poor in spirit? Is this someone who is dejected/depressed? Someone who has lost their way, turned from God? What's going on with your soul that you would call being "poor in spirit"?

Peter Woods

Micah 6; Psalm 15; Matthew 5; 1 Corinthians 1

The word for "blessed" in biblical Greek is *makarioi*. *Makarios* is the noun. It is a word popular as a name in Greek-speaking culture. It has been the name of three Cypriot Archbishops:

- Makarios I, archbishop of Cyprus from 1854 to 1865.
- Makarios II, archbishop of Cyprus from 1948 to 1950.
- Makarios III, archbishop (1950–1977) and president of Cyprus (1960–1977).

The last Archbishop Makarios also became the President of Cyprus. When you read about his life it seems that he was well beloved of the Cypriot people, even though he led Cyprus through a tumultuous time in their history. It is a tricky thing to take spiritual values into the realm of politics.

Micah tells it plainly: "He has told you, O mortal, what is good; / and what does the Lord require of you / but to do justice, and to love kindness, / and to walk humbly with your God?" (Micah 6:8 NRSV).

Psalm 15 suggests that honesty is the value that permits access to God.

Jesus suggests that the blessed *(Makarioi)* are those who are not powerful and influential, and Paul in the Corinthian passage points out that God has a different logic for ranking and status. Some Christians have taken this to mean that Christ followers should stay out of positions of power and politics. Total separation of Church and State is their value and demand.

That raises a question. If the blessed, good, humble and wise people described in today's scriptures stay away from roles of social responsibility, to whom are those tasks left? Can the people of God, the *Makarioi,* afford not to get involved? The third Archbishop of Cyprus was blessed enough to try. What about we blessed ones, who know what is good?

Lowell Grisham
http://lowellsblog.blogspot.com/

Prayers of the People

Officiant: Blessed God, whose foolishness is wiser than human wisdom and whose weakness is stronger than human strength, pour out your blessing upon your creation as we pray: "Lead us to do justice and to love kindness; and to walk humbly with our God."

Intercessor: Fill your church with your blessing, O God, that we may hunger and thirst for righteousness, and strengthen our mission to proclaim Christ crucified, the power of God and the wisdom of God. Lead us to do justice and to love kindness;

and to walk humbly with our God.

Inspire our leaders with purity of heart that they may see with godly vision and become peacemakers, children of God. Lead us to do justice and to love kindness;

and to walk humbly with our God.

Look with mercy on the meek and poor in spirit and protect all who are persecuted falsely throughout the world. Lead us to do justice and to love kindness;

and to walk humbly with our God.

Bless our community with your grace, that we may be compassionate peacemakers, pure in heart and willing to suffer for the sake of your healing and reconciling work. Lead us to do justice and to love kindness;

and to walk humbly with our God.

Visit us with your grace and strengthen those who call upon your help, especially _____. Comfort all who mourn as we remember _____. We give you thanks for all the blessings you bestow upon us, especially _____. Lead us to do justice and to love kindness;

and to walk humbly with our God.

Officiant: O God of unchangeable power and eternal light: Look favorably upon your whole Church, that wonderful and sacred mystery; by the effectual working of your providence, carry out in tranquility the plan of salvation; let the whole world see and know that things which were cast down are being raised up, and things which had grown old are being made new, and that all things are being brought to their perfection by him through whom all things were made, your Son Jesus Christ our Lord; who lives and reigns with you, in the unity of the Holy Spirit, one God for ever and ever. **Amen.**

NOTE: Closing prayer is from the *Book of Common Prayer* (1979), 515.

Melissa Bane Sevier
http://melissabanesevier.wordpress.com

Walk (Micah 6)

"He has told you, O mortal, what is good; / and what does the Lᴏʀᴅ require of you / but to do justice, and to love kindness, / and to walk humbly with your God?" (Micah 6:8 NRSV).

This time of year, I become a lot more conscious of walking. Walking is normally a pretty natural thing for me. I don't think much about it when I put one foot in front of the other.

We've had a lot of snow and ice lately, though, and walking takes more concentration. The church parking lot can get really icy, especially after cars have packed down the snow. Church floors are slippery when people track in snow on their shoes. Even at home I take the porch steps one at a time, then walk through the yard to avoid cement and pavement. Once in the yard, walking is fun, but different. I like to make interesting footprints, to take long strides, to jump (when I think the neighbors aren't looking), and then to retrace those same prints back to the house.

The prophet Micah says God's people are called to walk humbly with God. Walking with God can be treacherous, easy, fun, or difficult. Sometimes it requires great concentration to decide what is the right thing to do, how to act in a tough situation. Sometimes it's easy; we know exactly what to do from the beginning. Sometimes it's frightening, because walking the right path can lead to change, and change isn't always what it's cracked up to be. Sometimes it is dangerous to pursue justice, or even to love kindness. When we challenge the societal norms, we can put ourselves at risk of being ostracized, or worse.

A friend had a fourteen-month-old baby who had not yet begun to walk. Out of concern for his development, she took the boy to the pediatrician who gave him a thorough exam. Everything seemed fine. A few tests. Again, no alarms. The doctor knows the family, which consisted, at that time, of two teenaged girls and the fourteen-month-old boy. "How much do the girls carry him around?" the doctor asked. "Almost constantly," said the mother. The doctor said, "Tell them not to carry him for a week." Within three days he had begun to walk.

Walking simply takes practice. The more we practice prayer, being kind, justice-making, the more natural those things become. That doesn't mean we won't make a wrong step, slip, or fall down. But we continue to walk with God anyway. The more we walk, the more at ease we become, even on the slippery days.

John Wesley's Notes on the Bible
http://www.ccel.org/ccel/wesley/notes.txt

Micah 6:8

"To do justly"—To render to every one their due, superiors, equals, inferiors, to be equal to all, and oppress none, in body, goods or name; in all your dealings with men carry a chancery in your own breasts, and do according to equity. "To love mercy"—To be kind, merciful and compassionate to all, not using severity towards any. "Walk humbly with thy God"—Keep up a constant fellowship with God, by humble, holy faith.

Thom Shuman
http://lectionaryliturgies.blogspot.com/

Call to Worship

We are blessed when we hunger for justice and thirst for reconciliation.
Our souls are nourished by God's hope and grace.
We are blessed when we grieve over the brokenness of the world,
choosing, as God does, to be with those who are weak and powerless.
We are blessed when we become God's fools,
willing to do what is right and good, not what is easy.

Prayer of the Day

The hills sing your hopes
and the valleys echo your dreams,
Holy God, of a world
where we catch sight of you
in the innocent hearts of children;
where we listen to the wisdom
of souls willing to be weak;
where we find the home we long for
in your heart's brokenness.

Teacher of our hearts,
when we are generous to the poor,
your kingdom of justice is built;
when we love kindness
more than we do power,
we are heirs of creation's grace;
when we walk hand-in-hand
with the humble-hearted,
we are in step with you;
when we share a picnic of hope and joy
with the forgotten of the world,
we follow you up the hill of faithfulness.

Wisdom of Weakness,
when our differences with one another
become stumbling blocks to life together,
you come
with your hopeful foolishness
so your children
might be at peace,
and a blessing of life
to a world in need of healing.

God in Community, Holy in One,
hear us as we pray as Jesus has taught us,
saying, **Our Father...**

Call to Reconciliation

Called to be weak,
we idolize the powerful;
called to be foolish,
we hunger for the world's wisdom;
called to be poor in spirit,
we thirst for more and more.
Let us confess to God how following Jesus is often a stumbling block for us.

Unison Prayer of Confession

How do we approach you, Exalted God, with our confessions? We make you weary with our inability to do justice for the poor and outcast. We gossip about those who are close to us, instead of being their loving friend. We make promises, and then go back on our word.

Forgive us, God of Hope, and bless us with your mercy. By your peace, we can do justice. By your love, we can act kindly. By your grace, we can walk with you as humbly, and hopefully, as did our Lord and Savior, Jesus Christ.

Silence is kept.

Assurance of Pardon

It is through foolishness that God makes us wise;
it is through weakness that God strengthens us to serve;
it is through forgiveness that God makes us whole.
**We cannot boast in what we have done, but only in the grace and joy of our God,
who showers us with mercy. Amen.**

Kathryn Schifferdecker

1 Corinthians 1; Matthew 5

When God acts, everything is turned upside down. Mary's song a few weeks ago spoke of the powerful brought low and the lowly exalted (Luke 1:52). Her son's vision is equally radical: "Blessed are the poor in spirit, for theirs is the kingdom of heaven. Blessed are those who mourn, for they will be comforted. Blessed are the meek, for they will inherit the earth" (Matt 5:3-5 NRSV).

The poor, those who mourn, the meek—they do not typically get much attention in our day. Their voices are drowned out by the voices of the powerful, the famous, the rich. And yet, the poor, the meek, those who mourn—these are the ones whom Jesus calls "blessed." Blessed not in the world's eyes but in God's eyes.

Paul proclaims the same radical vision of a world turned upside down. To a congregation keeping score over spiritual gifts, Paul writes of a different way of being in the world. It is not the powerful or the wise whom God chooses to show forth God's power. The Corinthians know this from their own experience: "[N]ot many of you were wise by human standards, not many were powerful, not many were of noble birth. But God chose what is foolish in the world to shame the wise; God chose what is weak in the world to shame the strong" (1 Cor 1:26b-27 NRSV).

When God acts, everything is turned upside down. Perhaps it's not surprising. What else would we expect from a God who chooses to be known in—of all things—the cross? That sign of shameful death is "a stumbling block" and "foolishness" to the wise, but to those who are called, "Christ the power of God and the wisdom of God" (vv. 23-24). This is strange and wonderful blessing indeed.

Martha Spong
http://marthaspong.com/

Matthew 5

In our house, quietly alone most of the time, lives an elliptical machine. Its paddles turn a big wheel, encased in a plastic shell. Each time I get on it, I push the paddles, and I hear the wheel spin, heavily. We put it together on the same weekend the Beatitudes were in the lectionary that year, and it struck me then that these verses have a familiar rhythm of their own. They come around, again and again. My mother used to caution me with verse 9, whenever a squabble broke out with my younger brother: "Blessed are the peacemakers," she said. I had no idea what that was supposed to mean. I only knew what my mother meant. Stop fighting with your little brother. It's your job to keep the peace, even if it means giving in to make the fight stop. Take the blame if you must.

It turned me off the Beatitudes, which being a clever girl I eventually found in my little New Testament. I read them all, and I thought they sounded sad, mostly. Still, it was clear they mattered, that I was supposed to attend to them. They reflect the human condition, the elliptical way of a spiritual life. We know we are working hard, but we wonder whether we are going anywhere.

I've gotten on the machine when some other member of the family used it last, someone stronger and taller, and found I could not make the paddles move at all. Unfortunately, it doesn't turn "on," the batteries don't activate, until the paddles go around. So in order to change the level of resistance from someone else's 6 or 7 to my level 1, I have to find a way to make the wheel spin first.

The way of Jesus will sometimes feel like the elliptical set unexpectedly at level 10.

When we feel as if someone is persecuting us for being the kind of person we believe we're meant to be, the kind of person God calls us to be, it's hard work to turn the wheel, to get things in motion again, to feel actually blessed by God in the moment of challenge.

When I have to get the actual elliptical started under those difficult circumstances, I remember that gravity is my friend, and I step on and let my weight carry the paddle down, hoping the batteries will come to life. Or I ask for help, if someone stronger is nearby.

In our effort to be disciples, we may need to let the weight of the moment carry the paddles around, slowly at first. We may need to ask for the help of others who have been there before. God blesses their faithfulness in the face of resistance. God will bless ours, too.

February 9
5th Sunday after Epiphany

Isaiah 58:1-9a, (9b-12); Psalm 112:1-9, (10); 1 Corinthians 2:1-12, (13-16); Matthew 5:13-20

Dan Clendenin
http://journeywithjesus.net

Isaiah 58

One of the most counter-intuitive facts of history is that blacks adopted the religion of their white oppressors, a religion that was often the primary means of their oppression. A significant number of the four million slaves freed after the Civil War lived into the 1940s. During the Depression, the Federal Writers Project hired people to interview and record first-person narratives from these former slaves, the last firsthand resource that could document their slave experiences. Today the Library of Congress houses two thousand such interviews, in their original "dialect" and broken English, in the simply titled *Slave Narratives*, portions of which are available on the one-hour film called *Unchained Memories: Readings from the Slave Narratives* (2003).

Unchained Memories uses original still photographs, contemporary re-enactments, slave music, a running commentary by Whoopi Goldberg, and, most notably and thus the film's title, dramatic readings of those original slave narratives by contemporary African-American actors and actresses like Oprah Winfrey. They recall the daily horrors of slave life from those who lived to tell of it—relentless work, horrendous housing and diet, the denial of education, sexual violence, and how the "masters" used Christianity to keep the slaves passive.

Neither the Civil War, the Emancipation Proclamation, nor the Thirteenth Amendment fully abolished what Abraham Lincoln called the "monstrous injustice" of slavery. After all, it was the *planters* who were reimbursed for their "losses," not the slaves. And as Isabel Wilkerson shows in her award-winning book *The Warmth of Other Suns* (2010), the years of reconstruction gave way to a Jim Crow south that was characterized by a "feudal caste system" of lynchings, terror, torture, and violence.

Maybe blacks accepted the gospel because they knew their Bibles well, especially prophetic texts like those from Isaiah 58. Whatever the reason(s), Lerone Bennett Jr. points out in *Before the Mayflower* (Chicago: Johnson Pub., 2003) that toward the end of the nineteenth century, the black church "quickly established itself as the dominant institutional force in black American life" (262). Martin Luther King, Jr. was a churchman, and there was never a time when he was not a pastor (at Dexter Avenue Baptist Church in Montgomery and Ebenezer Baptist in Atlanta).

A few years ago I celebrated Black History Month by reading some primary materials on the subject. Of the many good options, I chose three slave narratives: *Narrative of the Life of Frederick Douglass* (1845), the *Narrative of Sojourner Truth* (1850), and *Incidents in the Life of a Slave Girl* (1861) by Harriet Jacobs. I also recommend Eugene Robinson's new book called *Disintegration: The Splintering of Black America* (2010), the seven-part PBS documentary on the Civil Rights Movement called *Eyes on the Prize*, and MLK's 1963 "I Have a Dream" speech (http://www.americanrhetoric.com/speeches/mlkihaveadream.htm).

John Wesley's Notes on the Bible
http://www.ccel.org/ccel/wesley/notes.txt

Isaiah 58:2

"Delight"—There are many men who take some pleasure in knowing God's will and word, and yet do not conform their lives to it.

Carolyn Winfrey Gillette
http://www.carolynshymns.com/

Up on a Mountaintop (Matthew 5)

Up on a mountaintop, Jesus sat down,
Teaching the people who gathered around:
Look for the blessings that God kindly brings;
God's loving kingdom is changing all things.

You are the salt and you're also the light.
Flavor God's world, with your faith shining bright.
Know that I've come here, God's word to fulfill.
Keep the commandments and follow them well.

Let go of anger, for it is a sin.
It will destroy you, both outside and in.
Even your thinking can lead you astray;
Whatever tempts you, just throw it away.

Keep strong the bonds between husband and wife;
Keep your commitments for all of your life.
Don't swear by heaven or by earth below;
Let "yes" be "yes" then, and let "no" be "no."

If any hurt you, then you may resist,
But not with hatred or weapon or fist.
God's way is stronger than any you face;
Stand up and love them! And give them God's grace.

Love those who hate you and pray for them, too.
God's mercy reaches out far beyond you.
Seek, as God's people, God's wholeness each day
So you can witness to God's perfect way.

NOTES
Biblical reference: Matthew 5
Tune: SLANE 10.10.10.10 ("Be Thou My Vision"), Ancient Irish ballad
Text: Copyright © 2011 by Carolyn Winfrey Gillette. All rights reserved.
This hymn is part of "The Sermon on the Mount: A Worship Service of Lessons and Songs" by Carolyn Winfrey Gillette.

Kathryn Schifferdecker

Isaiah 58; Matthew 5

"You are the salt of the earth," says Jesus. "You are the light of the world" (Matt 5:13a, 14a NRSV). Who, me? Salt and light for the *world*?! I'm lucky if I manage to get the kids off to school and get myself together for the day. I'm not a savior. I'm not, well, *you*, Jesus.

But it's not about me. It's about God and my neighbor. "Let your light shine before others, so that they may see your good works and give glory to your Father in heaven" (v. 16 NRSV). If we claim to worship God, in other words, it matters how we live, because how we live reflects the character of the God we worship.

That seems a self-evident truth, but Christians seem too easily to forget it. How often do we make our day-to-day decisions (what to eat, what to buy, how to treat the stranger) based on our Christian convictions? Does our faith make a difference in how we live, or are we, for all intents and purposes, agnostics from Sunday noon to Saturday night?

It's about God and our neighbor. Isaiah prophesies to those who have forgotten the character of the God they worship. They fast but they neglect justice. They pray to God but they ignore God's children in need. "Is not this the fast that I choose: / to loose the bonds of injustice / …to share your bread with the hungry, / and bring the homeless poor into your house?" (Isa 58:6a, 7 NRSV).

True worship must involve more than an hour or two a week. True worship must involve our whole lives, lived out in service to God and our neighbor. We can't do it alone, of course, but in the midst of it, we have the promise of God's presence: "Here I am" (Isa 58:9b NRSV). Where God leads, God provides.

Suzanne Guthrie
http://www.edgeofenclosure.org

"Let Your Light so Shine" (Matthew 5)

Somehow my righteousness, and that of my community, must exceed that of the most ardent practitioners of the law. The jots and tittles remain in place, but I am called to penetrate the meaning, to see the whole in its layers of depth and context; to love the spirit of the law over and beyond the letter of the law.

> Is not this the fast that I choose: / to loose the bonds of injustice, / to undo the thongs of the yoke, / to let the oppressed go free, / and to break every yoke? / Is it not to share your bread with the hungry, / and bring the homeless poor into your house; / when you see the naked, to cover them, / and not to hide yourself from your own kin? (Isaiah 58:6-7 NRSV)

Loving the law draws the devotee into ever-widening modes of consciousness. Every new context engages my understanding and my compassion. I have to understand creatively what to do in the face of every new challenge. I am called into Light to make known the Light.

Men, women, and even children throughout history sacrificed themselves to bring forth the Light. "Be of good comfort, Master Ridley, and play the man; we shall this day light such a candle, by God's grace, in England, as I trust shall never be put out," says Hugh Latimer to Nicholas Ridley as they are burning at the stake in 1555. In twentieth-century Nazi Germany, after the disappearance and arrests of many church members and just before his own arrest, Martin Niemoller preaches on this same text of the bushel and the lampstand. He says, "We are not to worry whether the light is extinguished or not; that is His concern: we are only to see that the light is not hidden away—hidden away perhaps with a noble intent, so that we may bring it out again in calmer times—no: 'Let your light shine before men!'"

And then?

> Then your light shall break forth like the dawn, / and your healing shall spring up quickly; / your vindicator shall go before you, / the glory of the Lord shall be your rear guard. / … if you offer your food to the hungry / and satisfy the needs of the afflicted, / then your light shall rise in the darkness / and your gloom be like the noon-day. (Isaiah 58:8, 10 NRSV)

I've got to awaken from the comfortable, respectable cocoon I've woven for myself and submit my own heart to the purifying fire. Somehow, I need to find a way to "speak truth to power" without fear, acting boldly in my own setting, to shine like a burning lamp to the world.

Ann Scull
http://seedstuff.blogspot.com

Listening Song

Newsboys, *"Shine"* on *Shine: The Hits,* compilation remix (USA: Sparrow Records, 2000). This song uses words directly from the gospel reading.

Discussion Questions: Plenary, Group, or with a Neighbour

1. Today, salt and light do not have the same meanings of preciousness and distinctiveness that they did in Jesus' day. What might Jesus say to us today if he was talking to us? "You are like…"

2. How can we "shine" and spread God's light on to those around us?

Brainstorm

Brainstorm definitions of the word *disciple*.

Stories

- *"Be a Copper Kettle."* This story can be found at http://www.comp.nus.edu.sg/~tankl/kettle.txt (accessed March 23, 2012). This is a story about reflecting Jesus' light on to those around us.
- *"Thermometers and Thermostats"* by Wayne Rice, *Hot Illustrations for Youth Talks* (El Cajon, Calif.: Youth Specialties, 1994), 198. If you can find a themostat and a thermometer as suggested to illustrate this story, you will find that you have an easily understood example of how Christians can be agents of change in the world.

John van de Laar
http://www.sacredise.com/

Matthew 5

I can't help feeling that in today's Church we have come to believe that we need to draw attention to ourselves in order to make an impact on the world. We buy television time, we build great auditoriums, and we try to ensure that we are always at the heart of the conversation, always being recognized and quoted. Yet, in spite of the huge religious marketing machine, our message—or rather, the message of Jesus—still seems to be getting lost.

Perhaps we've misunderstood what Jesus meant about letting our lights shine. Perhaps we haven't really thought through all the implications of salt and light—neither of which is valuable in itself. Look straight into a light and it damages your eyes. Eat salt alone and all you get is a huge thirst. These two things exist, not to be used for their own sakes, *but for the difference they make to other things*. It's not the light we want to look at—it's the world that the light brings into vibrant focus and color. It's not the salt we want to taste—it's the variety and richness of the flavors already contained in our food that the salt brings out.

In the Sermon on the Mount, Jesus seems to take for granted that the Pharisees are genuinely seeking to live "righteously." That's why he uses them as the standard for his followers to exceed. But, there is one thing that irks him about the religious elite of his day: their constant need to put their religion on public display (see Matt 6). The problem with public shows of religion is this: when the message of faith is constantly shouted out, people stop listening and start examining the lives of the shouters. And when they find the inevitable failure to practice what is being preached, they simply tune the message out.

But a salt-and-light conspiracy does not draw attention to itself. It simply reveals the world as it is and shows what can be done about it, not through loud, attention-getting words, but through quiet, momentum-gathering actions. All we need is a heart that finds the "color" and "tastiness" in life wherever it can be found, and that invites others into the experience, no matter who they may be. And, like salt and light, we are forgotten in the sheer joy of seeing and tasting, so God gets the glory.

This is why both Luke and Mark link the salt image with the daily work of living compassionately and justly. For Mark it's about living in peace (Mark 9:50) and for Luke it's about thoughtful, committed self-sacrifice (Luke 14:33-35). If we're looking for personal adulation, then we better stay clear of the Sermon on the Mount. But, if we're willing to give away our reputation and our desire for affirmation in favor of making the world a little more whole and compassionate, a little more just and true, then the salt-and-light conspiracy is the way to go.

Peter Woods

Matthew 5

I stood on the barren piece of land where a vibrant community of people had lived. The area is called District Six, once populated by a multiethnic community that was quintessentially Cape Town: colorful, exotically indigenous, and as spicy as its Malay cuisine.

That was before Apartheid came, the infamous system designed by Christian, White South Africans to keep the races apart and favor the minority. During the implementation of Apartheid, District Six was systematically bull-dozed to the ground and all sixty thousand of its residents forcibly removed. Each race was taken to its allocated ghetto.

When I stood on the barren piece of land, it was December of 1999 and the Parliament of the World's Religions had come to South Africa to celebrate the diversity of the faiths of the world in this country that had recently been healed of the scourge of Apartheid. Nelson Mandela was president. The Parliament held many of its sessions in the area of old District Six. One session in particular was held on a still barren tract of land awaiting restitution claims to be concluded.

Jewish delegates of the Parliament created a large patch of salt about three by three metres that we had to walk through to get to the open land.

Salt on the land renders it barren for many years. In South Africa the salt of segregation created barrenness: created by Christians who had lost their understanding of justice for all. We still worshiped on Sundays, but separately. We still prayed, but only for our own group concerns. We had become bland, heartless, and barren.

In this week's readings, Isaiah, the psalmist, and Paul all chorus the words of Jesus against religion that loses its heart for justice. It is as worthless as a salted, barren, and bulldozed field.

February 16
6th Sunday after Epiphany

Deuteronomy 30:15-20; Psalm 119:1-8; 1 Corinthians 3:1-9; Matthew 5:21-37

Julie Craig
http://winsomelearnsome.com

Deuteronomy 30

A friend of mine always sends her kids out the door by saying to them, "Make good choices; I love you; remember who you are." In our house, we shortened that considerably. When our kids became adolescents and were leaving the house now without us to watch over them, the standard sending remark was this: "Don't do anything stupid."

My kids know—because they were raised in our home, with our values—what *"Don't do anything stupid"* means. It means mind your manners, be kind to others, remember right from wrong, do the best and highest you can in any situation, avoid trouble.

A few years ago we took our then–seventeen-year-old daughter to New York City. On our first night there, we were in the Whole Foods store on 7th Avenue, near our Chelsea hotel, during the madness of evening rush hour. We found the appropriate checkout lane, waiting our turn, when we saw a young woman, not much older than our daughter, who had her arms full of items plus had a full basket of things on the floor that she was scooting with her foot as she inched her way up the line.

The problem with this picture is that all around her, everywhere she could possibly look, were signs that read "5 items or less." As you can imagine, the crowd was growing restless watching her—the crowd of people who had followed the rules and only had five items or less in *their* arms.

The girl got to the checker, who looked at her with utter disdain. The young woman seemed nonplussed by the whole event, and just looked at the checker with a puzzled look on her face. The crowd grew even more restless, and the checker made the young woman leave the line and stand in another one.

Minutes later, we were standing out on a very crowded 7th Avenue. I turned to my daughter and said, "Dear, when you are living on your own in a big city, and I'm not there to watch over you, please don't do what she did." And my daughter replied with, "Clearly her mother never taught her the rule *'Don't do anything stupid!'*"

Our texts for today are chock full of instructions, rules for living, admonitions to live out our highest, best selves. Moses, in his valedictory, or farewell speech, is letting the children of Israel know that they must cross the Jordan without him. Their forty long years together are about to end, and they must make the final portion of the journey with a new leader. And, like a loving parent, Moses wants the Israelites to live to their highest, best, most Yahweh-like selves, in order that they might prosper in the land that God has promised to them—the land that they can practically, *finally*—see off in the distance. He wants them to not do anything stupid.

Liz Crumlish
http://somethingtostandon.blogspot.co.uk/

Deuteronomy 30

Moses' speech in Deuteronomy 30 is some speech from a man who, when God called him, could barely speak. Moses has come a long way. And so have the people he leads. They have been through a lot together and they have learned a lot together. Moses implores them to always keep in mind the God who has directed their lives, the God who calls them to live in love—loving God, loving each other, and loving their neighbor.

The King's Speech is an award-winning movie about the life of King George VI. It is the true story of how the king, who was never expected to accede to the throne, overcame major speech difficulties. With the help and friendship of an unorthodox speech therapist, he overcame an impairment that had inhibited and plagued his life. The speech therapist believed in him and persisted in his work with and encouragement of the king until he was able to address the nation with confidence in a trying time of war. The king was finally able to find his voice and become a leader.

In 2011, thanks to extensive world media coverage, we were enabled to witness the Egypt of today finding voice. As the world looked on, voices raised for justice brought down a thirty-year-long dictatorship. Cries of "Get out!" became cries of "Freedom!" Persistent voices for justice were heard, and Egypt was changed forever.

One image that captured the world's empathy was an image of Muslims at prayer, surrounded by Christians joining hands, forming a human chain to protect their brothers and sisters at prayer. And then there were some wonderful images of the celebrations in Tahrir Square in Cairo—of people cleaning up. Cleaning up because they recognized that the achievement of the freedom they demanded is not the end of their journey but only the beginning. Everyone is now required to play their part in rebuilding a nation and in ensuring that what they build is true democracy.

And that's where the challenge lies. Building on the foundations that have been laid. Building freedom. Building justice. Finding voice is important. But it is not enough. Throughout history we have heard enough voices raised—and listened to—that seek power. But that power has not always been built on justice. And so we have oppressive regimes all around the world. Often these regimes started out with hope, attracted supporters by fine orations—but then perpetrated evil. Voices are important. But in voices raised there must be sounds of truth and of justice.

Moses' exhortation to the Israelites is for them to choose life by building on the commandments of God—to practice love and justice, to walk in the ways of truth. And the exhortation for us today is to remember whose we are and whom we serve—wherever we are.

Paul Nuechterlein
http://girardianlectionary.net/

Matthew 5

These first four of six antitheses—where Jesus poses traditional law versus God's law of Love that he came to fulfill—are more fruitfully understood through the interaction of the two pillars of Mimetic Theory, a biblical anthropology (from Stanford scholar René Girard; for more on Girard see my essays in this volume: Lent 1A [March 9] for the first pillar; Epiphany 2A [January 19] for the second). The first pillar is that human beings desire according to the desiring of others, which leads to reaching for the same objects of desire (*vis-à-vis* "mimetic desire") and thus sow the seeds to human conflict. The second pillar involves the sacrificial logic that founds and shapes human culture: attempting to substitute a lesser or sanctioned violence for the unwanted violence arising from our mimetic desire. The violence ensuing from mimetic desire threatens to unravel human community; sacrificial violence is what we trust to cohere human community.

Jesus fully understands this biblical anthropology; Mimetic Theory unpacks it for modern ears such that we can make use of it in more fully understanding these antitheses between traditional human law and the fulfillment of God's law in love. A deeper understanding of the Ten Commandments can also assist with understanding these antitheses. Human beings are always at jeopardy of breaking the final commandment against coveting, the law against desiring according to our neighbor, because we are hard-wired for mimesis. Breaking the tenth commandment increases our risk to break the others, because the rivalry generated by Mimetic Desire results in increasing envy, resentment, lust, and anger (and ultimately violence). So in the First Antithesis, Jesus poses the anger caused by mimetic rivalry (coveting) as on a continuum with slandering our neighbor (ninth commandment) and even murdering our neighbor (sixth commandment). Likewise with the Second and Third Antitheses, lust is akin to the breaking of the seventh commandment on adultery, of which divorce is the humanly legal extension.

45

The problem of human violence must be addressed at its root. The ultimate solution is the Greatest Commandment: to love the Lord your God with all your heart and soul and mind. In other words, the only solution to mimetically catching our desires from each other is to catch the desire of God the Father's "complete" love (v. 48), which is fulfilled in Jesus through the communication of the Holy Spirit. Otherwise, we are left to continue our sacrificial solutions of human law based on human councils of judgment (v. 22) and on sacrificial solutions—both in the frightening image of the fires of Gehenna where, Jeremiah 7 tells us, God's people resorted to the fires of ritual child sacrifice, and the more comically characterized, lesser sacrificial violence of amputating one's own hand or eye. Any solution less than following the complete love of the Father coming into the world through the Son—such as the anthropological powers of sacrificial logic that lead to state-sanctioned sins like divorce (adultery) or execution (murder)—is from the "evil one" (Matt 5:37). These lesser solutions characterize all of our lives if not for the "complete" love of the Father of Jesus Christ that graciously rescues us.

Matthew L. Skinner

Matthew 5

In Matthew 5:21-37, Jesus builds on his previous statement that he has come to "fulfill" "the Law and the Prophets" (v. 17). When he says "you have heard that it was said" and refers to Torah, Jesus is interpreting those laws, not abrogating them. He also is working toward what he says in verse 48, that the goodness envisioned in his interpretation of the law is a reflection of God's own perfection or fullness.

Jesus appears to make the law even more far-reaching, with sharper teeth, when he likens anger to murder and lust to adultery. The "righteousness" (v. 20) he commends involves more than avoiding certain actions; it reaches into the thoughts and emotions that dwell within us. Jesus was not the first Jew to recognize that the law is about more than forbidding certain egregious behaviors but also about cultivating an interior disposition or character. Jesus' point is that God's design for human flourishing extends to all aspects of how we live, and to all of who we are. Implied in the commands Jesus issues are promises: the reign of God he enacts proposes to encompass all of our existence. Righteousness involves more than how we act; it includes how we perceive the world, our neighbors, and ourselves.

Many listeners hear condemnation in these verses. This makes sense, given how many "hidden" though common thoughts Jesus names. The task for preachers is crafting a sermon able to do more than just levy accusation. Jesus cares about the deep and multiple dimensions of righteousness because he believes that God's own goodness is capable of saturating and reordering all aspects of human existence. The "kingdom of heaven" Jesus announces reminds us that God is committed to what is best for us and for our neighbors.

Todd Weir
http://bloomingcactus.typepad.com/

Matthew 5

I like to call this section of Matthew "The Pirate Ship Sermon." Imagine if we take the command too seriously to pluck out our eye or cut off our hand if they cause us to sin. Our congregations would look like Blackbeard's crew, with eye patches, peg legs, and hooks for hands. Those outside the church would see us as a cult of self-mutilation. While this would be an absurd religion, at least the effects of our sins would be visible on the outside, rather than buried deep within. A preacher could more easily see the struggles of the congregation, rather than having them buried underneath our Sunday clothes and Sabbath smiles designed to conceal what we really think and feel.

Jesus often unmasked the dangers of outward piety that tries to cover inward spiritual deformity. Sometimes we hide our spiritual failings so well, that even we can no longer see the evidence. Jesus notes that we can feel content if we avoid the obvious big sins of the Ten Commandments, like murder and adultery. As long as we don't kill anyone, or sleep with someone outside of marriage, we are still good people and on the way to heaven. The problem with this thinking is that it becomes a slippery slope when we don't pay attention to the inward attitudes that lead to deeper trouble.

Self-righteousness is often the first sign we are ignoring our inner self. When we find ourselves looking down on the murderers, adulterers, or even people who are poor, we are separating ourselves not only from them but also from our own inner turmoil. Anyone can find someone worse to look down upon, in order to feel better about him- or herself. I have worked with former murderers and drug dealers in the homeless shelter. The murderer looks down on the child molester, and the drug dealer says at least they did not sell to kids. The alcoholic says at least I did not smoke crack. Looking down on the bigger sinner will not lift us up. We must deal with ourselves.

Jesus said that if we are angry with our friend and do not deal with it, we are already harboring the attitudes that lead to murder. If we look around with lust or greed, our foot is on the path. But how do we know we are doing this? Our shadow is deeply buried to keep us from facing our inner pain. The best way I know to examine ourselves is to pay attention to what we judge most in others. Whatever annoys or angers us most in others is often what we most dislike in ourselves, and yet we do not recognize it or want to deal with it.

John Wesley's Notes on the Bible

http://www.ccel.org/ccel/wesley/notes.txt

Matthew 5:22

"Whosoever is angry with his brother"—Some copies add, without a cause—But this is utterly foreign to the whole scope and tenor of our Lord's discourse. If he had only forbidden the being angry without a cause, there was no manner of need of that solemn declaration, I say unto you; for the scribes and Pharisees themselves said as much as this. Even they taught, men ought not to be angry without a cause. So that this righteousness does not exceed theirs. But Christ teaches, that we ought not, for any cause, to be so angry as to call any man...fool. We ought not, for any cause, to be angry at the person of the sinner, but at his sins only. Happy world, were this plain and necessary distinction thoroughly understood, remembered, practiced!

February 23
7th Sunday after Epiphany

Leviticus 19:1-2, 9-18; Psalm 119:33-40; 1 Corinthians 3:10-11, 16-23;
Matthew 5:38-48

Teri Peterson
http://clevertitlehere.blogspot.com

Leviticus 19; 1 Corinthians 3; Matthew 5

It is not uncommon to find ridiculousness in the pages of Scripture. In addition to complex metaphor, vivid imagery, and storytelling that raises even twenty-first-century eyebrows, there's also stuff that just plain makes no sense. Why on earth would you leave part of your harvest in the field—you need the food and income! And besides, isn't that just enabling the poor to be lazy? How could you give to everyone who begs from you—isn't that a recipe for ending up a beggar yourself? Why would you pray for people who want you dead, or invite someone you don't like to a dinner party—that certainly is not in your own best self-interest.

And there we have it, of course: self-interest. Large swaths of the Bible are nonsensical because we're supposed to take care of ourselves, reward ourselves, pay ourselves—first. We have been taught to serve our own happiness, which means doing more, getting more, having more, even if we have to close our eyes to the person standing at field's edge or strike back at someone who tries to take what's ours.

So of course Scripture makes no sense to those of us who are "wise in this age," because "the wisdom of this world is foolishness with God" (1 Cor 3:18-19 NRSV)! In our world's view, it's foolishness to sacrifice to provide for others, but in God's view it's foolishness *not* to. In the world's view, it's silly to offer active non-violent resistance when it's easier to hit back, but in God's view it's the violent response that's ridiculous. We insist on independence, but in reality we "belong to Christ, and Christ belongs to God" (v. 23 NRSV). We strive for our own perfection, but Jesus asks us to strive for God's perfection—perfection of love, justice, compassion (Matt 5:48). Perfect holiness is loving our neighbors as we love ourselves, not loving ourselves *(or God)* to the exclusion of our neighbors . . . or worse, at their expense.

What about those of us who don't have fields in which to leave gleanings, or who do not often directly experience oppression or violence, or who can't name an enemy or persecutor? While we may need a lesson on the cultural issues inherent in turning the other cheek (so we don't interpret it as "be a doormat"), we rarely have opportunity to practice it literally. Ditto on fields and vineyards. But lying, allowing social status to influence judgment, and justice for laborers? Living in an unjust system? Wondering how to handle people who resist our dreams or our full humanity? Sharing our love and lives only with those who love us in return? Those are everyday matters.

Jesus calls us to a higher way than our natural inclination. He does not do away with the law, nor does he make Scripture easier to swallow. He simply casts off literal-legalistic interpretation, which frees us to read those things that make no sense in a new light, the light of God's wisdom, however foolish it may appear.

Natalie Sims
http://lectionarysong.blogspot.com

Psalm 119
Give us life in God's way; teach us your ways; keep us on the path.

"You Are Holy ,You Show Us the Way / Hamba Nathi" (Traditional Zulu)—There are a lot of translations and variations of this song. It's very joyful, and a good base for writing your own lyrics for different liturgical uses (e.g., benedictions, processionals). Make sure you teach the congregation the pronunciation, so they don't freak out when they see the word "Mkhululi." I like this translation (http://rockhay.tripod.com/worship/music/hambanathi.htm) best, but am not sure where it's available.

"And on This Path" (Linnea Good)—In our congregation, we sing it as a gospel-style song with big chords and a groovy bass part; it's really joyous!

"The Grace of God Is Like a Road" (Michael Hudson)—Really beautiful words sung to a very familiar Celtic hymn tune (THE GIFT OF LOVE, which is very similar to O WALY WALY). Highly recommended. I would even print these words for the congregation to take home with them and meditate with during the week. A good song to sing after the sermon. Lyrics (http://www.stgeorgesepiscopal.net/Bulletins/2011/2011_01/2011_01_16/05_30_Bulletin.pdf).

"I Want Jesus to Walk with Me" (African American spiritual)—I don't usually suggest Jesus songs for the Hebrew Scriptures, but this is such a beautiful song, and meditative, so I think it could work. I especially like Eric Bibb's version (http://www.youtube.com/watch?v=59FfyEbDPAw).

Ever in Your Understanding (Isaac Everett)—This book is one of my sure resources for the Psalms; each Psalm is read over improvised music based on the main chord, and the congregation joins in the sung refrain. If your musicians are not great improvisers, they can simply play the chord progression of the Psalm refrain (gently) during the read verses. Sample music (https://www.churchpublishing.org/products/index.cfm?fuseaction=productDetail&productID=6226)

"We Will Go with God / Sizahamba Nnaye" (Traditional Swaziland)—A simple song from Swaziland. Good for the end of the service. Video with pronunciation and parts (http://www.youtube.com/watch?v=VunGjb_mJmQ&feature=related).

John Petty
http://progressiveinvolvement.com

Matthew 5

"If anyone strikes you on the right cheek, turn the other also" (v. 39 NRSV). How would someone land a right hook on someone else's right cheek? They can't. The only way to do it is by backhanding the person. The backhand is an insult, an expression of dominance. It says: I can humiliate you, and you can't do a thing about it.

If someone backhands you on the right cheek, Jesus says, lift your head back up, turn your cheek and expose the left one as well. You have dignity as a human being. Don't let someone else take that away from you. Stand there with head held high.

"If anyone wants to sue you, and take your shirt, let him have your coat also" (v. 40 NASB). The coat, or outer garment, was sometimes used by the (very) poor as collateral for a loan (Deut 24:10-13). If the coat was used for collateral, it had to be returned to the person by nightfall so they could sleep in it. The next morning, however, the person's creditors could come and get it again.

The situation Jesus describes is one in which a destitute peasant is getting pestered to the point of being sued for his underwear. If you're getting sued for your underwear, give it up.

Nakedness was considered shameful in the ancient world, and anyone who viewed a naked person was also shamed. Giving your "coat also" is confrontational. It says: I'm willing to strip off my clothes. I expose myself, and *you,* as a way of exposing the whole oppressive system.

Jesus' message is that these laws are unjust, and the Lord God is not on the side of your oppressor. "Give your coat also" is an expression of disgust at the whole rotten system that perpetrates poverty and denies dignity. "You can't take my coat; I freely give it"—this is a way of asserting personal agency in the face of dehumanizing oppression.

"Whoever shall force you to go one mile, go with him two" (v. 41 NASB). This refers to the practice of *angereia*. The Romans had a law by which they could make their subjects carry a soldier's gear for one mile. This is what allowed the Romans to make Simon of Cyrene carry Jesus' cross (Mark 15:21).

Pressing Jews into service was widely practiced throughout the country—and widely resented. Abuses were so widespread, in fact, that Rome later applied some limits. You know things are bad when even Rome thinks it's too much.

In martial arts, one takes the energy of one's opponent and uses that energy against them. Jesus encourages something like it. The Romans could compel you to carry gear for one mile, but *only* one mile. Carry the soldier's pack another mile, and that soldier may have some explaining to do to his superiors.

Suddenly, the upper hand gets shifted. Going the "extra mile" is an assertion of independence and personal autonomy in a situation that is ordinarily dehumanizing.

Marci Auld Glass
www.marciglass.com

Matthew 5

We, as a culture, and often even as a church, have bought into the myth that violence can be "cured" with more violence.

And you can think about that what you will, but Jesus is pretty clear. "You have heard that it was said, 'An eye for an eye and a tooth for a tooth.' But I say to you, Do not resist an evildoer. But if anyone strikes you on the right cheek, turn the other also" (vv. 38-39 NRSV).

Before we look at what I think Jesus means by this, let me say what he isn't saying. If you, or someone you love, is in an abusive relationship, Jesus is *not* saying that you should just take the abuse.

What he *is* saying is that when you encounter violence, you are *not* to respond with violence. The word translated as "resist," as in "do not resist an evildoer" should conjure up images of armed resistance, not submission. So Jesus is *not* telling us to continue to put up with violence. He is *not* telling us to submit to it. He is telling us to resist violence, but not with more violence.

If this violent world in which we live is to be different, it has to start with us. We have to break that cycle. Because whether we're righteous or unrighteous, evil or good, we are all God's children on whom the sun rises and the rain falls. All of us. No exceptions.

And while Jesus is most certainly concerned about justice for the weak, the poor, the marginalized, he is also concerned about justice for the powerful, the rich, and the mighty. Because here is the truth woven throughout the Sermon on the Mount: *there is no justice for one of us unless there is justice for all of us.*

So, let's take some "eye for an eye" scenarios:

If you steal my cow, my family will take one of your cows.

If you kill my sister, my family will kill your sister.

If you bomb my village, my village will bomb your village.

We can recognize a sort of justice in that *quid pro quo* system. But Jesus wants us to understand that the underlying problems that lead someone to kill, steal, or destroy will not be fixed or redeemed with an eye for an eye. Jesus doesn't call us to break that cycle of reciprocal violence to be clever. He calls us to practice non-violence so that *everyone* has a chance at redemption. It isn't about one side winning or one side losing. Both sides must realize there is only one side, that we are all children of God. An "eye for an eye" doesn't allow for that.

NOTES: Adapted from "Resistance," a sermon preached by Marci Auld Glass (http://marciglass.com/2011/02/13/resistance/).
The book *I Shall Not Hate* by Izzeldin Abulaish provides a powerful illustration of non-violence as seen through the Gaza violence.

Julia Seymour
http://lutheranjulia.blogspot.com

Matthew 5

"Be perfect, therefore, as your heavenly Father is perfect" (v. 48 NRSV).

"Therefore you are to be perfect, as your heavenly Father is perfect" (v. 48 NASB).

"Therefore, just as your heavenly Father is complete in showing love to everyone, so also you must be complete" (v. 48).

"In a word, what I'm saying is, *Grow up*. You're kingdom subjects. Now live like it. Live out your God-created identity. Live generously and graciously toward others, the way God lives toward you" (v. 48 The Message).

No matter how loose a translation one might consult, there is no escaping the high standard for behavior set by Jesus in this verse. Since most of us know that we fall short of perfection, it often seems as if we do not even want to try. We dismiss the standard as impossible and consider the case closed.

It is as though we cannot win the marathon, so we are not willing to try the one-mile walk or the 5K. It is as if we cannot speak Spanish, so we do not offer even a *gracias* to someone who might appreciate the effort. We understand that we cannot be Ansel Adams, so we will never even take a picture at a birthday party.

Effort matters. The work of our hands, the words of our mouths, the energy of our determination is, in part, how God accomplishes God's purposes in the world. We are not only called to be co-creators, disciples, co-workers in kingdom; we are equipped and guided to that work. Yet we allow the fear of failure to stop us short.

There is no failure in grace. There is only growth. The gift of sanctification is that God expects to be shaping us, God is planning to work on us, God is bringing us into who we are supposed to be. When we stop short, we put ourselves in God's place because we act as though we know exactly how much we are capable of doing and no more.

Are you greater than God? Are you greater than God's effort in you? Are you resisting shaping because of the limitations of your own understanding, or are you yielding through trust in the strength and promise of Christ? If you are alive, the Spirit's work of bringing you to perfection is still happening. Do not second-guess the work of the Lord.

Matthew L. Skinner

Matthew 5

At verse 38, the tone of Jesus' "you have heard that it was said" statements takes a slight turn. What is the proper response to those who mean to harm, oppress, or persecute Jesus' followers? The Old Testament's multiple references to "an eye for an eye" may have been intended to prevent excessive penalties for offenses. Do they also imply that retaliation is always within an injured person's rights?

Jesus rejects such an implication and instead advocates love for one's enemies. Such a love extends beyond passive forbearance of opponents; it calls a person also to pray for oppressors.

We misunderstand Jesus' point if we take him to commend a victim's compliant acceptance of gratuitous abuse. Such an interpretation does not square with the broader Gospel's portrayal of Jesus as a healer determined to alleviate suffering.

For one thing, the responses Jesus commends in these verses have a way of exposing injustice, not simply suffering under its weight. What kind of person slaps two cheeks? What does it say about those who take another's "shirt" (tunic), probably as a marker for an unpaid loan, *and also* that person's outer "coat"? If a soldier conscripts you to carry something for a mile, how far in excess do you need to go before his abuse becomes plain, even embarrassing to him? Humiliation can cut two ways.

Second, some of the abuse described here (especially in vv. 43-47) comes as a consequence of following Jesus. Jesus does not praise random suffering, but he does acknowledge that disciples should expect persecution. Those who respond to it, not with retaliation, but with genuine love, begin to participate in the same righteousness that Jesus himself exemplified.

John Wesley's Notes on the Bible
http://www.ccel.org/ccel/wesley/notes.txt

Matthew 5:40-41

Where the damage is not great, choose rather to suffer it, though possibly it may on that account be repeated, than to demand an eye for an eye, to enter into a rigorous prosecution of the offender. The meaning of the whole passage seems to be, rather than return evil for evil, when the wrong is purely personal, submit to one bodily wrong after another, give up one part of your goods after another, submit to one instance of compulsion after another. That the words are not literally to be understood, appears from the behaviour of our Lord himself (see John 18:22).

March 2
Transfiguration Sunday

Exodus 24:12-18; Psalm 2 or Psalm 99; 2 Peter 1:16-21; Matthew 17:1-9

Dan Clendenin
http://journeywithjesus.net

Matthew 17

Some readers dismiss this story as a bizarre fiction. A different reading tries to have its cake and eat it, too. It purges the story of offensive elements while retaining some kernel of truth—for example, interpreting the transfiguration as an embellished tale, as a truth communicated by myth or metaphor, or even as a misplaced and reinterpreted account of the resurrection. But this strategy is easier said than done. Its tendency, as history has shown, has been to make the ancient story look and sound suspiciously like the modern critic.

Decades after the transfiguration, Peter appealed to their terrifying experience precisely to rebut criticisms that the early believers followed "cleverly invented stories" as opposed to "eyewitness" accounts of actual events (2 Peter 1:16-18 NIV 1984). The details of the story—exactly six days after Peter's confession that Jesus is the Christ (Mark 8:27-30), the identification of Mount Hermon in present-day Syria, which reaches 9,000 feet, the secluded and private nature of the incident, the palpable fear they exhibited, Peter's impulsive outburst, and their confusion about something so essential as the resurrection from the dead—all these unflattering details suggest that the evangelists were writing history and not myth or metaphor, even if the story, like so many stories in the Gospels, is easier to describe than to explain.

It's true that people of their time and place enjoyed a worldview that's different from ours, but this doesn't mean that Christians back then were inherently more credulous than we are today. I find it hard to fathom why the evangelists would propagate a story that they knew was false, and knew that their detractors could falsify, knowing that a needlessly ludicrous claim would harm their cause, and knowing, as they surely did for the first 250 years of the church, that making outrageous claims would earn them social ridicule, political marginalization, and physical persecution. Peter and the disciples would have been wrong to deny an experience that they had, no matter how bizarre or difficult it was to comprehend and explain.

It's easy for Christians who have become over-familiar with the Gospel texts and traditions to domesticate and diminish them—to tame the ineffable, trivialize the indescribable, to cut and trim God down to our size so that we can manage God. The transfiguration of Jesus belies all the ways we dilute the stringent wine of the Gospel. The blinding light and the voice from the clouds challenge faith that has turned tepid, perfunctory, and bored.

Suzanne Guthrie
http://www.edgeofenclosure.org

"Tabor Light" (Matthew 17)

A high mountain. The cloud of Presence. The voice of the Most High. The disciples fall into ecstasy. They see time disassemble. They see Jesus, Moses, and Elijah outside of time talking about something that will happen in time, Jesus' "exodus."

And the light! The Orthodox call it "Tabor Light." It is the light that transfigures Moses, so that he has to wear a veil. It is the light that blinds Paul on his way to Damascus. It is the light at the boundary of the soul, alluring us in meditation to continue deepening and remaining faithful, even when prayer is dark.

Augustine writes about the light in his soul:

> With you as my guide I entered into my innermost citadel, and was given power to do so because you had become my helper (Psalm 29:11). I entered and with my soul's eye, such as it was, saw above that same eye of my soul the immutable light higher than my mind—not the light of every day, obvious to anyone, not a larger version of the same kind which would, as it were, have given out a much brighter light and filled everything with its magnitude. It was not that light, but a different thing, utterly different from all our kinds of light. It transcended my mind, not in the way the oil floats on water, nor as heaven is above earth. It was superior because it made me, and I was inferior because I was made by it. The person who knows the truth knows it, and he who knows it knows eternity. Love knows it.
> (Augustine, *Confessions*, book 7, chapter 10, Oxford World's Classics, trans. Henry Chadwick [UK: Oxford University Press, paperback 1998], 123.)

Pseudo-Macarius (fourth century) also writes about the light, once integrated fully in the soul:

> [S]o also when the soul is perfectly illumined with the ineffable beauty and glory of the light of Christ's countenance, and granted perfect communion with the Holy Spirit and counted worthy to become the dwelling-place and throne of God, then the soul becomes all eye, all light, all face, all glory, all spirit.
> (Pseudo-Macarius, *Spiritual Homilies*, Alphabetical Collection "H," 1, 2 [Paris: *Coptic Apophthegms*, 1894] as quoted in *Celebrating the Saints: Devotional Readings for Saint's Days* [Harrisburg, Pa.: Morehouse Publishing, 2001], 251.)

Further integration is necessary, however. Coming down from the mountain, or up from the "innermost citadel," the soul's lingering light must deal with life's dangerous and heartbreaking challenges. Face set toward Jerusalem, the journey continues.

Ann Scull
http://seedstuff.blogspot.com

Two Useful Images

(a) A photo taken in the Australian high country where it snows in winter. You can find the image at http://seedstuff.blogspot.com.au/2011/02/transfiguration-of-jesus-march-6.html (accessed March 27, 2012).

Sometimes, as on the day this photo was taken, the light up there is clearly different and the mountains seem to glow.

(b) A photo taken looking down Duck Arm on the Gippsland Lakes at sunset with 2 Peter 1:16 added as text. You can find the image at http://seedstuff.blogspot.com.au/2011/02/transfiguration-of-jesus-march-6.html (accessed March 27, 2012).

Listening Song

Newsboys, *"Shine"* on *Shine: The Hits,* compilation remix (USA: Sparrow Records, 2000). This song uses words directly from Matthew 5; however, seeing it is a song about shining, it fits in with the transfiguration story very well.

Kids' Story

Weslandia by Paul Fleischman (New York, HarperCollins, 1999). This is a children's story that is both profound and appealing to all ages. Using the knowledge he has gained, Wesley has the courage to be the person he knows he can be; just as the transfiguration event gave the disciples the courage to later share the gospel and to be the people God wanted them to be. Use these two stories together to provoke people into thinking about the person God wants each of them to be.

Discussion Topic

Share a time when you have experienced the presence of God.

Stories

- **"The Job Applicant"** by Wayne Rice, *Hot Illustrations for Youth Talks* (El Cajon, Calif.: Youth Specialties, 1994), 126–27. This is a story that challenges us to "Listen to him!" (Matthew 17:5) and to learn to listen to him through and despite the noise and busyness of our lives.
- **"The Boy and the Circus"** by Wayne Rice, *Hot Illustrations for Youth Talks* (El Cajon, Calif.: Youth Specialties, 1994), 56–57. This poignant little story warns us not to be like the frightened disciples on the mountain, and set our sights too low, when it comes to understanding what God has to offer us.

Adult Response

Give everyone a pencil and a postcard with a mountain pictured on one side and a blank space on the other. These are easy to make with any reasonable sort of publishing software and a clipart image, one of your own photos, or mine (see above). Ask people to imagine ways we can "climb the mountain." Where are the special places and times in our lives in which God can speak to us? Encourage people to write a prayer, draw a picture, compose a poem, or put down a resolution that reminds them of these special places and times. Playing a piece of music while people work by themselves is often helpful. For this worship response, I used Robert Prizeman, "Jubilate" on *Libera* (London: Warner Classics, 1999).

Matthew L. Skinner

Matthew 17

The transfiguration occurs at an important junction in the Gospel narrative. Jesus has just raised the question of his identity and predicted his death and resurrection. The cross begins to emerge as Jesus' unavoidable destiny. Here, recalling Jesus' baptism, another episode of divine approval takes place. God endorses what Jesus has just said, confirming that the cross is neither a failure nor a mistake.

The transfiguration does not appear to be an attempt to reassure Jesus. The voice from the cloud (indicating God's presence) speaks not to him but to his three disciples. The moment is for them. They receive a privileged glimpse into Jesus' majesty, symbolized by his dazzling face and clothes. Perhaps they are offered, if only for a split second, Jesus arrayed in clear splendor—a striking contrast to the confusion and struggle that plague them throughout this Gospel.

Moses and Elijah were remembered as Israel's greatest prophets. Each met God on Mount Sinai (or Horeb). Each had a role to play in God's imagined future, according to Deuteronomy 18:16-20 and Malachi 4:4-6. Perhaps, then, the disciples also glimpse God's future—the presence of God's accomplished spokespeople symbolizes the ultimate accomplishment of God's purposes. The cross, then, is not merely inevitable for Jesus. It will become the means by which God's intentions for humanity are brought to fruition.

The transfiguration raises many questions yet answers few. It offers enough of a glimpse to prod us into continuing the journey with Jesus, to see when and how this majestic future will materialize. It points us toward the cross, here at the cusp of Lent, even as it makes us remember our own moments of spiritual transcendence or clarity, where perhaps we spied a hint of God's undeniable reality. And so we press on.

John van de Laar
http://www.sacredise.com/

Matthew 17

Have you ever felt that you had understood something clearly, only to discover that you had missed the point? This has happened to me a few times. School mathematics and more than a few arguments come to mind. It takes time to understand well, and if we don't take it we usually end up in pain. But, if we are willing to listen, we always find that the truth is only too willing to reveal itself.

Matthew's account of the transfiguration is a case in point. Peter moves from an uninformed opinion about the Messiah in 16:22 to an inappropriate response to the glorification of Jesus in 17:5. In the first instance, still basking in the glow of his faith declaration, Peter rebukes Jesus for predicting that the Messiah must die. In the second, in the midst of the glorious manifestations, Peter seeks to capture the moment. But neither the lights and smoke, nor even the glorification of Jesus, were the point.

Matthew's Gospel is built on one simple truth: Jesus is the promised "prophet like Moses," and he teaches that the law is fulfilled when it captures the heart and leads to lives of justice, compassion, and peace (see the Sermon on the Mount). The point for Matthew is that the *eschaton*, the end-time reign of God, has come. It seems that Peter is just beginning to understand this when he makes his declaration, but then he fails to perceive the nature of this new reality. He still believes that a dead Messiah is no Messiah, and that God's reign must overthrow Rome.

On the mountain Peter is given the signs that show him the truth of Jesus' Messiahship. Two eschatological characters appear with Jesus—Elijah, prophesied to come before the Messiah (hence the discussion on the way down the mountain in vv. 10-13), and Moses. If there was any doubt that Jesus was the "one like Moses," the parallels between this trip up the mountain and Moses' journey to receive the law are striking. Three friends are named as companions, the cloud of smoke appears, God's voice is heard, and both Moses and Jesus shine brilliantly in God's presence. The message is clear—the eschaton truly is among them, and it will be established through the sacrifice of Jesus and of those who follow him.

We still struggle with this revelation of God's reign. We still portray God's Messiah as a conquering general rather than a self-sacrificing servant. We still view God's reign as an empire that destroys all others, instead of the divine reality that transforms by grace. Like Peter, we need to be cautious in our assumptions about God's reign. Like Peter, we need to listen more, watch more, and open ourselves to this startling new reality. Heaven knows, our world is longing for those who see God's reign more clearly and are willing to pay the price to live it out.

John Wesley's Notes on the Bible
http://www.ccel.org/ccel/wesley/notes.txt

Matthew 17:1-9

"Tell the vision to no man"—Not to the rest of the disciples, lest they should be grieved and discouraged because they were not admitted to the sight: nor to any other persons, lest it should enrage some the more, and his approaching sufferings shall make others disbelieve it; till the Son of man be risen again—Till the resurrection should make it credible, and confirm their testimony about it.

March 5
Ash Wednesday

Joel 2:1-2, 12-17 or Isaiah 58:1-12; Psalm 51:1-17; 2 Corinthians 5:20b–6:10; Matthew 6:1-6, 16-21

Liz Crumlish
http://somethingtostandon.blogspot.co.uk

Joel 2; Matthew 6

For many years, the practice of donning ashes at the start of Lent seemed, to me, to be at odds with Jesus' exhortation to perform our spiritual disciplines in secret. For many, that will be the only time of the year when we make a public spectacle of our repentance, perhaps even our faith. As I grew up, it wasn't a discipline observed in my Presbyterian upbringing. However, the first time I did participate in this ritual, having ashes placed on my forehead by a beloved Roman Catholic colleague, I was so moved by the experience that I vowed to seek the opportunity to make this observance accessible wherever I ministered. There is something in the donning of ashes that speaks of change for us and the world around us—a symbol of change that needs to be publicly displayed and not hidden away behind locked doors.

The dark smudge on my forehead
feels dry and grainy.
Felt cool and damp as it was placed there.
Already it has changed.
Remember you are dust
and to dust you shall return.
Dry, sobering words.
God forbid that any should forget
their humble beginnings
or equally humble, inevitable end
Summed up in a smudge of ash!
Sobering if that were all:
Remember that you are dust
and to dust you shall return.
But, there's more.
In those ashes
lies not just a salutary reminder
but an exhortation—
a call to turn from sin
and live out the gospel,
an affirmation
that, from those humble beginnings,
we are called to great things

Turn from sin and live out the gospel
transforming the dirty smudge on my forehead
into an aspiration of service
changing its weight and import
into a sign of hope
that this ancient holy day ritual
still has import.
In a world rushing on to the next thing
ashes become
symbols of love
carrying all the potential
to spread love
as the gospel is lived out
in ordinary people
in humble people
who don ashes
to change the world.

Chuck Aaron

Psalm 51; Matthew 6

Reading Psalm 51 in conjunction with the passage from Matthew highlights the sharp contrast between the genuineness of the psalmist and the potential for self-aggrandizement against which Jesus warns. The psalmist experiences true remorse, relying solely on God's character and mercy for forgiveness. Jesus, by contrast, describes those who practice a false religiosity in pursuit of admiration.

Most contemporary Christians would locate their faith somewhere between the two poles of these passages. Politicians and business leaders sometimes parade their religiosity for votes or the lure of customers, but average churchgoers rarely make a show of long prayers for attention. Many in church shy from praying in public at all. Most giving to a church remains anonymous, although some people give ostentatiously. Christians rarely fast, with potlucks drawing nice crowds.

Few Christians face their sins with the same remorse as the psalmist. They make excuses, rationalize, obsess over sins against them, and rely on cheap grace. These two passages give the preacher an opportunity to speak about authentic faith in the heart, and the ways that prayer, giving, and fasting can feed such faith. The psalmist seeks to restore a broken relationship with God, characterized by contrition and a deep desire to change from within. The religious activities Jesus mentions can feed that opportunity to grow and change, if the Christian uses them wisely and faithfully. An Ash Wednesday sermon drawing on these two passages could explore the things that prevent Christians from obtaining the genuine faith and repentance of the psalmist, while redeeming the practices that Jesus warns can become distorted. Praying, giving, and fasting should lead one to a deeper relationship with God that serves as its own reward. These actions also connect the Christian to others, especially to those in need.

Julie Craig
http://winsomelearnsome.com

Psalm 51

I remember the first time I celebrated Ash Wednesday as a pastor. I had forgotten to buy ashes—a fact I discovered when I met with my clergy women's group the Monday before Ash Wednesday—so in a panic, I decided to make some.

I couldn't find any leftover palms in the church building, since the congregation had had a pulpit-supply preacher the previous year who hadn't saved any back, of course. I decided that ashes were ashes, and I would find some yard clippings from my back yard to burn.

The weather turned cold on Tuesday, but I knew I should burn the clippings outside just in case any noxious fumes would be created. So I built a fire in an old coffee can on our little kettle grill, and laid the clippings in. I had some fits and starts, since the clippings were not 100% dry, but eventually the clippings all turned to a grey ash.

Unfortunately, the wind kicked up as I was carrying the can back to the house, and I found out the hazard of DIY ashes. A fine, gray film blew everywhere—on me, on the back deck, and all over the kitchen when I finally made it into the house. I hurried to set the can down and shut the back door, but the damage was done. Everything that those ashes came into contact with was covered with a fine gray dusty coating.

Our mortality touches every part of us. There is no aspect of our being that is not left vulnerable to our finitude. As I washed my hands and arms, and wiped down the kitchen counters, I recalled the words of the psalmist:

> Have mercy on me, O God, / according to your steadfast love; / according to your abundant mercy / blot out my transgressions. / Wash me thoroughly from my iniquity, / and cleanse me from my sin. / For I know my transgressions, / and my sin is ever before me. / Against you, you alone, have I sinned, / and done what is evil in your sight, / so that you are justified in your sentence / and blameless when you pass judgment. / Indeed, I was born guilty, / a sinner when my mother conceived me. / You desire truth in the inward being; / therefore teach me wisdom in my secret heart. / Purge me with hyssop, and I shall be clean; / wash me, and I shall be whiter than snow. (vv. 1-7 NRSV)

Todd Weir
http://bloomingcactus.typepad.com/

Psalm 51

We sometimes think of Lent as the annual visit to the doctor's office to make sure we are spiritually healthy, expecting little to be wrong. But King David, in Psalm 51, is not coming in for a check-up. He is not asking, "Am I doing OK, doc?" He says,

> I know my transgressions and my sin is ever before me. / Against you, you alone, have I sinned, / and done what is evil in your sight, / so that you are justified in your sentence / and blameless when you pass judgment. / Indeed, I was born guilty, a sinner when my mother conceived me. (vv. 3-5 NRSV)

David is more like a patient waiting for a heart transplant. "Create in me a clean heart, O God, / and put a new and right spirit within me" (v. 10 NRSV). Listen to the verbs—wash me thoroughly, cleanse me, purge me, deliver me, restore me, teach me. He is a man in anguish, describing his feelings as his very bones have been crushed. Like a patient with a faulty heart valve, he knows that the great physician must do something radical with his heart.

Since we begin Lent by having ashes smeared on our foreheads, it is hard to miss the point that we are all sinners. But like a patient waiting on a heart transplant list, I wonder if God's grace will really touch me and heal me. Will I survive long enough for my name to be called? If I make it through surgery alive, will the new heart take to my chest or will it be rejected by my flesh? I don't doubt that I'm a sinner. My bigger problem is I'm not sure I trust the great physician to heal me. I don't have David's passion and trust in the mercy and steadfast love of God. Maybe that is my biggest sin. I'm afraid to say, "Restore to me the joy of your salvation, / and sustain in me a willing spirit" (v. 12 NRSV). My fear is that I will cry out and nothing will happen.

I can relate to David's sense of desolation, for I once spent a year attending church but not having the nerve to go to the communion rail, and for five years I thought I would never step in a pulpit. Eventually I came to know what I should have always known. There is more grace in God than sin in me. God did not cast me away from divine presence or take the Holy Spirit from me. I find it hard to believe that my sin is just blotted out, but I am blessed for I have heard joy and gladness from the Lord. I am washed, and though I may still be in the spin cycle, yet shall I dry. Hear me and believe, God abounds in steadfast love, and there is more grace in God than sin in you.

John Wesley's Notes on the Bible
http://www.ccel.org/ccel/wesley/notes.txt

Psalm 51:4

"Thee only"—Which is not to be, understood absolutely, because he had sinned against Bathsheba and Uriah, and many others; but comparatively. So the sense is, though I have sinned against my own conscience, and against others; yet nothing is more grievous to me, than that I have sinned against thee.

Teri Peterson
http://clevertitlehere.blogspot.com

Matthew 6

There's a certain irony in reading this Matthew passage on Ash Wednesday. There aren't many times when Mainline Protestants can truthfully be accused of showy religious practices, and the one time a year when we do put on an outwardly visible mark, we first are admonished to beware of practicing our religion before others. But it is important to read the rest of the sentence—Jesus doesn't say, "don't practice your faith where other people can see," he says, "don't practice your religion to draw others' attention" (Matthew 6:1). If the purpose of our faith practice is to make an impression on others, to garner attention for ourselves, then we *do* need to beware—there is no benefit in that practice. Jesus was neither the first nor the last to say so! Isaiah rails against showy religion too. He says to forget about the outward trappings that do nothing but bring glory to us, and instead to look to practices that glorify God—feeding the hungry, correcting injustice, giving of ourselves.

Jesus said the same—notice he didn't do away with the practice, only with the prestige and worldly benefits. Jesus says "*when* you give" and "*when* you fast" and "*when* you pray." He assumes we will do these things, assumes we will practice our faith, assumes we will continue to seek a relationship with God, even if no one is watching and waiting to praise our piety.

Will we?

We are entering a season when it's tempting to either drag friends and family through our caffeine- and dessert-deprived wilderness along with us, or to ignore it because we're somehow above the spiritual disciplines of Lent. Wherever along that spectrum we fall, these readings invite us to another way. Joel calls us to "tear your hearts and not your clothing" (2:13 CEB)—to recognize that we have not lived as God's covenant people; we have followed other ways, we have broken God's heart. This is one of the things we can feel in that gritty ash cross, but if our only sign of that recognition is on the outside, we have still missed the point and the opportunity in the practice. "Return to me with all your hearts" (2:12). Return—related to "repent," the word of Lent. But to repent, to turn, to return, is a wholehearted endeavor, though our hearts may be torn and broken. It requires all of us; it's not something we can do halfway. Half-hearted faith, the faith of torn clothes and proudly worn ashes, easily becomes showy religion that reaps only immediate rewards. But the ashes of a torn heart make room for a life-changing relationship with the most merciful, compassionate, patient, forgiving Love—a Love that will give us new hearts and new lives, if only we will live in the new kingdom.

March 9
1st Sunday in Lent

Genesis 2:15-17; 3:1-7; Psalm 32; Romans 5:12-19; Matthew 4:1-11

Chuck Aaron

Genesis 2–3; Matthew 4

Lent serves as a time set aside by the church for self-examination, repentance, spiritual growth, and preparation for Easter. All four of the passages assigned for this Sunday interpret the doctrines of sin, temptation, and guilt. Psalm 32 poignantly describes the potential physical effects of denied sin. The Romans passage reflects theologically on the introduction, spread, and pervasiveness of sin. Then Paul proclaims the work of the Messiah to break the power of sin, over people and creation.

The Genesis passage and the Matthew passage both explore sensitively and carefully the experience of temptation. Both texts seek to determine the nature of temptation and the deepest thing(s) people desire in temptation. In Genesis, the two desire to leave innocence and plunge themselves into the world of good and evil. The terms *good* and *evil* imply more than right and wrong, suggesting that the couple desires the sophistication of the darkness of life. Although the reading stops at v. 17, the whole passage contains the awful insight that even though people should not be alone (v. 18), they betray each other at the first opportunity. The Matthew passage expands the understanding of temptation to include power and presumption about one's relationship with God.

When the reader compares the Genesis and Matthew passages, one of the interesting insights that emerges is that temptation can occur in times of plenty and abundance, as in the garden in Genesis, and in times of deprivation, as with Jesus' hunger in the wilderness. Peer pressure, as in the garden, or loneliness, as with Jesus, can facilitate temptation. Temptation arises within the human heart in a variety of situations.

Jesus experiences again the temptations of Israel in the wilderness. Just as his obedience redeems Israel's failure, so it redeems the failures of the contemporary church.

Barbara Dick

Genesis 3; Matthew 4

Temptation is such a loaded word. When I was growing up, I viewed temptation as one of those nasty things you didn't talk about in mixed company. It was as if, in the act of being tempted, a person was already in sin. Resisting temptation involved thinking "pure" thoughts and avoiding media that dealt with "certain subjects." Living in a middle-class suburb, it was fairly easy to distance myself from temptation as I understood it. I was comfortable, secure, naïve, and sheltered; temptation had very little opportunity to get at me.

But those external influences have gotten more insistent. Today, I know of no means for avoiding external temptation in daily life. We are bombarded by it every moment of every day in television, movie product placement, pop-up ads, billboards, website banners. Use this product and you will have friends, mates, wealth, happiness. Take this pill, and you will be thin, fit, healthy. And it's about more than advertising, of course. For our consumerist society to succeed, we are told we must give in to temptation. If we don't, the economy will suffer, people will lose their jobs, and the stock market will crash.

So, what is the difference between the first humans and Jesus? Why did they give in? Why could he resist, and how can we? As we grow in experience and understanding, we learn that resisting temptation is more about being present in our choices than it is about fighting external influence. The first humans reacted to pretty fruit and ate; Jesus considered alternatives, and made conscious choices. The Holy Spirit works in our lives to help us to respond rather than react, to make space in our hearts and brains for more informed decision making about purchasing, relationships, lifestyle, love, and service.

Carolyn Winfrey Gillette
http://www.carolynshymns.com/

Our Lord, You Were Sent (Matthew 4)

Our Lord, you were sent to a place wild and vast
To ponder your mission, to pray and to fast;
Then hungry and weary, you faced night and day
The subtle temptations to turn from God's way.

How could it be wrong to want bread on the shelf?
To seek, in one's serving, to first serve one's self?
But by God's own word you remained ever sure:
It's only in God that our lives are secure.

How could it be wrong to step out and to dare,
To prove with great drama the depths of God's care?
But you knew God's word, true since all time began:
It's wrong to expect God to work by our plan.

How could it be wrong to just once bow the knee,
To shake hands with sin to achieve victory?
Yet you made it clear that no matter the cost:
Your path was obedience, your way was the cross.

Our Lord, in your struggle you chose to obey;
God's word filled your heart and you trusted God's way.
Now risen, you save us from sins that destroy;
You give us your Spirit, your peace and your joy.

NOTES
Biblical Texts: Matthew 4:1-11; Mark 1:12-13; Luke 4:1-13
Music: FOUNDATION 11.11.11.11 ("How Firm a Foundation"), American Folk Melody, Funk's *Genuine Church Music,* 1832
Text: Copyright © 2000 by Carolyn Winfrey Gillette. All rights reserved.
Also published in *Songs of Grace: New Hymns for God and Neighbor* by Carolyn Winfrey Gillette (Nashville: Upper Room Books, 2009), 13.

Paul Nuechterlein
http://girardianlectionary.net/

Genesis 2–3; Romans 5

"So when the woman *saw* that the tree was...to be desired..." (Gen 3:6a NRSV, emphasis added). The narrator of Genesis 3 seems to intuit that the woman did not just happen to desire the fruit, but that the serpent interjected that desire. Up until that time she was content to not eat of the forbidden fruit. But when the serpent persuaded her how desirable it was, the woman caught her desire from the serpent, and then the man from the woman. The paradisial love of the Creator was traded for the envy of fellow creatures.

This beautifully illustrates the core principle of René Girard's Mimetic (Greek: *mimeomai,* "imitate") Theory: that we *see* our desires—but not in the way we might think. Mimetic Theory suggests that we do not see the object in itself as desirable, but rather we see the other person desiring the object, which in turn fuels our desire.

The Ten Commandments (where *desire* is translated as *covet*) also clearly illustrate the mimetic understanding of desire. The tenth commandment begins with a specific list of objects of desire typically possessed by our neighbor, and concludes with "or anything that belongs to your neighbor" (Exod 20:17 NRSV). The commandment does not say we cannot desire objects but that we are forbidden from desiring according to our neighbor.

It has long been recognized that human beings learn by imitation. In the last twenty years, neuroscientists have identified *mirror neurons* as a core part of the cortex in the human brain. Our brains are hard-wired for imitation. Girard was the first to strongly thematize the fact that we also learn *desiring* by imitation—with the resulting negative tendency to reach for the same objects of desire. The nature of human desiring tends to lead us toward coveting, where we become rivals with one another for the objects we desire—as toddlers: toys; as nations: land and resources.

Mimetic desire is also confirmed by the current Western culture of consumerism. Advertisers understand mimetic desire implicitly. They do not simply show us the desirability of their products. They show us peers desiring their products. "Be like Mike" was the Nike byline during the Michael Jordan years. And the upshot is a culture based on making us all rivals of one another—of "keeping up with the Joneses."

But there is another Way, another Culture, God's Culture in Jesus Christ. Romans 5 shows us Paul's typology of the first Adam and second Adam. The first Adam falls prey to desiring according to our neighbor, a downward spiral into coveting, conflict, and violence; and all the Adams and Eves are caught in that same fallen desiring—"life in the flesh." But the second Adam—Jesus—comes to incarnate God's loving desire, which is never conflictual. Imitating Christ, we are able to live "life in the Spirit"; we live according to God's Love in Jesus Christ that leads us to desire our neighbor to flourish—to love our neighbor as ourselves.

John Wesley's Notes on the Bible
http://www.ccel.org/ccel/wesley/notes.txt

Romans 5:14

"As by one man sin entered into the world, and death by sin; so by one man righteousness entered into the world, and life by righteousness." As death passed upon all men, in that all had sinned; so life passed upon all men (who are in the second Adam by faith), in that all are justified. And as death through the sin of the first Adam reigned even over them who had not sinned after the likeness of Adam's transgression; so through the righteousness of Christ, even those who have not obeyed, after the likeness of his obedience, shall reign in life. We may add, As the sin of Adam, without the sins which we afterwards committed, brought us death; so the righteousness of Christ, without the good works which we afterwards perform, brings us life: although still every good, as well as evil, work, will receive its due reward.

Thom Shuman
http://lectionaryliturgies.blogspot.com/

Litany for Lent
O Christ,
led by the Spirit
into temptation's wilderness,
you teach us
to turn our backs
on the wrong ways of the world,
so we can follow.
Walk with us, Lord Jesus.

O Christ,
Wellspring of wonder,
you let go of your glory,
so you might hold
our shattered hearts.
Cradle us, Lord Jesus.

O Christ,
grace-full and truth-full,
you empty yourself
becoming the bread,
which makes us whole;
you are living water,
which bursts the banks
of our faded dreams.
Fill us, Lord Jesus.

O Christ,
Shatterer of death's grip,
into our despair, you bring hope;
into our fear, you come with peace;
in our loneliness, you become our brother.
Save us, Lord Jesus.

Jesus Christ, Lamb of God:
have mercy on us.
Jesus Christ, Mercy of God:
pour our your grace upon us.
Jesus Christ, gift of salvation:
grant us your peace.

Silence is kept.

You hold nothing, nothing!
back from us, Gardener of Grace.
Your very self came to us,
your very heart was broken for us,
your life was poured out for us,
in Jesus, our Brother.
Seeking to do your will,
sharing your truth,
singing of your faithfulness,
proclaiming good news,
we follow Jesus into the wonder of your kingdom,
praying as he taught us, saying, **Our Father...**

Call to Reconciliation

Like a parent, God sets boundaries for the children of God. Like children, we want to do things our own way, and so we become easy prey for the evil one. But Jesus our Brother shows us how to find the will, the strength, to resist and to know the mercy of God. Together, let us confess our sins, so God might fill us with hope and joy.

Unison Prayer of Confession

God of Eden's morning, Lent is a hard time for us. In a culture that showcases success, you call us to sacrifice ourselves for others. In a world that promotes power, you invite us to deny ourselves. In a society that encourages us to "feel good," you point us to the struggles of our sisters, the burdens our brothers bear.

By your mercy, forgive us, Hope of our lives. As we journey with Jesus, may we learn the steps of discipleship. As we listen to his call to obedience, may we learn to say no to all that tempts us. As we see his suffering, may we live out the good news that has come to us through our Lord and Savior, Jesus Christ.

Silence is kept.

Assurance of Pardon

Alone, we would be easily controlled by sin and temptation. God has given us the free gift of grace, so we are set free to live as disciples.

This is the gift that brings us hope; this is the gift that brings us joy; this is the gift that brings us life. Thanks be to God, we are forgiven! Amen

March 16
2nd Sunday in Lent

Genesis 12:1-4a; Psalm 121; Romans 4:1-5, 13-17; John 3:1-17 or Matthew 17:1-9

Natalie Sims
http://lectionarysong.blogspot.com

Genesis 12
Abram and Sarah's travels and the promise of the future.

"One More Step Along the World I Go" (Sidney Carter)—A good fun kid's song from Sydney Carter which many of their parents will remember. Lyrics and a slow sound sample (http://www.oremus.org/hymnal/o/o797.html).

"God of Abraham Lead Us" (Bernadette Farrell)—I love this energetic call and response with the response "Lead us to your kingdom." Just don't try to sing all seventeen verses! Choose what you like, or what fits your congregation this week. You can sing with a cantor and response, or your congregation could split in the middle and one half sing the cantor part. Lyrics (http://www.blogger.com/www.beaumarisblackrockunitingchurch.org.au/service29-6-2008.pdf).

"To Abraham and Sarah" (Judith Fetter)—Excellent words of being a pilgrim people, sung to the familiar tune THORNBURY.

"God of Abraham and Sarah" (Gertmenian)—Salvation history in one song with a focus on justice, healing, courage. Fits well with all themes for this week. Could also be sung to NETTLETON if you want a familiar tune.

"The Living God Be Praised" (Daniel ben Judah, translated by Max Landsberg and Newton Mann)—A new translation of "The God of Abraham praise." Excellent words and a familiar tune (LEONI).

"Be Thou My Vision" (Eighth-century Irish)—Most recent hymnals are fairly inclusive in their language for this. Note that the High King imagery is quite important in terms of Irish history. This has been changed in some hymnals because it is masculine, but its use is based on an ancient story of St. Patrick refusing to follow the High King Logaire, but choosing instead the "High King of Heaven." Probably worth telling this story to your congregation! Lyrics, tune, and a little of the story (http://www.cyberhymnal.org/htm/b/t/btmvison.htm).

"The Kingdom of God Is Justice and Peace and Joy in the Holy Spirit" (Taizé Community)—A nice, joyful Taizé chant. Sheet music and sound samples of parts for practice (http://www.taize.fr/en_article499.html).

"God It Was Who Said to Abraham" (John Bell)—Easy Celtic-style tune. Good story words. "God it was who said to Abraham 'Pack your bags and travel on!'" Note that God is masculine; this may have been addressed in more recent editions of *Love from Below*. Lyrics and sheet music (http://www.hymnprint.net/jpg/GC_701-1.jpg); slow sound sample (http://www.hymnprint.net/audio/GC_701.midi).

Marci Auld Glass
www.marciglass.com

Matthew 17
The incarnation of God in the person of Jesus of Nazareth is offered as a gift to us. And in the transfiguration, the gifts to the disciples are comfort, encouragement, and preparation for the journey ahead—the journey to the cross, where their friend will be tortured, suffer, and die.

This gift of transfiguration doesn't mean they are more inclined to make the journey. Peter offers to build dwellings on the mountain, presumably so they can stay and not make the journey to the cross. But Jesus reaches out, touches them, and says "Get up and do not be afraid" (v. 7 NRSV).

While most of us are not likely to have stood on a mountaintop in quite the same way as the disciples did, I suspect all of us have had, or will have, such a moment. We tend to think of "mountaintop experiences" as good moments, highlight moments.

But the mountaintop might also appear to be a cliff edge. News comes to us—bad news of one kind or another—whether diagnosis or divorce or loss of another kind—and we can't see where the path goes or what the path looks like. But we see the valley, way below our perch on the crumbling mountainside, and we know we have to get to the bottom, somehow.

Like Peter, we decide we'd just as soon not journey down that path. We want to pitch tents and stay right there on the mountainside of denial, hoping that a new highway will be built to keep us from having to take the road indicated on our map of bad news.

But Jesus comes to us, touches us, and tells us, "Get up and do not be afraid."

He doesn't say that the journey won't be exactly as bad as we fear it will be. But in his presence, in his transfigured, bright, shiny glory, we are reminded that we are not alone. That the very presence of God is with us on the journey. We see him face to face. The journey to the cross, the journey to death, the journey to loss, the journey to pain is one we only take in the presence of God.

One of the gifts of ministry is the privilege I have of being invited into your lives in those moments when the world is turned upside down by harsh and horrible news. And as I see you move down the mountainside, down a path you would never voluntarily tread, my prayer is that you will feel Jesus put his hand on your shoulder and say, "Get up and do not be afraid." Because nothing makes the bad news go away. But God's presence in our lives gets us through it and then opens us up to beauty and grace, giving us new paths on which we journey together.

In this season of Lent, we, together, are people journeying to a cross we don't want to see, and we are not alone. "Get up and do not be afraid."

NOTE: Adapted from "Face to Face," a sermon preached by Marci Auld Glass (http://marciglass.com/2011/03/06/face-to-face/).

John Petty
http://progressiveinvolvement.com

Matthew 17

Our vision is clouded. "Now we see through a glass, darkly," said St. Paul (1 Cor 13:12 KJV). In the transfiguration, however, the veil is pulled back for a glimpse of the universe's essential spiritual reality, the centrality of Jesus in the world of light.

Matthew tells us that this occurred "after six days" (17:1 KJV) following Jesus' remarks about suffering and the way of the cross. In keeping with the Matthean theme of Jesus as the "new Moses," the "six days" recalls Moses being on the mountain six days in Exodus 24:16. "Six days" also recalls the beginning of creation, and anticipates the seventh day when God's work was completed and God rested. Here, "after six days," Jesus himself is the embodiment of the seventh day, the completion of God's work.

On the mountaintop, Jesus is "metamorphosized" (*metamorphothe*). In a glimpse of Easter, Jesus is transformed. It is a sign of the resurrection—a "vision," Matthew will say, of a transformed world.

The idea of some kind of existence beyond the grave was certainly not new in Israel. People commonly thought that, after death, people became some kind of spirit, or ghost, or even angel. Resurrection, however, was about transformation—a translation of the cosmos that is both radically new, and radically renewed—indeed, "a new heavens and a new earth."

Peter suggests the building of three booths. Unlike Mark, Matthew adds no note of direct disapproval of Peter's remark. Peter's proposal to "institutionalize" the vision is simply brushed aside. The voice and the cloud intervene while Peter is still speaking.

The voice from heaven recalls the voice that spoke at Jesus' baptism, and, in Matthew, speaks exactly the same words with the addition of: "hear ye him" (v. 5 KJV). The exhortation to "hear" recalls Deuteronomy 18:15, and Moses saying that someday God would bring another prophet like Moses: "He's the one you must listen to."

Hear him when he is shining in glory between Moses and Elijah, and hear him as well as he is hung between two criminals on the cross. Hear him when he talks of the way of the kingdom, and hear him when he says to "go and do."

The disciples adopt a posture of worship. Grammatically, the expression is curious: "They fell on their face" (v. 6 KJV). "They" and "their" are plural, but "face" is singular. Possibly, Peter, James, and John represent all of humanity. Faced, so to speak, with the great chasm between human beings and Ultimate Spiritual Reality, the only appropriate posture for the human race is prostration.

The three disciples were also "struck with great fear" (*ephobethesan sphodra,* v. 6 author's translation). "Great fear" is a not uncommon reaction to manifestations of the divine. Matthew says that "Jesus came and touched them" (v. 7a KJV). Just as Jesus' touch cures a leper in 8:3, cures Peter's mother-in-law in 8:15, raises Jairus's daughter in 9:25, and healed two blind men in 9:29, so his touch here calms the fear of the disciples.

"Arise, and be not afraid" (v. 7b KJV). On the strength of his touch and the power of his word, the disciples are able to lift up their eyes (v. 8).

Suzanne Guthrie
http://www.edgeofenclosure.org

"Nicodemus by Night" (John 3)

Don't wait till you know the source of the wind before you let it refresh you, or its destination before you spread sail to it. It offers what you need; trust yourself to it.
(William Temple, *Readings in John's Gospel* [The MacMillan Press LTD, first published in two volumes, 1939, 1940, first Issued in St. Martin's Library, 1961], 46.)

Nicodemus comes to Jesus by night, perhaps so that he won't be seen by his highly critical Pharisee brothers, but perhaps also in a state of intellectual or emotional obscurity. Cautious, concrete, literal-minded, entrenched in his beliefs and practices, Nicodemus is genuinely curious and humble in light of Jesus' signs.

In his encounters with people, Jesus finds the weak spot as the locus of transformation. For Paul it is the mysterious "thorn" in his side. Paul begs God to remove it, but hears instead, "My grace is sufficient for you, for power is made perfect in weakness" (2 Cor 12:9 NRSV). For Peter, it is his threefold denial. After the Resurrection, Jesus will ask three times, "Do you love me?" (John 21).

For Nicodemus, it is his knowledge: "How can?" "But?" Jesus meets the Pharisee's literal-mindedness with a frustratingly wild metaphor. "The wind blows where it chooses, and you hear the sound of it, but you do not know where it comes from or where it goes. So it is with everyone who is born of the Spirit" (3:8 NRSV).

Jesus confronts Nicodemus's knowing with the essential necessity of unknowing. God can be loved, says the author of the *Cloud of Unknowing,* but not thought.

I love Nicodemus, I suppose, because my own intellectual struggles eventually exhausted themselves into a dark love of unknowing.

When we realize that we do not have to be clever,
powerful or successful
in order to be loved, then we can live in truth,
come to the light and be led by the Spirit of God.
(Jean Vanier, *Drawn into the Mystery of Jesus through the Gospel of John* [Mahwah, N.J.: Paulist Press, 2004], 88.)

Chuck Aaron

John 3

The first reading and Gospel reading for this day present two significant theological statements. The Genesis passage, which defines Israel's purpose as a blessing to all the families of the earth, serves as a corrective to both a sense of entitlement on the part of the chosen people and the passages that describe the annihilation of the indigenous people. God gives Israel the ultimate goal of blessing all the families of the earth.

One could hardly overstate the familiarity of John 3 and its terminology. That familiarity gives the preacher the opportunity to push the congregation to a deeper understanding of the insights of this text. John skillfully uses conversations to commence theological discussions. Nicodemus serves as a real character and also as a means to open the dialogue about the role of the Spirit in the development of faith. Readers will find the words about "born anew [from above]" (v. 3) the most familiar phrase from this passage. The metaphor of birth speaks to the sense of renewal that the Spirit enables in the life of faith. Unfortunately, the phrase has taken on the connotation that everyone must come to the faith in the same way, with a dramatic experience.

The preacher can affirm that the Spirit enables this sense of renewal in a variety of ways. The passage affirms the unpredictability of the Spirit, which "blows wherever it wishes" (v. 8). The passage goes on to affirm the healing (citing the story from Numbers 21) and love of God. Rather than supporting a demand of a single kind of experience, the passage celebrates the renewal, love, and healing of God. Some hearers will find reassurance in the message that many types of experience can qualify as being born anew; others may find a needed push to rethink long-held assumptions.

Julia Seymour
http://lutheranjulia.blogspot.com

John 3

Arguably, John 3:16 is one of, if not the, most well-known Scripture citations. I say citations, because I'm not always certain that people understand the verse or its purpose. Paired with verse 17, these two lines in John summarize God's action in the world through Jesus. However, in their popular context (posters, athletic events, road signs), these two sentences become all about human action.

Whenever we talk about human action, it is easy to make the created the first movers, forgetting that only the Creator initiates relationship. Consider the verbs of the sentences: "God so *loved*...[God] *gave*...[God allows people to not] *perish*...*have* eternal life. God *did not send* the Son...to *condemn*...but in order that the world *might be saved* through him" (vv. 16-17 NRSV, emphasis added). All the verbs, except for *believe,* belong to God.

God is the primary actor, the initiator, the Sender and Redeemer. Yet, all the pressure in contemporary thought is placed on believing and non-believing. When the emphasis becomes on what *we* do, the understanding shifts to God as responder. Thus, in popular imagination, our ability to believe or not is what either frees or ties God's hands.

Our ability to believe does not undo what is true. Our failure to perceive cannot trump God's prerogative. Our doubts and fears cannot diminish the sustaining work of the Holy Spirit. Our discomfort with the Word does not make the historical Jesus or the limitless Christ a non-reality.

In the season of Lent, we are often compelled to consider the areas where we have fallen short of the glory of God. And we all have done so. What if we allowed ourselves to be carried in the hope of the verses, in their specific lack of condemnation? What if the bright white of resurrection peeked into the deep purple of this season through the trust that we are not greater than God? God's actions are stronger than our inaction. Christ's love overturns our affection. The Spirit's wind blows where it will and none too weakly. If we allow ourselves to trust in the truth of the verbs in the sentences that belong to God, perhaps we will find ourselves being brought ever more fully into the one verb that belongs to us.

John Wesley's Notes on the Bible
http://www.ccel.org/ccel/wesley/notes.txt

John 3:5

"Except a man be born of water and of the Spirit"—Except he experience that great inward change by the Spirit, and be baptized (wherever baptism can be had) as the outward sign and means of it.

March 23
3rd Sunday in Lent

Exodus 17:1-7; Psalm 95; Romans 5:1-11; John 4:5-42

Chuck Aaron

Exodus 17

The reading from Exodus contains themes that can connect with any of the other readings. The psalm, of course, comments directly on the episode in the first reading. The psalmist places words directly into the divine mouth, exhorting the reader not to allow hearts to harden. The psalm focuses on the recalcitrance of the people. It comes down heavy on guilt, but the sensation of unrelenting thirst can have a powerful effect on people, opening the discussion to a pastoral approach. Although the psalmist portrays the Lord as "despising" (v. 10) the people, the rest of the Pentateuch presents God's love, care, and choosing of the people. The Exodus passage and the psalm can serve as encouragement to trust, rather than give up on God.

If one reads the Exodus passage in light of the deprivation of the people in their thirst, the Romans passage provides a pastoral approach to situations of hardship. A preacher could proclaim the missed opportunity of the escaped slaves to build character through endurance to find hope.

The motif of thirst connects the first reading with the reading from John. In the wilderness, the experience of thirst leads to a lack of trust in the Lord. In John, routine thirst leads to an encounter with Jesus. A dialogical reading of the two passages affirms thirst as both a physical deprivation and a spiritual need (understanding thirst as a metaphor for spiritual longing). Thirst reminds the reader of vulnerability and need, for which we should trust God. Thirst (physical or metaphorical) can lead to either a lack of faith or an experience of divine presence. The church has a responsibility to minister to people dealing with physical deprivation and spiritual longing.

Melissa Bane Sevier
http://melissabanesevier.wordpress.com

Traveling in Circles (Exodus 17)

Here's my take on what really happened…

We beat the Egyptians. Happy Dance. Happy Song. All our problems are gone!

Free from the burden of our past!

But…in the wilderness.

The young ones start to whine. I'm hungry. I'm thirsty. How much longer to the Promised Land?

Are we there yet?

Then the grownups join in.

It starts with a few people. Hey, do you guys have some extra cans of chick peas? Flour? Olive oil? My stomach is growling.

So, Moses, we were just wondering, because our kids were asking: Just how long do you think it'll be before we get to this terrific place?

I'm not really sure, says Moses. But I'm thinking a month. Maybe two. Six or eight months tops. Definitely not more than a year.

A YEAR?! Moses, what are you thinking? We were better off in Egypt. We were oppressed, sure, but we weren't thirsty. You said we were going to the Promised Land flowing with milk and honey. They don't call this a wilderness for nothing. A little milk or honey or just plain water would be nice right about now. We are just walking in circles when we expected a straight line to the new, better life. We're going to starve, following you, following God...

Things used to be better in the good old days of Egypt. The people just kept looking back. Back over the sea. Even if it was better, easier in Egypt, you can't go back. You might as well look forward. A new life comes at the cost of familiarity. We move ahead with the uncertain future, but with the certainty of God's presence.

Sometimes forward is great—a new school, a new job, a marriage, a baby. Sometimes forward is horrendous—an illness, a death, the loss of something important, frightening times. But no matter how much we want to go back, it just isn't possible. The sea has closed up behind us and there's no way back.

God did not abandon the Israelites to the desert. There was manna ("what is it?") and water from a rock. One day at a time, with just what they needed, they began to make their way through the wilderness. One day at a time, they got up and ate. They drank. They lived. They breathed. Nothing exciting or glamorous. Just one day at a time.

God's help also comes to us one day at a time. It is the manna of people reaching out to us. It is God's gift in the person who sees our difficulty and steps in to help in some small way. It is the water of a moment of peace in the middle of a troublesome week. It is God's gift of beauty or joy or memory or purpose or strength.

Even though we're walking in circles, we're able to keep going. One day at a time.

Lowell Grisham
http://lowellsblog.blogspot.com/

Prayers of the People

Presider: Gracious and loving God, we are the people of your pasture and the sheep of your hand: Hear our prayers as we call upon you, for you, O Holy One, are a great God; you are great above all gods. Let us come before God's presence with thanksgiving, and raise a loud shout with psalms.

Litanist: Your Church, O God, has been justified by faith, and we have peace with you through our Lord Jesus Christ in whom we boast of our hope of sharing your glory: Nourish us with the water of eternal life and feed us with the bread of Christ, that the Church's food may be to do the will of God and to complete Christ's work. Let us come before God's presence with thanksgiving,

and raise a loud shout with psalms.

Give to our leaders the wisdom of Moses and let all who lead or hold authority in the world grow in faith, that they may use their power to speak hope to the outcast and marginal and to bring drink to all who thirst. Let us come before God's presence with thanksgiving,

and raise a loud shout with psalms.

Let your harvest of righteousness abound in our community that we may be a spring of water gushing to eternal life, bringing comfort, hospitality, and relief to all who are near us. Let us come before God's presence with thanksgiving,

and raise a loud shout with psalms.

Let your spirit and truth go forth into the world to uphold and protect the vulnerable, the poor, and those who live in places of strife and conflict. Let us come before God's presence with thanksgiving,

and raise a loud shout with psalms.

Guide all who suffer thorough the wilderness of their pain, especially _____. May their suffering produce endurance, and endurance produce character, and character produce hope that does not disappoint because God's love has been poured into our hearts through the Holy Spirit that has been given to us. Come, let us sing to the Holy

71

One; let us shout for joy to the Rock of our salvation, offering grateful thanksgivings, especially for _____. While we were sinners, Christ died for us, reconciling all humanity to God: Give your water of eternal life to all who have died, especially _____. Let us come before God's presence with thanksgiving,

and raise a loud shout with psalms.

Presider: Guide your Church to draw comfort from the deep wells of your refreshing presence, O God, that we may share in Christ's work of reconciliation and give unto others the living water of your Spirit, through Jesus Christ our Savior, who with you and the Holy Spirit lives and reigns, One God, in glory everlasting. Amen.

Beth Quick
http://bethquick.blogspot.com

Exodus 17

• Human nature is so perfectly exhibited by the Israelites. We tend to find things to gripe about no matter what is going on. "They are almost ready to stone me," Moses admits (v. 4 NRSV). Perhaps pastors sometimes feel that way when trying to lead congregations out of the wilderness and into the vision that God has laid before the people. How can we get over our griping, count our blessings, and forge ahead?

• The name *Massah and Meribah* is summed up as indicating the question of the people, "Is the LORD among us or not?" (v. 7b). Hopefully, that should be a rhetorical question: the answer is yes. And if God is among the people, then the people should respond with faith.

Psalm 95

• This is a good call-to-worship psalm, and that's what it is, in part.

• Note the switch in voice between verse 7 and 8: First the psalmist is speaking, then God is speaking first-person.

• The second part refers to the people wandering in the desert after the exodus from Egypt. God is depicted as moody, temperamental. I like the first half better!

Romans 5

• "Since we are justified by faith, we have peace with God" (v. 1 NRSV). That's an interesting if/then statement. Both parts on their own are not necessarily surprising, but that the first causes the second is an interesting play on words. What does it mean to have peace with God? Trusting that it is our faith—not our faulty, failing works—that brings us to God and God's grace, we can rest at peace with God.

• "And hope does not disappoint us" (v. 5 NRSV). What do you think about that? Has your hope ever disappointed you? If you're like me, you can probably think of times that you would say yes to this question, so what does Paul mean here? Has your hope in God ever disappointed you?

• "Right time" (v. 6 NRSV). The Greek word is *kairos*, which means *God's* right time for action, not just any regular time.

John 4

• This is a daring conversation for the woman at the well: Jesus is a Jew and a man. She and Jesus both cross boundaries to talk. Note that this is one of the longest conversations in the Gospels.

• Even though Jesus offers living water, he first asks the woman for a drink. He asks her to give him something, even as he offers the immeasurably valuable to her. Give and take. God seeks that kind of relationship with us.

• "For we have heard for ourselves" (v. 42 NRSV). We don't like to believe from another person's information. We always want to hear it firsthand, from a credible source. That's sensible, right? It's hard to let go of those rules to come to belief through faith. How do we figure out when it's right and when it's foolish to insist on seeing for ourselves?

Martha Spong
http://marthaspong.com/

John 4

In Japan, in the weeks after the 2011 earthquake and tsunami, the troubles at Fukushima Daiichi nuclear plant continued, and 150 miles away in Tokyo, mothers were being warned not to mix their babies' formula with tap water. Although authorities advised the residents not to hoard, it happened. They hurried to buy up bottled water, understandably. If the water is not safe for infants, why chance it for anyone else? Every hour of every day, the people of Japan had to think about what really mattered and what they really needed to survive and how to care for the people they loved most.

In the aftermath of disaster, we all stop and think about what matters to us. We don't even have to be directly touched by the disaster. Just knowing there is death or mayhem brings us up short, causes us to look more keenly at our children, our parents, our friends, and our loves. After September 11, people ended marriages and began them, because whether you were unhappy or happy, life was too short to stay in the first or lose a chance at the second.

But the most dramatic moments in our lives will all be followed by the need to go, the next day, back to the well and draw more water from it.

It must be so shocking. He tells her everything she had ever done. He tells her the story of her complicated life. He doesn't blame her or anyone else for it. He simply names it.

And that's the key to this story. The rest is a lot of possibly confusing metaphor, in addition to numerous parenthetical attempts at explaining what everything means and how poor even the disciples are at understanding Jesus. The Samaritan woman is smart enough to engage with Jesus about the water. It must be a pleasure to talk with someone who catches on so quickly! He even reveals to her that he *is* the Messiah. The disciples don't understand him. They don't get that he is speaking in images when he talks about food. They don't get him.

The Samaritan woman does. She goes back to the city, illuminated by their short conversation, and she spreads the word, and it has to be with an air of certainty that convinces people, or at least makes them curious, because they go out to meet Jesus, and he stays and wins hearts and souls.

Even so, the next day, that woman must go back to the well, for the regular, ordinary water needed in her household, where she lives with whoever isn't her husband. The work of being alive goes on, day after day. And although Jesus told her the hour was near, we are still waiting.

John Wesley's Notes on the Bible
http://www.ccel.org/ccel/wesley/notes.txt

John 4:14

"But the water that I shall give him"—The spirit of faith working by love, "shall become in him" an inward living principle, "a fountain." Not barely a well, which is soon exhausted, "springing up into everlasting life," which is a confluence, or rather an ocean of streams arising from this fountain.

March 30

4th Sunday in Lent

1 Samuel 16:1-13; Psalm 23; Ephesians 5:8-14; John 9:1-41

John Wesley's Notes on the Bible

http://www.ccel.org/ccel/wesley/notes.txt

1 Samuel 16:11

"Keepeth sheep"—And consequently is the most unfit of all my sons for that high employment. Either therefore he did not understand David's wisdom and valour, or he judged him unfit, by reason of his mean education. And God so ordered it by his providence, that David's choice might plainly appear to be God's work, and not Samuel's, or Jesse's. David signifies beloved: a fit name for so eminent a type of the Beloved Son. It is supposed, David was now about twenty years old. If so, his troubles by Saul lasted near ten years: for he was thirty years old when Saul died. Samuel having done this went to Ramah. He retired to die in peace, since his eyes had seen the salvation, even the scepter brought into the tribe of Judah.

Todd Weir

http://bloomingcactus.typepad.com/

Psalm 23

"The LORD is my shepherd, I shall not want" (v. 1 NRSV). Can you imagine a state of being content, satisfied so that you "shall not want"? No worries, no fears, no headaches . . . I shall not want. That would be an advertising agency's worst nightmare. What would they do if people didn't have infinite wants that constantly needed filling? Our consumer-driven economy would fall apart. In 2008, 70 percent of America's GDP was consumer spending, the highest in the industrialized world, compared to Europe, where consumer spending was only 50 percent of GDP ("Consumer spending accounts for two-thirds of U.S. economy," Annie Baxter, host [Minnesota Public Radio, http://minnesota.publicradio.org/display/web/2008/10/29/gdp_numbers_consumer_spending/, accessed June 2012]). I shall not want? Are you nuts? It is our job to want, to be consumers. We must save the world with our spending, even if it means going into great debt.

When it comes to the word *want,* we really have to keep our wits about us. "I shall not want" is not a promise of a consumer or materialistic paradise, nor is it the freedom from the troubles of the world. (Remember the table is prepared for us in the presence of our enemies and we still walk through the valley of the shadow of death, and it doesn't say no evil will touch us, just that we won't fear it.) So what exactly does Psalm 23 have to offer that is better than the mall?

Reading the Psalm to myself in the King James Version, something struck me that never occurred to me in the hundreds of times I have heard this psalm. In the first three verses, notice the person for "God." God is mentioned in the third person five times as "he" or "him." Now look at what happens in the last three verses. There the poet shifts to the intimate form "Thou," and God is again mentioned five times.

This clarifies for me what it means to say "I shall not want." The spiritual life is a movement from looking to God from a distance, a third-person God who is far away from us, to experiencing God as "Thou." We all have to start somewhere with God. We have some idea or hint of a divine being as we rest in a green pasture, or as we look at the still waters of a pond on a gorgeous day. We have moments in worship, perhaps when we light candles on

Christmas Eve, when our soul is restored. As we read Scripture and listen to sermons, we find wisdom to be on the right moral path. And then at some moment in our lives we come face to face with the reality of death, evil, enemies that would hurt us. In these times we need a God we can call "Thou." As we pass through these times, we come to know the true nature of God as a living presence, a good shepherd, who will walk with us. Then we know the true blessing of saying, "I shall not want."

Natalie Sims
http://lectionarysong.blogspot.com

Psalm 23: Alternatives to "The Lord's My Shepherd"

"Are You a Shepherd?" (Ruth Duck)—Good and joyous. Lots of images of God: shepherd, teacher, mother, father. A catchy chorus. Good for kids.

"Like the Sun upon My Skin/God's Mercy" (Sheree Anderson)—A beautiful ballad about identifying God's mercy in the beauty of creation. Lyrics, sound sample, and songbook available here (http://www.wholenote.com/tunein.html).

"23rd Psalm" (Bobby McFerrin)—A beautiful feminine rendering of the Psalm. From the album *Medicine Man*. Listen to it on YouTube (http://www.youtube.com/watch?v=t5WadVmFe0o&feature=related). If you'd like to sing it, it's also in the Unitarian Universalist book *Singing the Journey* and *Music for Liturgy* from St. Gregory of Nyssa Episcopal Church.

"Shepherd Me O God" (Marty Haugen)—A nice reworking of the 23rd Psalm. The chant could also be used on its own as a response to a reading of the psalm: "Shepherd me O God beyond my wants, beyond my fears, from death into life."

"With a Shepherd's Care" (James Chepponis)—Very nice words with feminine and masculine images for God. Would be very straightforward to sing.

"You Lord Are Both Lamb and Shepherd" (Sylvia Dunstan)—Beautiful words. Can be sung to many tunes. I like it to PICARDY or WESTMINSTER ABBEY.

"In God Alone My Soul Can Find Rest and Peace / Mon Ame Se Repose" (Jacques Berthier)—A very beautiful chant from Taizé. Music and sound samples for practice here (http://www.taize.fr/en_article468.html). Good for kids.

"It All Depends on Where I'm Going" (Colin Gibson)—Good words of God's constant presence through all of life's travels, sung to a simple Celtic-style tune (TE HORO). Full music and lyrics here (http://homepages.ihug.co.nz/~Serlewis/wshp/dpnd.htm).

"Come and Find the Quiet Centre" (Shirley Murray)—A good song for the beginning of worship. I would prefer to sing this to one of the more traditional melodies or BEACH SPRING.

"Come Away from Rush and Hurry" (Marva J. Dawn)—Excellent words of resting in a sacred space to the familiar tune BEACH SPRING.

"My Shepherd You Supply My Need and Holy Is Your Name" (Isaac Watts)—Responsive psalm with sung refrain to the tune of the first line of Brother James' Air.

Chuck Aaron

John 9

The rich narrative in John 9, based on the healing of the blind man, contains many themes that a preacher could develop into useful sermons. Because of the length of the story, the preacher has the choice of basing the sermon on the whole narrative or focusing on sections or ideas within the narrative.

Verses 1-7, which recount the miracle itself, address the common assumption that everything has a reason behind it. The disciples assume that the blindness represents a consequence of sin. Jesus shifts the attention from events behind the blindness to God's ability to display mighty works. This part of the narrative opens a discussion on the difference between looking for a reason behind everything to looking at how God works in every situation. This shift takes the responsibility off of God and off of punishment for sin, which frees the reader to anticipate God's healing and grace in every situation.

As the conversations develop in the rest of the narrative, Jesus' opponents exhibit a number of ways of evading the evidence of God's grace and power in the healing. The presence of the healed man vitiates their arguments, but they refuse to see what is directly in front of them. Although those outside the church mount arguments against faith, the passage really speaks to insiders. Those within the church use evasions to avoid fully responding to Christ's claims on them. Contemporary readers do not have any evidence as clear and irrefutable as the blind man in the narrative. The preacher will need to articulate the evidences of divine presence available to the congregation. Some examples include the sacraments, the Holy Spirit, and the witness of the church. A sermon on these conversations might achieve the goal of enabling the congregation to see the ways they hold back from full commitment.

Thom Shuman
http://lectionaryliturgies.blogspot.com/

Call to Worship

Here, in this place, with these people,
we find the One who leads us into God's Kingdom.
Here, in God's Kingdom, with our sisters and brothers in Christ,
we find a Feast prepared for us.
Here, in God's sanctuary, at this Table,
we eat of the goodness which heals us; we drink of the mercy which is God's gift.

Prayer of the Day

Shepherding God:
you create life
from the mud of the earth;
you draw forth light
from the shadowed corners of chaos;
your goodness and mercy
are our closest friends.
Great is your name.

Jesus our Shepherd:
you open eyes
shuttered by sin
and prejudice;
you heal lives
shattered by bitterness;
you create pools of still grace
in our stress-filled hearts.
Great is your love

Holy Spirit,
our companion in every darkened valley:
you plant seeds of goodness and mercy
deep within our souls,
that we would bear fruit for others;
you awaken us from
our troubled sleep,
that we might be a light to the world.
Great is your peace.

God in Community, Holy in One,
hear us as we pray as Jesus taught us, saying,
Our Father...

Call to Reconciliation

How quickly we notice the mistakes of others, but never see our own faults! Before we judge others, we need to pray that our blindness might be healed by God's gracious love. Please join me as we pray together, saying,

Unison Prayer of Confession

God our Great Shepherd: it is easy for us to lose sight of your kingdom and your way for us. We hope that love conquers hate, that light shines in our shadows, that life is stronger than death—yet our lips are filled with bitter words, our lives are weak and shallow, the darkened corners of the world beckon to us.

Have mercy on us and lead us to the still waters of your grace and the healing garden of your heart, Tender Shepherd. Restore our sight to see you living with us, restore our hope that we might trust you, restore our speech that we might praise you for your great gift to us in Jesus Christ, our Lord and Savior.

Silence is kept.

Assurance of Pardon

With a gentle touch, with the anointing of the Holy Spirit, with the joy of love, God reaches out to forgive us and make us whole.

Touch us, Eternal Spirit;
heal us, Light of Love;
fill our lives with new meaning, God of joy,
as we receive your forgiveness and grace. Amen.

Martha Spong
http://marthaspong.com/

John 9

This week I got a message from Jesus. Or more precisely, a "tweet." On Twitter, I wrote: "I believe my own willful stubbornness will play a part in this week's sermon about Jesus and the Man Born Blind."

You see, I had made the connection that blindness takes many forms. Jesus heals the man but is more interested in the spiritual blindness besetting all the people he meets. But I was banging my head against the text, complaining to anyone who would listen about the implication of verse 3 that God might actually set up a man to be born blind in order to teach the rest of us a lesson.

Then, imagine it, there came a response from Jesus—well, not Jesus, but someone on the Internet using the Twitter nickname JesusofNaz316 and employing Jesus-like rhetorical flourishes. And he or she, because who really knows, wrote back to me: "Who sinned that you were born stubborn?"

That made me laugh. I got the reference to verse 2, "Who sinned, that this man was born blind?"

I replied: "No one. I hear it was so God's works might be revealed in me."

I was born stubborn, blindly and blindingly stubborn, so that God's works might be revealed in me. We each have innate characteristics, and we also have inherent qualities, some of which may work against our understanding, our seeing. But however we were born, God's works can be revealed in us.

God didn't set up the parents to have a blind child or the man to have a life as a beggar. I know this. The prophets knew it long before Jesus came. We just get confused about it sometimes. Some of us are born to be short, or redheaded, or left-handed, or gay. In the past, some of those things have been considered the result of sin on someone's part. But we live in the era of science. We know better. Even a tenth-grade biology student can tell us a little about genetics. They know that we are only beginning to understand the full range of things coded in our DNA and where exactly to find them. Maybe someday they'll find stubbornness. The more we know, the brighter the light of understanding shines.

However we are born, we are flawed and fragile simply by virtue of being human. And even so, God's works can be revealed in us.

"You were born entirely in sins" (v. 34 NRSV), the Pharisees say to the Man Who Now Can See. And they dismiss his testimony about the way God's works had been revealed in and through Jesus. They bang their heads against the truth. I've been right there with them. Sometimes it's the only way I can get to it.

Who loved, that this man was born Jesus? He was born Jesus, Christ, that God's works might be revealed in him for all of us to see. He was born Christ, Jesus, that God's work of love might be known in him.

John van de Laar
http://www.sacredise.com/

John 9

Sight is a choice. Too often we avoid what we would prefer not to see, refusing to question, closing our eyes to new perspectives, and, in the process, avoiding life. When we see wrongly, we hurt others and ourselves, but when we see clearly, we discover life and deep connection with God and others.

It is tragic when religion blinds us to truth, but this occurred even in Jesus' day. The religious leaders in this pericope adopt amazingly circular logic: Jesus healed on the Sabbath, which is forbidden work and therefore sin. But God doesn't hear sinners, so he couldn't have healed. But, he did heal....No wonder Jesus challenged the Pharisees for *choosing* blindness.

The question of sin is central here. A core belief of the time was that sickness was a punishment from God, so the disciples wondered whether the man's or his parents' sin was to blame. Perhaps this is why the man was a beggar. His parents were close enough to be called in for questioning, yet they weren't caring for their disabled son. Were the disease and the associated blame ripping this family apart? The parents offered no defense of their son, preferring to protect their place in the synagogue. Perhaps, when the Pharisees finally declared the blind man a sinner they were relieved.

The sin question also gets directed at Jesus, with the Pharisees quick to pronounce in the affirmative. But they have seen neither Jesus nor the blind man clearly. In his extended narrative, John confirms that neither Jesus nor the blind man is a sinner (see especially 10:21). If this passage teaches us anything, it is that we need to be careful not to allow our sin-focus to blind us to what God is doing.

The Gospel seeks to reveal Jesus as God's sent one, inspiring faith in the Man more than his miracles. The blind man is the model. He goes from blindness to seeing (9:7) to belief in Jesus as a prophet (vv. 11, 17, 25) to relationship with Jesus—true sight and true faith (vv. 35-38)! He may begin by *seeing*, but he ends with *understanding* (Greek: *blepo*).

Those who see like this become "sent" ones. Jesus explains that the man's blindness would glorify God (v. 24) and informs his disciples that they must work as *sent* ones (v. 4). Then he *sends* the man to wash his eyes in the pool of Siloam (which means "Sent," v. 7). Finally, the man testifies that Jesus comes from God (vv. 30-33). Though the Pharisees cannot recognize Jesus as sent by God, this man does, and becomes, himself, a sent one.

The Gospel presents Jesus as the one whom God *sent* to bring true sight and lead us into the light where we discover relationship with God. The starting point is to acknowledge that we do not see and need our eyes to be healed. Then, when our eyes are opened we inevitably become "sent ones" who let God's light shine to those who still need to see.

April 6
5th Sunday in Lent

Ezekiel 37:1-14; Psalm 130; Romans 8:6-11; John 11:1-45

Chuck Aaron

Ezekiel 37; Romans 8; John 11

Coming near the end of Lent, three of these passages (Ezekiel, Romans, and John) explore dimensions of death and affirm the ways God empowers life.

The dramatic oracle in Ezekiel evokes the image of a battle scene, with dead bodies of the defeated lying grotesquely on the ground. All that remains of the bodies are the dry bones, with no possibility of life. In powerful, unforgettable imagery, the dead bones receive all of the tissue they need, and the breath of life. The oracle assures the dejected, devastated community that God can restore them to vitality.

In Romans, Paul contrasts the Spirit with selfishness. Selfishness leads to a moral and emotional death, within both the individual and the community. Paul encourages the church to allow the Spirit to work within to counteract the influence of selfishness. Paul invokes the power of God who raised Jesus to affirm the Spirit's ability to empower life morally, psychologically, and even physically.

John's narrative of the reanimation of Lazarus conveys the divine power over life and death, including the present reality of life for the individual and the church. Jesus brings Lazarus back after all hope had vanished, and in the absence of faith by those at the tomb. Lazarus's emergence from his tomb enables belief, the goal of John's Gospel.

The readings for this day give the preacher the resources to talk about sin and death on several levels: community despair, moral decay and selfishness, and physical death itself. For all of these situations, God brings hope, healing, strength, and life. The preacher can use all of the passages to bring out the different dimensions, or focus on one dimension, affirming God's power to work and restore in them. God's work begins now, but reaches fullness in God's time.

John Wesley's Notes on the Bible
http://www.ccel.org/ccel/wesley/notes.txt

Ezekiel 37:7

"Came together"—Glided nearer and nearer, till each bone met the bone to which it was to be joined. Of all the bones of all those numerous slain, not one was missing, not one missed its way, not one missed its place, but each knew and found its fellow. Thus in the resurrection of the dead, the scattered atoms shall be arranged in their proper place and order, and every bone come to his bone, by the same wisdom and power by which they were first formed in the womb of her that is with child.

Mike Lowry

God's Power (Ezekiel 37)

In slightly altered form a conversation comes back to me. We stood visiting in his driveway. There was an edge of desperation in his voice. "It's not as if I haven't tried. I've tried again and again. People say stupid things to me like, 'if only you had the will, you'd quit drinking.' I've got the will; what I lack is the power!"

The need for power is true for many aspects and avenues of our lives besides the obvious chains of addiction. Where we are powerless, God moves. God's power comes at the end of our own striving, in the midst of our "dry bones"—perhaps the clearest biblical reference—offered to the people of God in Ezekiel's time. People are defeated and discouraged. Life is so bad it is as if they live in a valley of dry bones. *Powerless* is the only word that accurately describes their situation.

Power comes for the powerless from the Lord! Scholars have long noted the connection between "breath" in Ezekiel 37 and the breath of God in Genesis 2:7. God's creative power is at work in the valley of our dry bones. Furthermore, the Spirit and power of God is not ours to command (note Ezek 37:7). Catch the sweep of this passage. It carries a tangible sense of the force of God in gracious strength. "The LORD's power overcame me. . . . Say to the breath, The LORD God proclaims: Come from the four winds, breath! Breathe into these dead bodies and let them live. . . . I will put my breath in you, and you will live" (vv. 3:1, 9, 14).

So powerful was this sense of the Holy Spirit for the early Christians that they realized the Spirit was in very fact God with them and for them. When they formed the Apostles' Creed so that the least educated could memorize and understand, they expressed the fundamental conviction that in the Holy Spirit, God is with us and for us in the Holy Trinity.

The preacher might wish to connect such conviction to God's power for the powerless in facing the cross as Good Friday approaches. Practical lessons abound for those of us who claim to be Christian. God brings life from the dead. The Lord triumphs at the scene of apparent disaster.

Teri Peterson
http://clevertitlehere.blogspot.com

Psalm 130, John 11

One year during Lent, we reversed the Advent candle tradition—at every worship service during Lent we blew out a candle, until the last was extinguished at the end of the Good Friday service. Though the days lengthened outside the sanctuary, inside the darkness was growing as we took this journey through wilderness, despair, and dark valleys. By the end of the season, we longed for the light of resurrection. We had learned to trust God in the wilderness and to be honest about our distress.

Mary and Martha have learned this lesson well. The disciples may be a little dense, but Mary and Martha are honest. Their tears fall even as they say "If you had been here, things would have been different." They don't hold back their grief, their disappointment, their dashed hope.

How often, when we walk into the valley of the shadow of death, do we find that God seems to have left us there alone? It sometimes seems as if God has a penchant for disappearing or for hiding just when we most need to know God's presence. We call into the darkness and get only darkness in return, and so often we give up. We stop talking to God, perhaps afraid that we shouldn't be angry or sad or despairing or lonely, perhaps tired of receiving no answer.

Mary and Martha called out to Jesus, and Jesus intentionally held back. When he did show up, they weren't shy about sharing their feelings. They already knew something we learn over and over again: God can take it. We can rail, shout, cry, and be real, because not only can God hold all of that, God rails, shouts, and cries right along with us.

It seems improper somehow, but throughout Scripture we see God's people expressing the full range of emotions—from joy to despair and everything in between. The psalmist even offers us words when our own fail. "Out of the depths I cry to you / . . . hear my voice!" (v. 1 NRSV). The darkness deepens, there's no way out. . . . Where are you? The candles are going out, one by one, and I feel alone . . . and "my whole being hopes" (v. 5). Not just my sad self, not just my intellectual capacity, not just "for the kids," but my whole being.

Sometimes it seems too soon to make that move. It can feel jarring, as in a piece of music that seems so dark and then moves to a brighter major key (for example, Rutter's setting of Psalm 130 in his Requiem—http://www.youtube.com/watch?v=Aw2WgpGxBk4). But even Rutter moves back and forth between darkness and light, between cello and oboe, between lower and higher voices. We know that feeling—the vacillation between despair and hope, the Mary and Martha experience of "if you had been here" mingled with "I believe." In many ways, this is Christian life: to hope even in the dark valley, knowing that life is indeed possible, and stronger than the darkness.

Natalie Sims
http://lectionarysong.blogspot.com

Psalm 130

"Out of the depths I cry to you, O Lord" (v. 1 NRSV).

I think it's critical that we provide songs for people to sing in difficult times. Here are some examples.

"Senzenina? / What Have We Done?" (Traditional South African)—It's good to let people ask this question. This beautiful chant from South Africa asks the question that we often ask when things go wrong beyond belief. It's important to know what the song means when singing it. If you have some part-singers in your congregation, this would be particularly good. It is also on the soundtrack for *The Power of One,* so you could also play the recorded music if appropriate. Free sheet music (http://www.humph.org/lw/concerts/13shakin/music/Senzenina.pdf).

"God When Human Bonds Are Broken" (Fred Kaan)—These words pick up an unusual theme, and fit really well with this reading. There are a couple of possible tunes, none of which are immediately familiar, but they are not difficult either.

"Out of the Depths O God We Call to You" (Ruth Duck)—A simple and honest hymn, which sings this psalm from the perspective of a community trying to work out its faith together. Excellent words and the tune (FENNVILLE) is quite straightforward. Lyrics and sheet music sample (http://www.hymnprint.net/).

"Wait for the Lord" (Jacques Berthier)—"Wait for the Lord, keep watch, take heart." A lovely simple Taizé chant. Sheet music, translations, and sound samples (http://www.taize.fr/en_article512.html).

"Out of the Depths" (Harding)—A simple four-part arrangement that would be nice if you have a choir or quartet that could sing it. Available for purchase, and you can view a sample PDF (https://www.melodicarts.com/melodi_carts/catalog/product_info.php?products_id=208).

"Precious Lord Take My Hand" (Thomas A. Dorsey)—A classic gospel song, familiar to many.

"How Shall I Sing to God" (Brian Wren)—The words are excellent, but the tunes offered are not straightforward because of the difficult meter; this might be a good song for your musicians to present to start teaching the congregation so they can remember it in more difficult times.

John Petty
http://progressiveinvolvement.com

John 11

Mary says exactly the same thing to Jesus that Martha had said: "Lord, if you had been here, my brother would not have died" (vv. 21, 32, NRSV). Jesus responds differently to Mary, however, than he did to Martha.

With Mary, Jesus does not engage in high-level theological discussion. Instead, surrounded by death and mourning, he is "deeply moved in spirit and emotionally agitated" (v. 33, author's translation). *Enebrimesato* has its root in the sound of a horse snorting, and expresses great anger. *Etaraxen* relates to fear and dread. Another possible translation: "He was enraged in spirit and agitated with fear."

Nevertheless, this is a necessary confrontation. True life and resurrection cannot deny the reality of death. Sorrow is a part of human existence. In response to the grief and sorrow he sees, Jesus is overcome by grief and sorrow himself. Out of love and compassion, he shares fully in the sufferings of life.

Suddenly, the conversation includes "they." No longer is Jesus talking with one person, either Martha or Mary, but now, when Jesus asks where "you" (plural) have laid Lazarus, "they" say "come and see" (v. 34 NRSV). This is ironic. The phrase "come and see" has been used to bring people to Jesus (1:46). Now, it is used to bring Jesus to face death. Confronting death, sorrow, and grief directly, Jesus weeps.

Jesus' anger and agitation continues as he comes to the tomb. "It was a cave" (v. 38 NRSV). In mythological language, caves are places of spiritual mystery and are symbolic of the womb. Going into a cave upon death is symbolic of return to God as Mother. It is also a way of saying that new life can emerge only out of the death of the old. This is *mortificatio,* a word common to the writings of medieval contemplatives and the psychologist Carl Jung.

Martha, identified as the sister of a dead man, speaks to the ghastly reality of death. "Lord, already he stinks" (v. 39b, author's translation). Jesus reminds her that if she "trusted" she would see the glory of God. (Jesus had not actually said this to Martha. He had said it to the disciples in verse 4.)

"Raise up the stone," he says—*arate ton lithon* (v. 39a, author's translation). "They raised up the stone, but Jesus raised up his eyes upward." Jesus speaks directly to God, the first time he does so in the Fourth Gospel. His prayer recalls the prayer of Elijah in 1 Kings 18:37: "Answer me, O Lord, . . . so that this people may know that you, O Lord, are God, and that you have turned their hearts back."

Jesus cries out "with a loud voice, 'Lazarus, come out!' The dead man came out" (vv. 43-44 NRSV). His sheep hear his voice (see John 10:27)! Lazarus—"the dead man"—is still wrapped in the garments of death. Jesus tells "them" to "unbind him, and let him go" (v. 44 NRSV). The major work of raising Lazarus is done, but the work is not completed until those who hear Jesus' command "unbind" Lazarus and free him from the restraints imposed by death.

Julia Seymour
http://lutheranjulia.blogspot.com

John 11

I did not know how I could go on living. My body vibrated from sheer exhaustion. My fingernails were torn and aching. They bled at the corners, and I could feel the throbbing pain up my arms, in my temples, and behind my eyelids. I hurt my fingers tearing my clothing when my brother died.

It is not just that my heart hurt, but that it kept breaking over and over. I needed help preparing the house for a funeral, and I would think to myself, "Lazarus can help me lift the..." "I hope someone brings olives because Lazarus enjoys..." "I must remember to ask Lazarus..."

But my brother was no more.

My sister, Mary, sat in the cool of the house, grieving, wailing, and refusing to be consoled, with many of our friends gathered around her. Our friends were here, except the one for whom we sent, the one who could have helped the most. The fact that Jesus did not come only deepened my grief. To know that perhaps Lazarus did not have to die, could have been healed, might still be with us—I could not bear to think it. Surely Jesus did not mean to wait so long; he must have been delayed.

When he came, our reunion with him was a blur of my anger and Mary's grief. We all went with Jesus to the burial place, believing he wished to mourn Lazarus as his own friend. Jesus lay his wind-reddened cheek against the cool of the burial stone and wept with abandon. Then he straightened, turned, and pointed to some men, "Roll the stone away."

I looked at Mary, but she was sobbing, so I said what had to be on everyone's mind, "Jesus, he will smell after four days in there. There is no need to enter the tomb."

He looked at me, with his look of love, and said, "Did I not tell you that if you believed, you would see the glory of God?"

Jesus picked the worst time for riddles.

Jesus prayed and Mary squeezed my hand and my sore fingertips burned from the pressure.

And there was our brother.

Jesus gestured for us to go to Lazarus and we scrambled to unwrap him and to touch him. People pressed forward in fear and amazement. As I unwound the bandages, I looked to Jesus, filled with the power of God to be sure and yet a man like any other. It was not easy to sort out my feelings about him, his work, his teaching.

I rejoiced to have my brother returned, but my hurt still burned. Why had Jesus allowed this to happen? Where was he when we needed him? I had come to rely so much on his presence. Can I learn to live with both a sense of abandonment *and* the joy and hope of resurrection? Do I want to?

April 13
Palm/Passion Sunday

Palm Sunday: Matthew 21:1-11; Psalm 118:1-12, 19-29;
Passion Sunday: Isaiah 50:4-9a; Philippians 2:5-11; Matthew 26:14–27:66
or Matthew 27:11-54

Beth Quick
http://bethquick.blogspot.com

Matthew 21

• Notice that here the crowds identify Jesus as a prophet.

• Can you think of current figures who have received such overwhelming support, only to quickly fall from grace shortly after?

• This is a passage that aches to be visually depicted in our congregations. That's why we wave the palms. We need to see it, experience it, and be part of it.

• Is the triumphant entry like a protest march? Upsetting the order of the day?

Isaiah 50

• "The tongue of a teacher, / that I may know how to sustain / the weary with a word" (v. 4 NRSV). Sustaining the weary with a word: that's a gift; that's power. Who can accomplish this feat? Isaiah, apparently! Seriously, this is the gift we're called to live into as preachers. With God's Word, we can sustain the weary.

• "I gave my back... / and my cheeks... / I did not hide my face" (v. 6 NRSV). Let us not think that there is nothing of Jesus' "turn the other cheek" teaching in the Old Testament, that the Old Testament only speaks of "an eye for an eye"—this passage shows us it's just not so!

Philippians 2

• "Let the same mind be in you that was in Christ Jesus" (v. 5 NRSV). Simple and clear.

• "Did not regard equality with God / as something to be exploited" (v. 6 NRSV). I find this such a unique statement. Imagine if Christ had used his equality to exploit? What would that look like? Perhaps this is what Satan tempted Christ to do—to exploit his equality.

• "Every knee should bend.../ every tongue should confess" (vv. 10-11 NRSV). This is a passage often used by people who are seeking to convert non-Christians and those of other faith traditions as proof or encouragement about the task at hand. Frankly, it makes me a bit uncomfortable. If the idea is that people will ultimately be moved to worship Jesus even against their will, I'm not sure I'd want to see that display.

Matthew 26–27

• I guess you have to ask: why this huge, all-encompassing text, when much of this material will be included later in Holy Week? The answer, on the practical side, is that many in our congregations won't be back again until Easter Sunday—won't be at Maundy Thursday or Good Friday. They need to know how we get from Palm Sunday to Easter Morning. But on a deeper level, for me at least, nothing beats the contrast of starting a sermon with the joy of the Palms and ending with the reality of the cross.

• This text as a whole is almost too huge to comment on. In worship, I typically let the text speak for itself. It doesn't need me to try to explain what it says, but speaks with a loud voice on its own.

Eric D. Barreto

Philippians 2; Matthew 21

On Palm Sunday, we acclaim the arrival of our king. The Gospel text in Matthew is sure to take a prominent place in worship. But notice in the midst of the joy of children entering the sanctuary with palm branches that Matthew's text contains within it both tragedy and acclamation. Jerusalem receives her long-expected Messiah, but the same people who here regale Jesus will soon revile Jesus. Faithfulness and faithlessness are never too far from each other.

But first is the acclamation. That God orchestrates Jesus' entrance into Jerusalem is clear in at least two ways. First, as when he directs the disciples to find a ready-made room for a Passover meal in 26:18-19, Jesus commands two disciples to go into a village and take a colt and a donkey. If anyone attempts to stop their seeming theft, they simply need to say that the Lord needs them. Second, for the twelfth time, Matthew explicitly ties Jesus' life to the prophets (v. 5). For Matthew, God is clearly in control of all things even as—or especially as—Jesus approaches the cross.

But soon will come the tragedy and the rejection of Jesus. Even as we wave our palm branches, the long shadow of Good Friday is on the horizon.

In Philippians, Paul points to this same Jesus as the very model for how our lives together should be led. By pointing to a Christ willing to empty himself and walk with us, by pointing to a Christ willing to die for the sake of obedience, Paul wants us to realize what it means to be a community of faith. This is the mind of Christ: to walk in obedience and humility as Christ did on the path to the cross. Neither acclamation nor rejection caused him to swerve.

Lowell Grisham
http://lowellsblog.blogspot.com/

Prayers of the People

Presider: Gracious and loving God, you have shown us that the way of the cross is the way of life, and through your Son Jesus you have taken upon yourself all of the evil, sin, and violence of the world, even death itself: Take into your divine heart the needs and concerns of your children, and hear us as we pray: Make your face to shine upon your servants, and in your loving-kindness save us.

Intercessor: As Jesus emptied himself, taking the form of a slave, humbling himself and being obedient to the point of death, so inspire your Church to follow faithfully in the way that he has led us, that we may share in his exaltation and resurrection. Make your face to shine upon your servants,

and in your loving-kindness save us.

As Jesus confronted the powers and principalities of the world—the kings and emperors and authorities of religion and state—so empower us to unmask all injustice, envy, violence, and greed, that your divine light may cast out all darkness. Make your face to shine upon your servants,

and in your loving-kindness save us.

As Jesus became one with the poor, the criminal, the outcast, and the dying, so send your resurrection grace unto all who suffer, that they may be comforted by the promise of your heavenly kingdom. Make your face to shine upon your servants,

and in your loving-kindness save us.

As Jesus carried his cross with compassion and humility for all of the sin and suffering of the world, so let us reach out to our neighbors in steadfast love and willing service. Make your face to shine upon your servants,

and in your loving-kindness save us.

As Jesus accepted pain, humiliation, contempt, and powerlessness with patient strength and steadfast hope, be present in your divine glory with those for whom we pray, especially ____. As Jesus gave himself to the Father in thankful surrender, hear our grateful hearts as we offer our prayers of thanksgiving, especially for ____. As Jesus humbled himself to the point of death, even death on a cross, so that his Name may be exalted above every name, so bring into his eternal glory those who have died, especially ＿＿＿. Make your face to shine upon your servants, **and in your loving-kindness save us.**

Presider: Through the humble trust of Jesus on the cross you have showed us the path of eternal life, O God: Give us courage and grace to follow his example of obedient love, to walk in the way of the cross, and to share in his glorious resurrection, that we may live in the power of his Spirit, now and forever. **Amen.**

Martha Spong
http://marthaspong.com/

Matthew 21; Philippians 2

Who is this? It's no wonder they asked.

We wave our palms and smile at the children and feel the joy of—well, what is the joy we're feeling, exactly? We're likely remembering being little children ourselves, going to church and having something to do that wouldn't happen any other day of the year, marching around the sanctuary and waving the palms. We feel festive! Palm Sunday is one of the few days in the church year when pastors wear red vestments and we use the red paraments. It's a party! Even good Americans, who would never want a king, love King Jesus riding into the city, and the sweet hosannas being sung, asking him to save us.

Who is this? A man on a donkey, riding into town, was not the amazing sight. It was the people around him and their clear adoration of him that got the attentions of the authorities, which set the events of the rest of that week in motion.

In the days to come, we will remember events more dramatic and less celebratory. We will follow Jesus to the upper room, and out to the garden of Gethsemane. We will hear him pray and feel his disappointment when his friends can't stay awake and wait for him even for an hour. We will shudder at his arrest and trial and crucifixion. We will wonder how anybody could think of betraying him.

Maybe for a minute we'll realize that we would have been just like the people around Jesus, as helpless to stop the earthly powers, as sleepy as the men and as silent as the women who followed him from Galilee into Jerusalem, the same friends and followers who started the week cheering for him.

Maybe, just maybe, we will step outside of our own stories and wonder how it felt for Jesus.

The letter to the church at Philippi stresses that Jesus lived the human experience right up to the end. He had both the form of God and the form of a human. He rode into Jerusalem on that donkey as both. He did not use the power of God to save the mortal body. He rode in that day prepared to take whatever would come.

And that makes me want to celebrate, although the form my joy takes feels as solemn as it does festive. We come to the end of Lent, to the beginning of this Holy Week, and we gather to worship God who loved us enough to be one of us: to live as one of us and to die as one of us.

Who is this? The whole city asked the question, says Matthew. It must have been on everyone's lips. And the answer is simply "the prophet Jesus from Nazareth in Galilee" (v. 11 NRSV).

They don't know who he is. Do we?

John Wesley's Notes on the Bible
http://www.ccel.org/ccel/wesley/notes.txt

Matthew 21:9

"Hoseanna" (Lord save us) was a solemn word in frequent use among the Jews. The meaning is, "We sing hosanna to the Son of David. Blessed is he, the Messiah, of the Lord. Save. Thou that art in the highest heavens." Our Lord restrained all public tokens of honour from the people till now, lest the envy of his enemies should interrupt his preaching before the time. But this reason now ceasing, he suffered their acclamations, that they might be a public testimony against their wickedness, who in four or five days after cried out, Crucify him, crucify him. The expressions recorded by the other evangelists are somewhat different from these: but all of them were undoubtedly used by some or others of the multitude.

Amy Persons Parkes

Matthew 26–27

Before I was born, it was decided where I would be buried. Enclosed by a single row of cedar trees that form a slightly tilted square, my graveyard adheres to the surroundings like a postage stamp marking an otherwise blank pasture. Because generations of my family lie beside one another, each one coming to rest in this place intermittently through my years, I have seen the ground of my death tilled often. And so, I wonder what Joseph of Arimathea must have felt when he "took the body [of Jesus] and wrapped it in a clean linen cloth and laid it in his own new tomb, which he had hewn in the rock" (Matt 27:59-60 NRSV). Having selected and purchased the burial place, having displaced the rock forming the grave, I wonder what odd mixture of pain and sad relief Joseph must have felt in putting the wrong body into the hollowed-out rock where his own body should have lain. The passion of Jesus Christ is our passion; and in the most authentic of ways, Joseph was the first person to experience the deep connection between Jesus' vulnerability and self-sacrifice and his own mortality. The firstborn of the dead enters into the womb of our graves before us, denying death's power over us. I have gazed down many a dark hole watching the contrast of color as the topsoil gives way to the deep burnt orange and red of Alabama clay. Let it be so that the first face peering back at me is that of Jesus, the one who enters into each of our graves before us. For Grannie and Grandmother, for Jon and Dianne, for Shelley and Gaye, when they saw the world to come, my hope is that they saw the One who had been there before.

April 17
Holy Thursday

Exodus 12:1-4, (5-10), 11-14; Psalm 116:1-2, 12-19; 1 Corinthians 11:23-26;
John 13:1-7, 31b-35

John Wesley's Notes on the Bible
http://www.ccel.org/ccel/wesley/notes.txt

Exodus 12:3

The solemn eating of the lamb was typical of our gospel duty to Christ. First, the paschal lamb was killed not to be looked upon only, but to be fed upon; so we must by faith make Christ ours, as we do that which we eat, and we must receive spiritual strength and nourishment from him, as from our food, and have delight in him, as we have in eating and drinking when we are hungry or thirsty. Second, it was to be all eaten: those that, by faith, feed upon Christ, must feed upon a whole Christ. They must take Christ and his yoke, Christ and his cross, as well as Christ and his crown. Third, it was to be eaten with bitter herbs, in remembrance of the bitterness of their bondage in Egypt; we must feed upon Christ with brokenness of heart, in remembrance of sin. Fourth, it was to be eaten in a departing posture v. 11, when we feed upon Christ by faith, we must sit loose to the world, and every thing in it.

Eric D. Barreto

Exodus 12; 1 Corinthians 11

The sharing of meals is a culturally and spiritually significant event. On Maundy Thursday, we remember and imagine anew the significance of mere bread and wine representing the promise and fulfillment of God's liberation. The Exodus account of the Passover carefully details the preparations of a lamb without blemish that will be a sacrifice, whose blood is a means of protection from the plagues raining down on Israel's oppressors. A few of the details in the passage might seem odd to many readers, but each has a theological rationale. For example, verse 4 makes provision for families too small to be able to consume a whole lamb. They were to join their neighbors and divide the lamb evenly. No one is to be excluded from this meal, and nothing must be wasted. The lamb is too precious to throw away its leftovers, and the challenges of escaping Egypt required the Israelites to pack light and be ready to move at a moment's notice (v. 11). The Passover was never intended to be eaten once but as "a day of remembrance" (v. 14 NRSV) of the promises God always fulfills.

The sharing of a meal in 1 Corinthians 11 is also a powerful moment of remembrance. The difficulty Paul faces is that some in the community were participating in this meal as they might any other meal. That is, his recitation of the Supper is not a first-time introduction to this practice but a reminder of its importance. Verse 26 reminds them that, whenever they share this meal, they "proclaim the Lord's death until he comes" (NRSV). The meal looks back to Jesus' death, reminding those who eat and drink of the great cost Jesus was willing to pay for our sakes, and looks forward to his return when all things will be made right.

Amy Persons Parkes

John 13

"Jesus replied, 'You don't understand what I'm doing now, but you will understand later'" (v. 7). With these words, Jesus defines *mystery*. The mystery of the eucharist and baptism. The mystery of the trinity, the virgin birth, death, and resurrection. Mystery is that which is completely understandable in the mind of God and is slowly, creatively, compassionately unveiled in the fullness of time to those who follow Jesus. How impatient we are with our own inability to comprehend what God is about and how God is acting in the world and in our lives at this very moment. If only we could "God-it" as easily as we "google-it."

Where are the occipital lobes of the brain? What symptoms will present from strokes in those areas?

How do you get a gerbil water bottle to stop leaking?

Is there any way to replace the heating element in the dryer without calling an expensive repair service?

The frequency and intensity of my questions directly correlate to my need for control in any given situation. Ultimately, I am not satisfied with the unknown because I cannot conquer and own what I do not understand. During my second year of seminary as I tried in vain to attend church without succumbing to paralyzing anxiety attacks, I was approached by my mentoring pastor to assist in serving communion. Wasn't my existential crisis enough to make me unfit to serve communion? I had no idea what that juice and bread was supposed to mean! And then came the wisdom of God through the pastor, "Nobody really knows what it means." We simply wait like Peter, like disciples, like little children, to hear the answer to our question, "What are you doing, Jesus?"

Ann Scull
http://seedstuff.blogspot.com

Two Useful Images

1. This image comes from Heartlight—a very useful free slide site: http://www.heartlight.org/gallery/2099.html (accessed April 16, 2012).

2. This image comes from an equally helpful free slide site, Image Bank: http://www.imagebank.org.uk/ibimage.html?md5sum=ae5c4f2db724232463316766388847a0 (accessed April 16, 2012).

Introductory Activity

Have a small laminated foot-washing picture for each person to hold throughout the service and take home afterward. Either image above would work well or visit www.paulajolly.com for a couple of great pencil sketches on this theme. Please abide by all copyright rules.

Response Activity

This works well as a change from foot washing or when there are congregational members who have mobility difficulties. It also takes a while to do, so have some meditative music playing in the background. Pass around cloves of peeled garlic and talk about how garlic leaves a reminder behind on your fingertips. Ask people to think of a disappointment or hurt they have either suffered or caused. Then pass a box of scented disposable towelettes or tissues around and ask each person to wash the hands of the person on their right. As they do so, ask them to pray for that person, asking God to remove the disappointment or hurt in that person's life.

John van de Laar
http://www.sacredise.com/

John 13

Many years ago I attended a Christian Artists' Retreat at which the "rules" included delegates serving meals to the international guest musicians. Immediately after this was announced, the keynote speaker, John Fischer, replied, "We are quite capable of serving our own meals. We are here to serve, not to be served."

The community of faith all too often conducts its affairs much like the world's empires, giving honor to those who are wealthy, powerful, or "great." Yet, Jesus embraced a completely different ethos. In chapter 13, we reach a defining moment in John's Gospel. There is much debate about the exact timing of this meal, but John clearly connects it with the Passover, indicating that what is about to happen is reminiscent of the great moment of Israel's liberation. The reader is to understand how Jesus fulfils the Passover salvation plan of God and how he gives insight into the nature of God and God's glory.

The act of washing feet was the work of slaves. Some Jews even insisted that it be reserved for Gentile, not Jewish, slaves (D. A. Carson, *The Gospel of John* [Leicester: Apollos, 1991], 462). Yet John describes Jesus' performance of this service as a demonstration of the "full extent of his love" (v. 1 NIV 1984). It may be, as Luke suggests (Luke 22:24), that they had been arguing about which of them was the greatest, making Jesus' undignified embrace of the role of slave even more challenging. Nevertheless, John describes this act as a response to Jesus' knowledge that God had given him "all authority" (Matt 28:18 NIV 1984), and connects it with both his self-giving death and God's glory. The implication is clear—this act, and the cross to which it points, reveals God's true glory, how God's authority is exercised and what God's nature is really like. It is significant that in the verses immediately preceding this pericope Jesus teaches that whoever sees him sees God (John 12:45-50). In this simple, shocking act, the Reign of God is revealed as the complete antithesis to the domination, coldness, and hierarchy of human empire.

But Jesus goes further. He insists that what he has done is to be normative for his followers. The love that he has just shown—and will continue to express on the cross—is his "new commandment" (13:34 NRSV) for them to follow. It is significant that even Judas—the "enemy"—was included in the foot washing. The "one another," then, expands to include all others. This, and only this, says Jesus, is the proof of our discipleship. Until we have wrapped the towel around our waists we have no business calling ourselves disciples of Christ. The tragedy is that we have failed to learn this, and have often turned faith into an empire of its own, along with violence, oppression, and injustice. Our world is literally dying for lack of this self-abandoning love. However, it's never too late for us to heed the call and enter the self-giving Reign of God with all the world-healing grace and love that it promises.

Suzanne Guthrie
http://www.edgeofenclosure.org

"Gethsemane" (Mark 14)

"Sit here while I pray...remain here, and keep awake" (vv. 32b, 34b NRSV).

I can't help but think the women were awake. First, they would not have had as much to drink at the Passover meal. Instead, they would have been negotiating with merchants for last-minute items, preparing the food, shooing away animals, soothing children who were awake past their bedtimes, and finally clearing away the debris of the meal and sweeping the borrowed space. Perhaps they came to the olive grove late, walking by themselves along the Kidron Valley in the moonlight.

By then it may have been too late to convince Jesus to rouse himself and walk with haste across the Mount of Olives toward the desert. By then Jesus may have already thrown himself to the ground in agony, sweating blood, weeping in mortal torment. Perhaps this was part of Jesus' plan. He had to face alone the coming contest with evil. Even Judas knew the women would stay behind to clean up. He knew the women would not obediently have let Jesus pray alone in danger, but would have argued with him to stop fussing and get a move on.

Nevertheless, the women and common sense remained in Jerusalem until too late, leaving Jesus alone in his agony.

Was it the kind of death he was going to die? He's not about to drink hemlock surrounded by admiring friends hanging on his every word. He faces the most obscenely cruel torture perfected over centuries by the cleverest people on earth, devised to maximize terror not only for the victim but also for the populace. Seven last words? Barely able to breathe, he will have just enough air to stay alive and suffer.

Did he believe he would redeem humanity by the offering of his body, by the shedding of his blood? Did he believe he would harrow hell and rise from the dead? Or did he sense the silence of God and wonder whether his mission had been yet one more messianic illusion? "Let this hour pass from me. Remove this cup from me" (see vv. 35-36). In these prayers, did he mean his death or something even more torturous, dangerous, difficult, and mysterious?

"Sit here while I pray...remain here, and keep awake."

Padre Pio writes, "How many hearts in the course of the centuries have responded generously to Thy invitation?...May this multitude of souls, then, in this supreme hour, be a comfort to Thee, who, better than the disciples, share with Thee the distress of Thy heart" (Padre Pio of Pietrelcina, O.F.M. Cap., *The Agony of Jesus in the Garden of Gethsemane* [Rockford, Ill: Tan Books and Publishers, 1974], 22).

When a friend suffers in agony, it is enough to be present and say nothing. And so, we do.

April 18
Good Friday

Isaiah 52:13–53:12; Psalm 22; Hebrews 10:16-25 or Hebrews 4:14-16; 5:7-9; John 18:1–19:42

Eric D. Barreto

Isaiah 52–53; Psalm 22; Hebrews 4; John 18

Lent draws to a close, and we are brought to the foot of the cross. How do we make sense of God's Messiah dying on a symbol of criminality and shame? If we are honest, this is not at all what any of us would have expected. The earliest Christians struggled to make sense of this crucial moment in Jesus' life. Execution on a cross was as shameful a death as anyone could imagine. What could this senselessness have to do with God? The Scriptures answer with one voice: everything. When Jesus looks most deserted and defeated, the promise of hope, love, and victory resounds most powerfully.

When early Christians turned to the prophets, they found exactly this tension in Isaiah's song of the suffering servant. Similarly, they turned to Psalm 22 and read a lament that could have been on Jesus' lips as he seemingly breathed his last. In these powerful cries for justice, our sisters and brothers found Jesus' shameful death and his exaltation standing side-by-side, not as contradictions but as the mysterious path God chooses to reach us, God's children. We are not alone in our distress. Jesus meets us in suffering and anguish, for he has walked with us, as Hebrews 4:14-16, 5:7-9 confesses.

This year, these hopes and expectations come together in John's extended account of Jesus' passion. Space does not allow for extensive exegesis of this long passage save this basic guiding principle. We ought not rush to the confession that God will deliver in Psalm 22 or the exaltation of God's servant in Isaiah. We ought not rush to the glory of Easter morning. Instead, walk in the steps of Christ, not in order to dwell on his torture and death but to reflect on the burdens he chose to bear for our sake.

John Wesley's Notes on the Bible
http://www.ccel.org/ccel/wesley/notes.txt

Hebrews 10:20

"By . . . a living way"—The way of faith, whereby we live indeed. "Which he hath consecrated"—Prepared, dedicated, and established for us. "Through the veil, that is, his flesh"—As by rending the veil in the temple, the holy of holies became visible and accessible; so by wounding the body of Christ, the God of heaven was manifested, and the way to heaven opened.

Julie Craig
http://winsomelearnsome.com

John 18–19

I should have seen the question coming. They always ask at this fabric store. I suppose it makes an otherwise boring job of measuring, snipping, ripping, and folding a little less tedious. If the person handling your fabric, and cutting it from the bolt can start up a conversation with you about how you are going to use the fabric maybe it benefits you too. Maybe you can begin to see the project take shape, right there in the store.

So I should have anticipated the question and perhaps prepared an answer, but I didn't. And when she asked me, quite innocently, what I was making out of those two yards of black poly-cotton blend, I hesitated for a few seconds, then stammered, "Um…a shroud."

Her eyes narrowed as she considered this. She began, ever so slightly, to ask a follow-up question, then it showed quite plainly on her face that she changed her mind. But really, what would one ask? And we stood there, wanly smiling at each other, agreeing to just let that matter drop.

But as she worked, I thought back to just a few minutes earlier. Had I really stood at all those bolts of black fabric, touching them one by one, considering weight, heft, drape? Could I really explain how such a thing could possibly matter when the task for the fabric—the thing the fabric was going to do—was to cover the cross on Friday?

Even more ridiculous—almost comical even—I had stood in line at the fabric store with all the other customers that day, surrounded by people buying cheery cottons printed with eggs and bunnies, and sherbet-toned polyesters that would become little girls' Easter finery within the week.

Later, when the fabric was hemmed and ready, and I took it to the church and practiced shrouding the cross on the Communion table, I realized the futility of such careful consideration of the fabric. Although, yes, the fabric was fine and did what it was supposed to do, no matter how weighty it was, the cross beneath it was recognizable. We can cover up the cross, but we cannot undo that terrible day any more than we can get to Easter morning without it.

Todd Weir

http://bloomingcactus.typepad.com/

John 18–19

Maybe you have never been asked to deny Jesus or had to lie about your faith to save your skin. But we have all faced our own "roosters." In a moment of inflated pride, I make my boast, defend my worth, react defensively to not lose face and cover my fear. I want everyone to know that I am right, I am just, I am true to my beliefs. But in the morning, the rooster's crow reminds me I am a fraud.

It always seems to be a shock to the sinner, when the moment of truth comes and failure is crowed with the dawn. With the servant in the parable of judgment, we ask:

> "Lord, when was it that we saw you hungry or thirsty or a stranger or naked or sick or in prison, and did not take care of you?" Then he will answer them, "Truly I tell you, just as you did not do it to one of the least of these, you did not do it to me." (Matthew 25:44-45 NRSV)

How could I have been so foolish, so blind, so insensitive, so pig-headed? I know what is right, but in that moment I must have been temporarily insane. Truth seems so clear looking backwards. But then Hell has been described as truth seen too late.

This is our human predicament, ignoring the truth until it is too late to act. In retrospect we see the futility of war after thousands of innocents die. Too late we see that the neglect of the poor diminishes the wealth of us all, and the failure to protect the rights of the weak eventually robs the whole of any shred of dignity. Too late we see we cannot undo the careless word that cut to the heart, the neglected duty that let others down. We thought it would be okay if we bent the truth a little, and later it is impossible make it straight again. Then we hear the rooster crow.

So in the dark hours of Gethsemane, this is my prayer. Let me see more clearly in the present moment. Prod me to hold my tongue, to admit my fault, to make peace before it is too late. Awaken me to the needs of others, to the need for justice, and to the possibilities to love and serve in the moment, so that I do not need a rooster to tell me the truth too late. Be Thou my vision, Lord, so that I may live in the hope of Easter dawn, to awaken with joy rather than regret.

Liz Crumlish

http://somethingtostandon.blogspot.co.uk/

John 18–19

"Tried and found wanting" is a curious phrase that is often used in judgment. A phrase that mainly says more about the one who uses it than the one to whom it is applied.

As Jesus was passed from pillar to post in his final days of trial, conviction, and execution, he was "tried and found wanting" by many different groups. Those who expected this Messiah figure to overthrow the repressive occupying forces were disappointed that he did not step up to the mark. Those who had already condemned him to death were thwarted by his refusal to use violence or to argue his case. Those who taunted him to save himself by coming down off the cross found their taunts echoing in an abyss. "Tried and found wanting."

When I have found myself in that discouraging predicament as, I believe, all pastors find themselves at some point, perhaps even frequently, I comfort myself with the reassurance that I am in good company!

Conforming to God's will involves, at times, disappointing the hopes of those around us and not bowing to the pressure of being sucked into some, at times, very noble causes. Why? Simply because there is a longer game to play. It is tempting to play up to expectations and, in the process, boost our own egos by the approval that attracts. Who would ever have imagined that God would pluck resurrection from the ashes of Good Friday? Precisely because our view is so limited, we have to trust God, who has a much bigger game plan than ours can ever be.

On this day that we dare to call *good,* let us imagine for a moment that we are one of those whom Jesus encountered in his last few days on his road to the cross. Which part of Jesus would we have "tried and found wanting"?

Even though we live in the light of the resurrection, are there times and places today when we are disappointed in the suffering servant who is our Saviour? Still, today, our Lord is "tried and found wanting." Still, today, as Christ struggles alongside us, when he looks into our eyes and into our souls, he is stung by the disappointment we nurture deep within.

At least the crowds he encountered on his journey to Calvary let their voices be heard. Better that than the simmering resentment harboured in the silence of today.

Amy Persons Parkes

John 18–19

As a child, gardens both beckoned and repulsed me. Beckoned, I followed Daddy's footsteps (step for step, for fear of crushing something he wanted to grow) to find the first, red-ripe tomato, ready to be eaten like a poor man's apple. Repulsed, I passed through the hog-wire fence and glared at the old coffee cans scattered among the rows filled with urine from my grandfather's chamber pot. Azaleas and bees. Sweet silver queen corn and striped brown burrowing worms. Fresh fried okra and sticking prickles. Beckoned and repulsed. After the incident with Adam, Eve, and a serpent, one might think it best for God to avoid gardens; but there Jesus was in a garden where he "often gathered…with his disciples" (John 18:2). And so, too, was Judas, one of Jesus disciples, "his betrayer, [who] knew the place" (v. 2 NRSV). On Good Friday, we remember Jesus' willingness to gather with us in humanity's garden where the kernels of faith and hope and love often take root and sprout alongside the seeds of greed and injustice and pride. The goodness of God in Christ will not abandon the garden of humanity where, from the same earth, the same heart, both devotion and deceit grow. Just as Jesus included Judas in his innermost circle, God is the same gardener who beckons us toward relationship despite our capacity to repulse, sting, burrow, and prick—even when we sting and burrow and prick him to death.

April 20
Resurrection Sunday

Acts 10:34-43 or Jeremiah 31:1-6; Psalm 118:1-2, 14-24; Colossians 3:1-4
or Acts 10:34-43; John 20:1-18 or Matthew 28:1-10

Mark Stamm

Acts 10; Matthew 28

What does one say about the Resurrection of Jesus? This event is proclaimed to us, yet it stands beyond understanding. The texts guide us in our speaking, however. Note first Peter's sermon to Cornelius and his household (Acts 10:34-43). He summarizes the mystery of Jesus' death and rising, and thus it is something like a first-century Easter sermon, but the context is even more revealing. He preaches it in a Gentile household, in a setting he had thought forbidden. God had other ideas. Resurrection breaks barriers, of death and all others. Into what unlikely contexts is God asking us to proclaim the gospel, doing justice and mercy?

Note that we usually read the Matthew 28:1-10 empty-tomb narrative as a separate pericope, and thus it is read apart from the Passion Narrative (chs. 26–27) and on separate days. Considering the wider context helps us hear it better. At the request of the religious leaders, Pilate had instructed the soldiers to make the tomb secure, and so the stone was placed and sealed (Matt 27:62-66). Here was an act of imperial authority, but Resurrection overruled it—the angel rolled away that stone "and sat on it" (28:2 NRSV). Remember, to sit was a sign of authority, and so here God's messenger represents a power that trumps the empire. In my fantasy about this text, I like to think of a little angel sitting on top of the rock swinging his legs, blowing raspberries at the guards. That image may go over the top, but do not fail to hear the defiant tones in this scene. This Gospel calls us not to fear, but to bold mission (vv. 6-7, 10).

Paul Bellan-Boyer

"Peter Began to Speak" (Acts 10)

There is so much going on today. As a people we are busy with the celebration of Easter. We, like those early friends of Jesus, have been through a week of Passion, high drama and brutal trauma, the terrifying and amazing mystery of a Lord who will not stay buried. Maybe this is why the church reads this early summary of what has happened.

With the perspective of a few months or years, Peter (and his chronicler Luke, with the advantage of a few additional decades) could put this wild, untamed, unexpected, unbelievable resurrection story into a context that people could hold onto, even if Jesus himself could not be grasped.

We do well to read the preceding verses and recall the story in which this mini-sermon is set. Peter is in the throes of an "indigestible" religious experience. The same God who opened the tomb has just opened the skies, showing Peter that God has erased the boundaries between clean and unclean.

The old certainties are broken open. God has been changing the rules, bridging old divisions—not just between Jew and Gentile but between empire and subjects, even between life and death. For God has been "preaching peace by Jesus Christ" (v. 36 NRSV).

Virtually any part of this speech might serve as a basis for preaching. But what sounds today like dogma is Peter telling a story, speaking to his audience, teaching about this Lord that he encountered. And just as important, Peter is also testifying about his own religious awakening, ongoing since Jesus called him.

This confession that Jesus is Lord over all is unthinkable, except by the power of God working miracles in and through him. Healing the oppressed. Raising from the dead. And forgiving those who believe in him. Including Peter. If Jesus can bring Peter back from Good Friday failure, how can we not believe in God's power to redeem the world?

Carolyn Winfrey Gillette
http://www.carolynshymns.com/

Come and Join the Celebration!

Come and join the celebration! Praise the Lord and gladly sing.
Hear the gospel proclamation: God in Christ changed everything!
Tell again the wondrous story; let your praises rise above.
God, we sing and give you glory for your everlasting love.

Sing with joy, for on a Sunday friends of Jesus went to grieve.
Soon they found his tomb was empty; telling others, they believed.
God of miracle and wonder, Jesus died and lives again.
Death has lost, for you are stronger; all creation sings, "Amen!"

God, we sing, for there is nothing that can keep your love away—
Not oppression, hardship, famine, things to come or things today.
Heights and depths cannot defeat us; death will never be the same.
Christ is risen! So you promise: we have life in Jesus' name.

Sing with joy, each generation! Sing with those who've gone before.
Join the kingdom celebration, old and young, both rich and poor.
We have life, for we're forgiven; where, O death, is now your sting?
Born of dust, we're claimed for heaven, so let all God's people sing.

NOTES
Biblical Texts: John 20:1-18 or Matthew 28:1-10
Tune: NETTLETON 8.7.8.7 D ("Come, Thou Fount of Every Blessing"), Wyeth's Repository of Sacred Music, 1813
Text: Copyright © 2010 by Carolyn Winfrey Gillette. All rights reserved.
This new hymn was commissioned by Grace Covenant Presbyterian Church in memory and honor of Ann Gettys Nash and was sung for the first time in their worship service on April 18, 2010, in Asheville, North Carolina.

Marci Auld Glass
www.marciglass.com

John 20

In John's Gospel, Jesus cares a lot about seeing and believing. All throughout the account, characters are told to look around them, to pay attention to what they see, so that they may believe in Jesus. In the beginning of the Gospel, as Jesus calls the first disciples, they are invited to "come and see" (1:39) as they join him on the journey. Once people see things in John's Gospel, they believe.

But then we get to the horrible visions of Holy Week. Betrayal, arrest, unjust condemnation, death on a cross, and burial in a borrowed tomb. *Who wants to see that?*

What are we supposed to see in those events? How are we supposed to believe in LIFE when we see only death? So, when Mary shows up that morning to weep at the tomb, *we get it.* Mary can't let go of Jesus. She isn't ready to let go of what she thinks she knows about life and death. She isn't ready to let go of control and live into unfathomable mystery. The world she lived in last week had problems, for sure, but they were familiar problems.

And then she sees Jesus standing there and hears him ask, "Woman, why are you weeping? Whom are you looking for?" (20:15a NRSV). And even as she supposes him to be the gardener, you wonder if she begins to see and believe as she hears his voice. Because she saw and heard Jesus call Lazarus out of the tomb. Because she heard him talk about being the Resurrection and the Life. Because she saw the signs of water into wine and the feeding of the crowd of thousands. Because she heard him telling the disciples all about his being glorified and ascending to God the Father.

You wonder if all of those moments in the past are beginning to be seen with new eyes, even as she continues to cling to the past. "Sir, if you have carried him away, tell me where you have laid him, and I will take him away" (v. 15b NRSV).

It is hard to let go of our belief in Death. But then Jesus calls her by name. "Mary." And that's what it takes for Mary to turn around, away from an empty tomb, and away from seeing and believing in death, to seeing and believing in LIFE. Being called by name. "Mary." She sees him in that moment and, finally, believes.

NOTE: Adapted from "Seeing and Believing," a sermon preached by Marci Auld Glass (http://marciglass.com/2011/04/24/seeing-and-believing/).

Paul Nuechterlein
http://girardianlectionary.net/

John 20

"[Mary] turned around and saw Jesus standing there, but she didn't know it was Jesus" (v. 14). Mary actually mistook her Lord for a gardener! (*Sarcastically*): Way to go, Mary!

But was it a mistake? John put Mary and Jesus in a garden on the first day of the week, reminiscent of another couple in a garden at the beginning of creation. Earlier John tells us that Jesus proclaimed with his dying breath, "It is completed" (19:30). Was Jesus proclaiming the sin-filled creation completed? In the dawning of the first day of a new week was Mary witnessing a fresh start for creation itself—renewed and redeemed?

In John's chronology, Jesus died on the sixth day of the *un*renewed creation. After resting on the Sabbath, Jesus is in the garden at the dawn of a new week with Mary, calling her by name and sending her forth with new purpose. She must not cling to Jesus, but rather must go with the apostles and proclaim a new beginning for creation, a fresh start in caring for God's creation. If at first she mistook Jesus as a gardener, it was the right mistake—he came as a gardener that we will finally hear our vocation of caring for God's creation. (*Enthusiastically*): Way to go, Mary!*

The *work* of creation did not end in the first garden. John's Gospel is full of examples of God still working. In both John 5 and 9, when Jesus is criticized for healing on the Sabbath, he responds, "My Father is still working, and I also am working" (John 5:17 NRSV). In John 9:3-6 Jesus rubs mud on the eyes of the blind man, reminiscent of the Genesis 2 creation of humanity out of the mud.** Finally, in John 14:12 Jesus says, "I assure you that whoever believes in me will do…even greater works than these."

John's Gospel begins, "In the beginning was the Word and the Word was with God and the Word was God" (1:1)—opening in the darkness of the first creation with Jesus, the Word. At the end, Jesus is again in the garden at the first light. But this is a new creation, bringing forth forgiveness and new life so that his disciples can begin their calling anew. Mary Magdalene wanted to cling to Jesus, but Jesus sends her out to be the first evangelist announcing the new creation (20:18). Way to go, Mary!

Now it's our turn. John's Jesus is saying to future generations of Mary Magdalenes, "I need you to be signs of that new life right here and now. I need you in whatever your calling in life—whether it's as husband or wife, parent or child, neighbor or citizen, as scientist, as teacher, as healer, as farmer, as builder, in whatever your calling—to care for one another and for the creation as I have cared for you. In the power of my name, you can do greater works than me."

NOTES:

*The basic concept of seeing John's Gospel as a story of New Creation comes from many of N. T. Wright's writings on the Gospel of John, e.g., *The Resurrection of the Son of God* (Minneapolis: Fortress, 2003), 662–82. The more particular idea of Mary making the right kind of mistake when mistaking Jesus for the gardener comes from N. T. Wright, *Twelve Months of Sundays—Year A* (London: SPCK, 2002), 54–55.

**See James Alison's magnificent essay on John 9, "The Man Blind from Birth and the Creator's Subversion of Sin," in *Faith Beyond Resentment* (New York: Crossroad, 2001), 3–26.

Thom Shuman
http://lectionaryliturgies.blogspot.com/

Call to Worship

This is the day:
when healing touches the suffering,
when loneliness discovers a family,
when peace caresses the stressed.
This is the day the Lord:
breaks free of death's clutches,
rolls away the stone,
folds the grave clothes into a neat pile.
This is the day the Lord has made:
the day of sin's defeat,
the day of resurrection,
the first day of the new creation.
This is the day!
Christ Is Risen! Hallelujah!

Great Prayer of Thanksgiving

The God of early mornings be with you.
And also with you.
People of the first day, lift up your hearts!
We lift them to the One who makes every day Easter.
People of Easter joy, give thanks to the One who is your salvation.
We offer our alleluias to the God of steadfast love.

We lift our praise to you,
Gardener of Creation.
On the first day
your Light split the shadows of chaos,
and all goodness flowed forth.
Gently and tenderly
you gathered up the dust of the earth
and shaped us into your image.
But the day came
when we chose
to run away from you,
preferring our petty schemes
to your dreams for us.
You sang to us through the prophets,
hoping we would join you
in the heavenly chorus.
But we kept silent,
believing our wisdom
was far superior to your love.
And when we dug our heels in
through blind stubbornness,
refusing to follow you,
you became one of us
that you might lead us back to you.

Therefore we join our glad songs of Easter with those
in every time and in every place who sing to you their praise:

Rejoice, heavenly powers!
Sing, choirs of angels!
Jesus Christ, our Lord, is Risen!

You alone are holy, Steadfast God,
and blessed is your Son, Jesus Christ, our Lord and Savior.
God's true Light,
he wandered the shadows of hell
to bring us out;
God's own Beloved,
he endured our sin,
to heal us forever;
God's own Glory,
he went into the grave,
that we might enter
the gates of righteousness.

As we remember you raising him
from the dead and giving us life,
we proclaim our faith:

Sin is conquered;
death is defeated;
Christ is risen!
Alleluia!

Here at this Table
we are nourished by your steadfast love, God of every morning.
As you pour out your Spirit
upon the bread and the cup,
fill us with the grace of Jesus..
As we have been raised to new life,
may we reach out to those who have fallen;
as we have been fed,
may we fill the hunger of the world;
as we have seen the empty tomb,
may we bear witness to the presence
of the Risen Lord in our lives.

Then, when we are united with all the saints,
may we gather around your Table,
one people, lifting our voices in praise to you,
Father, Son, and Holy Spirit,
one God, forever and ever. Amen.

Julia Seymour
http://lutheranjulia.blogspot.com

John 20

How glorious that moment must have been for Mary Magdalene in the garden. How powerful that the word of resurrection for her grieved spirit was the sound of her name of Jesus' lips. The hope for resurrection for all people is that the Living God calls them from darkness into light by name.

Yet how quickly that joy must have turned to confusion when Jesus put a physical distance between them. How her countenance must have fallen when he said, "Do not hold on to me, because I have not yet ascended to the Father" (v. 17 NRSV). Jesus' relationship with all his disciples, including Mary, had been one of physicality. They ate together, walked together, fished together. They struggled through crowds and dawdled through empty byways, tearing the heads of grain as they passed.

Jesus touched to heal, to welcome, and to comfort. His touch was something that Mary knew, like the sound of his voice calling her name. But her touch was also something *he* knew. The warmth of a hug, the peace of a kiss, the intimacy of closeness in prayer and praise.

Even John's high Christology cannot escape the fact that God had a body, a body that came and lived among and loved other bodies. Even as death is defeated and the promise of resurrection and restoration is unfolding, there is grief that the body of Jesus cannot remain in this life, in this creation. Perhaps Jesus cannot allow Mary, or any of the other disciples, to touch him, because *he* cannot handle it. As long as there is space between them, he can ascend and complete the work that was begun in him in the beginning.

The power of resurrection moves us because we believe that it happened to a real body and that it will again. The power of resurrection moves God because it happened to Jesus' real body, which had been nursed, fed, tended, wounded, and raised. For a few years, through that body, the Trinity had the relationship with creation that was longed for since the beginning. The Word made flesh spoke names, brought healing, and created a communion. Ascending meant putting distance in that relationship again, which likely grieved the Trinity, evidenced in Jesus' words to Mary. Real presence brought a bond that no other word had been able to do.

John Wesley's Notes on the Bible
http://www.ccel.org/ccel/wesley/notes.txt

John 20:17

"Touch me not"—Or rather, Do not cling to me (for she held him by the feet). Detain me not now. You will have other opportunities of conversing with me. "For I am not ascended to my Father"—I have not yet left the world. "But go immediately to my brethren"—Thus does he intimate in the strongest manner the forgiveness of their fault, even without ever mentioning it. These exquisite touches, which every where abound in the evangelical writings, show how perfectly Christ knew our frame.

April 27

2nd Sunday of Easter

Acts 2:14a, 22-32; Psalm 16; 1 Peter 1:3-9; John 20:19-31

Dan Clendenin
http://journeywithjesus.net

Psalm 16

You know a good prayer when you hear it. The best prayers, those that are most authentic and heartfelt, those shorn of tired cliches and pious platitudes, are often our shortest prayers. The writer Anne Lamott insists that she has prayer down to one word: "Help!" (*Plan B: Further Thoughts on Faith* [New York: Riverhead Books, 2005], 37). The psalmist for this week utters a prayer notable for its brevity, tenderness, and power. It is just five words, and you can pray it at any time, at any place, for any reason: "Keep me safe, O God" (v. 1 NIV 1984). It is a prayer rich with pastoral and political ramifications.

The psalmist's prayer implicitly acknowledges what we all know from experience, that far too much of our world, for far too many people, is not a safe place. For many the world is a horror of devastation and destruction, vulnerability, and sorrow. In a favorite hymn of mine, "A Mighty Fortress Is Our God," the Protestant reformer Martin Luther (1483–1546) admitted that ours is a "world with devils filled, that threaten to undo us." Still, the Hebrew psalmist is confident about the God whom he worships; a God who counsels and instructs, and to be sure he will not abandon us (see vv. 7, 10). In an unsafe world God is a God of protection, preservation, and refuge.

In 1910, a leading British pundit, Norman Angell, wrote *The Great Illusion,* which rightly argued that national economies had become so interdependent, so much a part of a global division of labor, that war among the economic leaders had become unimaginably destructive. War, Angell warned, would so undermine the network of international trade that no military venture by a European power against another could conceivably lead to economic benefits for the aggressor. He surmised that war itself would cease once the costs and benefits of war were more clearly understood. Angell was correct, economically speaking, but just a few years after he published his book, World War I, a Great Depression, then World War II, unleashed catastrophic consequences, economic and otherwise, for all the world.

Christian prayer to stop war is thus both a pastoral and a political act. We pray for soldiers and civilians alike, for governments and diplomats, for peacemakers and treaty negotiators, for Iraqis and Congolese, Palestinians and Chechens, as much as for Americans: "Lord, keep us safe. Somehow. Some way. Save us from our warring impulses. Please, keep us safe."

Paul Bellan-Boyer

"It Was Impossible for Jesus" (Acts 2)

Did that title catch your attention? I hope so, because it's hard to preach someone else's sermon, especially one that midwifed the church into being and led to three thousand baptisms. Peter's preaching is set in the day of Pentecost.

The apostles, inspired by the Holy Spirit, have the attention of Jews from all over the Mediterranean who are in Jerusalem for the festival. Many of these are likely pilgrims who had come for Passover, fifty days ago, when Jesus was killed.

Peter is dealing with several impossibilities. First, all the powers that put Jesus to death seven weeks ago (the Roman empire, the religious and local authorities, the forces of order) are still in place. Second, the apostles, seemingly drunk with the Spirit, are speaking in strange tongues. And most of all, they are saying crazy things, prophecies from the Scriptures mixed with those impossible claims about Jesus.

Rising from the dead? Well, maybe you could believe that—or at least hope for it. But Jesus of Nazareth? An impossible Messiah. His kingdom had been, like so many others, conquered by Rome. He had been judged. He had been crucified as the most wretched of slaves, an utterly defeated rebel.

And yet, there is something about the way they tell this story that catches people's attention. Yes, they were on fire with the Holy Spirit. And this Spirit is also part of Jesus! Jesus drew these disciples together and held them together, and they will carry his story to the world. While Jesus opened up a new world of possibilities, Peter recognizes that the bottom-line impossibilities are what give backbone to his proclamation. It was impossible for Jesus not to love God's people. It was impossible for Jesus to walk past injustice. It was impossible for Jesus to abandon his friends. And it was impossible for him to be held in death's power. Hallelujah!

Mark Stamm

Acts 2; John 20

Acts 2:14a, 22-32 brings us a portion of Peter's sermon delivered on the church's first Pentecost. Does it seem out of place, perhaps better suited for Pentecost Sunday? The text is fully appropriate when one considers the ancient tradition of the Great Fifty Days. Indeed, Eastern Orthodox Christians call their service book for Eastertide the *Pentecostarion*. Hearing Peter's sermon reminds us that Easter faith is lived in the power of the Spirit.

The Second Sunday of Easter offers the John 20:19-31 reading each year of the three-year cycle. What should we hear? Note that the disciples were gathered together, but that the doors "were locked for fear of the Jews" (v. 19 NRSV). Jesus came and stood among them anyway. As we are told, Thomas was not there on the evening of the first day; for that matter, neither were we. Now here we are a week later, standing with Thomas and listening to the text. We should not be too hard on this one who has long been called "the Doubter." The other disciples had seen the Risen Lord and had testified to that fact, yet the doors of their assembly were still shut a week later (v. 26).

This text is about believing and that shape of believing (v. 25). Indeed, "that you may come to believe" (v. 31 NRSV) is the goal of John's Gospel. What does believing mean? Preachers should not assume that they and others have a well-developed understanding of what believing means. Although the disciples had received the Spirit and were given a commission to forgive sins, they were still huddled in their room. What manner of believing is that?

What locked doors are we standing behind? Can we trust the Risen Christ to help us move beyond them?

Barbara Dick

1 Peter 1; John 20

Today's Gospel and epistle texts have to do with believing without seeing. In the famous story of "doubting Thomas," Jesus praises those who will believe without seeing (John 20:29). Peter writes to encourage those who already believe without seeing to stay strong as they face suffering and persecution (1 Peter 1).

What does it really mean to believe in something we have never seen? The easiest examples are metaphorical; we will never actually see love, hope, and trust, and yet we believe in them. If we did not, we could not function in the world.

But how does that work with faith? It seems that our faith is often stronger when we are in distress. Faith becomes an active partner in the fight against depression, sorrow, fear, and rage. It can be harder, however, to conjure up a strong faith when we battle inertia, boredom, and apathy, those insidious weapons of passivity. Perhaps it has to do with a view of faith as a battle banner rather than a way of living. Do we see faith as something other, outside of us, that we have to find or attain so we can make use of it? Or do we see faith as an aspect of character, an innate trait—like a sense of humor—that fills and informs our living? Rather than having faith, we are called to become faith. That puts faith—along with love, hope, trust, and the rest of the fruits of the spirit—into an entirely different category. As the body of Christ, we are called to shine with the light of faith, to become living testimony of God's love in the world. Ah! So faith is not a tool; it is an identity. It is not put on for battle; it fills our lives with light and love.

Carolyn Winfrey Gillette
http://www.carolynshymns.com/

When Thomas Heard from Jesus

When Jesus heard from Jesus, "Now come and follow me,"
He surely went with gladness, for there was much to see.
He witnessed Jesus' teaching and saw his healing touch;
He found a faith to guide him, a friend he loved so much.

When Jesus spoke of heaven, bold Thomas dared to say,
"We don't know where you're going! How can we know the way?"
He wanted understanding of what he could not see.
Then Jesus reassured him, "The way is here—through me."

When crowds began to murmur and leaders raised their cry,
Brave Thomas spoke out firmly, "Let's go with him and die."
He ate at Jesus' table, partaking wine and bread;
Yet later with the others, he saw the cross and fled.

What joy on Easter evening when many saw the Lord!
Yet Thomas was not with them and would not trust their word.
When Christ appeared before him, his doubts were quickly gone;
He gladly knew that evening the joy of Easter dawn.

That man of faith saw Jesus at breakfast by the sea;
At Pentecost he witnessed so others would believe.
O Lord, may we—like Thomas—keep growing day by day;
Increase our faith and guide us, for Lord, you are the Way.

NOTES
Biblical References: Matthew 10:1-4; Mark 3:13-19; Luke 6:12-16;
John 11:11-16; 14:1-7; 20:19-29; 21:1-7; Acts 1:12-14
Tune: AURELIA ("The Church's One Foundation"), Samuel S. Wesley, 1864
Text: Copyright © 2012 by Carolyn Winfrey Gillette. All rights reserved.

Melissa Bane Sevier
http://melissabanesevier.wordpress.com

Seeing Is Believing (John 20)

I once spent a week in New York state helping chaperone a youth mission trip to a church camp. We took one day off and went into New York City on the subway, carrying bag lunches.

None of the youth had ever been to New York City. At Grand Central Station, I began my day of counting to eighteen (the number of youth) from the back of the group. In those days before cell phones, we didn't want to lose anyone.

Right out of the station, we were struck by how many people were living on the streets asking for handouts. The excitement of being in the city turned into something different. Instead of noticing the buildings, the stores, the crowded streets, I watched as our kids watched the homeless. Most pedestrians were walking right on by, understandably. They walked down this street and others like it every day.

But for a bunch of kids from Louisville, Kentucky, people asking them for money was anything but normal. They stopped. They spoke to the street people. Then they came to talk to me.

"Is it OK if we give our lunches away?"

"What?" I said.

"We want to give our lunches to these folks. They are hungry."

"Look," I said. "Do you know how expensive lunch is in New York? If you give away your food you may not be able to afford both souvenirs and lunch." I didn't want them to complain later because they didn't have money. "Okay," they said. Okay?

I watched as eighteen youth, one by one, gave their lunches to people they'd never met. Some took the food and gave a blessing. Some said nothing. Some refused. Our young people shook hands with the hungry. Sometimes they sat down next to them and talked for a few minutes. Finally we moved on. But we were a different group. The rest of the day our young people spoke to just about every person they saw sitting on the sidewalk. It was a slow way to move down the streets of New York.

We went to the Hardrock Café at lunchtime. Some of the youth ordered food; some just drank a coke; some ate nothing, or just bought a T-shirt. Not a single one complained about not having enough money.

This Sunday we read the story of Thomas, who had trouble believing Jesus could still be among them. There had been a crucifixion, after all. Yet, he came face to face with the risen Jesus. "Have you believed because you have seen me?" Jesus asked. "Blessed are those who have not seen and yet have come to believe" (v. 29 NRSV).

We'd been working at a church camp, and if we expected to see Jesus anywhere, we expected to see him there, where kids came for Christian education. But that day, eighteen teenagers saw Jesus in people they met on the city sidewalks. I saw Jesus in eighteen young people I already knew.

John Wesley's Notes on the Bible
http://www.ccel.org/ccel/wesley/notes.txt

John 20:23

"Whose soever sins ye remit"—(According to the tenor of the Gospel, that is, supposing them to repent and believe) they are remitted, and whose soever sins ye retain (supposing them to remain impenitent) they are retained. So far is plain. But here arises a difficulty. Are not the sins of one who truly repents, and unfeignedly believes in Christ, remitted, without sacerdotal absolution? And are not the sins of one who does not repent or believe, retained even with it? What then does this commission imply? Can it imply any more than 1. A power of declaring with authority the Christian terms of pardon; whose sins are remitted and whose retained? As in our daily form of absolution; and 2. A power of inflicting and remitting ecclesiastical censures? That is, of excluding from, and re-admitting into, a Christian congregation.

May 4
3rd Sunday of Easter

Acts 2:14a, 36-41; Psalm 116:1-4, 12-19; 1 Peter 1:17-23; Luke 24:13-35

Beth Quick
http://bethquick.blogspot.com

Acts 2

• This, like last week's reading from Acts, continues as an account of the reaction of the crowds to Peter's speaking at the festival of Pentecost.

• "God has made him both Lord and Messiah, this Jesus whom you crucified" (v. 36 NRSV). This is interesting phrasing by Peter—does he believe that Jesus was not innately the Messiah, but only chosen to take on that identity? Hmm…

Psalm 116

• This text was just in our lectionary cycle for Maundy Thursday—hopefully it looks a little familiar to you! What makes it different to read this psalm during Holy Week and then during the days of Easter?

• "I love the LORD, because he has heard my voice" (v. 1 NRSV). Do we love people "because" of something? Or does our love, even for God, go deeper and beyond a "because"?

• "I will pay my vows to the LORD" (v. 14 NRSV). This phrase is repeated in this psalm. It seems the psalmist feels he must pay God back for hearing his voice, his supplications. Does God need to be paid back? Does God want to be paid back? I don't think God wants to feel "owed" as much as loved.

• "Loosed my bonds" (v. 16 NRSV). What has you bound up?

1 Peter 1

• "Purified your souls by your obedience to the truth" (v. 22a NRSV). What does it mean to be obedient to truth? Does it mean to always tell the truth? To go out of your way to share truth? To act on the truth that you know?

• "Genuine mutual love" (v. 22b) is literally *philadelphian,* in Greek, "brotherly love."

• "Love one another deeply from the heart" (v. 22c). The word *deeply* has the sense of intense, zealous love.

Luke 24

• "How he had been made known to them in the breaking of the bread" (v. 35 NRSV). I like this phrase. There are so many accounts in the Scriptures of Jesus sharing meals with people—isn't it appropriate that it is over a meal that these two recognize him after the resurrection?

• "Beginning with Moses and all the prophets, he interpreted to them the things about himself in all the scriptures" (v. 27 NRSV). Ah, if only that conversation had been recorded into the Scriptures!

• I always wonder, in texts like this, and in Mary's seeing Jesus at the resurrection, and the disciples seeing Jesus walking on water—how can they not recognize one around whom they have centered their lives? What keeps them from seeing and knowing Jesus for who he is? When do we fail to recognize Jesus standing right in our midst?

John Wesley's Notes on the Bible
http://www.ccel.org/ccel/wesley/notes.txt

Acts 2:38

The gift of the Holy Ghost does not mean in this place the power of speaking with tongues. For the promise of this was not given to all that were afar off, in distant ages and nations. But rather the constant fruits of faith, even righteousness, and peace, and joy in the Holy Ghost. Whomsoever the Lord our God shall call—(Whether they are Jews or Gentiles) by his word and by his Spirit: and who are not disobedient to the heavenly calling. But it is observable St. Peter did not yet understand the very words he spoke.

Mark Stamm

Acts 2; Luke 24

Acts 2:14a, 36-41 continues the reading through the narrative of the church's first Pentecost, this week giving us the conclusion of Peter's sermon, which is then followed by the call to repentance (*metanoia,* or turning) and baptism in the name of Jesus Christ. Here one finds another connection of our lives to that of the Risen Christ—in the baptismal covenant we enter the life and mission of Jesus. Resurrection is about what happens to us, along with Jesus, and it always points us toward mission.

The Luke 24 narrative on the Emmaus Road brings us the third and final Resurrection appearance narrative for this year's cycle. In the fourth week, the focus shifts to the church's experience of life in the Risen One, but the shift is already occurring in this text. Here we have the story of the Risen Christ who shares scriptures (v. 27) with the disciples and follows that by making himself known to them in the breaking of the bread (v. 35). What can we hear in this and other post-Resurrection texts that we have not heard before? Perhaps that is the wrong question.

Jesus came among them and they did not recognize him (v. 15). How odd. It helps to read this text from the perspective of those disciples. Notice that their conversation also happened on the first day of the week, that is, on the day that the church traditionally gathers. Could it be that Jesus is in the room with the church today, and we do not recognize him? What might prevent such recognition? Our greed? Despair? Lack of imagination? These are better questions. We respond best in the faith shared within the Baptismal Covenant, that is, in turning toward Christ and his vision for the world.

Lowell Grisham
http://lowellsblog.blogspot.com/

Prayers of the People

Presider: Christ is present with us, in us, and through us. In faith let us offer the prayers of our hearts, as we set our faith and hope on God saying: We offer you the sacrifice of thanksgiving; and call upon your holy Name.

Litanist: Fill your baptized people with spirit, O God, and make our hearts burn within us, that we may know you as you are revealed in the opening of the Scriptures and in the breaking of the bread. We offer you the sacrifice of thanksgiving;

and call upon your holy Name.

Protect our nation from futile ways and the pursuit of power, that our people may be obedient to your truth and manifest genuine mutual love. We offer you the sacrifice of thanksgiving;

and call upon your holy Name.

Fulfill your promise of life for everyone and comfort those who live entangled in the cords of death, that Christ may turn their suffering into glory. We offer you the sacrifice of thanksgiving;

and call upon your holy Name.

Stay with us and accept the concerns and needs of this community, that our eyes may recognize you as the stranger along the way, and we may be filled by your teaching and your eucharistic presence. We offer you the sacrifice of thanksgiving;

and call upon your holy Name.

Hear our prayers for those for whom we intercede, especially _____. Share our joy and thanksgiving for the blessings that we offer you, especially for _____. Welcome into your eternal banquet those who have died, especially _____. May they know the glory of the risen Lord. We offer you the sacrifice of thanksgiving;

and call upon your holy Name.

Presider: O Risen One, take, bless, and break and give our lives and our prayers to God as an offering of your eucharistic life, O Christ, that you may be recognized throughout the world, in the unity of the Holy Spirit, one God forever and ever. **Amen.**

Melissa Bane Sevier

http://melissabanesevier.wordpress.com

The End of a Terrorist (1 Peter 1)

I remember so clearly the day that Osama bin Laden was killed by U.S. Navy SEALs. As the news became public, reaction varied around the world. Crowds cheered. Others stood solemnly. Many prayed.

Then criticism started. Those who cheered were criticized for being exuberant over the death of another human being. Those who didn't cheer were criticized for not cheering. My personal reaction was, I suppose, one of relief. I really had no impulse to gather with others, but I admit to being glad this particular page had been turned, even if the chapter wasn't fully over yet. Even if the end of the book will never be written in human history.

Maybe we can come together on one point at least: the end of a life whose singular purpose appeared to be creating fear and terror makes us focus once again on how destructive and viral such values are. The destruction of 9/11 came swooping unbidden back into our memories on hearing of the death of this one terrorist. The virus of terror tends to be less obvious, and, if we let it, will seep into every nation, political party, and human heart. If terror engenders hatred, violence, or injustice, it has accomplished its vile purpose.

Fear makes us behave in strange ways. We become angry and vengeful. We decide to hate a certain group of people, a certain race, a certain religion, a certain nationality. But if God truly judges all impartially, then will we not be judged on how we act and speak? There is no end to the cycle of violence. Terror depends on that. There is no end unless we end it.

We can show peace and live peace. We can speak peace and share peace. We can refuse to hate and can endeavor to understand. Any of these actions reduces the power of terrorism.

A life that was lived by the sword has found its terminus by the sword. Let us take a moment to recommit ourselves to ending the need for swords.

"If you invoke as Father the one who judges all people impartially according to their deeds, live in reverent fear during the time of your exile" (v. 17 NRSV).

Martha Spong

http://marthaspong.com/

Luke 24

After Hurricane Katrina, I traveled to the Gulf Coast on a mission of pastoral relief to a United Methodist minister whose house had been devastated by flooding during the storm. My presence for two Sundays allowed her time off to work on rebuilding her home. The second Sunday, we celebrated Communion. I checked in with Pastor Leah, because I wanted to be sure to do it right. My style for presiding is a loose combination of what I observed in my Baptist childhood and my UCC adulthood, with little training in anything orthodox and a leftward theological leaning that caused me to avoid saying "body" and "blood" in favor of "the bread of life" and "the cup of blessing."

So I asked a lot of questions. I learned that the people came forward, and I learned that Pastor Leah would tear the bread herself and then hand a piece to each person. After all, she said, the bread, Christ's body, is not taken by us, but given for us.

Instead of improvising words of invitation and a Communion prayer as I might do at home, I followed the expected liturgy carefully. I was not there to bring them some new way of doing things, but to keep them going as best I could. I worried a bit about being coordinated enough to hold the plate and tear the bread and hand it to each person while remembering to say the words they expected to hear: "The body of Christ, broken for you."

When the first person in line came to me, and I tore the bread, I had one of those moments of intense surprise, as if the bread itself were saying to me, the way my son does, "Oh, snap!"

Yes, it was a "snap" moment, and it reminded me of that greatest "snap" moment ever, on the road to Emmaus. Two of Jesus' followers are walking to Emmaus on Easter evening, when a man falls in beside them. The reader knows from the beginning it is Jesus, but Cleopas and friend do not recognize him. They tell him about all the events that have taken place and how they grieve for their master, saying they never believed he would die, for he was to redeem Israel. And although they have been told the story of the empty tomb, they cannot put together all the pieces of the story until Jesus begins to explain the words of the prophets, all while they are walking along the road.

Snap! Their eyes are opened, and they recognize him! It happens in the breaking of the bread.

Snap! As I tore those pieces of bread at the church in Mississippi, Christ's presence became real and erased all my worries about getting Communion "right" that day.

Snap! What is Jesus telling you?

Paul Bellan-Boyer

"Their Eyes Were Opened" (Luke 24)

Have you had moments when God's vision began to take hold, opened your horizon, struck home in a way that made sense, that gave hope and changed your view of the world, of the faith, of yourself?

It happened along the road to Emmaus. Those disciples could be us, Cleopas and his companion (a man or a woman?). Jesus reached them. "Were not our hearts burning within us while he was talking to us...while he was opening the scriptures to us?" (v. 32).

Walk for a moment with them. They have left Jerusalem with Jesus' gruesome death and the women's hard-to-believe story of resurrection fresh in their minds. Within the past week they had gone to conquer Jerusalem for God and been dashed against the stones of temple and empire, and now...

I think of one of my greatest teachers, who "opened the scriptures." He helped the text—and God's possibilities—come to life for me and many others. He preached justice, non-violence, and the beauty of God's love for the world, and helped us see that this was God's word, right there in the Bible. But when we left the presence of the master, somehow it was never quite as easy as when our guide and the gift of his spirit were right there with us. The journey with Christ has a tension between the promise that Jesus will be with us always and our experience that we often seem to walk alone.

Yet with my beloved teacher and friend, as with Jesus, once the Scriptures have been opened, all manner of things open up. Yes, we find God, but we also find our neighbors and ourselves.

The Scriptures lead the Emmaus disciples to open their hearts in hospitality, and that is when it all breaks open. In the breaking of bread, these disciples find all they need. They can't wait to share the good news. May it be so for us.

May 11
4th Sunday of Easter

Acts 2:42-47; Psalm 23; 1 Peter 2:19-25; John 10:1-10

David Lose

Acts 2; Psalm 23; John 10

When we read Luke's description of the early church, it's easy to become either nostalgic—"Those were the good old days…" or depressed—"What are we doing wrong?"

Before falling prey to either reaction, however, it's worth considering that we now live in a culture that no longer assumes church attendance is either expected or obligatory. That is, people no longer go to church because they feel they should. Instead, they give their time, energy, and resources to those activities and institutions that make a real difference in their lives.

So perhaps we should ask people what they want, what they need, even what they crave from their faith communities. My guess is that the variety of answers we receive will have one thing in common: we want life, real life, a life of meaning and purpose, a life characterized by fulfillment, generosity, and love. Which is exactly what Jesus promises in the Gospel reading today: "I came that they may have life, and have it abundantly" (John 10:10 NRSV).

There are still "thieves and bandits" promising life to our people but failing to deliver. They can set the context for our preaching. In response to the false promise of acceptance—if you become thin or beautiful enough—that animates so many diet fads, the Gospel promises unconditional acceptance. In response to the false promise of escape in the face of hardship that drives many to drugs and alcohol, the church offers a community that shares all in common (Acts 2:44)—including joys and suffering. In response to the false promise that contentment comes by having more stuff, the church reminds us that "the LORD is my shepherd, I shall not want" (Psalm 23:1 NRSV).

The audience craving abundant life has never been larger. Let's offer it.

Paul Escamilla

Psalm 23

Psalm 23 is a mainstay for memorial occasions, a gentle companion to help us make our way toward an assurance that we go not alone through valleys, and loved ones are forever held in the care of the Good Shepherd. Many have been comforted in a time of loss through reading or hearing this beautifully poetic prayer. So how does this psalm find its way into the lectionary for Eastertide? A certain word gives us a clue. It is drawn from the Latin Vulgate translation of the same phrase immortally rendered in the KJV as "my cup runneth over": *inebrians.* You'll recognize in that Latin verb the makings of our English word "inebriated." "My cup runneth over" may indeed be a euphemism for having a whale of a good time.

The coarser implications of that observation aside, let's look at the word in context: "You prepare a table before me / in the presence of my enemies… / my cup overflows" (v. 5 NRSV). A picture begins to emerge that transforms this pastoral into a declaration of transcendence and triumph: In the very presence of my enemies, my cup is filled to the brim, and even over; I enjoy its every delight. Even in company with the many reminders of my vulnerability, my mixed record of relationships, and my checkered history of challenging unjust systems or hurtful individuals, my spirits soar, for I know God reigns, and goodness and mercy are ever near.

One recalls Paul and Silas in prison—*singing* (Acts 16:25); or Bonhoeffer, held in Hitler's clutches, writing of a "great future" (Dietrich Bonhoeffer, *Letters and Papers from Prison* [NY: Touchstone edition, 1997], 15); or the psalmist praising a God who turns mourning into dancing (30:11). Come what may, God the shepherd will be my companion, and that good news, that deeply grounded and transcendent assurance, is not merely hand-holding comfort; it is Easter's news.

Suzanne Guthrie
http://www.edgeofenclosure.org

"The Beautiful One"

"Tell me, you whom my soul loves, / where you pasture your flock" (Song 1:7 NRSV).

William Temple, in his devotional commentary on John's Gospel, translates the Good Shepherd as "The Beautiful One" (*Readings in St. John's Gospel* [MacMillan, 1955], 5). He admits the exaggeration, but wants to convey the implied attractiveness in the word *good*. Jean Vanier, in his commentary (*Drawn into the Mystery of Jesus through the Gospel of John* [New York/ Mahwah, N.J.: Paulist Press, 2004]), also alludes to the beauty implicit in this passage. Beauty attracts; we want to dwell in the beauty of holiness, to be beautiful for others and to draw out their own beauty. Vanier writes, "To become a good shepherd is to come out of the shell of selfishness in order to be attentive to those for whom we are responsible so as to reveal to them their fundamental beauty and value and help them to grow and become fully alive" (Vanier, 189). Other archetypal traits of the Good Shepherd include knowledge both expansive and interior, practical and sapiential.

> The symbolism of the shepherd also contains the sense of a wisdom which is both intuitive and the fruit of experience. The shepherd symbolizes watchfulness. His duties entail the constant exercise of vigilance. He is awake and watching. Hence he is compared with the Sun, which sees all things, and with the king. Furthermore, since, as we have stated, the shepherd symbolizes the nomad, he is rootless and stands for the soul which is not a native of this Earth but always a stranger and pilgrim. In so far as his flock is concerned, the shepherd acts as a guardian and to this is linked knowledge, since he knows what pasture suits the animals in his charge. He observes the Heavens, the Sun, the Moon and the stars and can predict the weather. He distinguishes sounds and hears the noise of approaching wolves, as well as the bleating of lost sheep.
>
> Through the different duties which he performs, he is regarded as a wise man whose activities are the result of contemplation and inner vision. (Jean Chevalier and Alain Gheerbrant, *The Penguin Dictionary of Symbols,* translated from the French by John Buchanan-Brown [London:Penguin Books, 1996], 873-74.)

Good Shepherd Sunday promises sentimental loveliness and nostalgia but instead delivers overwhelming challenges. I think it's nearly impossible to meditate on Jesus' discourse on the Good Shepherd without hearing Ezekiel 34:1-31 in the background: waking up to the corruption of the bad shepherds, seeking accountability in the causes of justice, and knowing the Holy One as Shepherd.

The timeless call to radical activism can't be separated from the good, or beauty, or wisdom.

Dan Clendenin
http://journeywithjesus.net

1 Peter 2

"Slaves, submit yourselves to your masters with all respect, not only to those who are good and considerate, but also to those who are harsh" (v. 18 NIV 1984).

This shocking verse is where the epistle for this week *should* start, with the first sentence of what is obviously a new paragraph. But it doesn't. The lectionary leapfrogs the submission of slaves in 2:18 and instead begins with the imitation of Christ in 2:19. How convenient. If we're honest, I suspect that we're glad for this avoidance strategy. Isn't submission to slavery an example of complicity with evil? Aren't Christians called to subvert injustice rather than submit to it?

Sprinkled throughout 1 Peter are important clues about that community's unique time, place, and circumstances. The author writes from Rome, but he doesn't use the word *Rome*. Rather, he uses the politically provocative code word "Babylon" (5:13). It's hard to think of a more derogatory epithet than that ancient empire that conquered and subjugated the Jews way back in 586 BCE. Similarly, John disparages Rome as "Babylon the Great, the mother of prostitutes and of the abominations of the earth" who is "drunk with the blood of the saints" (Revelation 17:5-6 NIV 1984).

The recipients of 1 Peter lived a thousand miles east of Rome, in what is now north-central Turkey. Peter refers to the believers as "aliens and strangers" (2:11 NIV 1984) to Rome's paganism. They belonged to their own peculiar "people and nation" (Rev 5:9). They didn't conform to the social conventions of the day. Their social marginalization, observes the author, earned them abuse, scorn, slander, and malicious gossip from pagan critics. Even "the name" Christian was offensive to their detractors (1 Peter 4:14, 16).

For about a hundred years after Jesus, Christians remained invisible to the greater Roman empire. But across the decades, they earned a reputation as an anti-social community that lived on the fringes of society. They were considered fanatical, seditious, obstinate, and defiant. The historian Tacitus (d. 117 CE) called them "haters of mankind."

Rome responded to Christian sedition and separatism with state persecution, sometimes sporadic and at other times by official policy. The first few sentences of the epistle describe how the believers "suffer grief in all kinds of trials" (1:6 NIV). They shouldn't be surprised by their "fiery trials" (4:12), he says, as if their persecutions are strange or unexpected. Indeed, he reminds them, "you know that your brothers throughout the world are undergoing the same kind of sufferings" (5:9 NIV 1984).

It's no wonder that these believers who suffered social marginalization and political persecution felt like "the end of all things is near" (4:7 NIV 1984). For some of them it was. The writer thus recommends a strategy of survival. Slaves should submit to their masters. Wives should submit to their husbands, and young men should submit to older men (3:1, 5:5). There was enough trouble in the world without looking for more. To make the best of a bad situation, sometimes compromise is necessary and wise.

Ann Scull
http://seedstuff.blogspot.com

Listening Song

Steve Grace, *"Better Days Ahead"* on *Better Days Ahead* (World Mission International, 2007).

Kid's Stories

Max Lucado, *The Song of the King* (Crossways Books, 1995). We can recognise the music of the king when we travel with his son. Kids love this story and it brings tears to the eyes of adults.

Elspeth Campbell Murphy, *Sometimes I Get Scared: Psalm 23 for Children* (USA: Chariot Books, 1980). Although the illustrations are a little dated, children find this book very reassuring because it makes Psalm 23 particularly relevant for children today. Each time I have used this book, a parent has asked to borrow it to read again to his or her child.

Youth: More Than Skin Deep

Kevin Johnson, *Could Someone Wake Me Up Before I Drool on the Desk?* (Minneapolis, MN: Bethany House, 1995), 73–74. Use this little story as is for teens or adapt it for adults. I often use the ideas in this book as sermon starters, and the basic idea here makes a great introduction to the Acts reading.

Film Clip

Dead Poets Society. Show the scene where Mr. Keating (Robin Williams) encourages the boys to tear out the first few instructional pages of their poetry books and challenges them to instead think for themselves. He asks them what verse they will contribute to the world. Relate this to how God calls us in the John reading and ask people to discuss together what their verse might be.

Drama

"A Podlich" in *Drama Resources 2,* ed. Lutheran Commission on Worship (Adelaide: Lutheran Publishing House, 1986), 74–77. This is a drama about the modern church that can be compared with the church in the Acts reading. The drama can easily be adapted or shortened for any congregation. The introduction to this drama book encourages us to use the dramas as a springboard for our own ideas.

Quotation: Teresa of Avila

"Lord, if this is the way you treat your friends, it's no wonder you have so few!" This makes a humourous yet thought-provoking introduction to the 1 Peter reading. It is said that she said this after falling out of her carriage into mud while visiting the poor on a stormy night or after falling off a bridge into a swollen stream. Either way, she wasn't having a good time. (http://ericsammonscom/blog/2009/10/15/the-quotable-st-teresa-of-avila, accessed March 28, 2012).

Response Activities

Sue Wallace, *Multi-Sensory Scripture* (UK: Scripture Union, 2005), 22–27. There are three excellent response activities in this book that can be used for our readings. **"Fridge Magnet Psalms"** and **"Psalm Calligraphy"** can both be used for any psalm but we often struggle to find something new to say about the well-used and well-known Psalm 23. These response activities challenge people to reword and reinterpret the psalm in a way that is meaningful to them. **"Abstract Art Bible Pictures"** lends itself to the 1 Peter reading. This is a response activity that can also be used in a variety of contexts for a variety of readings. To that end, I collect postcards and art and photography books.

John van de Laar
http://www.sacredise.com/

John 10

The quest for good leadership is a universal struggle. Good leaders bring life, peace, and joy. Poor leaders don't. Some even seek power for no other reason than to control and fleece those under their (lack of) care. In his Gospel, John presents Jesus as the ultimate leader who loves and brings life to his followers, who, in turn, are called to lead and love those under their care. This is the message of this week's Gospel reading.

This section does not stand alone. It is part of a much longer discourse, and flows out of the preceding narrative. The John 9 story of the Sabbath-healing of the man born blind sets up Jesus' statement about making the blind see and the sighted blind. In reaction, Jesus is challenged by Pharisees who ask if his words apply to them. His response begins the discourse that continues, uninterrupted, into John 10—"If you were blind, you would not be guilty of sin; but now that you claim you can see, your guilt remains" (9:41 NIV).

While this story appears to be part of the sequence beginning in chapter 7 at the time of the Feast of Tabernacles, 10:22 seems to indicate that the Shepherd discourse happened a few months later at the Feast of Dedication (or Hanukkah), which commemorated the Maccabean confrontation of true and corrupt leaders (about 160 BC). Since the Ezekiel 34 prophecy about the wicked shepherds of Israel was customarily read at this festival, it makes sense for this to be the setting for the shepherd discourse. But, John certainly wants to keep the connection with the blind man in our minds (see 10:21).

In the discourse of John 10, the "blind" religious leaders of the previous chapter are Ezekiel's wicked shepherds and Jesus' thieves. Jesus, mixing his metaphors, claims to be the opposite. He is the good shepherd who enters through the gate with the gatekeeper's permission. He is the gate through which the sheep enter to find safety and protection, and go out to find pasture. He has the interests of God's people at heart, unlike the thieves who "steal, kill [*thuo:* literally "sacrifice"], and destroy" the sheep (John 10:10a). Bad leaders *sacrifice the sheep* on the altar of their own greed, power-hunger, or need for control. Jesus *sacrifices himself for the sheep* that they may find abundant life. It's a simple test of leadership: who gets sacrificed, the sheep or the shepherd?

Every person is a leader in some sense, and we are all called to be "good shepherds" who lay down our lives for our "sheep." To the extent that others are sacrificed or damaged by our needs for control, power, or material gain, we are less "shepherd" and more "thief." But, insofar as we lay aside our needs, insofar as we embrace sacrifice so that others don't have to, we are the good shepherds that Jesus calls us to be. And only in this way can we, and those we lead, find life.

John Wesley's Notes on the Bible
http://www.ccel.org/ccel/wesley/notes.txt

John 10:3

"And the sheep hear his voice"—The circumstances that follow, exactly agree with the customs of the ancient eastern shepherds. They called their sheep by name, went before them and the sheep followed them. So real Christians hear, listen to, understand, and obey the voice of the shepherd whom Christ hath sent. And he counteth them his own, dearer than any friend or brother: calleth, advises, directs each by name, and leadeth them out, in the paths of righteousness, beside the waters of comfort.

May 18
5th Sunday of Easter

Acts 7:55-60; Psalm 31:1-5, 15-16; 1 Peter 2:2-10; John 14:1-14

Liz Crumlish
http://somethingtostandon.blogspot.co.uk/

Acts 7

When my adult child, in a rare moment of sharing (he is still a teenager) describes to me some of the exploits that are a part of his performing in a punk band, involving mosh pits and crowd surfing, I sometimes have to put my hands over my ears and sing loudly in order to block out the worrying pictures that he describes so vividly. While I appreciate his confidences, sometimes there are things I would rather not know! A clear case of too much information.

Stephen, one of seven men recruited by the early church to "wait on tables" so that the disciples would not be deflected from preaching the word, was guilty of sharing too much information. Finding his preaching voice, he speaks too clearly to the religious institutions of the day, indicting their practice, inflaming their anger to the point where they want him dead.

In order to stone Stephen, these good, religious people had to cover their ears to his preaching. They had to immunize themselves from his sharing of the vision he was receiving in the grip of the Holy Spirit. It would not have satisfied their appetite to quell his prophetic preaching if they took on board the justification he experienced in martyrdom. They needed to taste blood.

As people of faith today, living in the light of the Resurrection, we too can find ourselves covering our ears—blocking out those things we simply don't want to hear about, those things that indict our way of life. We, too, by closing our ears to the things we do not want to hear can find ourselves surrounded by the ugliness of rocks poised to attack, especially when those things we want to blot out call into question our dearly held traditions of faith.

Surely, as resurrection people, our mission is to seek new ways to listen and to respond and to discern the prompting of the Spirit of the risen Christ in all of life.

Todd Weir
http://bloomingcactus.typepad.com/

Acts 7

"Lord, do not hold this sin against them" (v. 60b NRSV). It is hard to comprehend Stephen's words at his martyrdom. My ministry was shaped by murder from the very beginning. The day after my ordination, a family from my church was kidnapped and murdered. It was a senseless crime. A commodities broker went through a bad trading streak and lost his client's money. The client turned him in to the authorities, the broker's wife left him, and his office furniture was repossessed all in the same day. He retaliated by kidnapping and murdering his client's whole family, including their eight-year-old daughter, all three members of my church, in a pathetic attempt to make the charges go away. He was a worse criminal than he was a commodities broker, because he was caught in their blood-stained car babbling a nonsense story about the mafia.

It was chilling that the murderer was an active member of a nearby church, pastored by a seminary friend of mine. This murderer taught Sunday school, led the youth group, and coached a soccer team. He was not some creepy thug or career criminal. As human nature goes, many people tried to piece together a portrait of a murderer that made him a monster all along. "He always had a mean streak, there was something creepy about him," the stories went. And yet the same people had willingly trusted their children to his care only days before without a thought. It is hard to accept the fact that someone so much like us could snap and be brutally cold-blooded; so he must not really be like us.

During the funeral a family member spoke of his great love for the deceased and called for the murderer's execution. A part of my heart was stone-cold from anger and grief, and ready to find a jagged rock to hurl into the face of the murderer. Yet the part of my heart that could still beat reminded me that when Christ commanded me to forgive, there was no fine print, no exceptions.

As fate would have it, twenty years later, I have worked in a transitional housing program that often helps people on parole re-enter society after incarceration. I have come to know several murderers. Some of them have gone through great sorrow and personal growth, and others have been selfish, nasty people. I try to help them all equally, whether I like them or feel like they deserve help, or not. I help them because of Stephen's words to not hold sin against his killers, because Jesus said, "Father, forgive them for they do not know what they are doing" (Luke 23:34a NRSV). I help them because a future Moses, another famous murderer, may be among them; I help them because at the time, they did not know what they were doing. But I cannot say I do not know what to do, because the Gospel is clear—forgive as I have been forgiven.

Dan Clendenin
http://journeywithjesus.net

1 Peter 2

In our politically correct culture, few opinions generate more hostility than ones like the words of Jesus from this week's readings: "I am the way, the truth, and the life. No one comes to the Father except through me" (John 14:6). Or consider Peter's words: "There is no other name [than Jesus] under heaven given to men by which we must be saved" (Acts 4:12 NIV 1984). Truly, Jesus is a stone that causes us to stumble and a rock of offense (1 Peter 2:8).

Radical religious pluralism sounds and feels good, and across the years I've always wanted to believe it. But I can't, because I don't think it's true. Instead, I've come to a number of conclusions that, although they don't "solve" the problem, guide my thinking.

1. Some religious views and practices are clearly false, harmful, and even despicable.

2. The claim that all religions teach the same thing is patently false; this is precisely what religions do not do.

3. Pluralism tries to solve this problem of contradictory truth claims in two ways. People like John Hick appeal to agnosticism (see *God and the Universe of Faiths* [Oxford: OneWorld Publications Ltd., 1973]). A second strategy identifies a "common essence" in all religions, some lowest common denominator in them all.

4. Christians need not reject everything about other religions.

5. The conundrum of relating ten thousand religions to one another is not a "Christian" problem. It's an equal opportunity problem that confronts every religion and person.

6. I agree with the liberal Jewish writer Michael Kinsley that it's not wrong or intolerant to try to convert other people (see http://www.time.com/time/magazine/article/0,9171,98949,00.html, accessed June 29, 2012).

7. A rule of thumb in Bible interpretation is to understand the complex and ambiguous parts of Scripture in light of simple and straightforward passages.

8. Instead of discarding what you don't like in Scripture and ending up with a Bible that reflects only your own biases (as did Thomas Jefferson), Christians should hold together two broad themes. First, God desires that no person should perish, and that every person be saved and come to a knowledge of the truth (1 Timothy 2:4; 2 Peter 3:9). Christ is the atoning sacrifice not only for Christians but for the entire cosmos (1 John 2:2). Peter anticipates the universal "restoration of all things" (Acts 3:21). Second, Christ alone is God's ultimate means of salvation (John 14:6; Acts 4:12).

9. Exactly how the universal love of God and the particularity of Jesus fit together isn't clear.

10. Finally, a long time ago I quit trying to understand everything and admitted the many limitations of my knowledge. At the end of the day, it's not the parts of the Bible that I don't understand that bother me, such as the many questions about religious pluralism, but the parts that I do understand, like loving God with my whole heart and loving my neighbor as myself.

Julie Craig
http://winsomelearnsome.com

1 Peter 2

Once upon a time, a baby girl was born. The exact date and place are not known. If they had been known, they might have been important to the story, but we will never know them, so we build the story without them. All her life, the story of the beginning of who she is and who she came to be did not begin like other birth narratives, with broken waters, or a hurried trip to the hospital, or a long labor or a Cesarean scar; although her birth might have included all or some of those things, none of them were a part of her story. It began with the phrase, "We chose you."

It was a popular mythology, for the adoptive parents, in an effort to make the child feel less stigmatized, to tell the child that she was chosen. The problem with that mythology is that it sets up unrealistic visions of a hopeful couple walking through a room filled with isolettes in which happy healthy babies lay just waiting to be picked. The parents look at each baby carefully, inspecting each one—perhaps they even pick up each baby and practice holding them until they come to the one that is just right for them. That one they choose, and a happy family is formed.

I have no recollection of that day, of course, but they tell me that it was a happy one. When they say that I was chosen, they are telling the truth. They made the choice to adopt me before they met me, back when they began the process. They may have had an image of what I'd look like, sound like, be like. They may have imagined me blonde or brown-haired, chubby and ruddy or fair and delicate. But what they were really imagining was not a set of features, but a real, live child. Their child.

"But you are a chosen race, a royal priesthood, a holy nation, God's own people, in order that you may proclaim the mighty acts of him who called you out of darkness into his marvelous light" (v. 9 NRSV).

The promise that we are God's children, chosen and precious, is this: God alone does the choosing, and God chose from before creation. We are chosen, not because of some specialness or gifts or talents or shiny features or skills that we have achieved. We are chosen for a purpose—in order that we might proclaim the mighty acts of the One who called us out of darkness into marvelous light. We are chosen for a life of service, and this impacts our life together as the church. This place is where we have the best and most frequent opportunity to be open and welcoming to all whom God has chosen, regardless of specialness or gifts or talents or shiny features, just as God has welcomed us. When God imagines us, it is not a set of features, but God's real live child.

Paul Escamilla

John 14

The Farewell Discourse of John 14–16 is often understood, to state the obvious, as a good-bye—parting words from a beloved teacher to his disciples. The opening words of this pericope, however, give us a somewhat different sense of what is occurring in this final message of Jesus to his disciples: "I go and prepare a place for you ... that where I am, there you may be also" (v. 3 NRSV). Jesus' last words with his "friends" (15:13-15) regard his plans to bring them to where he is going. At one level, we hear these words and think "heaven"; and heaven knows this passage has been infinitely helpful in conveying to the bereaved a sense of eternal home for loved ones who have gone before.

At a different level, however, Jesus appears to have another end in mind: he is cultivating a present-day spiritual orientation, one he articulates as the discourse unfolds. The "place" he goes to prepare is, in part, *right here among his followers*. It is the beloved community on earth, in real time, in which fear is dispelled (14:1, 27), great works are accomplished (14:12), the Spirit is, as the creed states it, "a very present help" (compare 14:26), love is foundational (15:12, 17), and joy is complete (15:11). In these conversations around good-bye, Jesus is inculcating a sense of how life in Christ, nurtured by the Father, guided by the Spirit, is to be lived by his friends and in his spiritual presence.

Such a transcendent vision is perhaps the most distant and yet daily gift that can be imparted from one to another, no less practical for being also proleptic. Jesus sees ahead, and wants us to see, too—heaven, yes; but also earth, and a devotion to the present beloved community that bears his name.

David Lose

John 14

Sometimes the most impetuous questions lead to the most revealing answers.

I don't actually know if Thomas and Philip intended to be impetuous, or if they were merely curious, or just frustrated. Whatever the case, not satisfied with Jesus' promise of a house with many dwelling places (v. 2), they push. "Lord, we do not know where you are going. How can we know the way?" (v. 5 NRSV), Thomas begins. And when Jesus answers that he is the way to the Father, and that if they know him they know the Father, Philip blurts out what would have been a nearly inconceivable demand for a faithful Jew to make: "show us the Father, and we will be satisfied" (v. 8 NRSV).

In other words, just make the immortal and invisible God visible. Just make the God whose name is too holy even to be spoken appear before our eyes. Just show us something that Moses and Elijah were never permitted to see. That's all.

And then it comes—Jesus' revealing response, the heart of John's Gospel: "Whoever has seen me has seen the Father" (v. 9 NRSV). John tipped his hand near the beginning of his account: "No one has ever seen God" (1:18a), he wrote, reminding us of something we have each learned through painful experience. When a loved one falls ill, when a job disappoints, when an important relationship fails, how deeply true we experience God's absence and invisibility. But John goes on, "God the only Son, who is at the Father's side, has made God known" (v. 18b).

So here we are, just hours from the cross, and Jesus tells us again: see me and you see God. In my pain, my suffering, my innocence, and my triumph, you see divine love made manifest and the almighty and invisible God revealed…for you.

John Wesley's Notes on the Bible
http://www.ccel.org/ccel/wesley/notes.txt

John 14:3

To the question concerning the way, he answers, I am the way. To the question concerning knowledge, he answers, I am the truth. To the question whither, I am the life.

May 25
6th Sunday of Easter

2014

Acts 17:22-31; Psalm 66:8-20; 1 Peter 3:13-22; John 14:15-21

Julia Seymour
http://lutheranjulia.blogspot.com

Acts 17

The apostles and missionaries of the early church often encountered people who were unable to comprehend the story of Christ without trying to put it into their context, which did not always work. There were many stories of gods and goddesses around already and it was easier to fit a powerful experience of healing or of the Holy Spirit into what one already knew than to try to learn something new.

What do we already know that we might try to make an experience of Jesus fit into? Consider the god of our time: the wallet. Debit/credit card—Do we try to make Jesus an instant-gratification experience? That whatever we need or want he can take care of instantly? Library card—Is an encounter with Jesus a privilege? Is it limited to people who have already applied and been pre-qualified to have the experience? Discount card—Do we add up points with Jesus, so that we can be redeemed? Notes and pictures—Is an encounter with Jesus a memento of a good feeling or a souvenir of a closeness, trapped in time but occasionally stirring up affection?

Paul sees how the people are trying to fit the experience of Jesus into the story they already know. What he does is draw them away from the story they know to the evidence of God in life, with which they are already familiar. Paul sees the altar that the Athenian people have erected to an unknown god. Even though they have the pantheon of Greek gods and goddesses, there is something in their hearts that realizes they cannot know everything, that they have not identified the source of all things. Paul identifies that restlessness, that openness, as the longing the Spirit has stirred up in each of us until we rest in God. Through Jesus, we come to understand the invitation and welcome of God and learn to recognize how in God, we live and move and have our being.

Like the people of Athens, we have to allow that Jesus does not fit into any category we might try to create. The other stories we may encounter in the world, the other stories that may be offered up as gods, do not offer these things on their own.

Like Paul, we are called to witness to the story of Jesus, the savior and hope of the world. What is the good news of that story? Reconciliation with God, the promise of peace, the words of eternal life, the hope of the life of the world to come, the forgiveness of sins, guidance in how to live and in how to die. No other story can do that.

Marci Auld Glass
www.marciglass.com

Acts 17

Paul shares the Good News of the Gospel with a crowd of Athenians in the marketplace, and his rhetoric is masterful. He doesn't insult them. He doesn't scare them. He invites them to see something familiar in a new way. He allows them to re-interpret their tradition in light of new information about Jesus. He encourages them to consider that the God for whom they have been striving who was unknown is now able to be known through the person of Jesus of Nazareth.

And Paul suggests that one of the reasons we were created by this now known God was so we "would search for God and perhaps grope for him and find him—though indeed he is not far from each one of us" (v. 27 NRSV).

I love this. What a gift. How would we live life differently if we considered that we were here on earth to search and grope and, perhaps, find God? Doesn't that remove any certainty we might try to bring to the faith journey? If we are here to be Searchers and Gropers and Finders, then we are not here to be Declarers and Fact Finders and People Who Live Without Mystery. It isn't our job to have all of the answers and get an "A" on the test of life. God created us to seek, to wander around in the dark with our hands out in front of us, hoping we'll stumble into the God we seek.

Paul calls the Athenians to imagine God, and themselves, in more lofty terms than they are used to doing. Rather than worshiping a God of stone or silver or gold, they are called to consider that we are offspring of God. And so the God we worship should be better than stone. And the people who worship God reflect God's love back to the world.

The tension in this text between known and unknown keeps us from settling with easy answers. Yes, God is closer to us than an "unknown god." We are offspring of God, who is nearby. We know about God through the life, death, and resurrection of Jesus, a man who was known. But for all we know about God, we are still groping in the dark, searching high and low and, *perhaps,* finding God.

How do you share the Good News of the Gospel? With a set of proscribed tenets to which the Athenians must adhere? Or do you invite people to stumble around in the dark with you, knowing that God is never far away?

NOTE: From "Searching, Stumbling Faith" by Marci Auld Glass (http://marciglass.com/2012/04/30/searching-stumbling-faith/).

Natalie Sims
http://lectionarysong.blogspot.com

Acts 17

Paul preaches in Athens; universal longing for God; call to repentance; universality of the gospel.

"God of My Breathing" (Richard Bruxvoort-Colligan)—Excellent words to a well-known hymn tune. Sample and lyrics (http://www.worldmaking.net/).

"Ground and Source of All That Is" (Richard Bruxvoort-Colligan)—This song is very beautiful and easy to sing. Lyrics and sound sample (http://www.worldmaking.net/).

"Longing for Light We Wait in Darkness (Christ Be Our Light)" (Bernadette Farrell)—This song is just excellent; joyous words and a soaring chorus, particularly if you have someone to sing the (really high!) descant part.

"Longing for You" (Elaine Loukes)—A simple chant of longing for God. Sound sample, lyrics, and songbook available (http://www.wholenote.com.au/songs/longing.html).

"Bring Many Names Beautiful and Good" (Brian Wren)—This is a beautiful song, but long. Try singing one verse unison, then one women, one men, then all together again, to keep people interested in what they are singing. Lyrics (http://www.oremus.org/hymnal/b/b198.html).

"Christ Is Alive Let Christians Sing" (Brian Wren)—Excellent words of Christ's saving, and still relevant grace. A couple of tunes are offered in different hymn books. I prefer TRURO. Lyrics and sound sample (http://www.oremus.org/hymnal/c/c055.html).

"God Is Here as We Your People" (Fred Pratt Green)—Great lyrics, but not inclusive in all sources. It's sung to the familiar tune ABBOT'S LEIGH. Sound sample and less inclusive lyrics (http://www.oremus.org/hymnal/g/g157.html).

"God of Many Names" (Brian Wren)—If this is new it will need to be taught to your congregation as the tune is not intuitive, but it is worth knowing. The chorus is particularly appealing to kids. Lyrics (http://www.blogger.com/www.canterburyumc.org/clientimages/26257/bulletins/twbull053109.pdf).

"Kamana O 'I' O" (Joe Camacho)—Fun Hawai'ian song; good words. The chorus is not too hard to sing in Hawai'ian if you teach it. Nice with guitar and/or ukelele. Sound sample (http://www.myspace.com/music/player?sid=86781897&ac=now).

"Shadow and Substance" (Daniel Charles Damon)—Good clear words of being Christ's community in all our diversity. A simple tune. Lyrics and sheet music (http://www.hymnary.org/hymn/WAR2003/599).

Teri Peterson
http://clevertitlehere.blogspot.com

To the Unknown . . . (Acts 17)

Most of the time, we are taught to fear You. Not knowing means we cannot prepare, cannot control, cannot manipulate, and those limitations mean we are afraid of what You might do and especially what You might require of us. We like to know things. Our intellects are practiced and ready to rationalize nearly anything, as long as it fits on a linear path and follows a defined plan.

But You defy our intellects. You remain shrouded in mystery even as You surround us and support us and seek us. Your breath is our breath, but we cannot figure out how. Our life is Your life, but we cannot explain the mechanism that makes it so. We long for connection to something greater, to You, and yet we tell ourselves it cannot be. So we build our altars, read books crammed with big words, and push aside hope because it is impractical.

Still You keep coming around, swirling and pushing and pulling and calling and inspiring and providing in ways we cannot understand. We look for the who/what/where/when/why/how, and You tell us a story. We ask for step-by-step instructions in what to do next and how to please You, and You offer us instead Your very self, made flesh to live our story alongside us. We seek a list of good deeds or appropriate sacrifices to get what we want, and You remind us that You, not we, are God, and nothing we can do will change Your grace or Your providence.

Perhaps we are right to fear the Unknown. Or perhaps what we really fear is what You mean for our lives. If it's true, if our life, movement, and existence is held by You, is *in* You, then we cannot be separated, we cannot be cut off, we cannot truly be lost. No wonder You demand everything of us—changed hearts and lives to go with our changed minds. No wonder You offer so much of Yourself to us—even life, suffering, death, and more. While we have been busy creating rules for how You can work, You have been busy loving us into life.

Perhaps You are not scary after all. And perhaps You are also not completely Unknown—and so we seek, and grope, and hope to find you: "Closer is He than breathing, and nearer than hands and feet" (Alfred Tennyson, "The Higher Pantheism," from *The Holy Grail and Other Poems* [London: Strahan, 1870], 202).

John Wesley's Notes on the Bible
http://www.ccel.org/ccel/wesley/notes.txt

1 Peter 3:18

"The just for the unjust"—The word signifies, not only them who have wronged their neighbours, but those who have transgressed any of the commands of God; as the preceding word, *just*, denotes a person who has fulfilled, not barely social duties, but all kind of righteousness. "That he might bring us to God"—Now to his gracious favour, hereafter to his blissful presence, by the same steps of suffering and of glory.

Paul Escamilla

John 14

If John 20 ("Receive the Holy Spirit," v. 22) is the Fourth Evangelist's equivalent of Luke's Pentecost as recorded in Acts 2, then John 14 is his Ascension. In Luke's ascension narrative, Jesus suggests the nature of the Holy Spirit as power: " . . . stay here in the city until you have been clothed with power from on high" (Luke 24:49 NRSV). In John's "ascension" narrative, known to us as the Farewell Discourse, Jesus characterizes the Holy Spirit somewhat differently: "And I will ask the Father, and he will give you another Advocate . . ." (John 14:16 NRSV).

NRSV's "Advocate" translates a Greek word better represented by the KJV's more arcane "Paraklete." *Parakleton* means, literally, "beside-caller." For John, the Holy Spirit is introduced not principally as a force within, a beacon in the near distance, a voice overhead, or a hand in the small of the back (as, for example, in Mark 1:12), but rather as a companion.

A world of impressions opens to us as we conceive of the Holy Spirit in such a way. The *Parakleton* walks beside the followers of Jesus to teach, remind (John 14:26), and bear the truth (v. 17). There is a certain "with-ness" to the witness of the Spirit. (The word "with" in "he abides *with* you" translates the same *para* we find in the compound *Parakleton*.) Further, the image of a beside-caller is suggestive of a segment later in the Farewell Discourse in which Jesus equates discipleship with friendship (15:14-15). Finally, one begins to imagine the teaching, reminding, truth-bearing work of the community of Jesus' followers as representing, embodying, and mediating the Holy Spirit. The beside-caller, who abides *with* us as would a friend, calls to us in a voice heard and recognized beyond but also beneath the voice of the beloved community.

David Lose

John 14

Advocate. Helper. Comforter. All these words are apt translations of the Greek *parakletos*. And each has its place as we live as Christians in the world that (a) God loves so much and yet (b) rejected God's Son and often rejects those who follow him.

Notice that Jesus promises to send "another Advocate" (v. 16 NRSV). Jesus is the first. The second one will continue his work by making him alive in our hearts and experience. Which isn't to say that this life will be easy. If it were, we would need no advocate, no one to stand up for us, to encourage, comfort, and help us. Some of those hardships are part and parcel of living in a broken world where illness and war are as much the norm as health and peace. And some of those hardships come from trying to keep Jesus' commandments.

Do we believe this? I suspect that many of us tend to think that God rewards faithfulness. But sometimes acts of mercy are met with suspicion, standing for justice is met with hostility, speaking a word of mercy is met with anger, and bearing witness to God's love is met with contempt.

This isn't an easy word, but it is a true one. Christian faith does not exempt one from the challenges—physical, emotional, or spiritual—of this world. What else, indeed, should those who follow the Christ who "suffered for sins once for all, the righteous for the unrighteous" (1 Peter 3:18 NRSV) expect? But faith does promise help amid the challenges, comfort amid our grief, and an advocate to stand with us and for us. For we are not left alone, as orphans, but are accompanied by the Spirit of the One in whom "we live and move and have our being" (Acts 17:28 NRSV).

John Petty
http://progressiveinvolvement.com

John 14

The word *parakletos* means "one called alongside." It is generally translated as "advocate" or "comforter." The word is closely related to the Hebrew *hacham,* which appears in Psalm 23:4 (KJV), for example: "Thy rod and thy staff, they comfort [*hacham*] me."

Jesus promises "another Advocate" (v. 16 NRSV), himself apparently being the first. The "advocate" will be "the spirit of truth." This is reminiscent of the worship of those who do so "in spirit and truth" (4:23-24). The way the Fourth Gospel uses it, *parakletos* combines the concepts of comforter, encourager, advocate, and defender.

The "advocate" will "remain" with the disciples—*menei,* a key, even ubiquitous, word in the Fourth Gospel. Everyone—Jesus, the community, the advocate, the Father—seems to abide, dwell, and remain in, with, and under one another.

Jesus will not leave them bereft, like orphans. They will see him, even though no one else will. What's more, the community's relationship with Jesus is the same as Jesus' relationship with the Father, the first such statement in the Fourth Gospel.

The community "knows" the advocate, and, "on that day," the community "will know" that Jesus is in the Father. The word is *ginosko*. *Ginosko* is knowledge through intimate experience—"mystical knowledge," you might say. It is not so much a reasoned-based "knowing," but more revelation-based "knowing."

The Fourth Gospel anticipates some of the trinitarian debate that would come two or three hundred years later. The Son is in intimate relationship with the Father, yet is distinct from the Father. Jesus has a direct relationship with the Father and a direct relationship with the community, though the community itself is in relationship with the Father indirectly, through Jesus.

The Father is utterly transcendent, known only through the Son. The Father is beyond space and time, and, therefore, beyond description. The eastern tradition calls this *apophatic* theology, which means that God can be described only in negatives, without name, without origin, without end.

The question is: If the Father is unknown, how can the Father be known? The Fourth Gospel asserts: The Father can be known through the Son. The Father cannot be known, but the Son can be known, and to know the Son is to know the Father.

There is a shift in verse 21. Until then, Jesus had been speaking to the community—the "yous" were all plural. In verse 21, Jesus speaks to the individual: "The one having my commandments and keeping them is the one loving me. The one loving me will be loved by my Father, and I will love that one and will manifest myself to that one" (author's translation).

The primary sense of the sentence is to enjoin both community and individual in loving one another and Jesus. It would be a mistake, however, to view this in an exclusive way. Jesus is not saying that God will not love others who don't love. The Fourth Gospel is underscoring the reciprocity of relationship. Those in mutual relationship with one another—those who *menei* together and with Jesus—will want to live out the very basis of that relationship, which is love.

June 1
Ascension of the Lord Sunday

Acts 1:1-11; Psalm 47 or Psalm 93; Ephesians 1:15-23; Luke 24:44-53

Matthew L. Skinner

Acts 1

Many people know that Jesus ascends to "God's right side" (see Acts 2:32-5). But what does that mean?

The expression is less about location and more about status. Jesus' ascension expresses his exaltation, his reception of authority. When Jesus is "taken up...into heaven" (1:11), the result is not his absence but his widespread influence. His rule extends across creation. He reigns over all. He has a role in everything. He can exercise authority over every other power.

In Acts, Jesus never fully explains why his ascension benefits his followers, yet great expectations surround the event. Jesus promises power to his followers. He describes their role as "witnesses" (he declares this; he does not request it). This role will result in their movement across cultural boundaries; what begins in Jerusalem will reach "the end of the earth" (v. 8). The implication is that the ascension puts Jesus in a position, or to a status, from which he can commission and assist this work, just as Acts 2:33 later makes it clear that Jesus pours out the Holy Spirit on Pentecost.

The ascension therefore marks an end to Jesus' face-to-face interactions with his followers, yet it also points toward the beginning of a ministry in which they will be active. God still has promises to keep and work to do, if indeed "everyone who calls on the name of the Lord will be saved" (2:21). According to Jesus, this work will occur, in part, through the "power" he bestows.

At the same time, the scene is not all about urgency. Once Jesus departs, two angelic figures call the apostles back to their senses. But no one rushes. The apostles return to Jerusalem, so they can wait. Jesus will empower their ministry, to be sure, but according to his timetable.

Martha Spong
http://marthaspong.com/

Acts 1

My teenage daughter loves manga, those Japanese graphic novels popular in this country, too. They read from back to front, and in her collection are numerous multivolume teenage romances. But she also has a Manga Bible, illustrated by an artist, Siku, whose other work includes *Judge Dredd*. I particularly love his approach to the Acts of the Apostles, which is in many ways the adventure story of the early church.

For the adventure to begin, the leader needs to depart. And so we begin the book of Acts with our heroes grieving. They are stricken. They stand slack-jawed staring up into the sky. An amazing and wondrous and supernatural event occurred, right in front of them, but it also bereaved them, for the second time. How will they go on?

I once sat with half-a-dozen normally talkative people in a Bible study, reading the Ascension texts. They had things to say about the epistle and the Gospel, but when we read the Acts passage, they fell silent. I asked a leading question. Nothing. That physical ascending hangs us up. For first-century people, it symbolized their cosmology. The divine was above, and Jesus had to get there somehow. Life was a stage, with God in the fly space. We may think we know better, but it's still hard to reckon exactly where God is. Among the stars? In our hearts? Somewhere in between?

I decided to re-read verses 9 and 10:

> When he had said this, as they were watching, he was lifted up, and a cloud took him out of their sight. While he was going and they were gazing up toward heaven, suddenly two men in white robes stood by them. (NRSV)

Everyone was listening earnestly, and then I said, "Suddenly two men in white coats stood by them." Someone looked surprised. Someone else laughed, nervously. Seriously, if you had just seen your friend and teacher, previously dead, whisked away into the sky, wouldn't you wonder if those guys in white were there to take you away?

Practical people don't like this story. It strains credulity. We like our Jesus in the flesh, telling stories, walking dusty roads, eating dinner with people. We don't like him somewhere indefinable. Yet it's a truth of our faith that he is more than our brains can rationalize.

Jesus assured the disciples, in his last words to them, that understanding the details doesn't matter so much. Go out and be witnesses, he says, fueled by the power of the coming Spirit. And that's really the point of the story. It's not about the ultimate disposition of the resurrected body of our Lord and Savior. It's the prelude, the overture, to the great adventure of being Christ's Church. Don't stand around staring up at the clouds. Get out there and share the Good News, in your words and your actions and on your blogs…and even in your graphic novels.

Melissa Bane Sevier
http://melissabanesevier.wordpress.com

Beam Me Up, Scotty (Acts 1)

"They said, 'Men of Galilee, why do you stand looking up toward heaven?'" (v. 11a NRSV).

Every now and then a fringe religious group predicts the end of the world as we know it. I may even make a few jokes about it from the pulpit. There is, though, some appeal to the getting-out-of-Dodge syndrome. The night before the big exam or year-end job review. When the boyfriend or girlfriend schedules a talk about "where this relationship is headed." Tax day. Wouldn't it be something to be sucked out of your existence here right at the moment when the state trooper pulls you over for speeding in a construction zone? To end up in a place that is all goodness and light just as the mugger demands your wallet? Not to have to go through another presidential election season?

Wouldn't that be something? The disciples thought so. They could see the handwriting on the wall. After what had happened to Jesus, how could they hope for a happy future? They were starting to hold their meetings behind locked doors for a reason. They wanted to know if things were about to get better because maybe—just maybe—Jesus really *was* going to bring down the Romans. And so they asked him. His less-than-satisfying reply was, in essence, "Nope."

"You have some work to do," he said, and then he was taken from them. And there they stood, looking up. Wishing, I'm sure, that they could've been taken, too. Maybe like Elijah in the fiery chariot. Or on a cloud, like Jesus. Really, a cloud would have been fine. But a couple of guys showed up and asked them why they were just standing there.

Whatever and whenever our end might be, it isn't yet. We can spend our time wishing, dreaming of a world to come, or we can see what's right in front of us. We can look up, or we can look around. We can hope in a life to come in the future, or we can realize that hope also has a quality of immediacy.

Those followers of Jesus had learned some things from him. Soon they were doing what Jesus did: healing, teaching, preaching, causing trouble (in a good way), trying to figure out how to be a community together even though they got on one another's nerves.

We would do well to follow their following. To imagine how God wants the world to be, and to start trying to make it look like that. Yes, Christian faith is all about hope. But hope is very much about the now. Stop looking up. Look around instead. "You have some work to do," said Jesus. We'd best get started.

Beth Quick
http://bethquick.blogspot.com

Acts 1

• The ascension is such an interesting part of what happens to Jesus, in that, for most, it is something we care about *least*. Where does it fit in our Christian faith? Is Jesus' ascension important?

• For me, the importance of the ascension is that we are now left without Jesus physically present—that means *we* have to do it now—we have to do the work that he has been teaching and teaching about. No excuses, no right-there Jesus to do it for us. Just the Holy Spirit to be our Advocate. Jesus' ascension means that Jesus is asking *us* to get to work.

• Luke says that Jesus gives instructions, and shares "many convincing proofs" (v. 3 NRSV), and is with them for forty days speaking about the kingdom. It is little verses like these that drive me crazy. Where is all this stuff Jesus said and did? Why didn't Luke record it? Why do we get to have only little snippets of somebody that we adore so much?

Psalm 47

• An audience-participation psalm: "Clap your hands" (v. 1 NRSV). There are lots of musical settings for these words, and no wonder—they make you want to sing and clap!

• In verse 3, God subdues people under "our" feet. Gives the whole psalm the tone of a war-victory psalm of praise.

• "He chose our heritage for us" (v. 4 NRSV). I like this verse. God chooses our heritage for us—God chooses our history, our people, our story. I believe we have free will, but I manage to balance that, tricky though it sometimes feels, with a clear sense that God has a hand in all that goes on in my life. Even better to think of it as a "heritage" God chooses for us.

Luke 24

• Luke's "Part 1" account of the Ascension. Compare and contrast it to his testimony in Acts. I think here, the account is more reflective, looking back—calling up Moses, the fulfillments of the Old Testament prophecies, talking about what has happened up to this point. Acts is forward-looking, setting the stage for what has yet to happen.

• "And they were continually in the temple blessing God" (v. 53 NRSV). Indeed! I think we just can't imagine what these first weeks and months for the disciples must have been like. What an emotional roller-coaster they must have been on! But finally they were driven just to give thanks that their friend and teacher was still going to be in charge of their lives.

• Looking back on Luke, and moving ahead into Acts, we must take what Jesus has lived, and then live it ourselves.

Sharron Blezard

Acts 1

Are you tired of singing Easter hymns and shouting "Alleluias"? I hope not, because the principle act of the body of Christ is to worship, praise, and give glory and honor to God. All that we do and are flows from this expression of our devotion to the risen Christ, whose mercy and grace give us reason for being and purpose for doing. We are the witnesses now, even though we did not see with our own eyes Christ's ascension into heaven. We are the witnesses through Spirit and truth. The grand narrative story of God's interaction with God's people is, for the moment, in our hands and on our lips and within our hearts and minds. Yes, we are the body of Christ in this day and age, in our own unique contexts and communities.

Just as those early disciples were clothed with the Spirit, so we too are dressed for discipleship and equipped for ministry. Today, Ascension Day, is a good day to celebrate the reality into which we die and rise daily. Both psalms appointed for the day are infused with praise and lively worship. Rich images abound—joyous singing, clapping, praising, and acknowledging the power, majesty, beauty, and holiness of God. The lesson from Acts, Ephesians, and Luke's Gospel all point to Christ as the focus of our life, worship, and witness.

How might you integrate this spirit of joy and praise into your community's worship today? What can your message and worship do to ensure those gathered that Jesus is working in their lives through the Holy Spirit's nudging presence? Truly God is worthy of our highest praise, deepest devotion, and faithful service. We are gathered, shaped, and sent into the world in Christ's holy name.

Lowell Grisham
http://lowellsblog.blogspot.com/

Prayers of the People

Presider: Christ has ascended high that he might fill all things: Listen to our prayers, O God, as we proclaim the riches of your glorious inheritance and the immeasurable greatness of your power for us who believe, saying, Clap your hands, all you peoples; shout to God with a cry of joy.

Litanist: O gracious God of our Lord Jesus Christ, the Father of glory, give to your church a spirit of wisdom and revelation as we come to know you, that we may be your witnesses to the ends of the earth. Clap your hands, all you peoples;

shout to God with a cry of joy.

You reign over the nations, O God, and the rulers of the earth belong to you: Put your power to work among those who hold authority throughout the world, that they may establish your peace and reconciliation among all people. Clap your hands, all you peoples;

shout to God with a cry of joy.

Fill our community with your blessing, that with the eyes of our hearts enlightened, we may know the hope to which you have called us. Clap your hands, all you peoples;

shout to God with a cry of joy.

Cover the earth with your grace, O compassionate One, that all who suffer from any threat or oppression may know the power of your goodness. Clap your hands, all you peoples;

shout to God with a cry of joy.

Receive our prayers for all for whom we are called to pray, especially _____. Hear our song of praise and thanksgiving as we lift our gratefulness to you, especially for _____. You raised Christ from the dead and seated him at your right hand: Receive into your divine dwelling those who have died, especially _____. Clap your hands, all you peoples;

shout to God with a cry of joy.

Presider: Almighty God, your Christ reigns far above all rule and authority and power and dominion, and above every name that is named: Put all things under Christ's feet and fill the earth with the fullness of him who fills all in all, through the power of your Holy Spirit, One God, for ever and ever. **Amen.**

John Wesley's Notes on the Bible
http://www.ccel.org/ccel/wesley/notes.txt

Ephesians 1:13

"Ye were sealed by that Holy Spirit of promise"—Holy both in his nature and in his operations, and promised to all the children of God. The sealing seems to imply, 1. A full impression of the image of God on their souls. 2. A full assurance of receiving all the promises, whether relating to time or eternity.

Abingdon Creative Preaching Annual

Thom Shuman
http://lectionaryliturgies.blogspot.com/

Great Prayer of Thanksgiving

The Ascended Lord be with you.
And also with you.
Lift up your hearts to the One
    who gives us a spirit of wisdom.
We open our hearts to Jesus,
    who opens God's words to us.
Clap your hands, God's people!
  Sing songs of praise to our God!
We sing praises to the One
    who blesses and blesses us!

We do indeed lift loud songs of joy
to you, Awesome God!
Everything in heaven, and on earth,
provides the proof we need
of your goodness and mercy.
But closing our hearts to such evidence,
we looked to our own wisdom,
devising foolish ways to save ourselves.
Patiently you waited, hoping
we would return to you,
but when you could no longer wait,
you came to us in your Word
made flesh and blood.

Therefore, with all your people
of every time and every place,
we sing our glad songs to you:

Holy, holy, holy. Sovereign over
    all the earth.
The riches of your glorious creation
    forever praise you.
Hosanna in the highest!

Blessed is the One who will return to us.
Hosanna in the highest!

All glory is due to you, God on High,
and blessings on your Son,
our Lord and Savior, Jesus Christ.
Stripping himself of glory
he came that we might be clothed
in the power of the Holy Spirit.
Wearing the thorny crown of death,
he is the Head of all the Church,
his Body made whole for the world.

As we remember his life, his service,
his death, his resurrection, his ascension,
we speak of that mystery called faith:

Christ died to reveal salvation for us;
Christ arose to reveal resurrection life for us;
Christ ascended and will return
    to reveal glory to us.

We will not stop giving thanks to you,
Generous and Wonderful God,
as we pray that you
would pour out your Holy Spirit
upon your children gathered at the Table,
and upon the gifts of the bread and the cup.
We are filled with Christ's presence,
so we may go to empty ourselves:
telling your story of grace and hope,
carrying your mercy to those
who cannot forgive themselves,
pouring cups of cold water,
embracing the untouchables of our time.

Then, when we gather at your feast in glory,
seated with our sisters and brothers from all time,
we will clap our hands, shouting our joy to you,
God in Community, Holy in One,
now and forevermore. **Amen.**

June 8
Day of Pentecost

Acts 2:1-21 or Numbers 11:24-30; Psalm 104:24-34, 35b; 1 Corinthians 12:3b-13 or Acts 2:1-21; John 20:19-23 or John 7:37-39

Dan Clendenin
http://journeywithjesus.net

Acts 2

Jesus promised a kingdom; what we got was the church.

The feast of Pentecost marks the birth of the church. After Christmas and Easter, Pentecost is the most important celebration of the Christian calendar. The term comes from the Greek word *pentekostos,* meaning fiftieth, from which one of the most important feasts in the Jewish calendar derives its name. Fifty days after Passover, Jews celebrated the "Feast of Harvest" (Exodus 23:16) or "Feast of Weeks" (Leviticus 23:15-21). Centuries later, after their exile to Babylon, Pentecost became one of the great pilgrimage feasts of Judaism, when Diaspora Jews returned to Jerusalem to worship.

Pentecost not only birthed the church; it begot a bureaucracy. Across the centuries, human institutions became the wineskins for Spirit-led inspirations, and therein lies both the wit and the wisdom in the irony between the difference between God's vibrant kingdom and moribund human churches.

It's easy to criticize the church as a deeply flawed organization, but the institutionalization of the Jesus movement was both inevitable and necessary. Nothing happens without Spirit-inspired people, but nothing lasts without institutions. How should they organize five thousand new converts? What was its main message? What constituted proper worship and why? Could Gentiles join what was initially a Jewish movement, and if they did should they observe the Mosaic traditions? Who would lead and why? How broad or narrow were its boundaries? What were reasonable procedures and protocols for feeding widows, collecting money for famine relief, sending out missionaries like Paul and Barnabas, or adjudicating disputes? In short, where was the Spirit of God blowing, where was the Spirit's fire burning, and how could you be sure? These and many other questions required that the movement of the Spirit become a bureaucratic organization.

From those first tongues of fire described by Luke until today, from small beginnings as a vibrant movement to ecclesiastical institutions that two billion Christians call home, that has been the perennial challenge—how do we facilitate the Spirit's fire without shattering the bottle or extinguishing the flame?

Although the institutional church recognizes the Spirit's voice primarily in its historical creeds, its biblical canon, and its apostolic clergy, "in the experiences of monks and friars, of mystics and seers,...the Montanist heresy has carried on a sort of unofficial existence" (Jaroslav Pelikan, *The Emergence of the Catholic Tradition: 100–600* [Chicago: University of Chicago Press, 1972], 108). The Spirit of God who hovered over all creation (Genesis 1:2) still blows when, where, and how it pleases (John 3:8). Two thousand Pentecost celebrations later we should heed Paul's advice: "Do not put out the Spirit's fire; do not treat prophecies with contempt. Test everything. Hold on to the good. Avoid every kind of evil" (1 Thess 5:19-22 NIV 1984).

In one of the most widely used hymns in the church, "Veni, Creator Spiritus" (http://home.earthlink.net/~thesaurus/thesaurus/Hymni/VeniCreator.html), attributed to the German Benedictine monk and priest Rabanus Maurus (776–856), Christians around the world have cried out, "Come, Creator Spirit!" Anytime is a good time to pray that prayer, but no time is more appropriate than Pentecost Sunday.

Matthew L. Skinner

Acts 2; 1 Corinthians 12; John 20

The readings for Pentecost are not created equal. None of them describes the Holy Spirit in the same way. Each offers a particular angle on the character and work of the Holy Spirit.

In Acts 2, the Spirit comes fifty days after Jesus' death, as a source of "power" (Luke 24:49; Acts 1:8) that creates a community of prophets—men and women, all endowed with ability to speak meaningfully about God's deeds.

In John 20, the risen Jesus breathes the Holy Spirit (in Greek, the same word can mean "spirit," "breath," or "wind") into his disciples just hours after he first appears to Mary Magdalene outside his tomb. This Spirit bears witness to Jesus. The specific "sins" from which Jesus' followers can now release people are the sins that John's Gospel describes repeatedly: unbelief, or an inability to comprehend the truth of the Father revealed in Jesus. The Spirit makes Jesus known (John 15:26-27).

In 1 Corinthians 12, the Holy Spirit gives gifts and forges unity. Paul insists that *one* Spirit equips Jesus' followers for *diverse* kinds of ministry. Nevertheless, these ministries hang together, since the Spirit unites believers into "one body."

The different perspectives offered in these texts accentuate the Holy Spirit's tendency to frustrate our attempts to define the Spirit's nature with precision. The Spirit unites us to Christ and to one another, even as that same Spirit equips and propels us to bear witness within and to the wider world. The Spirit, as described by these texts, never acts as an independent agent. Instead, it always connects us to Jesus; it always manifests Jesus. Also, because of the Holy Spirit, Christians are not independent agents. All these texts describe the Spirit operating in a corporate setting. God the Spirit is no one's private possession.

John van de Laar
http://www.sacredise.com/

Acts 2

We can't know exactly what the first disciples experienced on the Day of Pentecost, but we do know the significance of this event. The Pentecost moment was really about a new perception and experience of the presence and power of God's Spirit. The sound of the wind was reminiscent of Ezekiel's reassuring prophecy of the valley of dry bones (Ezekiel 37:1-14). The flames that rested on each head would have reminded the disciples of the pillar of fire that guided the Israelites through the desert (Exodus 13:21, 22). As these phenomena opened them to the Spirit's activity, they finally began to understand Jesus' message of the Reign of God.

Pentecost was an agricultural feast—the end of the barley harvest and the wheat harvest's beginning. It expressed thanksgiving for another year of provision and prayer for the harvest to come. But it also commemorated the giving of the law at Sinai, fifty days after the Passover. For the gathered disciples, Jesus' words about the fields being ripe for harvest must have had a familiar ring (Matthew 9:37-38). The new (or fulfilled) law that he had taught and demonstrated was now being written on their hearts (Jeremiah 31:31-34).

The Reign of God that was manifest on that day was welcoming in the extreme. In the Babel story, arrogant human beings had been separated from one another by the confusion of their language, but here the curse is reversed and all barriers are overcome. This Kingdom is for all. Peter boldly expressed this new insight as he quoted Joel's promise of the Spirit poured out on "all people" and the salvation of "everyone" who calls on God's name. But, perhaps it was only when he received his vision of the sheet of food descending from heaven, and watched the Gentiles he was preaching to receive the Spirit (see Acts 10–11), that he really understood how radically inclusive this Kingdom is. But once they had caught the vision, the disciples spread the message to the whole world, including women, eunuchs, slaves, Gentiles, soldiers, revolutionaries, and even those, like Saul, who were deeply opposed to the way of Christ.

There is no question that God's Spirit is unrestrainedly active in human affairs. What we need is not so much an outpouring of the Spirit as an awakening to the Spirit's power and presence, and to the radically welcoming Reign of God. As we worship this Pentecost Sunday, we must ask: Are we willing to allow ourselves to be overwhelmed by a vision of God's radically inclusive Kingdom, and to begin to live it out through Spirit-empowered acts of welcome, compassion, grace, and service? Are we ready to have Christ's law of love written on our hearts, to have our way illumined by the Spirit's fire and to be blown into unexpected relationships by the wind of the Spirit? If we can answer yes, even just a little, the Pentecost experience will come to us, and we will never be the same.

John Wesley's Notes on the Bible
http://www.ccel.org/ccel/wesley/notes.txt

Acts 2:4

"And they began to speak with other tongues"—The miracle was not in the ears of the hearers (as some have unaccountably supposed), but in the mouth of the speakers. And this family praising God together, with the tongues of all the world, was an earnest that the whole world should in due time praise God in their various tongues. "As the Spirit gave them utterance"—Moses, the type of the law, was of a slow tongue; but the Gospel speaks with a fiery and flaming one.

Carolyn Winfrey Gillette
http://www.carolynshymns.com/

Pentecost Had Come

Pentecost had come and in that time of grace,
Jesus' friends were gathered in a meeting place.
Suddenly the Spirit came in wind and flame,
Sending men and women out in Jesus' name.
Spirit, come upon us, too!
Give us gifts to share for you.
We live in a world in need;
Send us where you daily lead!

All around the city joy was in the air;
People gathered in the streets from everywhere.
Soon they heard some preaching and the news was good!
There, in every language, they all understood.
Spirit, move through every land
Till all know and understand:
Jesus died and rose—it's true!
Now we have new life in you.

Peter told the crowd to turn and be baptized;
Thousands heard the words he spoke and changed their lives.
Daily they sold what they owned to help the poor;
Day by day the church was growing more and more.
Spirit, change the way we live.
Teach us how to gladly give
Guide us, as we seek to be
Faithful in our ministry.

NOTES
Biblical Text: Acts 2:1-47
Tune: ARGENTINA 11.11.11.11 refrain ("Canto de Esperanza/Song of Hope"), Argentine folk melody
Text: Copyright © 2010 by Carolyn Winfrey Gillette. All rights reserved.

Ann Scull
http://seedstuff.blogspot.com

A Useful Image

A photo of my lounge room fire with a line from the Third Day song below on it. You can find the image at http://seedstuff.blogspot.com.au/2011/06/pentecost-june-12-enough-for-everyone_05.html (accessed April 6, 2012).

Listening Song

Third Day, *"Holy Spirit"* on *Third Day* (Brentwood, Tenn.: Reunion Records, 1996). This band fits the Southern/Christian rock genre that all members of a congregation can usually enjoy.

Kids' Story

Andrew McDonough, *"Webster, the Preacher Duck"* (Unley, South Australia: Lost Sheep Resources, 2007). This book, which encourages us to be doers as well as hearers of God's word, is one of a brilliant series for young and old. Laugh and learn—and as it says on the title page, "Any similarities between the characters in this book and the old ducks in your church is purely coincidental."

Worship Service

Julie Pinazza, *Worship Is for Everyone* (Adelaide: Open Book, 2000), 13–17. Julie Pinazza uses children's story books to explore faith for all ages. Here she uses the Acts reading together with a storybook by Marcia Vaughan and Patricia Mullins, *The Sea-Breeze Hotel* (Sydney: Margaret Hamilton Books, 1991).

Film Clip

Edward Scissorhands (USA: 20th Century Fox, 1990). As the Corinthians reading points out—everyone has a gift. Show the clip where Edward trims the bushes into a dinosaur.

Dramas

Verena Johnson, *"Pentecost Photos?"* in *Let's Make Another Scene* (Adelaide: Open Book, 1995), 73–74. This drama, based on Acts 2, is lots of fun. Verena Johnson, *"What's a Holy Spirit?"* (77–80). This drama is also based on Acts 2 and lots of fun. You can turn the whole congregation into the chorus, if you project the words or hand out printed copies of the drama to everyone.

Story

Wayne Rice, *"Too Helpful,"* in *More Hot Illustrations for Youth Talks* (Grand Rapids: Zondervan, 1995), 161–62. This funny little story is based on the Corinthians reading and our ability to know how and when to use our gifts.

Illustration

Craig Brian Larson and Leadership Journal (eds.), *750 Engaging Illustrations for Preachers, Teachers, and Writers* (Grand Rapids: Baker Books, 2002), 78. This is an easily understood illustration (entitled *"Church"*) of the power of the Holy Spirit as seen in Acts 2.

Poem

Herbert F. Brokering, *"Acts 2:1,"* in *In Due Season* (Minneapolis: Augsburg, 1966), Summer section.

Sharron Blezard

John 20

Are you a S.A.D. Christian? I'm talking not about a state of emotions but rather about a state of being, living, and thriving. S.A.D. Christians are living paradoxes; they walk wet in the world, and they are on fire for Christ because they are "Spirit Activated Disciples." Yes, that's right—Spirit Activated Disciples—S.A.D. Christians. Today's lessons from Acts, 1 Corinthians, and John's Gospel all allude to the Spirit as the animating force and constant presence among God's people in this world. S.A.D. Christians have been around and active since the resurrected Jesus breathed the Spirit on those first amazed and terrified followers. S.A.D. Christians were present at Pentecost and went from there into the whole world to share the good news in every time, in all places, and with different gifts and strengths.

Spirit Activated Disciples will be present at this week's Pentecost celebration, too. They will be hungry for the Word, hungry for a word about how to live their identity in a broken yet beautiful world. They will come open-handed to Christ's table hungry for the bread of grace and the wine of forgiveness. God will be present, Christ will be present at his supper, and the Spirit will again be blowing among those gathered in each faith community.

Hear the words of Jesus speak to you: "Peace be with you. As the Father has sent me, so I send you" (v. 21b NRSV). Are you ready to experience a conflagration of holy hope? Are you willing to be showered in the affirmation of baptism? Will you go from worship into the world as a Spirit Activated Disciple equipped to be Christ's hands and feet in your time and place? Go in peace as one body, of one mind, with the same Spirit.

Suzanne Guthrie
http://www.edgeofenclosure.org

"Receive the Holy Spirit" (John 20)

"You make the winds your messengers; / you make fire and flame your ministers" (Psalm 104:4).

In his study of mysticism, *The Idea of the Holy,* Rudolf Otto describes both a sense of awe and a sense of dread when encountering the numinous. Like wind and fire in nature provoking situations of danger or comfort, wind and fire in Scripture symbolize Divine Presence evoking awe, terror, and fascination.

In mystical progression, Pentecost is the analogue for the union of the soul with God. As Catherine of Sienna describes, the soul dwells in God "like the fish in the sea / and the sea in the fish" (Catherine of Sienna, trans. Susan Herzko [N.Y.: Paulist Press, 1980], 211).

And yet, I think it is impossible to approach Pentecost without a sense of dread. The conferring of the Holy Spirit is the same motion as the commissioning as Apostles. We are "sent" with the Good News to the "ends of the earth" as bearers of Good News. But Good News is real change, and change is dangerous and often not received well, as tradition illustrates. In the case of the Apostles, preaching the Good News resulted in torture and martyrdom.

What fire purifies you with awe and fascination and dread? "The wind bloweth where it listeth, and thou hearest the sound thereof, but canst not tell whence it cometh, and whither it goeth; so is every one that is born of the Spirit" (John 3:8 KJV). Where are you sent?

Here's a well-known prayer by Mychal Judge, the Franciscan brother and NYFD chaplain, one of the first who died on the ground beneath the twin towers on 9/11/01: "Lord, take me where you want me to go, let me meet who you want me to meet, tell me what you want me to say, and keep me out of your way" (Michael Ford, *Father Mychal Judge: An Authentic American Hero* [Mahwah, N.J.: Paulist Press, 2002], 18).

June 15
Trinity Sunday

Genesis 1:1–2:4a; Psalm 8; 2 Corinthians 13:11-13; Matthew 28:16-20

Matthew L. Skinner

Genesis 1–2; 2 Corinthians 13

Trinity Sunday sermons fall flat when preachers attempt to explain trinitarian theology. Instead, consider bringing people into an encounter with God, who—as trinitarian doctrine attempts to articulate—is both beyond our comprehension and relational. God transcends our deepest thoughts, and yet God chooses to be active among us, for us, and within us.

Genesis 1 and Psalm 8 give a brief tour of the cosmos, naming God as the source of all things. The language is soaring; the scale massive. These passages accentuate God's power, for God creates with words and holds dominion over all things. Yet this God does not remain aloof, as if such power exists for its own sake. God shares creative tasks and caretaking tasks with humanity. God the Creator is Other—over all things; and yet God is also among us, caring for us and willing to trust us with God's own work.

Paul's words to the Corinthians help us encounter this God, the same one we meet in Jesus Christ. The words Paul uses—"Jesus Christ," "God," "Holy Spirit"—mean little on their own. Paul's larger emphasis is on the other words: "grace," "love," "fellowship." These are things we can experience, or feel. Paul insists that God is the *source* of them. God can bring them into our own experiences, to heal us.

It is striking that 2 Corinthians ends as it does. In 2 Corinthians 10–13, Paul wrote contentious things to a community that was beginning to turn against him. The concluding verses hold out hope that reconciliation might still occur. Does Paul just trust his and the Corinthians' goodwill? No, he trusts God to provide grace, love, and the possibility of communal harmony. God does not grant these things from afar. God has already come and enacted them among us.

Liz Crumlish
http://somethingtostandon.blogspot.co.uk/

Psalm 8

Beaches have always been a place of refuge, sometimes a place of escape for me. I enjoy a bracing walk along the beach even on stormy days. And I love to stand on the beach in the dark, listening to the power of the waves and the scraping of shingle underfoot. I have often uttered psalms of praise while on the beach.

I am aware, however, that this source of great pleasure for me can also be a place of terror and destruction. The rawness that excites me creates havoc when the force of nature escapes careful control. The God to whom I offer praise is the same God whom others curse in the face of loss and devastation wrought by nature.

Out of affluence, many of us can rejoice in Psalm 8—rejoice at our position just a little lower than divine beings and rejoice at all that God has placed before us and over which we have dominion. But this psalm sounds so different for many others—those who, in the daily struggle for mere survival, experience little of that sense of blessing, far less any degree of power. Or those who have experienced this psalm used to exploit the rich resources of the earth, disregarding the need to share or be mindful of successive generations who will inherit a world so ravaged by its previous inhabitants.

The trinitarian nature of this psalm grounds us in our place in life. We exist in relationship with God, with creation, and with all God's people. The recognition of that co-existence should guide us in right living. The church, at its best, lives in relationship with the creator, takes seriously the responsibility to care for the world around, and is aware of our interconnectedness, each sustained by and dependent on the other.

Sharron Blezard

Genesis 1–2; Psalm 8; 2 Corinthians 13

Stop! Don't do it! Resist the urge this Sunday to try to explain or justify the doctrine of the Holy Trinity. Instead, consider embracing the marvelous mystery of God by exploring how God chooses to be revealed to us.

Scripture recounts God's relationship with humankind, and this week's lessons invite us to engage with awe and wonder the mystery of God: from the first creation account in Genesis and its vivid spoken progression from chaos to creative order to a lively hymn of praise in Psalm 8, celebrating God's majesty and the wonder of creation. The short readings from 2 Corinthians and Matthew's Gospel provide fertile soil to speak of the relational aspects of the Triune God as the one who creates, redeems, and sustains, particularly as evidenced within the body of Christ.

Consider ways to meld image, word, and participation in worship. Let the body of Christ "stretch" its relational muscles by engaging in conversation about how they see and experience the three expressions of God in the life of the church and in their own lives. If your congregation is uncomfortable with dialogue during worship, invite them to use different-colored sticky notes to share how they see God, Jesus, and Spirit at work, posting their observations on a designated wall so that all may see and share. Put a special emphasis on passing the peace today. Finally, incorporate the trinitarian blessing (2 Corinthians 13:13) during Holy Communion. In addition to bread and wine, provide an assisting minister to lay hands on those who desire to receive this blessing.

Yes, the Trinity is mystery, but God is always personal and relational. Living together as the body of Christ we point to God, embracing the unexplainable reality and living in the spirit of holy love and peace.

Julie Craig
http://winsomelearnsome.com

Matthew 28

I'm a sucker for a good love story. I like good stories in general, but a good *love* story—that's something I really like. The trouble with most Hollywood love stories is the predictability. Boy meets girl. Girl spurns boy's affections. There's a conflict that drives boy and girl apart—often involving another love interest for either boy or girl—and it seems as if all is lost…until. Until the 89th minute of the movie, or the 287th page of the novel—often involving a dénouement of the third wheel in the relationship—which brings boy and girl back together, forever and ever, until death do they part. The end. Roll credits. Close the book.

Having participated in a love story or two, and having been the shoulder that has gotten cried upon by persons who have been involved in a love story or two, I can tell you that it almost never happens the way Hollywood and/or Random House conceives it.

Years ago I became infatuated with a fictionalized story of plural marriage I watched on a cable television show. What makes the show a study in one way to understand God is that the characters in the plural marriage all believe not only that there is enough love to go around but that living a life in which we do not share love with as many people as we can has cosmic implications for both this life and the one that comes after this one on earth.

Now, I don't think that plural marriage, or polygamy, or whatever you want to call it is a good idea—in fact, I'm pretty sure it's against my religion, and yours too. It's illegal, probably immoral, and definitely messy.

But…what if? What if we as a community lived our lives with these two ideas: that there *is* enough love to go around, and that what we do with that love has implications of cosmic proportions? Today is Trinity Sunday, that day when we stop to consider the shape of love, as expressed in how we conceive the idea of a God in three persons.

What if this shape of love is a reminder that there is enough love to go around—that God's love for us and for the world is too immense and too outrageous to be contained in one name for God, one way of thinking about God, and we must take seriously the vows we take when we baptize children, including the promise to love and support their parents in the raising of them, believing that our failure to do so has cosmic implications? It's a big job. But there is plenty of love to go around.

Paul Nuechterlein
http://girardianlectionary.net/

Matthew 28

The Trinity can be difficult to understand. In discussions I often notice that many people choose to simply accept it as a mystery. The word *Trinity* never appears in the New Testament; however, *mystery* (Greek: *mysterion*) does—most often in a way opposite from how it is generally used today. The New Testament primarily speaks of God as a mystery *revealed* through Jesus. The Great Commission of Matthew 28 compels us to proclaim the mystery of God as loving Father *revealed* in the Son through the Holy Spirit.

So why has the Trinity developed into something that obscures the mystery that Matthew proclaims has been revealed? Because, if we accept a *re-veiling* instead of a *revealing* by covering this revelation of *who God is,* then we can also cover over the revelation of *who we are* and turn responsibility for our "righteous" violence back over to the gods. Our responsibility for our own violence can once again go underground, hidden beneath a veil of the wrathful gods who command us to do violence.

A key passage in this regard appears in 1 Corinthians as Paul explains his proclamation of "God's secrets" (1 Cor. 2:1, *mysterion*) solely through the simple language of Christ crucified:

> We talk about God's wisdom, which has been hidden as a secret [lit., "a mystery kept secret"]....It is a wisdom that none of the present-day rulers have understood, because if they did understand it, they would never have crucified the Lord of glory! (1 Cor 2:7a, 8)

If humans had known that the work of the cross in the power of the Spirit was to reveal our sacrificial mechanisms, then we never would have crucified Jesus, for the last thing we want is for acts of sacred violence to be revealed as *our* violence, not the gods'.

Human nature compels us to hide from harsh truths. With our violence revealed through the cross, we want to proclaim the *mystery-accepted* once again, rather than name the *mystery-revealed*. The Athanasian Creed, written at the climax of developing historical creeds, is a perfect example. In it, the cross becomes progressively lost. After a lengthy discourse on the philosophical mystery of the persons of the Trinity that believers are told they must simply accept as true or suffer hell, we are then told of Jesus that "He suffered death for our salvation." No Pilate, no cross. This creed, written after Constantine made Christianity the imperial religion, allowed the "present-day rulers" to obscure the cross from our eyes and to once again wash their hands of the responsibility of state-sanctioned violence. And when substitutionary atonement is added to the mix, state-sanctioned violence can then hide behind God-sanctioned violence.

I believe an evangelical anthropology (see my essays in January 19, and March 9) that unveils our human responsibility for violence is a crucial step in renewing our experience of *who God is*. To ponder the Trinity without knowledge of *who we are* risks the danger of having things hidden once again in the "mystery" of the God revealed in Christ Jesus.

John Wesley's Notes on the Bible
http://www.ccel.org/ccel/wesley/notes.txt

Matthew 28:19

"Disciple all nations"—Make them my disciples. This includes the whole design of Christ's commission. Baptizing and teaching are the two great branches of that general design. And these were to be determined by the circumstances of things; which made it necessary in baptizing adult Jews or heathens, to teach them before they were baptized; in discipling their children, to baptize them before they were taught; as the Jewish children in all ages were first circumcised, and after taught to do all God had commanded them.

June 22
2nd Sunday after Pentecost (Proper 7)

Genesis 21:8-21; Psalm 86:1-10, 16-17; Romans 6:1b-11; Matthew 10:24-39; Jeremiah 20:7-13; Psalm 69:7-10, (11-15), 16-18

Rick Morley

Genesis 21

Abraham's life was complicated. When his wife, Sarah, appears to be barren, she tells Abraham to go and conceive a son with Hagar, the slave. Being the obedient husband, he listens to her, and Hagar conceives and bears a son. This is supposed to be a good thing, but it immediately sparks jealousy and threatens to tear the home apart.

Of course, Hagar's life is also complicated. She is moved around the chessboard like a pawn. As a slave, she is given to a man to conceive a son without ever being asked her opinion in the matter. And, when she does in fact bear a son, she and her son bear the brunt of jealous anger. She can't win.

I suppose one could say that Sarah's life is complicated too. God had promised her husband a son who would be the father of many nations, and yet she didn't seem able to fulfill that promise. When her slave-girl does what she isn't able to do, who can rightly blame her for her jealousy?

The world of Abraham, Sarah, and Hagar seems so amazingly foreign to us today. But, while the specifics of their daily life are exotic, our family situations and home lives aren't any less complicated. Complicated lives are the norm.

And yet, in the midst of chaos, God brings calm and order. God comes to Abraham and says, "do not be distressed," and he comes to Hagar and says, "do not be afraid" (vv. 12, 17 NRSV).

When we stand in the midst of stress, swamped by complexity, we are not left alone, but God comes to us. God brings us peace, and bids us to let go of our fears. Just as he did for our foremothers and forefathers.

Julia Seymour
http://lutheranjulia.blogspot.com

Genesis 21

We live in a world of connections, wherein we can so easily be in touch with anyone whom we have ever met. Yet we still pass many people, content to stay mutual strangers. Despite our vast repositories of information and contacts, it is likely that you do not know what happened to the sister of the young man that your cousin dated in high school. You probably do not know the story of the mother of the man whom your parent did not marry. The saga of third cousin of the neighbor who moved away ten years ago is lost to you and to yours.

So be it. We cannot know everything. We cannot know everyone. We can, however, remember that their stories, even unknown, touch up against our own through God. We think frequently about how God is shaping us, about God's promises to those in our particular faith community and to us, about God's work in what is our known world. What about God's work that goes on, unknown to us?

Did Isaac ever wonder what happened to the dark-eyed teenager he remembered so faintly from his childhood? Did Ishmael ever speak of his half-brother whom he enjoyed making laugh? Did Abraham tell Isaac of his folly? Did Hagar tell her son of Abraham and of Sarah and of her broken heart? Did both boys grow up, knowing of God's promises to their parents and their role in fulfilling them? And, if they knew, did they imagine God making the same promise with regard to each of them?

Isaac and Ishmael are both signs of God's providence and commitment. In human history, they represent two significant personal, political, and religious streams whose currents have significantly shaped the sands and rocks of time. If Isaac had known that Ishmael was also the start of a great nation, what might he have done differently? If Ishmael heard of the twin promises, did it soothe the ache of rejection or fire up his frustrations at his father and at Isaac?

God's promise to Hagar is a powerful and significant promise. Offered to a woman in the worst of circumstances, watching her child die, it is not a hurried consolation prize, but a powerful offer of hope and future. While Ishmael may have been second place in some households, in the eyes of his creator, he still mattered, as the offspring of Abraham *and* as the offspring of Hagar.

All of creation, including all people, receives this promise of hope and a future. God considers each person worthy of shaping, of wholeness, and of salvation. We are called into seeing that worthiness in one another. Furthermore, we are called into working together toward the fulfillment of those promises. We do not always know the stories of the people around us, but we can know the promises that have been made to them. God is with them. We cannot pretend their stories do not matter.

Natalie Sims
http://lectionarysong.blogspot.com

Genesis 21

The casting out of Hagar and Ishmael coupled with the Gospel reading including Christ's words that he came not to bring peace but a sword makes me think that it would be good to pray for peace among the three faiths descended from Abraham.

"Hope of Abraham and Sarah" (Ruth Duck)—A song of unity for Islam, Judaism, and Christianity. "So may Torah, cross and crescent, each a sign of life made new, / point us t'ward your love and justice, earth at peace and one in you." The tune, CAELAN, is straightforward (and new!), but more familiar alternative tunes, such as ABBOT'S LEIGH, can be used.

"Peace, Salaam, Shalom" (Pat Humphries)—A beautiful and simple chant with two cantor lines over the top. The congregation could easily sing the basic round even without the cantor lines as a meditative focus. Sheet music available for free (http://www.seattlepeacechorus.org/songsheets.htm).

"Salaam" (Sheva)—A cool, recorded song that couples Jewish and Muslim prayers for peace.

"May Peace Be with You / Salamun Kullaheen" (Traditional Lebanese)—Simple chant in English and Arabic. I reckon this would be a good one for our congregation to learn.

"When Trouble Strikes and Fear Takes Root" (Iona Community)—Actually based on Isaiah 49, but the parallels with the hopelessness of Hagar and God's love for her children make it worth singing this week. The tune is a straightforward English folk tune.

"God! When Human Bonds Are Broken" (Fred Kaan)—These words pick up an unusual theme, and fit really well with this reading. Words of healing of relationships. The tune is not familiar, but it works very well and should not be too difficult if a little time is taken to introduce it to your congregation.

"By Gracious Powers so Wonderfully Sheltered" (Dietrich Bonhoeffer)—All sources seem to have different tricky tunes, but I think the words fit well to "O Perfect Love."

"I'm Gonna Stick with You" (Richard Bruxvoort-Colligan)—How do you present this reading to kids? No idea, but if you choose to focus on being a faithful friend (in contrast to Sarah), this is a fun song about friendship for kids to sing.

Teri Peterson
http://clevertitlehere.blogspot.com

Genesis 21

Isaac received his name because he caused laughter in his parents' lives. It seems that laughter is restricted, though, since when Ishmael laughs, it causes not happiness but rage. Sarah sees Ishmael and Hagar laughing and feasting as they celebrate Isaac's weaning, and it is too much to bear. Though Ishmael exists only because Sarah gave her slave Hagar as a concubine for Abraham, and though his status as second-wife's-son is below Isaac's, he is still the firstborn, and his laughter cuts into Sarah's heart.

So out they must go, out into the desert with only a little food and a day's water. If Hagar had doubts about this God of Abraham's, they have been confirmed now—this is a God who cares only for his own kind, not for outsiders or those who are mistreated. She will have no part in the covenant God is making with his people—she is literally and figuratively cast out. Her last meeting with God resulted in instructions to put up with Sarah's abuse (Gen 16), and now she must know for certain that this God not only allows but encourages pain, grief, and heartache. It seems unlikely she (or anyone else who feels outside of grace) would be interested in adding this God to her already heavy desert burden.

Finally God takes notice…of Ishmael's cries. Never mind that Hagar has been lifting her voice in grief and despair, God has heard the cries of her son and remembered the promise to make him a great nation as well, to pay heed to his status as Abraham's son even if no one else will. That paternity is what will save Hagar as well as Ishmael. By this point Hagar must be wondering if she matters at all—a foreigner with dark skin and different language, a slave turned concubine, an outcast. God's messenger has even had the audacity to ask "What's wrong?" What isn't wrong? God is making covenant partners and has left her out, casting her into the desert. Is there any good news to be had?

There is a well. And actually, the presence of shrubs under which to place a child also means the presence of water. The haze of grief and despair can sometimes cloud our vision, but even so God offers what we need. God opens Hagar's eyes, and she sees her well of salvation right in front of her, and she is strengthened to go on, to find a way forward as a part of God's great story, rather than as a footnote. How often do we resign ourselves to the bit part, eyes closed to the possibility of good news or clouded by resentment and despair of injustice ever being overcome? There is a well, even in the desert, for those whose eyes are open to see, and perhaps there will be laughter too.

Kathryn Schifferdecker

Romans 6; Matthew 10

The lectionary texts for today might be summarized with Bonhoeffer's title, *The Cost of Discipleship*. Jeremiah laments his prophetic vocation, which has made him an object of ridicule and hate. Paul speaks of being "buried with [Christ] by baptism into death" (Rom 6:4a NRSV). And Jesus himself proclaims, "Whoever does not take up the cross and follow me is not worthy of me. Those who find their life will lose it, and those who lose their life for my sake will find it" (Matt 10:38-39 NRSV).

These are hard words. Take up the cross? Lose my life? That's not what I signed up for. I prefer Jesus' saying about having life and having it abundantly (John 10:10). But perhaps these sayings are not mutually exclusive. What if the abundant life is the life we find when we take up the cross and follow Jesus? What if that is our real and true life? What if a life lived in self-interest is a life already lost?

Paul seems to be saying a similar thing as he speaks of "our old self" being crucified with Christ Jesus so that "we might no longer be enslaved to sin." Having participated by baptism in Christ's death and resurrection, "you also must consider yourselves dead to sin and alive to God in Christ Jesus" (Rom 6:6, 11 NRSV).

Death and resurrection, in other words, are not about just the end of our lives. Death and resurrection have to do with our lives here and now. The cost of discipleship is the death of our old self-centered selves along with the scorn and hate that such a new way of life will provoke in others (something Bonhoeffer knew well). But the fruit of discipleship is resurrection—abundant life here and now, and the promise of new life in the world to come.

John Petty
http://progressiveinvolvement.com

Matthew 10

The disciples of Jesus are encouraged not to fear three times in five verses (vv. 26, 28, 31). Despite the difficulties they face, their movement cannot be stopped, Jesus tells them. Even if you go to prison, even if you are oppressed, the message will be revealed and "become known" (*ginoskio*, v. 26 NRSV).

These are words for a beleaguered community, one that feels itself under siege, one where people must speak in whispers—"in the dark"—under threat of real violence from those who can "kill the body" (vv. 27, 28a).

Invoking the devil, the one who is able to "destroy both body and soul" (v. 28b) means that Matthew's community should see their struggle as being fundamentally spiritual. Yes, they are enduring political and social oppression. Yes, they are under the boot of Rome. These earthly powers, however, are really doing the devil's work.

Then, the discourse turns more positive. Sparrows were the cheapest edible birds. Two of them could be bought for an *assariou,* which is one-tenth of a drachma, or one-sixteenth of a denarius.

Yet, "not one of them will fall to the ground apart from your Father" (v. 29 NRSV). In the phrase "your Father," Matthew reminds his readers of God's providential care of all creation, including *them*. Do not be afraid because—Matthew wryly notes—you are of more value than many sparrows.

If Jesus' followers acknowledge him in front of others, then Jesus will do the same on behalf of them "before my Father in heaven" (v. 32). Note that "*your* Father" has now been changed to "*my* Father." This expresses Jesus' son-ship, and indicates that it is precisely through his son-ship that his followers also become sons and daughters.

Regarding these difficult sayings about family, Matthew's fundamental message is that, contrary to our own assumptions, we are people being formed by the future and not the past. The kingdom of heaven is coming, a kingdom in which all relationships will be relationships of equality, not hierarchical, as in a family. Traditional power relationships will be upended—"the last will be first, and the first will be last" (20:16 NRSV)—including those of the family where father and mother stand "higher" than son or daughter.

To be dominated by one's family is to be dominated by the past. Indeed, considering that a person's DNA goes back hundreds of thousands of years, we are—in a manner of speaking—in "bondage" to our family and in "bondage" to our past in quite literal ways.

To the one who had said he wanted to bury his father before he could follow Jesus, Jesus said, "Let the dead bury their own dead" (8:22). Jesus would not let people be dominated by their past. They are to step out from their past, with its hierarchical power relationships and its bondage to tradition. These are "old wineskins" that are not able to hold the "new wine" (9:17).

John Wesley's Notes on the Bible
http://www.ccel.org/ccel/wesley/notes.txt

Matthew 10:27

"Even what I now tell you secretly is not to be kept secret long, but declared publicly. Therefore, What ye hear in the ear, publish on the house-top"—Two customs of the Jews seem to be alluded to here. Their doctors used to whisper in the ear of their disciples what they were to pronounce aloud to others. And as their houses were low and flat roofed, they sometimes preached to the people from thence.

June 29
3rd Sunday after Pentecost (Proper 8)

Genesis 22:1-14; Psalm 130; Romans 6:12-23; Matthew 10:40-42;
Jeremiah 28:5-9; Psalm 89:1-4, 15-18

John Wesley's Notes on the Bible
http://www.ccel.org/ccel/wesley/notes.txt

Genesis 22:12

"Now know I that thou fearest God"—God knew it before, but now Abraham had given a memorable evidence of it. He need do no more, what he had done was sufficient to prove the religious regard he had to God and his authority. The best evidence of our fearing God is our being willing to honour him with that which is dearest to us, and to part with all to him, or for him.

Marci Auld Glass
www.marciglass.com

Genesis 22

I am furious. I have sojourned with him all across the Middle East. I forgave him when he tried to pass me off as his sister. *Twice.* We've had some good times too, for sure. He stood by me in my barrenness. Even after God promised we would be the ancestors of more offspring than we could count, Abraham stood by me. He even agreed to my ill-conceived plan to have a child through my maid, Hagar.

But at long last, well past anyone's expectation of childbearing, I gave birth to Isaac. When you wait one hundred years for a child, he is treasured indeed. Which brings me back to my fury.

The boys have just returned from what I thought was your standard father/son weekend at Mt. Moriah, and Isaac told me a chilling tale. Apparently *his father* tied him up and put him on an altar. And, apparently, *Abraham* took out a sharp knife and was going to KILL MY BABY BOY! Isaac saw the blade of the knife headed toward his body!

I guess I am supposed to be thankful the angel got there just in time to stop Abraham from carrying out this sordid story. But I can't be thankful right now. I am furious. What was this "exercise" supposed to prove? That Abraham was obedient? Or that Abraham was insane? Why weren't Abraham's many years of sojourning and obedience enough to prove his faithfulness?

We are going to have a talk, *you can be sure*. If Abraham wants to watch his son grow up, he's going to have to learn new ways to talk with God. He's going to have to learn to suggest God find some other ways to prove his point. He's going to have to talk back to God, because God can take it. But I'm about done. Because my poor son is devastated. How do you recover from having your father tie you up and nearly sacrifice you on an altar?

I'm going to go for a long walk. I'm going to keep saying to myself, *"God would never have let this happen. God did not let this happen,"* until my fury abates. I'm going to let Isaac eat all the ice cream he wants.

And when I calm down *(please, God, let me calm down)*, I will pray that I can see redemption in this story. Because I don't now. I will pray to see blessing as I kiss Isaac goodnight and smell his hair as I hug him, thankful he came home from this horror story. I will pray for the strength to forgive Abraham for his faithfulness. I will pray I have the courage to invite him back into the house and out of the not-proverbial-but-very-real-doghouse, so I can console him. And when I calm down, I will pray to God this never happens again to any mother, or that *at least* the presence of God is tangible with them through the horror.

NOTE: "Sarah's Fury" by Marci Auld Glass (http://marciglass.com/2012/04/30/sarahs-fury/).

by Thom Shuman
http://lectionaryliturgies.blogspot.com/

who forgives God?

when
    in that hedgerow
    woven tight with the
        vines of despair,
            the thorns of loss
            pricking at us,
    we find no ram
    caught by its horns;

when
    we cling desperately to
        each other as our
            child is wheeled
            toward the surgery,
        where her life is placed
        in the hands of strangers,
    and no angel comes
    running down the hall, yelling
            'wait!'

when
        we have mailed the letter
    to that old friend whose
        heart our anger broke
            all those years ago,
    but no word of pardon comes;

when
    the doctor comes into
        our room, but the words
    uttered are not
            "it's benign";

when
    there is no last minute
            reprieve
        in the sentence of
            loneliness
    which has been pronounced
            upon us;

when,
    do we forgive
you?

Rick Morley

Genesis 22

The story of the sacrifice of Isaac is about as scary as it gets in the Bible. There are, of course, bloodier chapters with high body counts. But lying helpless beneath Abraham's knife was a child. When I consider preaching this passage, I always wonder if there are going to be many children in church that Sunday.

It's also a story that confronts our understanding of the goodness of God. What kind of God would ask this of a father? What kind of God would put a child through that? One could even say that this story is embarrassing, presenting a disdainful picture of God.

However, if we can put our revulsion on hold for a moment, I do think that the sacrifice of Isaac has at least two important things to say. First, the whole thing is really about Abraham's faithfulness. The first verse of this passage is "God tested Abraham," and a few verses later we find that Abraham passed the test. His commitment to God is so broad and deep, he is willing to go to any lengths. Abraham's obedience to God is a thing to behold.

141

Second, this is one of those texts that reminds us that we don't have a neat and tidy little religion that is country-club-respectable in all ways at all times. Sometimes life, even a life of faith, can go horribly wrong. But the story doesn't end there. The story goes on. Isaac goes on to live a life of faith, and he becomes the father of Israel.

There is always the possibility of redemption. Even in a thicket on top of a hill. With a knife in the air over the wide-eyed stare of a child. Even there.

Paul Nuechterlein
http://girardianlectionary.net/

Genesis 22

The story of Abraham's near sacrifice of Isaac is among the passages of Scripture most difficult to understand. Modern readers try to put themselves into the psyche of Abraham—how could a person actually consider sacrificing his son on an altar? But we need to make a shift from the usual psychologizing of this text. It is immensely helpful to begin by alerting ourselves to the anthropological fact that child sacrifice was actually very common in Abraham's cultural milieu.

This is more clearly illuminated by the evangelical anthropology of Stanford scholar René Girard (see my essays in February 16 and March 9). His cross-centered anthropology is crucial in its unveiling of the logic of sacrifice as foundational to human culture. First, we need to recognize that contemporary cultures still practice child sacrifice of a sort, even though it is no longer part of a religious ritual. Our modern versions of child sacrifice have to do with being willing to send our children into the fray of sanctioned violence to fight for the freedoms we hold dear—in the United States, for example, it is defending the Constitution as a sacred truth with the blood of our sons and daughters.

Second, many Christians through the ages have seen a link between Genesis 22 and substitutionary theories of atonement. Since Girard's Mimetic Theory calls into question the truth of substitutionary atonement, it offers to shed new light on the story of Abraham's near sacrifice (see my essay in January 19).

The key to preaching this text, then, is to argue that the correct reading of this story is that Abraham passed the test of faith not by listening to the voice of the false gods of sacred violence at the story's opening, but rather by listening to the voice of Yahweh, "the LORD's messenger" (v. 11), at the story's close. This is vastly different from the test that the narrator sees—that Abraham is obedient in his willingness to sacrifice his son. The narrator nevertheless leaves us a clue in the words used for God. *Elohim*—the standard word for god in Hebrew, referring to any and all gods, even false gods—commands the sacrifice at the beginning of the story. The messenger of *Yahweh,* the special name for God in Hebrew, bids him stop the sacrifice as the knife is raised in the air. From our anthropological vantage point, we may say that Abraham passed the test in hearing the true God's voice telling him, stop, don't kill. All the major prophets take this even a step further: that Yahweh does not want sacrifice at all but rather compassionate justice (e.g., Hosea 6:6; Micah 6:6-8; Amos 5:21-24).

And now, almost two thousand years after the voice of our risen Savior forgiving us for our numerous slaughters brought together on his cross, are *we* ready to pass the test? Are we ready to find and practice ways to peace beyond sending our children to be sacrificed in war? What could happen in our world if two billion people who claim Abraham as their religious father could finally recognize what this test of faith is really all about?

Kathryn Schifferdecker

Jeremiah 28

The story of Jeremiah and Hananiah is worth exploring in a sermon. In order to do so, though, one must provide some context. In Jeremiah 27, God tells Jeremiah to wear a yoke on his neck to symbolize his message to the king of Judah: submit to the "yoke" of the king of Babylon.

The problem that Jeremiah faces (aside from the fact that he has to walk around Jerusalem with a yoke on his neck) is that he brings a message of judgment to a people who desperately want to hear of peace. Their king and nobles deported to Babylon along with the temple vessels (in 597 BCE), the people of Jerusalem want to regain a sense of security. So when Hananiah breaks the yoke on Jeremiah's neck, declaring that the Lord will likewise "break the yoke of the king of Babylon" (Jer 28:4), the people want to believe him.

Even Jeremiah wants to believe him. "Amen! May the LORD do so; may the LORD fulfill the words that you have prophesied" (v. 6 NRSV). But Jeremiah knows that past prophets spoke more often of judgment than of peace. He knows that the word of the Lord is "like fire" and "like a hammer that breaks a rock in pieces" (Jer 23:29 NRSV). The prophet, then, who preaches only what the people want to hear is suspect. Jeremiah's words are proven true, of course, by the Babylonian exile in 587 BCE.

Who are the false prophets in our day? The issue is always a matter of discernment, of course, and one's own preaching is not immune from judgment. Still, it is worth asking: What voices within and outside the church lead people to trust in false gods instead of following the One who judges justly and who also, with overflowing mercy, redeems?

Carolyn Winfrey Gillette
http://www.carolynshymns.com/

A Prophet Has a Lonely Task

A prophet has a lonely task—
To help the world to see anew,
To name injustice, then to ask
What God is calling us to do.

On city streets among the poor,
In places spoiled for oil or coal,
At yet another time of war,
A prophet seeks the nation's soul.

O Lord, you taught us: Hear their shout!
Receive their call to turn from sin!
When others seek to shut them out,
The church must welcome prophets in.

For in our welcome, Lord, we'll find
A living faith, a new world-view,
A life more peaceful, just and kind,
A church that gladly welcomes you.

NOTES
Biblical Reference: Mark 6:1-13 and Matthew 10:40-42
Tune: WAREHAM LM ("The Church of Christ in Every Age"), William Knapp, 1738
Alternate Tune: CANONBURY LM ("Lord, Speak to Me, That I May Speak")

July 6
4th Sunday after Pentecost (Proper 9)

Genesis 24:34-38, 42-49, 58-67; Psalm 45:10-17 or Song of Solomon 2:8-13; Romans 7:15-25a; Matthew 11:16-19, 25-30; Zechariah 9:9-12; Psalm 145:8-14

Julia Seymour
http://lutheranjulia.blogspot.com

Genesis 24; Song of Songs 2; Matthew 11

The book most of us grew up calling *Song of Solomon* is now more frequently being referred to as *Song of Songs*. In church tradition, Solomon either wrote the verses or they had long been attributed to him. This attribution was, in part, because it is kind of a racy book and, according to biblical sources, Solomon knew his way around a...*ahem*...bedchamber (see 1 Kings 11:3).

However, as the book has begun to be more deeply read and examined, it is clear that sixty percent of the book is written from a woman's point of view. In fact, though the action of the book can be a little difficult to follow at times, the female narrator has a distinct voice as she makes her case for being allowed to be with the man she loves.

That worried feeling that you have right now—that I might start talking about sex—that feeling has accompanied biblical interpreters for years when they come to the Song. A book that so frankly approaches human desire and physical longing makes everyone a little nervous. When clergy were mostly male and celibate, a book heavy with feminine sexuality couldn't be interpreted as anything but allegory.

Thus, allegorical interpretation was *the* way to read the Song. It was interpreted as a demonstration of God's love for Israel, Christ's love for the church, or even the Spirit's love for the individual soul. Unfortunately, when we interpret the Song allegorically, we miss a truth about how human relationships reveal divine love. In some way, this book's uncomfortable stanzas about the desires of the body help us in our struggle with what it means to be human.

Most of us have absorbed and internalized negative ideas about bodies, about sex, and about our physical selves. Often unable to separate those feelings from what we think about God, one of our greatest spiritual temptations is to believe that God is interested only in our souls. Then we can either ignore our bodies, to their detriment, or we can say what we do with them doesn't matter.

If God didn't want us to have bodies, God wouldn't have given them to us. If our physical selves didn't matter, then God would not have sent the Son, *in the flesh,* so that we might know more fully God's love. The consolation of the body is how those around Jesus experienced God (see Matt 11:16-19). It's how Isaac was comforted after his mother died (Gen 24:67). Furthermore, if God had no interest in our bodies, then we would be able to do God's work with our minds alone.

Song of Songs deserves our attention as the deep, erotic hymn to human love that it is. This hymn of hymns helps keep our bodies at the forefront among our gifts from God. If we disdain our bodies, how can we love the body of Christ?

Rick Morley

Romans 7

Paul's Letter to the Romans is a great theological treatise, but it's also a letter from one Christian introducing himself and his understanding of the Gospel to a church he had yet to personally meet. Paul is well known, though he knows full well that such notoriety is a double-edged sword. Romans is Paul's way of setting the record straight on who he is and what he believes.

Paul obviously poured a lot of time and effort into the theological and rhetorical composition of the letter. Then he takes a deep breath, places both hands on the pulpit, and gets down to the nitty-gritty.

There are things that he knows to be the "right thing" to do, and yet he fails time and time again to do them. There are things that he knows to be the "wrong thing" and yet he does them anyway.

If he has lost anyone in the deep compositional contours of the discussions on faith and the law, he has the attention of everyone in the church with those lines. Because who can't identify with that? Who hasn't hurt another or God or themselves so badly and so stupidly? Who hasn't thought themselves to be "wretched" (v. 24 NRSV)? Who hasn't banged their forehead with their fist and said, "Why in the world did I do that?!"

But Paul doesn't leave us to wallow in our self-hatred. He boldly proclaims that those things aren't the end of the road. For we have a rescuer, a savior: Jesus. Such actions and inactions, however stupid they are, demonstrate the condition of sin within us. But with Jesus as Lord, sin doesn't have the last word. We all have sinned and fallen short of the glory of God, and yet God's grace far exceeds even our most wretched moment.

Natalie Sims
http://lectionarysong.blogspot.com

Romans 7

It's really hard to do what's right. Obedience. Discipleship.

"Guide My Feet While I Run This Race" (African American Spiritual)—An excellent civil rights song. Would work well as a meditative prayer for guidance or as an uplifting call to action at the end of the service. Lyrics and clunky sound sample (http://www.hymnsite.com/fws/hymn.cgi?2208).

"In the Lord I'll Be Ever Thankful / El Senyor" (Jacques Berthier)—A joyful and bouncy Taizé song. Works well in English, German, and Spanish at least. Good for kids. Sheet music, translations into many other languages, sound samples (http://www.taize.fr/spip.php?page=chant&song=322&lang=en).

"Who Will Speak if We Don't" (Marty Haugen)—Excellent challenging words. Also available from GIA publications.

"The Summons" (Iona Community)—A classic. Don't sing it too slowly or it really drags and takes forever! Lyrics (http://www.spiritandsong.com/compositions/30338).

"Make Me a Channel of Your Peace" (Sebastian Temple)—A very well known and beautiful song.

"Three Things I Promise" (Brian Wren)—Beautiful words of seeking to live faithfully from Brian Wren. The set tune is unfamiliar, but very beautiful, and if not familiar to your congregation would make a good reflective piece (for the congregation to sing in later weeks). You could also sing it to PROSPECT or WAREHAM.

"We Will Follow (Som'landela)" (Traditional Zulu)—Groovy African song. Sample for listening (http://www.mennolink.org/cgi-bin/search.cgi?bk.sts.03.txt&track=15).

"I'm Gonna Live so God Can Use Me" (African American Traditional)—Good simple tune and meaningful words. Easy to sing and play around with. Good for kids, non-readers, and for people for whom English is a second language.

"Save Us in the Time of Trial" (Shawn Whelan)—Reflective song about trying to follow Christ in the face of temptation. Chorus is particularly straightforward and chantlike. Reference recording, lyrics, and songbook available (http://www.wholenote.com.au/songs/saveusinthetimeoftrial.html).

Kathryn Schifferdecker

Romans 7; Matthew 11

We hear about yokes again this week. Last week, Jeremiah walked around Jerusalem wearing a yoke, calling on

Judah to submit to Babylon. This week, Jesus uses a similar image to convey a dramatically different message: "Come to me, all you that are weary and are carrying heavy burdens, and I will give you rest. Take my yoke upon you, and learn from me; for I am gentle and humble in heart, and you will find rest for your souls. For my yoke is easy, and my burden is light" (Matt 11:28-30 NRSV).

Hearers of this text today may have mixed reactions. On the one hand, rest sounds like a wonderful promise in our frenetic lives. On the other hand, taking on someone's yoke implies servitude, which is not something we aspire to. We are not slaves to anyone.

Or are we? Consider Paul's letter to the Romans. "I am of the flesh, sold into slavery under sin. I do not understand my own actions. For I do not do what I want, but I do the very thing I hate....I can will what is right, but I cannot do it" (Rom 7:14b-15, 18b NRSV).

Paul's dilemma sounds all too familiar to a person caught in the throes of an addiction. But it may also ring true for others. We too often fail to live up to the ideal image we have of ourselves. We disappoint ourselves and those we love. We sin.

Like the Israelites freed from Egypt, perhaps it is not a matter of *whether* we will serve someone. Rather, it's a matter of *whom* we will serve. "Choose this day whom you will serve," says Joshua (Josh 24:15 NRSV). The yoke of slavery to sin. Or the yoke that Jesus offers, which is true freedom. The choice is clear.

Teri Peterson
http://clevertitlehere.blogspot.com

Matthew 11

Few of us use yokes anymore—we often have to explain that a yoke is equipment used to hitch animals together and to something else, such as a plow. Machines do so much of our farming, and so few people work the land, that a yoke is an antique, a museum piece, not an everyday item.

However, for Jesus and the people in his community, the yoke was both everyday *and* held double meaning. The most obvious is the agricultural, but there was also the example of Isaiah 58: "Is not this the fast that I choose: / to loose the bonds of injustice, / to undo the thongs of the yoke, / to let the oppressed go free, / and to break every yoke?" (v. 6 NRSV). A yoke is a system, often a system of bondage—whether that system is economic, political, or intellectual. Sometimes people are put under the yoke by an oppressive power, as the Israelites had been by the Babylonians, or as they were under the Romans. Sometimes the yoke is a choice—by choosing to follow a particular teacher, one took his yoke upon oneself. The yoke was the system of teachings, the teacher's philosophy. And sometimes a system that should be life-giving—like the Torah—is turned into an oppression, as we see with the wise and intelligent—the Pharisees and the scribes—who have made the good law of God into a religious and political system that oppresses people and needs to be broken.

So Jesus calls all of us who are caught in those systems, especially those weary of following all six hundred thirteen laws to the letter and still wondering about the grace of God, especially those who believe God's love has to be earned, to come to him and trade that yoke for another.

I always thought the point of breaking the oppressive yoke was to be free. But we all know that isn't exactly true—as Bob Dylan said, we "Gotta Serve Somebody." The question is: will we be yoked to the letter of the law? To the economic and political system? Yoked to our possessions? Social status? Desires? Yoked to our limited understanding of God, or to what we think the good life looks like? Or will we slip into the empty side of Jesus' yoke and partner with him in the work God has in mind for the world?

When a farmer has a new animal to train, the new animal is yoked together with an experienced one. That way the new animal learns the way while the experienced one carries most of the burden. Eventually the new animal becomes so experienced that it follows the way willingly, and finds the work easy, the burden light.

Are we willing to take Jesus' yoke upon us? Are we willing to submit, knowing it means we cannot continue to pull our other burdens (however much they may look like blessings), to walk with Jesus until we are so trained that our lives won't go any other way?

John Petty
http://progressiveinvolvement.com

Matthew 11

The religious leadership condemned the leaders of the people. John the baptizer came as an ascetic, yet his opponents called him a demon. Jesus came "eating and drinking" but that didn't suit his opponents either so they attacked him personally as well, calling him a glutton and a wino (see vv. 18-19).

This is typical of the approach the powers-that-be often use to manipulate public opinion. When they are criticized, they attack their accusers personally. They assault character. The accusers are themselves accused of insufficient piety—"demon"—or some variation of libertinism—"glutton and wino." *Ad hominem* attacks are the oldest trick in the book.

"Yet wisdom is vindicated by her deeds" (v. 19 NRSV). Matthew is associating the works of Jesus with the wisdom of God. The works of Jesus we have seen in Matthew's Gospel—gender equality, open table fellowship, non-violent resistance to Rome, critique of hierarchy—demonstrate God's true wisdom in action in the world.

In a moment of special revelation (*kairos*), Jesus says, "I thank you, Father." *Exomologoumai* (I thank you) has a sense of celebration and joyous affirmation. "Because you have hidden these things from the wise [*sophon*] and the intelligent, and have revealed [*apocalypto*] them to infants" (v. 25 NRSV).

True wisdom issues in following the Way of Jesus. This way has been "hidden" from those who are "wise and intelligent," but "revealed" to the insignificant. It is God's "gracious will" to reveal the ways of the kingdom to the marginalized. This is yet another affirmation of what, today, we call "preferential option for the poor."

Despite the opposition his followers face, the sense of Jesus' speech is joyous. "All things have been handed over to me by my Father," he says. The "Lord of heaven and earth" has delivered over "all" [*panta*], everything, the entire universe and everything in it—to Jesus (vv. 27, 25 NRSV).

Jesus encourages the people to take up his "yoke" (vv. 29, 30). *Yoke* was a common image for Torah and the Mosaic Law. Instead of Torah, however, we are encouraged to take up Jesus' yoke and "learn" from him.

The "yoke" of Jesus is to learn his Way and follow it. In marked contrast to the way of earthly rulers, both political and religious, Jesus is "meek and lowly in heart" (v. 29 KJV).

"You will find rest for your souls" (v. 29 NRSV). *Anapausin,* which appears also in verse 28, means not only rest but also sabbath rest, the kind of rest that puts a person on the road to recovery. It has a sense of not only rest but also refreshment. Following the Way of Jesus—open table fellowship, dignity for all—will set a people on the path of true life.

"For my yoke is lovingkindness" (v. 30 author's translation). The word is *xrestos*—"goodness, benevolence, pleasant, worthy, loving, kind," or, even better, "active benevolence in spite of ingratitude."

Egalitarian living is "lighter" than hierarchical living. Living in light of the freedom and dignity of every person, and especially the poor, is not a "burden" but is, in fact, the way of true rest and true refreshment.

John Wesley's Notes on the Bible
http://www.ccel.org/ccel/wesley/notes.txt

Matthew 11:28

"Come to me"—Here he shows to whom he is pleased to reveal these things to the weary and heavy laden; ye that labour—After rest in God: "and are heavy laden"—With the guilt and power of sin: "and I will give you rest"—I alone (for none else can) will freely give you (what ye cannot purchase) rest from the guilt of sin by justification, and from the power of sin by sanctification.

Thom Shuman
http://lectionaryliturgies.blogspot.com/

Great Prayer of Thanksgiving

May the Lord of rest be with you.
And also with you.
Weary, come yoke yourselves to the Lord of life.
We join our hearts with God's Heart of compassion..
Gladdened, come lift your songs to the One who loves us.
Thanksgiving overflows from our hearts.

At the first moment of time,
you drew from the deep wells
of gentleness and goodness,
Compassionate Creator.
You wandered the fields,
planting seeds that blossomed
into rainbows of beauty;
you walked in evening's coolness,
scattering stars and moons
into the blue-black skies.
All that you made
was given to us that
we might eat, drink, and dance
with you forever.
But we did not understand
all that you offered,
choosing to sit in sin's marketplace,
as death played its
mournful tunes for us.
You offered us rest
from our wandering ways,
whispering to our souls
through the prophets' heartaches.
When we could not, or would not,
turn back to you,
you sent Jesus to
rescue us from ourselves.

With every generation before us,
with all who will come after us,
we lift our voices in praise:

Holy, holy, holy, God of the weary soul.
Creation celebrates your name in all generations.
Hosanna in the highest!

Blessed is the One who offers our souls rest.
Hosanna in the highest!

Holy are you, God of every moment,
and blessed is Jesus Christ,
friend of the forsaken, Savior of all.

Graced with glory,
he humbled himself to come to us,
to lead us back to you.
Yoked with your heart,
he came to bear our burdens,
so we might find rest
in your hope and healing.
Fed by your love,
he came to eat and drink
with all outsiders,
so we might dance
in your kingdom of love.
Embraced by your gracious will,
he handed himself over to death,
carrying the heavy burden of our sins,
so the joy of resurrection
might be revealed.

As we remember his life, his death, his rising,
as we come to the meal prepared for us,
we celebrate that mystery of faith given to every generation:

Christ died, gentle and humble to the end;
Christ rose, delighting in the new life given to him;
Christ will return, offering us the yoke of resurrection.

To what shall we compare your grace?
You pour it out upon us,
and the simple gifts of the Meal,
through your gentle Spirit.
You feed us with the Bread of hope,
not that we might be satisfied,
but so we would go forth
to embrace the outcasts of our world,
eating and drinking with them,
offering your love to them.
You tilt the Cup of mercy to our lips,
not that we might become smug,
but so we would be dissatisfied
   until the broken are healed,
   until the homeless are sheltered,
   until the hungry are fed,
   until the lost are found,
   until the least are celebrated.

Then, when the last moment of time has come,
and creation is restored to goodness and beauty,
we will sit at the Table with the Lamb,
with all the sinners and saints,
with all the winners and losers,
with all our sisters and brothers,
celebrating your peace and joy forever and ever,
God in Community, Holy in One. **Amen.**

July 13

5th Sunday after Pentecost (Proper 10)

Genesis 25:19-34; Psalm 119:105-112; Romans 8:1-11; Matthew 13:1-9, 18-23; Isaiah 55:10-13; Psalm 65:(1-8), 9-13

Cameron Howard

Genesis 25; Romans 8

Both the Genesis text and the Romans text for this week build arguments based on dichotomies. In Romans, Paul contrasts "flesh" (CEB: "selfishness"), which is hostile to God (v. 7), with "Spirit," which is life-giving (v. 6). It is easy to see that Paul has a point he wants to prove, and he crafts an argument to support his point. By drawing this stark contrast between two separate ideas, he pulls his readers toward affirming one pole—"Spirit"—over the other.

We sometimes forget that narratives also argue for a certain point of view. Although Jacob and Esau are twins, the text describes them as opposites. Esau knows hunting, while Jacob dwells in tents. Esau is a man of the open country, while Jacob is a man of quiet. Esau is loved by their father Isaac, while Jacob is loved by their mother Rebekah. Esau acts hurriedly and rashly, a characterization underscored by the quick succession of five Hebrew verbs in v. 34; translated strictly in order, they read, "He ate, and he drank, and he got up, and he left, and he despised...." Jacob, by contrast, is shrewdly calculating, refusing to hand over the stew until Esau hands over his birthright.

The dualism in the Genesis text pulls us toward affirming Jacob over and against Esau, and toward reaffirming Jacob's characteristics over Esau's. The story's national overlay, wherein Jacob is ancestor of Israel and Esau is ancestor of Edom, also asserts a pull on our political consciousness. Storytelling is advocacy, and this advocacy is inherently neither good nor bad. It is, nonetheless, powerful, and so we should tune our ears to the force of our own rhetoric. What stories do we tell—as a church, a family, a community, a nation—that advocate for a certain point of view?

Melissa Bane Sevier
http://melissabanesevier.wordpress.com

Running in the Dark (Psalm 119)

Sometimes I run in the dark.

In the winter, the sun comes up so late that a morning run nearly always begins in darkness. This time of year I do all my jogging early, before the day gets too hot. Sometimes I run before the sun has begun to rise, either because my schedule demands it or because it is already warmer than I like, and I want to finish early.

Most of the path I cover has no streetlights, so when it's dark I need a lamp of some kind. I wear one of those (very dorky) little forehead lights that attaches around my head with an elastic strap. As soon as the morning sky gives enough light for me to see without the lamp, I take it off and carry it the rest of the way (thereby reducing the dork factor, should I be seen by anyone I know).

The headlamp gives me freedom to run without fear of falling over a speed bump or tree root, ensures that drivers can see me when I'm crossing a street, and enables me to exercise when otherwise I'd be stuck at home.

Our generation in this country isn't much accustomed to the darkness. Unless the power is out, we merely have to flick a switch and the lights come on. What a luxury.

Even so, being in the dark, figuratively, is part of the human condition. We never know just what's coming next. Even less do we know what the distant future holds. We plan our schooling, imagine what job we'll have, look for long-term relationships, save for retirement. I am confident in saying that no one's life has ever turned out exactly how they'd imagined it when they were young.

Because we are in the dark about what's coming, we need lights. People to whom we can go for advice or help. Friends who encourage. Family who are our home even when we're far away. God, who never leaves our side. These lights help us find our way. Alone on an unlit pathway, we trip over our own feet, find ourselves in unsafe situations, grope in the darkness. With the light of God's presence, we are less afraid, more sure of our footsteps, secure that we are headed in the right general direction.

"Your word is a lamp to my feet / and a light to my path" (Ps 119:105 NRSV).

We run in the dark, but not alone. With light, we begin to see with growing clarity what was there all along: purpose, meaning, love, faith, hope. As the pathway continues to unfold before us, every switchback brings something new and unforeseen. Around every turn, God is already there, holding the lamp.

Beth Quick
http://bethquick.blogspot.com

Genesis 25

• "Two nations are in your womb, / and two peoples born of you shall be divided; / the one shall be stronger than the other, / the elder shall serve the younger" (v. 23 NRSV). What a pre-natal message for a mother to receive! Rebekah doesn't see a problem in having a favorite of these children—she chooses the stronger. But for my own mother, I know there is nothing worse than when her children are fighting with each other. She can't choose, she just wants everyone to get along! How would you receive this news, personally, and on behalf of the people it would affect?

• I've always thought Jacob and Rebekah were pretty nasty and scheming in this storyline—but you have to admit, Esau is not too bright to give up ("despised" [v. 34 NRSV]) his birthright for some stew. I guess we often are willing to sacrifice something of value for our immediate pleasures, even to our own detriment.

Psalm 119

• "Your word is a lamp to my feet" (v. 105 NRSV). This is a great praise chorus/camp song made popular by Amy Grant. It is also, in my mind, a good view to hold of Scripture: A lamp to my feet and a light to my path. I think the words put Scripture in its appropriate place: illuminating our way by God's word, without our becoming idolatrous of the Bible.

Romans 8

• "There is therefore now no condemnation" (v. 1 NRSV). These are such awesome words! We are *not* condemned by God in the midst of a world that is *so* condemning.

• "Christ Jesus has set you free" (v. 2). *Freedom* and *free* are words tossed around a lot today. How are we free in Christ? Is this the same or different from freedom we talk about in political circles today?

• The limits of law are clear when held up next to the amazingness of God's grace.

Matthew 13

• Jesus' parables are amazing things, because they are always more than they seem. We like to decode everything in them, saying, this equals this and that equals that, knowing what each image corresponds to. But parables don't really work that way, piece by piece. We must take them as a whole.

• Where do you see yourself in this parable? Rocky soil? Parched by the sun? Good soil?

• If God is the sower, then why doesn't God sow seed only in the good soil? God sows wastefully, extravagantly, without worry about using up too much. Can we be so free with our resources? With our love?

Lowell Grisham
http://lowellsblog.blogspot.com/

Prayers of the People (Genesis 25 & Psalm 119)

Presider: Gracious God, you sow your gifts abundantly upon the church and upon the world, inviting all to live with such depth that we may produce abundant blessings for your creation: Hear our intercessions on behalf of all who need your nurturing love, as we pray: Your word is a lantern to our feet and a light upon our path.

Intercessor: There is now no condemnation for those who are in Christ Jesus: Spread your grace generously within your Church, O God, that it may be rooted deeply in your love and walk according to your Spirit. Your word is a lantern to our feet

and a light upon our path.

Bring light and understanding to our leaders and to all in authority that they may resist the things of the flesh and set their minds on your Spirit, which is life and peace. Your word is a lantern to our feet

and a light upon our path.

Our community is troubled with the cares of the world and choked with the lure of wealth: Free us with the Spirit of life and peace, that we may bear fruit with abundance. Your word is a lantern to our feet

and a light upon our path.

Bless with your divine fecundity all who wish to have and to nurture children, and bring your gift of peace and reconciliation to all families in conflict. Your word is a lantern to our feet

and a light upon our path.

Protect all who are threatened by poverty, hunger, violence, famine, or disaster, that they may be relieved from their anxiety and restored to their birthright as your children. Your word is a lantern to our feet

and a light upon our path.

We offer to your extravagant love those people and concerns that fill our hearts, remembering especially _____. We give you thanks for the blessings of this life, especially _____. We pray for those who have died, especially _____; knowing that he who raised Christ from the dead will give life to their mortal bodies also through his Spirit that dwells in us.

Presider: Almighty God, you have planted your Spirit within all creation: Nurture and bring to fruition your graceful intention to accomplish that which you purpose and succeed in the thing for which you have sent your word, that life and peace may grow into the abundance that fills the world with your joy, through Jesus Christ our Savior. **Amen.**

Safiyah Fosua

Matthew 13

There it is in verse 4, a reference so subtle we could easily miss it. Seed fallen on the ground and eaten by birds! A crust of bread in a park, an old French fry in a parking lot—that is just what birds do. It sounds so ordinary. Perhaps that is the point, that we can be so easily sidetracked by the ordinary, routine things of life.

In the parable, birds are not the only thing that can go wrong with the seed of the word. The list reads: rocky ground (v. 5), hot sun (v. 6), and thorns (v. 7). Something about each suggests the catastrophic. What a tragedy that perfectly good seed could be destroyed in such ways! We go out of our way to avoid the catastrophic, but the birds? It is no accident that Jesus has chosen them, and that they are first on the list. Birds in the wild are not cuteness and endearment, they also hold potential to be destructive. Ask the farmers who go to great lengths to pull in the welcome mat at planting time, or ask your neighbor who may be attempting to reseed her lawn. When Jesus interprets the parable, his choice of words is jarring. He calls the birds the "evil one," who "snatches away what is sown in the heart" (v. 19 NRSV).

Jesus is talking to people who "flock" to hear him, and birds are first on the list. They are there to remind us that we are more likely to be tripped up by something small and ordinary than by hard-heartedness or by hardship or by the lure of the world's treasure.

Paul Nuechterlein
http://girardianlectionary.net/

Matthew 13

Speaking in support of funding low-cost housing for homeless people, a sixty-six-year old County Resource Development Director shared how abuse had stolen his childhood; how he eventually found himself a twice-divorced alcoholic living in a cardboard box. After turning his life around, helping people find housing became his passion. I consider his life a perfect example of how suffering can become good soil for the seed of God's Love, increasing a hundredfold.

Jesus showed how suffering could be good soil for the seed of God's Love. Under Roman imperialism his people were horribly oppressed, yet instead of using military power or invoking God to destroy the Romans, Jesus taught his people to experience God as *Abba*—a Father, even "Daddy"—who asks his children to care for one another ensuring *everyone* has enough. In the midst of their suffering, Jesus planted the seed of God's Love in the soil of their hearts to take root so they could begin understanding how God's power of love would bring God's kingdom into this world through their caring for one another as sisters and brothers.

In his Gospel, Matthew discloses suffering as the good soil, especially in the way he tells us how Jesus begins and ends his teaching ministry. Matthew begins Jesus' teaching with the Beatitudes (5:1-12) and Matthew ends Jesus' teaching with the judgment of the sheep and the goats (25:31-46).

Jesus' message is an unusual seed needing unusual soil to grow bountifully. How do *we* become good soil for God's Love? *Not* by our own efforts, but by God's bountiful grace. The Sower continues to sow graciously everywhere, that seed may land on the parts of our lives where we are most vulnerable—in the midst of our own suffering where our lives connect to the suffering and death of Jesus. And it lands in the midst of the suffering of others, not necessarily that we may end their suffering (though that may be an outcome), but rather that we can love our sisters and brothers within it, sharing their suffering to help ease their burden. This is what the hundredfold yield looks like in our lives: God's household coming *down* into this world in the suffering of the Risen Christ, wherever God's children are working to ensure that the least of this family has enough.

Martha Spong
http://marthaspong.com/

Matthew 13

When I married at age forty-one, one of the gifts I received was a hydrangea, the kind that grows someday into a beautiful umbrella of pink blossoms. I delighted in it. Despite our young dog's scrabbling at its roots, and rude winters freezing it in a bent-over position, it blossomed abundantly. We staked it and pruned it and relied on it, until after a not-so-bad winter, the wedding-present hydrangea, aged seven-and-a-half, simply did not put forth leaves or buds. I stood beside it downhearted, wondering what I could have done differently. How could I have saved it?

In the fall, when it became clear that my marriage would not outlast the hydrangea, friends came from all over the country to stand beside me, and—in the way that people have when they want to help us, but the real problem can't be solved—they fell to doing tasks around my house. They painted and raked and mowed the lawn and tried to fix the icemaker and filled the freezer with lasagna portioned into little containers. In the midst of a flurry of yard work, a dear one offered to clear out the dead tree. I agreed, turned away to consider a lilac that needed pruning, and a moment later turned back to see it was already out of the ground, like an oversized twig in her hand. Whatever happened to my hydrangea had happened at the root.

Truly I tell you, it is not wise to spend our time assigning roles in the parable of the hydrangea. It is enough to say its death reinforced my sense that something was over.

I find it to be the same with Jesus and his metaphors. What if we just let the images wash over us instead of being in a hurry to assign parts to ourselves and to others as if they were absolutely unchangeable? Suppose we meditate for a moment on the idea that the Good News of God's love is forever being sown in the world...scattered widely without regard for likely climates or soils, strewn wildly even in the places it is least likely to be received.

A sower went out to sow, and on any given day that least likely place might be any of our hearts.

But now and then, thankfully, we are the soil where God's seed takes root. Now and then, thankfully, we are the seed that makes contact and grows where someone is hungry for God's grace. Even occasionally, we are the ones to put a hand into the bag slung over our shoulders, the ones who fling the seed of Life and Love into places where it assuredly takes root.

John Wesley's Notes on the Bible
http://www.ccel.org/ccel/wesley/notes.txt

Romans 8:5

"Mind the things of the flesh"—Have their thoughts and affections fixed on such things as gratify corrupt nature; namely, on things visible and temporal; on things of the earth, on pleasure, (of sense or imagination,) praise, or riches. "But they who are after the Spirit"—Who are under his guidance. "Mind the things of the Spirit"—Think of, relish, love things invisible, eternal; the things which the Spirit hath revealed, which he works in us, moves us to, and promises to give us.

July 20
6th Sunday after Pentecost (Proper 11)

Genesis 28:10-19a; Psalm 139:1-12, 23-24; Romans 8:12-25; Matthew 13:24-30, 36-43; Wisdom of Solomon 12:13, 16-19 or Isaiah 44:6-8; Psalm 86:11-17

John Wesley's Notes on the Bible
http://www.ccel.org/ccel/wesley/notes.txt

Genesis 28:12

[Christ] is this ladder: the foot on earth in his human nature, the top in heaven in his divine nature; or the former is his humiliation, the latter is his exaltation. All the intercourse between heaven and earth since the fall is by this ladder. Christ is the way: all God's favours come to us, and all our services come to him, by Christ. If God dwell with us, and we with him, it is by Christ: we have no way of getting to heaven but by this ladder; for the kind offices the angels do us, are all owing to Christ, who hath reconciled things on earth and things in heaven [see Col 1:20].

Cameron Howard

Psalm 139; Matthew 13

The parable of the weeds appears in the New Testament only in the Gospel of Matthew, and the allegorical interpretation at vv. 36-43, with its emphasis on judgment, carries a particularly Matthean flavor. The interpretation addresses a question that was alive and well in the early church and that continues to challenge communities of faith today: why does evil persist in the world?

The interpretation in vv. 36-43 does not reconcile with any satisfaction why the evil and the good cannot be separated sooner rather than later, only stating that eventually they will be. What is left to us is a suspicion that it is not so easy to sort out the two as we might think. Indeed, evil has become so systematized, so intertwined with our daily lives, that we cannot even buy a pair of shoes without participating in the exploitation of one of our brothers and sisters somewhere in this world. What Matthew reads as judgment we may also read as blessed relief: the day is coming when we will indeed extricate ourselves from the systems that, whether we will them to or not, oppress our neighbor.

Psalm 139 reminds us of the intimacy with which God knows us. God knows better than we know ourselves that we are just like Paul: "For I do not do the good I want, but the evil I do not want is what I do" (Rom 7:19 NRSV). Until the inbreaking of God's kingdom, when we are freed from our persistent relationship with evil, we pray with the psalmist, "See if there is any wicked way in me, / and lead me in the way everlasting" (v. 24 NRSV)

Dan Clendenin
http://journeywithjesus.net

Romans 8

The only favoritism that God shows is unconditional love for each person and every nation. Paul reinforces this point in this week's epistle. The eastern Orthodox tradition reminds us that Jesus is the *pantocrator*—the lord not just of people but of all things seen and unseen. Paul combines candor and hope to describe the ambiguous history of all creation. On the one hand, he acknowledges cosmic suffering. On the other hand, he exudes confident hope. Believers should live in eager expectation, because our future glory will far eclipse our present suffering. The ultimate destiny of all creation is liberation and freedom, adoption and redemption. The scale and scope of this future hope includes not only each person and every nation but "the whole creation" (vv. 12-25; 1 John 2:2).

There's an expansive logic to the Christian good news. God *created* "all things...in heaven and on earth, visible and invisible, whether thrones or powers or rulers or authorities" (Col 1:16 NIV 1984). He seeks the *worship* of all things "in heaven and on earth and under the earth" (Phil 2:9-11 NIV 1984). He will "*reconcile* to himself all things, whether things on earth or things in heaven" (Col 1:20 NIV 1984; emphasis added). He will *sum up* or *bring together* "all things in heaven and on earth" (Eph 1:10 NIV 1984). God delights in bestowing his fatherly favor on "his whole family in heaven and on earth" (Eph 3:15 NIV 1984). On earth, under the earth, and in heaven: God was in Christ "reconciling the *cosmos* to himself" (2 Cor 5:19 author's translation).

The redemption of the entire cosmos is a scandalous idea that faces significant objections. It shocks our sense of justice—doesn't Hitler deserve punishment? It seems to undermine ethics—don't our moral choices have eternal consequences? Universalism has had its adherents, but it's always been a minority position in the church. Most important of all, there are many texts, like the Gospel for this week, that speak of hell and judgment.

For these reasons universalism is best seen as a pious hope rather than a dogmatic certainty. You have to be crazy to teach it but impious not to believe it. The most presumptuous thing we can do is claim to know the mysteries of God. Judgment is God's alone. Still, the psalmist for this week rejects the dualist notion that anything exists outside the presence of the omnipresent God of infinite grace and perfect love. Which is to say that we rightly long for the day when death will be destroyed and God will be all in all (1 Cor 15:28).

Safiyah Fosua

Matthew 13

The passage tells us that the weeds appeared when the plants were old enough to bear grain. This suggests that weeds and grain had been growing side-by-side, indistinguishable—appearing to be of the same crop—for some time through various stages of their development. Since at least the time of the KJV translation, scholars have speculated that the weeds in this parable were tares, a useless, perhaps poisonous plant known for its resemblance to wheat until it matures.

When Jesus explained the parable of the Weeds in the Wheat, he assigned parts to everything and everyone except the "servants" (v. 27). What of their part? It appears that the servants, well-intentioned as they were, suffered from lack of information. They were unaware of the origin or the destiny of the mysterious weeds that appeared in what was otherwise a good field.

Jesus' answer gives us a glimpse into the nature of their problem. By this time, the weeds were so deep-rooted and so mingled in with the good crop that uprooting them would likely destroy the good wheat plants near them. The slaves simply did not see enough of the big picture to know how to take a helpful part in this drama.

We have only to look at our pews or our denominations for the obvious application. None of us is perfect. And, if we consider Wesley's doctrine of Christian perfection, none of us is ever fully mature. Here we sit, side by side, shoulder to shoulder on church pews, at different stages on the spiritual journey. We are mere mortals and simply *do not know enough* to uproot or "give the boot" to people suspected of being weedy. Added to our dilemma, at casting call, Jesus assigned someone else the part of Reaper.

Suzanne Guthrie
http://www.edgeofenclosure.org

"Wheat and Tares" (Matthew 13)

The Rev. Dr. Martin Luther King, Jr., said that we begin living only when we rise above our individual concerns to the broader concerns of humanity (see http://www.goodreads.com/author/quotes/23924.Martin_Luther_King_Jr_).

And how can true concern flourish without our realizing we're all in this mess together? Our roots inexorably tangled, whatever affects one directly affects all indirectly.

Good guy/bad guy exclusiveness limits the possibilities of continual conversion, reconciliation, maturing in faith and compassion. For example, let the tares represent all that is within the human character that stifles solidarity with all of life on this fragile planet. Only working together, accepting our inexorable connectedness, can we survive.

But I also have the responsibility to confront the tares in my own being, my own heart. The burning of the tares begins long before the final day. Sins, mistakes, flaws, all kinds of soul-debris fuel the continually smoldering fire. Once in a while some chunk of the psyche loosens and falls out of hiding, letting in the air and stirring up a new conflagration. My life work includes letting in the light, the air, accepting the fire of purification, not for my own sake alone, but for the sake of the whole.

Acknowledging the interconnectedness of life in the life cycle of my genesis, my entangled growth amongst the tares, my transfiguration, my fruit bearing, and my dying, let me sow peace, love, pardon, truth, faith, hope, light, joy.

Lord make me an instrument of your peace
Where there is hatred, let me sow love;
Where there is injury, pardon;
Where there is error, truth;
Where there is doubt, faith;
Where there is despair, hope;
Where there is darkness, light;
And where there is sadness, joy.
O Divine Master grant that I may not so much seek to be consoled, as to console;
To be understood, as to understand;
To be loved, as to love.
For it is in giving that we receive,
It is in pardoning that we are pardoned,
And it is in dying that we are born to eternal life.
(Prayer by an anonymous Norman, c. 1915, called "The Peace Prayer of St. Francis" [found on a St. Francis Holy Card during World War I].)

Carolyn Winfrey Gillette
http://www.carolynshymns.com/

To What Can the Kingdom of God Be Compared?

To what can the kingdom of God be compared?
A mustard seed falls where a field's been prepared,
And there, where predictable plantings should be,
There grows up a wild bush—as big as a tree!
God of love, here on earth, hidden things still surprise:
Loving deeds…signs of birth…faithful, Spirit-filled lives.
Your reign is amazing, your ways still astound,
Just like that new life springing forth from the ground.

A small bit of leaven will change the whole bread:
A poor woman sees that her neighbors are fed,
A church reaches out to the youth in the town,
A man shares his faith and God's blessings abound.
God of love, here on earth, hidden things still surprise:
Loving deeds…signs of birth…faithful, Spirit-filled lives.
Your reign is among us, creation is blessed,
When even a few faithful lives change the rest.

While some look for treasure or one priceless pearl,
God's reign is the gift wise ones seek in this world.
A girl sells possessions to help those in need;
A boy chooses faithfulness rather than greed.
God of love, here on earth, hidden things still surprise:
Loving deeds…signs of birth…faithful, Spirit-filled lives.
Your reign is a treasure that wise ones pursue;
May we seek your kingdom in all that we do.

NOTES
Biblical Reference: Matthew 13:31-33, 44-52
Tune: TO GOD BE THE GLORY 11.11.11.11 with refrain ("To God Be the Glory"), William Howard Doane, 1875
Text: Copyright © 2011 by Carolyn Winfrey Gillette. All rights reserved.

Ann Scull
http://seedstuff.blogspot.com

A Useful Image

This is a Heartlight free image based on Psalm 139:10-12. You can find the image at http://www.heartlight.org/gallery/397.html (accessed April 16, 2012). I think this image is fascinating—I can spend hours looking at it.

Listening Songs

Rachael Lampa, *"Live for You"* on *Live for You* (Nashville, Tenn.: Word, 2000). Rachael Lampa sings in the Contemporary Christian Music/Pop genre. This song is based on our response to God's words to us in the psalm and God's challenge to Jacob in the Genesis reading.

Third Day, *"I've Always Loved You"* on *Time* (Franklin, Tenn.: Essential Records, 1999). This song is based on God's words to us in Psalm 139.

Discussion to Introduce Genesis Reading

Show a group of road signs (go, stop, detour, U-turn, danger, caution, rough road ahead) and ask people to pick the one that best describes their relationship with God at the moment. Reassure them that there are no wrong answers because our relationship with God is also a journey. Jacob could have used every one of the road signs at some time or another of his life. Ask them to share their road sign with a neighbour.

Film Clip

Shrek (Dreamworks, 2001). Show the clip near the end of the film when Shrek sees the princess when she is her real self. Connect this with the psalm and how God sees us as we really are and loves us.

Drama

Verena Johnson, *"A Tare-ible Quarrel,"* in *Let's Make Another Scene* (Adelaide: Open Book, 1995), 48. As you may have guessed from the title, this drama is based on the Gospel reading. Discussion:

1. Is there a lesson here for us as a church?

2. Why are we unable to judge who are wheat and who are weeds?

3. What does Matthew teach us about human accountability?

4. What injustice makes you angry?

Prayer

"Midday Prayer" from a New Zealand prayer book and found in Susan A. Blain, Sharon Iverson Glouwens, Catherine O'Callaghan, and Grant Spradling (eds.), *Imaging the Word Volume 2* (Cleveland: United Church Press, 1995),

245. This goes well with the Gospel reading. Meditation: Project the prayer with images and the following music: Lisa Gerrard and Patrick Kennedy, "Amerigin's Invocation" on *Immortal Memory* (London [possibly]: 4AD, 2004). This music fits the modern classical/world fusion genre and colours the words of the prayer beautifully.

John van de Laar
http://www.sacredise.com/

Matthew 13

It may not seem like it, but, in this week's parable, Jesus speaks directly and comfortingly to humanity's loss of hope. The story would have been familiar to his hearers. They knew about the weeds that, in the early stages of growth, were indistinguishable from wheat. They knew the frustration of enemies planting such weeds in good wheat fields. They knew the dangers of trying to remove the weeds—because the good could not easily be distinguished from the bad, and the roots would intertwine. Jesus explained that the parable was about the evil one who "plants" wicked people in the world, who cannot immediately be rooted out and judged because they are indistinguishable from the righteous. Only at the "end of the age" can God finally separate the wheat from the weeds and deal with them as they deserve.

Jesus' hearers were tired that evil was rampant among them, seemingly allowed to continue without consequence or judgement. They may well have applied this parable to their Roman overlords and the corrupt religious establishment. Almost every response to this situation was one of despair. From the Pharisees and Sadducees who cooperated to preserve their influence and wealth, to the Essenes who withdrew into their own separated community, to the tax collectors who actively collaborated with the oppressors, to the zealots who sought to overthrow Rome by force of arms—all held a basic doubt that God was at work in the world or that evil would finally face its judgement.

But Jesus challenges this loss of hope: Don't lose faith in the people around you. Those who appear as weeds may actually reflect God's life, and those who appear as wheat may be anything but. It's not up to you to rip out the weeds or decide who's in and who's out. And you need not fear being "corrupted" should a "wheaty" looking weed slip past your notice.

Don't lose faith in yourself. Those "weeds" you're ashamed of may yet turn out to be seeds of life and the "wheat" you take pride in may be far less significant than you think. Don't judge your own heart too quickly or severely.

Don't lose faith in God. God does intend for goodness and love to win. God does intend to deal with evil and bring the cosmos to wholeness. But God's timetable is driven by grace and compassion. So don't allow your loss of hope to cause you to adopt evil methods or attempt to enact God's judgment prematurely. Trust that God's Reign is at work even if it doesn't seem so.

It's a tough parable, but it is the Gospel. There is always hope, because what may look like a weed can very well have the life and goodness of wheat surging up unseen within it. Our task is not to judge—not ourselves or others or the world or God's work in it. Our task is simply to trust, to believe, and to hope.

July 27
7th Sunday after Pentecost (Proper 12)

Genesis 29:15-28; Psalm 105:1-11, 45b or Psalm 128; Romans 8:26-39;
Matthew 13:31-33, 44-52; 1 Kings 3:5-12; Psalm 119:129-136

Marci Auld Glass
www.marciglass.com

Genesis 29

When I read this story, I feel like I've read someone's diary and exposed the hidden secrets of a family. It just doesn't seem right. Surely Rachel and Leah deserve some privacy so that they can deal with the consequences of their father's shady business practices without witnesses?

Presumably, Rachel prepared to be a bride as she watched Jacob work those seven years to earn her hand, perhaps even reminding Leah that nobody had come forward to marry her.

And even if Leah had a momentary victory at the last-minute switch on the wedding night, surely there was also humiliation for her the morning after, when Jacob ran from the tent, outraged at the deception. Had she perhaps hoped that in one night together, he would have reconsidered and changed his mind?

Even Jacob, the trickster who had lied and fooled his father, claiming his older brother Esau's birthright—even Jacob might not want this story read in every pulpit in the land. Because here, the trickster met his match.

When Jacob complained about the wife swap, Laban said, "This is not done in our country—giving the younger before the firstborn" (v. 26 NRSV).

Can't you just hear the rest of the sentence? "You thought you were so clever fooling your father for your brother's inheritance with just a pot of beans and the hair of a goat wrapped around your hand, but I just showed you how it's done! You didn't even know you'd married the wrong daughter until the morning! We do things the right way around here! Oldest wins."

Yes, you can see why Jacob probably wasn't thrilled when these pictures were put in the family album. But here they are.

From Adam, Eve, and the talking serpent at the beginning, all the way through the dysfunction of Jacob's sons at the end, Genesis is full of family stories that we might like to shove under the proverbial rug. And God is working right through the dirty laundry, betrayal, and trickery to tell the Divine story.

We know this to be true—that God works through highly flawed people and families. We even have it in Scripture. And yet, we continue to argue that only perfect people should lead us. Or we say that God doesn't need this person or that person to serve the church because we have decided that they sin more than the rest of us. Or we decide we will go back to church once we've gotten things figured out.

But if God seems perfectly content to work through people like Jacob and Laban, why do we pretend we're not like them? What grace do we need to accept in our lives so that we can offer our true selves as God's servants? What do we need to do so that we can then share that grace with others?

NOTE: Adapted from "Wife Swap—Genesis Style," a sermon preached by Marci Auld Glass (http://marciglass.com/2011/07/24/wife-swap-genesis-style/).

Cameron Howard

1 Kings 3

When God says to Solomon, "Ask whatever you wish, and I'll give it to you" (1 Kgs 3:5b), our first mental image may look less like the Lord appearing in a dream and more like a genie popping out of a bottle. Solomon, however, is not confused by God's approach. He responds, not with a list of demands, but with a prayer. He acknowledges the relationship God has had with his father David (v. 6), God's agency in his own kingship (v. 7a), his own shortcomings (v. 7b), and the enormity of the task before him (v. 8). Only then does he make his request.

Solomon could have asked for so many things. The text acknowledges three—"long life, wealth, or victory over your enemies" (v. 11), but we can surely think of more. We hope deeply that our own national and international political leaders will, like Solomon, ask for a "discerning mind" (v. 9) rather than for money, fame, or power. Yet Solomon's prayer is also an important model, in form even more than in content, for those of us outside of political leadership.

God grants Solomon's request for wisdom, but Solomon has already demonstrated his wisdom by asking well. He is already cultivating the quality that he desires God to give him. Prayer is not an exercise in wish-fulfillment; it is, rather, an orientation of the whole self toward God. When Psalms 119 and 128, like so much of the wisdom literature, exhort us to walk in God's ways, the implication is that we actively practice the good, rather than passively receiving it. Instead of asking God to grant us wishes, we must start down the path of the new life we seek, knowing that it is ultimately God who grants us a safe and fulfilling journey.

John Wesley's Notes on the Bible
http://www.ccel.org/ccel/wesley/notes.txt

Romans 8:33

The term *elect* was of old applied to all the members of the visible church; whereas in the New Testament it is applied only to the members of the invisible.

Julie Craig
http://winsomelearnsome.com

Romans 8

The first time I was to preach this text, I was not yet a pastor. I was filling in for a friend of mine who was going to be out of town for the Sunday, so she had asked me to preach, though I was still just a seminary student.

On the way to the airport to leave town, a tragic thing happened, and though my friend survived, the circumstances of her life were shattered. I found this out less than twenty-four hours before I was to preach. My sermon was written. I'm sure I did some editing, but I was not yet confident enough in my preaching skills to change the passage. I don't remember much of what was said, but I do remember that when I read these words of Paul, "We know that all things work together for good for those who love God, who are called according to his purpose" (v. 28 NRSV), I felt as though I had been slapped in the face, which is usually not a good feeling for a preacher when bringing the good news to the church.

I also feared I had just slapped the congregation in the face—those good and gentle people who were trying to care for their pastor in the midst of a horrific time. This text seems to argue the case for an omnipotent God, who is in charge and in control, yet the text does not appear to wrestle with the questions of what happens when bad things happen to God's good people.

A God who is in charge and a God who loves without limit are inextricably intertwined. One cannot tell where God's omnipotence ends and God's providence begins. This is a complicated set of ideas in a world where babies die and levees break and earthquakes happen and economies fail and those in power crush the weak and helpless.

One would have thought that the incarnation would have settled the question, that a God willing to become mud that breathes is a God willing to be both omniscient and omnipresent, a providential God whose believers never suffer. In the absence of that reality it is easy for us to imagine our temporary circumstances to be a measure of God' love—or lack thereof—for us.

Luckily, Paul keeps bringing us back to the big picture. And so when Paul says something like "What then are we to say about these things? If God is for us, who is against us?" (Rom 8:31 NRSV), it is a reminder that the good news is about more than measuring God's love by our momentary, transient, temporary circumstance. Or any human measure at all.

I am grateful to Paul—Jesus-obsessed, much-misunderstood Paul—for the reminder.

Liz Crumlish
http://somethingtostandon.blogspot.co.uk/

Matthew 13

Words, words, words—the world is full of words. And pictures too—the click of a mouse allows us to be privy to another's world, eavesdropping on their words and their pictures. Such is the wonder of the blogosphere where we can loiter largely undetected or interact, if we choose, with complete strangers in other parts of the world. We are afforded a glimpse of sometimes intimate moments in the lives of others and are, more often than not, free to comment—to congratulate, commiserate, or encourage.

The contemporary Facebook, Twitter, and Google retellings of the Christmas and Easter narratives provide entertaining, creative insights into how those stories might have been communicated in this age of social networking. Imagine how creative Jesus might have been with that vast network of communication at his disposal. It would have been impossible to keep up with him. But, then again, that notion that some might fall behind or that others might be excluded completely might lend credence to the theory that Jesus would have eschewed such technology in favour of plain old face-to-face conversation.

That's not a decision he had to take, but he did get pretty creative with the means available to him. Jesus used the familiar things of folks' everyday worlds and wove incredible tales that made folk stop in their tracks and look at life in a whole new way. Sometimes that wasn't a challenge that they relished. But Jesus' speech was plain and his message clear to those who would listen.

Of course there were those who chose to be dense, those who preferred not to see life in the way Jesus portrayed it as well as those who refused to see beyond a pretty story. The trouble is that the parables Jesus told were rarely pretty and were always incisive, providing damning social commentary on people's lives. Many people had difficulty facing the harsh truths that he laid out in his parables and chose, instead, to kill the messenger. Such are the perils of being a prophet—or even the son of God.

Safiyah Fosua

Matthew 13

The kingdom of heaven is like a tiny seed that grows into a large tree . . . get it? Well, how about yeast mixed in with the flour? Well then, how about an extremely valuable pearl that someone discovered was hidden in a field? In this series of parables about the Kingdom, Jesus sounds like a storyteller reaching for word pictures to describe a concept beyond the reach of his audience.

When the parable is read today, I am not sure that we find the kingdom of heaven any more accessible because of cultural distance from some of the examples. I think that all of us understand a pearl of great price, but I am not so sure that the mustard-bottle generation understands a mustard seed. Nor do I think that the bakery and bread-machine-from-a-box generation understands yeast.

Those who bake quickly learn that the mysterious action of yeast is not automatic. Ask bakers how to take care of yeast so that it remains effective. They will tell you not to place the yeast in hot liquids, or the rising dough in a place that is too warm lest the yeast die. After a time, yeast that is not fed becomes exhausted of its own meager resources and dies. And, of course, the baker must give the yeast time to do its work. Depending upon the kind of yeast, it could take a good portion of an hour or a good portion of a day for yeast to yield the desired results. Yeast works with conditions in her contract. Yeast cannot get too warm, yeast must be fed, and yeast takes time.

We are yeast.

Todd Weir
http://bloomingcactus.typepad.com/

Matthew 13

To what would you compare the Kingdom of Heaven? It is like finding the technology stock you bought in the 1980s for fifty dollars and suddenly realizing you are a millionaire. It is like the owner of DeBeers finally finding the perfect diamond and selling a billion-dollar empire to have it. It is like the harassed physician, tired of the HMOs, selling home and BMW and finding bliss in a mission in Congo. It is like an addict waking up with a clear head, free to choose a new life.

What will we tell our congregations about the Kingdom of Heaven? What makes this Kingdom any better than what can be gotten at the mall? Is it bigger than the consumer paradise promised every seven minutes while we watch the latest sitcom? Is it something that can be had only in the next life, so we must patiently suffer in this life to earn it? Will we be any closer to the Kingdom of Heaven if our party's political agenda is enacted, if our kids pray in school and have the Ten Commandments etched in twenty tons of marble at the town hall, or if we properly observe separation of church and state? If we double the new member classes and exceed the demands of the annual budget, will we be any closer to the Kingdom of Heaven?

Sure, these may sound like silly questions. But I confess that I regularly let things less valuable than the Kingdom of Heaven take on ultimate importance. As much as I wish to shove this thought into my unconscious, worldly success too often is my measure of the Kingdom of Heaven. I can easily settle for much less than the life Jesus has to offer. Our churches and our spiritual lives suffer from an anemic view of what being a Christian can be. A paltry view of the Kingdom of Heaven in our midst is more defeating than doctrinal error or, God forbid, a lack of funds. When we start to complain about the hymn selection or meet far into the night about carpet colors, it is time to rise up and say, "What is the Kingdom of Heaven like?"

Jesus did not go to Websters' Dictionary for a precise definition of the Kingdom of Heaven. Precision has its place, but here he means to stimulate the imagination. Our life with God is better than the most breathtaking thing we can imagine. We plant tiny seeds, we search the fields for it, we scour the marketplace and when we find the divine presence, nothing else can compare. It seems that the searchers in these brief parables were not quite expecting what they found. They didn't know their seeds would grow so well, they stumbled across the treasure while working the field, and while looking for fine pearls they found one so incomparable. They were searching and working, but found more than their imagination.

August 3
8th Sunday after Pentecost (Proper 13)

Genesis 32:22-31; Psalm 17:1-7, 15; Romans 9:1-5; Matthew 14:13-21; Isaiah 55:1-5; Psalm 145:8-9, 14-21

John Wesley's Notes on the Bible
http://www.ccel.org/ccel/wesley/notes.txt

Genesis 32:25

"The angel prevailed not against him"—That is, this discouragement did not shake his faith, nor silence his prayer. It was not in his own strength that he wrestled, nor by his own strength that he prevails; but by strength derived from heaven. That of Job illustrates this [Job 23:6]. Will he plead against me with his great power? No; had the angel done so, Jacob had been crushed; but he would put strength in me: and by that strength Jacob had power over the angel [see Hosea 12:3]. The angel put out Jacob's thigh, to shew him what he could do, and that it was God he was wrestling with, for no man could disjoint his thigh with a touch. Some think that Jacob felt little or no pain from this hurt; it is probable he did not, for he did not so much as halt 'till the struggle was over, v. 31, and if so, that was an evidence of a divine touch indeed, which wounded and healed at the same time.

Beth Quick
http://bethquick.blogspot.com

Genesis 32

• We all wrestle with God, but there are lots of ways to go about it. Jacob's approach is great—Jacob wrestles, holds his own, and demands a blessing. How do you wrestle with God?

• What are your names? What do they mean? Who named you?

• Are you willing and able to ask God to bless you? Demand it, even?

• "I have seen God face to face" (v. 30 NRSV). Have you? When? Where? How?

Psalm 17

• This psalm fits well with our passage from Genesis, because the psalmist, like Jacob, is bold and demanding. The psalmist declares himself to be free from deceit, able to withstand testing, feet not slipping from God's path.

• Sometimes we need to be bold with God—not for God's sake, but for our sake. Fear of God's justice has its place, but confidence in our status as God's beloved children with whom God seeks relationship also has its place.

• Read the in-between verses too, 8-14, in the NRSV. They include the phrase "apple of the eye." Did you know that was from the Bible?

Romans 9

• This is a little snippet of Scripture. What is here? Paul's passion that his people, the Israelites, would hear God's message. He has "great sorrow and unceasing anguish" (v. 2 NRSV) for them as he worries about their salvation. Who do you worry about? Whose walk with God are you anguished over, hoping that they find the hope you have found?

Matthew 14

• Food holds such a critical place in the Scriptures. Jesus talks about being spiritually fed lots of times. But he doesn't overlook the importance of alleviating literal hunger!

• Some look at this as a literal miracle. Others read this passage as a miracle of sharing and abundance in a more figurative sense. Either way, it is a miracle indeed. People were hungry and then were fed. People were enabled to stay and hear Jesus preach.

• There was more than enough to go around. This is a great statement for today—we live in a world of abundance, but perceive ourselves to be in a world of scarcity. Jesus tries to show us our abundance. Can you see it?

Lowell Grisham
http://lowellsblog.blogspot.com/

Prayers of the People (Genesis 32; Psalm 17)

Presider: Out of your abundance, O God, you bless us and feed us. Have compassion upon the multitudes who need your care, and touch all for whom we pray with the abundance of your grace, as we say: Incline your ear to us and hear our words; show us your marvelous loving-kindness.

Intercessor: Your church, O Holy One, is the eucharistic community of your Son Jesus Christ: Grant us the presence of your Spirit as we take, bless, break, and give our lives to your intentions. Incline your ear to us and hear our words;

show us your marvelous loving-kindness.

The nations live in fear and anxiety, O God: Visit our leaders and strive with them in their fears, that they may choose your paths of peace and reconciliation. Incline your ear to us and hear our words;

show us your marvelous loving-kindness.

Let your generosity bless this community, O Gracious One, that all who are ill may be healed, the hungry fed, and those needing fellowship find steadfast hospitality and care among us. Incline your ear to us and hear our words;

show us your marvelous loving-kindness.

Listen to our prayers for all the world, that your abundance may fill those living with scarcity and your presence may bless all people. Incline your ear to us and hear our words;

show us your marvelous loving-kindness.

Touch our sorrows and the unceasing anguish of our hearts as we bring our prayers to you, especially for _____. With grateful hearts we bring you our thanks, especially for _____. With faith we remember those who have died, especially _____. Incline your ear to us and hear our words;

show us your marvelous loving-kindness.

Presider: Visit us in our fear and fill us with the abundance of your grace, O God, that all the world may feel and know the goodness of your presence, in the power of your Holy Spirit, through Jesus Christ our Savior. **Amen.**

Prayers of the People (Track 2—Isaiah 55; Psalm 145)

Presider: Out of your abundance, O God, you bless us and feed us. Have compassion upon the multitudes who need your care, and touch all for whom we pray with the abundance of your grace, as we say: You are loving to everyone, and your compassion is over all your works.

Intercessor: Your church, O God, is the eucharistic community of your Son Jesus Christ. Grant us the presence of your Spirit as we take, bless, break, and give our lives to your purpose. You are loving to everyone,

and your compassion is over all your works.

You call nations that do not know you and they shall run to you, O Holy One: Visit the leaders of the nations that they may uphold all who fall and lift up those who are bowed down, sharing your divine graciousness and compassion with all humanity. You are loving to everyone,

and your compassion is over all your works.

Let your generosity bless this community, O Gracious One, that all who are ill may be healed, the hungry fed, and those needing fellowship find steadfast hospitality and care among us. You are loving to everyone,

and your compassion is over all your works.

Listen to our prayers for the world, that your abundance may fill all who live with scarcity and your presence may bless all people. You are loving to everyone,

and your compassion is over all your works.

Touch our sorrows and the unceasing anguish of our hearts as we bring our prayers to you, especially for _____. With grateful hearts we bring you our thanks, especially for _____. With faith we remember those who have died, especially _____. You are loving to everyone,

and your compassion is over all your works.

Presider: Visit us in our fear and fill us with the abundance of your grace, O God, that all the world may feel and know the goodness of your presence, in the power of your Holy Spirit, through Jesus Christ our Lord. **Amen.**

Cameron Howard

Isaiah 55; Psalm 145; Matthew 14

Isaiah 55, Psalm 145, and Matthew 14 all testify to abundance, to the enough-for-all economy that characterizes the kingdom of God. Walter Brueggemann has famously contrasted the Bible's "liturgy of abundance," demonstrated in the loaves and fishes story, with the "myth of scarcity" propagated by the economic powers of the world (Walter Brueggemann, *Christian Century* 116.10 [1999]: 342–47). Brueggemann's work awakens our consciousness to the *radical* nature of these texts, which provide powerful counter-testimony to the messages of acquisition, materialism, and hoarding of resources dominant in our culture.

It is ludicrous to say, as Isaiah 55:1b does, "Come, buy... / without money and without price" (NRSV). The notion of commerce, of buying anything at all, relies on a transaction, an exchange. In our economy, buying without money is just buying on credit: pay nothing now, pay more later. But God does not adhere to our economy. The disciples want Jesus to send the crowds from the deserted place where they are gathered into the villages, so that the people can purchase their supper before it is too late (Matt 14:15). Jesus holds them back from participating in the world's economy, demonstrating instead how the kingdom of God does business.

Folk singer John McCutcheon sings a song that testifies to the abundance found at the dinner table of a large family. "Calling All the Children Home" describes a mother standing in the doorway calling her children in to dinner, where "There was always just enough, there was always room for more" (John McCutcheon, "Calling All the Children Home," *Live at Wolf Trap,* 1992, compact disc). God's abundance is like that mother's table, which is characterized not only by *just enough* but also by radical hospitality: *always room for more.* We have five loaves and two fish in this world; if we will bless them and break them, they will be enough.

Melissa Bane Sevier
http://melissabanesevier.wordpress.com

Balancing Act (Matthew 14)

[Jesus] withdrew from there in a boat to a deserted place by himself....When he went ashore, he saw a great crowd; and he had compassion for them and cured their sick....[T]he disciples came to him and said, "...The hour is now late; send the crowds away so that they may go into the villages and buy food for themselves." Jesus said to them, "...You give them something to eat." (Matthew 14:13-16 NRSV)

It's one of my favorite Jesus stories, because in it he experiences what is common to most of us. He is tired, and he is grieving, having just heard about the beheading of his friend and cousin John (called the Baptist). He must be sick of the crowds. If there were ever a need for some alone time, this is it. He heads to a lonely spot, maybe a favorite place.

When he steps off the boat, there they are. Can't he just catch a few minutes, a half a day maybe, when he isn't needed to do something? A day to curl up with a good book and a cup of tea. Why don't these people get a life? For pity's sake.

Jesus looks at them, though, and he can't turn away. He turns *toward* them instead and heals the sick, and then they are hungry and he feeds them. All of them. More than five thousand. Whew. This emotionally drained giver finds he has more to give, because the need is great.

Sadly, though, the lectionary reading ends there, with the count of how many were fed. I think that's exactly the wrong place to end it. I always make sure to read the next verse and a half: "Immediately he made the disciples get into the boat and go on ahead to the other side, while he dismissed the crowds. And after he had dismissed the crowds, he went up the mountain by himself to pray" (vv. 22-23a, NRSV).

Yes, Jesus sends the disciples and the crowd away and finally makes the time to be alone.

Sometimes you have to keep giving. There are things that must be done because others are depending on you, and because it is right for you to do them. But you can't keep operating that way forever. We can only go on and on for so long before our souls call out to us to stop and wait for a while. To catch our breath. To look around and see where we are and how far we've come and where we are going.

Finding rest and renewal doesn't often come easily. It may be more like a dance between the responsibilities and the peace that both call to us. Like Jesus, we keep searching for the balance.

Martha Spong
http://marthaspong.com/

Matthew 14

I was just out of college when a boy I knew growing up was killed during a robbery at the Radio Shack where he worked. I had not seen him for many years. He was not a part of my daily life. I have to admit that as young teenagers, we did not get along. But Al was part of the fabric of my early years. His older sister babysat my little brother and me, and their father worked with our father, and I spent a lot of time at their house. Al's death left a shocking hole in the tapestry of the life I knew, threatening my sense of who was safe and who was not. And so despite the distance in time and relationship I had to take more than a moment to remember Al, to pray for his family, and to consider my own life.

Jesus withdrew to do the same thing, feeling depleted and shocked, bound to be considering his own mortality. John, who prepared the way for him, had been murdered as part of a palace plot, beheaded as the prize requested by a young girl at her mother's instigation. King Herod let it happen because he felt ashamed and embarrassed by his life and the truth John told him about it.

Jesus heard this terrible news about a barbaric death, and he needed to get away. Perhaps he felt he had nothing to give, but the people followed and somehow he found what they needed, although his own tank needed filling.

In my usually safe neighborhood, we woke one summer morning to find someone had tried to siphon gas from our cars. The latch on a neighbor's fuel hatch was broken, and although mine is electronic, the digital message I saw when I got in the car let me know someone had been fooling with it. I asked the neighbor how much gas they could have gotten, and he told me, "Not much, I was running on empty."

I wonder how many people who followed Jesus that day felt the same way: empty, a little desperate, willing to trust a guy who was popular with crowds but had come out of nowhere to attract so much attention.

And I wonder about Jesus, emptied out by shock and sadness, yet moved by compassion to help those who needed what he could give. I think of him, moving through grief to heal others. I think of him, touching people who needed filling, not just with fish and bread, but with hope. It is the hope we receive when we share the broken bread and the outpoured cup. That tank is never on empty.

Safiyah Fosua

Matthew 14

The two fish and five loaves of bread in today's passage have gradually morphed from symbol to cliché. So many *God-will-provide* sermons have been preached about this passage that our parishioners have become numb to the gifts that the feeding of the five thousand offers to hearers in the twenty-first century.

In our rush to experience the miracle, we often forget that Jesus and the disciples were on their way to a quiet place to tend to their own emotional and spiritual needs. Matthew, Mark, and Luke are careful to remind us that John the Baptist had just been beheaded. Nevertheless, Jesus and company were overtaken by the sick, the needy, and the curious. What was intended to be a period of retreat was quickly transformed into a *long* day of ministry.

Most of the people who attend your churches do not live in a constant state of food insecurity or great want. But needy people are with us today; relentlessly calling the parsonage on the pastor's day off. Here, with needs so great that pastors and leaders scarcely have time to pray, their constant tugging reveals that the passage is as much about spiritual hunger as it is about physical hunger. It is also about fatigue and feelings of inadequacy when leaders face their own spiritual needs.

The passage contains not one, but essentially two stories. The first: that Jesus and the disciples were somehow able to push past their own emotional and spiritual needs to respond to the pressing needs of the masses. The second, more familiar story: that God is able to meet *every* need of the people who come in search of something more. Both scenarios, only possible by the power of God.

August 10
9th Sunday after Pentecost (Proper 14)

Genesis 37:1-4, 12-28; Psalm 105:1-6, 16-22, 45b; Romans 10:5-15;
Matthew 14:22-33; 1 Kings 19:9-18; Psalm 85:8-13

Dan Clendenin
http://journeywithjesus.net

Genesis 37

The story of Joseph in Genesis 37–50 begins when he was seventeen and ends with his death in Egypt at the age of one hundred ten. That's ninety-three long years, many spent in exile from his family. The story features three sets of two dreams, all six of which are construed as divine messages. Joseph had two dreams as a teenager, one about sheaves of grain and another about the stars in the sky. Both of them foretold that he would rule over his older brothers. The next four dreams feature Joseph as the interpreter of dreams, although he insists that it's God who gives the interpretation. He deciphers a good dream by the cupbearer and a very bad dream by the baker, and then Pharaoh's two dreams about future years of feast and famine.

These six dreams turned Joseph's life into something of a nightmare. Some of the deepest hurts that we experience come from our own families, often through no fault of our own. Such was the case with Joseph. His brothers resented their father's favoritism, epitomized in his "coat of many colors" that privileged him above them. So they sold Joseph to Midianite merchants (slave traders?), who in turn sold him to an Egyptian official named Potiphar. This began thirteen years of slavery and imprisonment for Joseph (vv. 2-3; 41:46). He was later tempted and falsely accused by Potiphar's wife. Languishing in prison for crimes he didn't commit, he was forgotten by the cupbearer, who had gained his own freedom thanks to Joseph.

As history unfolded, though, roles were reversed. Joseph's brothers and family were demoted to beggars in a famine, whereas he was elevated to Pharaoh's second-in-command. When their fratricide was exposed, the brothers fully expected retaliation. But in contrast to the brothers, who tried to kill him out of jealousy, Joseph forgave his brothers out of a sense of God's providence.

Joseph believed that God had a providential purpose in the private wrongs that he had suffered: to preserve a remnant that would fulfill the promise to Abraham. "Don't be afraid," assured Joseph. "Am I in the place of God? You intended to harm me, but God intended it for good" (Gen 50:20 NIV). At least four times Joseph reassured his nervous brothers that it was God, not his brothers who had sent him to Egypt (Gen 45:5, 7, 8, 9). It's an astounding and radical idea, that nothing that I experience happens without divine design and permission.

The Joseph story shows how God uses our worst sins, sufferings, and failures in redemptive ways. This is risky business. There's a thin and mysterious line between honoring God's providence and calling evil good. We should also be wary of enabling or excusing bad family behaviors instead of correcting them. Nor should we ever turn a blind eye to injustice as if it doesn't matter. Nevertheless, Joseph moved beyond these legitimate concerns and discerned a larger purpose of good in the evil that he suffered.

Cameron Howard

Genesis 37

Genesis 37–50 is often described as a novella, because rather than reading as a collection of separate stories, the chapters cohere with a broad shape to tell the story of Joseph and his family. If we do take Genesis 37–50 as a whole, then chapter 37 reads as a masterful introduction to the narrative. We learn that Jacob is a tattletale (v. 2), his father's favorite (v. 3), and a dreamer (vv. 5-11) whose night visions have him ruling over his brothers. We learn that Joseph's brothers resent him so much that they conspire to kill him, and end up selling him for twenty pieces of silver (v. 28). Most of all, in a poignant line heavy with foreshadowing, we learn what will unfold for us, the readers, as the story continues; we, along with Joseph's brothers, "shall see what will become of his dreams" (v. 20 NRSV).

We have read ahead; we know that Joseph's dreams will be fulfilled, that he will save his brothers' lives, and that the family will be reunited and reconciled. Nonetheless, it is worthwhile to linger in that uncertainty as if we are reading the story for the first time, remembering the doubt, anxiety, and fear it raises in us as readers. With Joseph on his way into slavery in Egypt, what will indeed become of his dreams?

Even today the world has dreamers: people with the ability to imagine a future—for themselves or for the world—that no one else dares see. And even today the world is good at silencing dreamers, out of fear that they may speak a world-changing truth. Think of the dreamers you know today; if you could read ahead, what will have become of their dreams?

Ann Scull
http://seedstuff.blogspot.com

A Useful Image
This is my image taken at Narooma on the southern coast of New South Wales, Australia, with the words of Romans 10:11b. You can find the image at http://seedstuff.blogspot.com.au/2011/07/proper-14-ordinary-19-august-7-risk-and.html (accessed April 16, 2012).

Listening Songs
Serene and Pearl, *"Deep Water"* on *Crazy Stories* (Franklin, Tenn: Forefront Records, 1995). This song goes very well with the Gospel reading.

Third Day, *"Call My Name"* on *Revelation* (Franklin, Tenn.: Essential Records, 2008). This song goes very well with the Romans reading.

Kid's Stories and Talk
Catherine Store and Chris Molan, **Miracles by the Sea** (Sydney: Methuen Australia, 1983), 161–62. Part of this book is based on the Gospel reading for today.

Felicity Henderson and Chris Saunderson, *"Joseph the Favourite,"* in *The Picture Strip Bible* (Milton Keynes, UK: Scripture Union, 2001), 18.

J.B.C.E, *"In a Hole,"* in *Life Plus Ideas for Worship* (Melbourne: Joint Board for Christian Education, 1996), 15. This is a great talk idea about Joseph and his predicament when his brothers put him in the pit.

Film Clip
Indiana Jones and the Last Crusade (Paramount Pictures, 1989). Show the scene near the end of the movie where Indiana Jones has to step out in faith trusting that a bridge, which he cannot actually see, is there. Discussion:

1. What does this clip teach us about risk and faith?

2. What does the Gospel reading teach us about risk and faith?

Drama
"Joseph and His Brothers," found at http://seedstuff.blogspot.com.au/2011/07/proper-14-ordinary-19-august-7-risk-and.html (accessed April 16, 2012). This drama is based on the Genesis reading—it is my drama, so I encourage you to change the wording to fit your congregation and culture.

Discussion

Len Woods, *"Favoritism,"* in *Life Application Family Devotions* (Wheaton, Ill.: Tyndale House, 1997), 104–5. There are some good discussion ideas in this short chapter based on the Genesis reading.

Story

"Cash the Cheque," found in Index 3118 from *Bible Illustrator for Windows Version 1.0d* (Parsons Technology Inc., 1990) or http://www.focusongod.com/Romans-15.htm (accessed April 16, 2012). This story is based on the Romans reading.

Poem

Peter Dainty, *"Joseph the Dreamer,"* in *The Electric Bible* (Suffolk: Kevin Mayhew, 2003), 30–31.

Response Activity: Meditation on the Gospel

Where do I feel that God is asking me to "get out of the boat" right now:

    a. in the work that I do
    b. in my family or in my relationships
    c. in my spiritual life with God
    d. something else

Safiyah Fosua

Matthew 14

The day had already been like an unwilling ride on a roller coaster. Weary disciples, needy crowds, distributing food to thousands; then, John tells us, there was politically dangerous talk of making Jesus king (John 6:15)! Next, the disciples faced a tumultuous storm at sea. Add to this the sight of Jesus walking on top of the waves!

The disciples were already feeling overtired, overwhelmed, and overcommitted. By this time they were so *over-stimulated* that they thought they were seeing a ghost and cried out in fear! Perhaps it was this over-the-top state of emotions that prevented them from even recognizing Jesus' voice when he attempted to calm their fears: "It is I; do not be afraid" (Matt 14:27 NRSV).

In the midst of this maelstrom of emotion, Peter, true to his nature, issued a challenge to the apparition that dared *to pass itself off as Jesus*. "Lord, if it is you, command me to come to you on the water" (v. 28 NRSV).

Come.

Peter *did* come. And, for a few glorious steps, he *did* walk on the water toward Jesus. When it occurred to Peter where he was and what he was doing, he fell. Test over.

Yes, *test over*. This is now the third time that the disciples are being tested on the same question: Will you allow God to move you beyond what you perceive to be a limitation? First it was fatigue and grief over the death of John the Baptist (Matt 14:8-14). Then it was the perception of scarcity with the feeding of the five thousand. This last test extended to the boundaries of the natural world! Don't worry. There was a re-test, later, when the disciples were sent out to perform miracles.

Suzanne Guthrie
http://www.edgeofenclosure.org

"Fear Not, You Are Mine" (Matthew 14)

"Fear not, for I have redeemed you; I have called you by name, you are mine. When you pass through the waters I will be with you; and through the rivers, they shall not overwhelm you" (Isa 43:1-2 RSV).

Terrified, the disciples think the figure coming toward them across the wind-stirred waters is a ghost. Recognizing Jesus, the terror intensifies. Jesus calls, "Fear not, it is I!" (*Ego eimi,* I AM.) Surely, the divine implication is still more terrifying.

Peter's impulse to walk on water is a line of thought I can't imagine. Did the others think to themselves, *Oh, I'd like to try that! Yes, Lord, call me out on the water too!* What made Peter think he could walk to Jesus across the water? *If it is you, command me to come to you on the water. And if it isn't you, if you're the devil, uh . . . I'll just drown!?*

"Come on out," says Jesus.

His impulses far ahead of his rational mind, Peter goes out and walks across the water. Then his brain catches up. Distracted, he loses . . . what? concentration? faith? trust? crazy-making adrenaline? The wind frightens him, he's gets back in the old groove, and down he goes. Peter shouts for help.

Jesus' response is often described as a rebuke, but I hear the comment differently. Playfully, Jesus compliments Peter, "Why did you doubt, ye of little faith? You *had* it!" Like a parent teaching a child to ride a two-wheel bicycle, you let go and the child sails off in perfect balance. But in a moment of self-consciousness, he falters and falls. The parent calls out, "You did it! You were doing it! You can do it!" I remember those milestones of praise and encouragement, wonder, pride, and celebration—even the bandages and ice pack over well-earned wounds. And, not long after, the child forgets ever learning to ride the bike as he and his friends tear off at dizzying speeds to explore a much-expanded world.

(I wonder why Jesus didn't insist that Peter try one more time?)

Jesus meets Peter's panic with an outstretched arm and the gentle encouragement of a loving parent. "Look! You transcended the deep. You see, your faith can move mountains! Why did you doubt?" Indeed. Why do you doubt?

Perhaps Peter's failure opens the way for a deepening of faith more secure than success might have offered. The loving Presence of the One lifts him from his terror. Peter may not remember how he walked on water, but he will remember how he was saved.

John van de Laar
http://www.sacredise.com/

Matthew 14

That night of the storm was a turning point for the disciples. It's shrouded in mystery. The Greek words are ambiguous and the circumstances so chaotic that an objective, clinical explanation is impossible. But Matthew's goal is to be anything but clinical. There are far greater miracles at stake than people wandering about on the surface of the sea.

It's not that a miracle did not happen, only that we cannot state its nature with absolute certainty. What we can declare is that Matthew's purpose is to reveal Jesus as the new Moses fulfilling the promise of the new covenant in which God's law is written on human hearts and God's presence is enjoyed by all. Matthew has already revealed Jesus as the bringer of the fulfilled law in the Sermon on the Mount, and the giver of the new manna in feeding the crowds in the wilderness. Now, he shows Jesus leading his people to freedom through stormy waters. Jesus offers a far greater exodus than Moses—from death to God's unquenchable life.

We enter the story as the crowds have been fed and sent home. Jesus' disciples are sailing back across the lake, and Jesus finally has some solitude in which to grieve John the Baptist's death. But his time is cut short when his disciples are overwhelmed by a freak storm. Characteristically, Jesus lays aside his own grief to rescue his friends. This is the first miracle.

The storm at sea is a small reflection of the storm of grief that Jesus and his followers are facing. It is also a small prophecy of the greater storm of crucifixion to come. Jesus demonstrates what he will later promise—his presence is always with them, and he will always be there to rescue them.

The second miracle is the disciples' response of worship. This is the critical point toward which Matthew has been working. Jesus is not just a "new" Moses. He is Moses' God—not just a re-interpreter of the law, but the Law-giver. This begins the shift that will ultimately lead to Peter's declaration in Matthew 16.

The disciples do not yet understand what manner of God Jesus is. John's Gospel indicates that Jesus sends everyone away in order to avoid an attempt to make him king. His followers have a long way to go, and Peter will have to endure worse failures, before they are ready to follow a crucified Messiah. Yet it's the failures that make Peter so effective in the end, and lead him to be the first to include the Gentiles. He knows that God welcomes all, because he has sunk and been rescued.

Hungry crowds, stormy seas, failed disciples, and rough crosses cannot deter God's purpose of bringing all things to shared wholeness in Christ. We, too, will fail, face storms, and have to endure crosses. But Christ's presence and purpose remains—and it's our worship that reminds us of who sustains us and gives us life.

John Wesley's Notes on the Bible
http://www.ccel.org/ccel/wesley/notes.txt

Matthew 14:30

"He was afraid"—Though he had been used to the sea, and was a skilful swimmer. But so it frequently is. When grace begins to act, the natural courage and strength are withdrawn.

August 17
10th Sunday after Pentecost (Proper 15)

Genesis 45:1-15; Psalm 133; Romans 11:1-2a, 29-32;
Matthew 15:(10-20), 21-28; Isaiah 56:1, 6-8; Psalm 67

Cameron Howard

Genesis 45

If Genesis 37 is the introduction to the Joseph novella, then Genesis 45 is the climax of the narrative. In the parlance of television makeover shows, this portion of the story is the "big reveal." When Joseph's brothers arrive in Egypt, he recognizes them, but they do not recognize him (Gen 42:7). He has been interacting with them ever since, and we readers—the "audience"—are in on the secret.

This passage is particularly striking in its contrast between Joseph's verbosity and the brothers' silence. Joseph has had time to process this turn of events. He has everything figured out, and he is quick to explain it all to them (Gen 45:4-13). The brothers, however, are terrified (v. 3). After Joseph's long speech, his weeping, and his embrace, "his brothers were finally able to talk to him" (v. 15).

One can hardly overemphasize the power Joseph holds over his brothers. He has been exercising that power in manipulative ways: insisting they bring Benjamin to Egypt and planting stolen goods in order to keep him there (Gen 42–44). A spontaneous outbreak of compassion and generosity was not Joseph's first response. But when Judah describes how deeply hurt their father will be if he does not see Benjamin again, Joseph's power play collapses. It is the discussion of Jacob's grief (Gen 44:18-34), not any obvious love or forgiveness Joseph has for his brothers, that finally dissolves Joseph's will to continue the deception.

The story is a poignant reminder of the interconnectedness of our human relationships. Joseph may have little personal regard for his brothers, but to manipulate them risks hurting Jacob, whom he loves profoundly. Acting not out of love but out of his brokenness, which mirrors our own, Joseph risks breeding more pain, even for the one he most highly regards.

John Wesley's Notes on the Bible
http://www.ccel.org/ccel/wesley/notes.txt

Genesis 45:5

"Be not grieved or angry with yourselves"—Sinners must grieve, and be angry with themselves for their sins; yea, though God, by his power, bring good out of them, for that is no thanks to the sinner: but true penitents should be greatly affected with it, when they see God bringing good out of evil Though we must not with this consideration extenuate our own sins, and so take off the edge of our repentance; yet it may do well thus to extenuate the sins of others, and so take off the edge of our angry resentments.

174

Julie Craig
http://winsomelearnsome.com

Matthew 15

What perhaps we all should do, at least briefly, to more fully understand what has happened out here on the street in front of this woman and the disciples is to give ourselves the dog's eye view. No matter what we know about the Canaanites, or about what has happened to Jesus previously in this Gospel, the sting of Jesus' comment to the woman is very real. We expect as much from the disciples—to them the woman must have seemed like an annoying insect, buzzing around them, asking for a favor, for healing of her daughter; all the while she is a Canaanite—a pagan, and a woman to boot. When Jesus does not immediately answer her pleas, the disciples assume that she is annoying him as much as she is annoying them, and they try to come to Jesus' rescue and get rid of her.

But then Jesus says what is perhaps the most troubling and puzzling thing we overhear him say in all of the Gospels—"It is not fair to take the children's food and throw it to the dogs" (v. 26 NRSV). In essence, calling her the dog, and we know instinctively that it is not a nice thing, not a very Jesus-like thing he just said. You see, dogs in the ancient Near East were not the fluffy poodles and sleek wiemaraners we have as our pets today. Dogs had a job to do in the tribes and towns and villages, however. Dogs ate the filth. They were the garbage collectors. You kept them around because you needed them, but you certainly didn't feed them, or touch them, or care for them. Dogs were on their own.

The woman, for her part, does not try to deny to Jesus that she is in exactly the position she is in. She knows who she is, and knows that to the disciples and anyone else standing around, she is the dog in that situation. A foreigner, a woman, and someone with trouble in her family. There are plenty of reasons for her to be excluded from the crowd that Jesus is talking to. And in the world of the Gospel of Matthew, a main focus of this new fledgling church is the issue of inclusion and exclusion. Who is in? Who is out? These seem to be the most important questions that Matthew wants to answer.

Some would say the miracle in this story is the healing of the woman's daughter. But if you look a little deeper into the story the miracle is that this woman approaches Jesus in the first place. From the dog's eye view—the point of view of this woman—we see that she has given up all that she has to come to this person she has heard about, this traveling Jewish teacher who—rumor has it—heals the sick and feeds the hungry; she has laid everything she is and everything she has at Jesus' feet.

Liz Crumlish
http://somethingtostandon.blogspot.co.uk/

Matthew 15

In my family, there were two maiden aunts who lived together. They were the family matriarchs. They kept the family together and whenever anyone was in need, Aunt Isobel and Aunt Lizzie were the first called on. They would always help out. From scrubbing floors to dishing out good advice, theirs was the place to go.

Eventually they both died and we assisted with the task of clearing the home they had shared. It seemed that everywhere you looked in the house, there were jars and tins and boxes of sugar. I don't think either of them actually used much sugar, but their cupboards were full of it. Because they had lived through the days of rationing that accompanied World War 2. They knew what it was to do without. And so, when times were good, they bought sugar. They would never be short of that again!

Perhaps that sounds just the tiniest bit eccentric, but these weren't two old, eccentric ladies. They were down-to-earth, hard-working ordinary folk. But folk who had known scarcity. And they bought into the idea that it might happen again. You just could never know. So they set about ensuring that, should sugar rationing ever come back, they would have plenty—and so would their family.

Walter Brueggemann suggests that the story of Joseph describes a pattern that is often perpetrated in our world economy today: an economy of scarcity (see *Collected Sermons of Walter Brueggemann* [Louisville: Westminster John Knox, 2011], 164–67). It went against all that Joseph and his people believed in, to imagine that their God would not continue to provide abundantly for them as had been the case for centuries. Yet Joseph bought into this idea of scarcity—and so his own kith and kin were uprooted and impoverished and became subject to the whims of a superpower.

The Gospel reading paired with this Old Testament story perhaps continues that theme. Can Jesus really be saying no to this poor woman who has asked for healing, not even for herself but for her daughter? Is he saying that God's mercy and God's love are not just for a particular people in a particular place—but for all people everywhere? Or was Jesus' hesitation drawing out the learning opportunity for the disciples, making it clear that this was a new regime in which God's love, God's healing, God's forgiveness, God's abundant grace—is for everyone?

All of us can so easily be seduced into believing that love is scarce, that resources are limited, that giving somehow diminishes us. And yet, the good news that Jesus came to live is that God's blessing multiplies whatever we have to offer—and, in God's purpose, there will always be enough. It's a lesson that we have to learn and a promise that we have to grasp hold of. For unless we take risks, we cannot find security. And unless we love we cannot know God's extravagance.

Safiyah Fosua

Matthew 15

This discussion about things clean and unclean follows a skirmish between Jesus and the Pharisees over ritual hand-washing. Surely there had been a time when all (or most) of the Pharisees' rituals brought them closer to God and pointed to an inward reality. But from Jesus' comments, it appears that these rituals had lost their ability to effect change in the lives of those who were observing them.

This episode raises questions about the observance of rituals in the twenty-first-century church. What makes rituals meaningful, and when should they be observed? Ideally, rituals are a dramatization of what has already happened in our lives, or what we pray will happen in our lives. Seen in this light, baptism, in certain Christian traditions, is a dramatization of an inward reality—the presence of God's saving grace in our lives through Jesus Christ. In worship, bowed heads or kneeling express humility and submission to God. Ritual does its best work when the worshiping community understands why it engages in ritual action, or when the action itself suggests the reason.

By the time of Christ, Pharisee rituals had changed from an aid to worship and discipleship into a tool of power and control. The Pharisees used their rituals to judge others. Those who did them well were in and those who did them poorly (or ignored their rituals altogether) were excluded and condemned.

Jesus' harsh commentary calls us back to the reason for the ritual in the first place—spiritual transformation. God is looking not at what goes into the mouth, but at what comes out of the mouth. The most important thing is not process or ritual, it is result.

Todd Weir
http://bloomingcactus.typepad.com/

Matthew 15

Think of the spectacle of seeing the Canaanite woman throw herself at the feet of Jesus. To even approach Jesus, she has broken several taboos. She is a Gentile approaching a Jew, a woman approaching a group of men in a gender-separated society, an outsider Canaanite. Maybe now we can better understand Christ's original response, when he says, "Let the children be fed first (referring to Jews) for it is not fair to give the children's bread to the dogs" (v. 26, paraphrased). There is no getting around the fact that Jesus has just "dissed" her. Jews considered dogs to be unclean scavengers. Every reference to dogs in the Bible is negative.

For a moment she is turned away by a great spiritual leader, which must feel like being turned away by God. That's why it is so hard when our feelings get hurt in church. We expect to experience the sacred grace of God when we come to church or approach a minister, and if we are hurt or overlooked for the moment, it affects our core spirit. Where else will we find the sacred in our lives? This is what disturbs us in this episode. How can Jesus compare anyone to a dog or say a thing like that? This story hits us in a place of fear that maybe God finds us to be really annoying. We don't belong, we don't deserve the bread, others are more important.

The great thing about the Canaanite woman is that she seems unfazed by everything working against her and quips back, "Yes, but even the dogs under the table deserve the crumbs" (v. 27, paraphrased). This woman understands the power of God's grace, for she believes so much that she knows a crumb from Jesus will suffice. And imagine, she isn't even on the church membership rolls! This is the only place I can find in the Gospels where someone wins a theological argument with Jesus. He tied the wisest scholars in knots, but not this woman. Maybe that's what Jesus wants her to do. If he had just healed her daughter at her request, the disciples would have been appalled and probably missed the point, but it is more dramatic to lose a theological argument to a Gentile, then heal her daughter. This unnamed woman gives us a wonderful example of how to approach God with both humility and boldness, a grounded trust in God's grace despite all the human obstacles that stand in the way of relationship.

We come to the communion table as God's children. We are getting the bread on top of the table, not crumbs off the floor. When you receive this morsel of bread handed to you on a silver platter, do you know the power of what you hold in your hand? This bread is a gift of grace that says God has not overlooked you, so make some room beside you for the Canaanite woman.

August 24

11th Sunday after Pentecost (Proper 16)

Exodus 1:8–2:10; Psalm 124; Romans 12:1-8; Matthew 16:13-20; Isaiah 51:1-6; Psalm 138

Marci Auld Glass
www.marciglass.com

Exodus 1–2

I wonder if Pharaoh ever had second thoughts about killing the Hebrew people's boy babies instead of their girl babies. Because if you read this story, the men aren't much of a problem. They are slaves. They are brutally abused. They build things for Pharaoh.

The women cause all of the trouble. Shiphrah and Puah, the midwives, were so important to this story that their names are recorded. Pharaoh's own daughter's name doesn't get recorded. Neither do Moses' parents. But all these many years later, we can thank Shiphrah and Puah *by name* for refusing to abide by Pharaoh's command. When summoned before him, and asked why the Hebrew boy children keep showing up on the playground, they make up a story and start talking about "lady parts," and you know how Pharaoh doesn't really want to hear about *that*. So they continue to go about their resistance to Pharaoh's infanticide policy. And God blesses them for quietly working for justice, no matter what their instructions had been.

But Pharaoh wants what he wants. And so the lives of all boy children are at risk. Moses' mother and father are in a bind. They have this beautiful son, but they cannot parent him. He will be thrown in the crocodile-infested river. They will likely face punishment as well.

His mother hears the command of Pharaoh to throw the child into the Nile and comes up with an idea. Perhaps she trusts that God would not have blessed her with this boy child if there weren't a plan for him. Perhaps she is so desperate with love for her baby that setting him loose on a small raft seems like a good plan. Whatever the case, Moses' mother obeys the letter, if not the spirit, of Pharaoh's command, and casts her son into the river. See why I'm wondering if Pharaoh had second thoughts about which gender he should have killed?

Here the Bible gives us our first illustration of open adoption. Like a birth mother who realizes that she cannot parent the child she loves, Moses' mother sets him loose on the waters of God's beautiful and dangerous world and trusts that there is life for him. And she weeps as she watches that flimsy raft float down the mighty river and wonders if she made the right decision.

Moses' sister follows the little boat from the riverbank, and when Pharaoh's daughter pulls him out of the river, she helpfully offers to go find a wet nurse. So Moses' two mothers meet and work out a plan to keep this baby alive, in Pharaoh's own house. The text doesn't report any further conversation between them, but I am certain there were, at least, knowing glances, a comforting hand on the shoulder, and assurances that life would continue, even when death seemed the only option.

NOTE: "Girl Problems" by Marci Auld Glass (http://marciglass.com/2012/04/30/girl-problems/).

Teri Peterson
http://clevertitlehere.blogspot.com

Exodus 1–2

A new king arose who didn't remember Joseph, and along with short historical memory this king has a taste for power and may be a little prone to anxiety. When he looks at census numbers and discovers that ethnic Hebrews outnumber ethnic Egyptians, he sees a recipe for trouble. He imagines the scenario where this all goes horribly wrong and manufactures a political crisis—so easy to do, after all—that he uses to spread his own fear through the whole nation: What if? What if? Soon the Egyptians hate, dread, fear their neighbors, so being ruthless is easy. Plus, with enough effort, maybe they'll begin to think of themselves the way we think of them—less than human.

But no. The spark of hope seems to grow stronger rather than weaker, the Hebrews continue to multiply and to grow. Desperate measures must be taken—Pharaoh orders the first biblically recorded ethnic cleansing campaign. And, of course, he calls on the women, the keepers of life.

These are no ordinary women—these are midwives. These women are charged with bringing life into the world, and they aren't about to follow an order to turn life into death, especially since they serve the God of Life, even Abundant Life. So they continue doing their jobs, just as before, bringing life and love into the world even if it is a world of ruthless oppression. They continue to fan the flame of hope, a small light in an increasingly dark time. They refuse to be intimidated by a manufactured crisis, and they blatantly disobey Pharaoh—the earthly authority, who considers himself powerful even over life and death. Soon they end up in the throne room, answering questions.

My favorite part of this story is the midwives' answer to Pharaoh's question. "Why have you done this when I told you to kill them?" he asks. Shiphrah and Puah, faced with earthly power, don't apologize, plead for their lives, or appeal to religion or politics. They look Pharaoh in the eye and do the last thing we expect of nice, proper ladies—they lie! They tell their made-up story convincingly enough that they leave the palace free women, able to continue their lives and their important work.

Soon their work leads infant Moses' mother and sister straight into Pharaoh's own household, through the compassionate princess. The hands of women are resourceful and strong, their wills are defiant and ingenious. Well-behaved women rarely make history, while these women allowed God's history to continue to be made.

Five women who defy expectations, politics, and fear, who choose to live with a little spark of hope rather than giving in to the darkness. Five women upon whose disobedience the entire future of God's people depends. Some with names long forgotten, some whose names live on in our collective memory. Five women who redeem an entire people with their courage in the face of power—because they live in the kingdom of God rather than the kingdom of fear, as an example for us all.

Julia Seymour
http://lutheranjulia.blogspot.com

Exodus 1–2

The story of the Hebrew midwives is a powerful one and worth considering in light of their motivations. Ancient Israelites do not believe in hell, a place of eternal punishment. So what spurs Shiphrah and Puah in their subversive actions? Why would they be afraid of God?

To be afraid of punishment, you have to know that you are doing the opposite of what is expected or commanded. Shiphrah and Puah know that God is about life, creating it, preserving it, flourishing life. God frowns on that which diminishes life and well-being. While the pharaoh may not know Joseph, the midwives know his story in their hearts. The knowledge of the providence of God through Joseph is enough to spur them on, both in choosing life and preventing death. The women of Israel know that the God of life offers blessing, and they try to put themselves and their children in the way of that blessing.

Without these women, the Hebrew people could have passed into a footnote of history. The only way that Moses exists, with a foot in two worlds, is through the bravery of the midwives, his mother, and his quick-thinking sister.

What would it look like for us to try to put ourselves in the way of God's blessing? What is the difference between choices for life and choices that prevent death? What would it mean to take seriously that we will be held accountable for our time, our talents, and our actions? Even knowing that we have been saved through Jesus Christ, we know that God is still working in us, still helping us to mature, and we know we are called to respond to that nurturing and shaping.

Shiphrah and Puah weren't necessarily thinking on the big scale. They were thinking about having to answer to God for what they had done, and they made a decision. Moses' mother wasn't thinking that her boy could save the Hebrew people, she looked at his little red face and saw her beautiful boy and focused on that. Pharoah's daughter didn't necessarily have a subversive plan against her dad, but she wanted a child of her own and Miriam's quick thinking made it possible.

The actions for life by any of us may change the course of history. However, the answer that we shall have to account for all we have done and left undone should give us pause. In a world of busyness, what are we really doing with our time? Does our schedule reflect the grace we have received? Does it reveal decisions for life?

Natalie Sims
http://lectionarysong.blogspot.com

Exodus 1–2

The oppression and attempted genocide of the Israelites. The birth of Moses, his hiding and his adoption.

"God Weeps at Love Withheld" (Shirley Murray)—Pretty full-on lyrics of lamentation that some may find difficult to sing simply because of the horrors it names. In the context of this story, I think this is okay. This is a really powerful story, let's not water it down. Lyrics (search for "God weeps"; http://gbgm-umc.org/umw/assembly/prayer_service.html). For the service this links to, they used the words as a responsive prayer.

"A Mother Lined a Basket" (Mary Nelson Keithahn)—Quite a remarkable song about the risks we take in letting children go. Lyrics (http://www.hymnary.org/text/a_mother_lined_a_basket).

"Inspired by Love and Anger" (John Bell / Graham Maule)—Strong song to a very familiar Celtic air (Salley Gardens). A big favourite. Lyrics (http://www.beswick.info/rclresources/L3B97Ser.htm; scroll down).

"O God of Every Nation" (William Watkins Reid)—Powerful words seeking God's redemption of the world. Can be sung to LLANGLOFFAN or PASSION CHORALE, both very familiar hymn tunes. Lyrics and a tune sample (http://www.oremus.org/hymnal/o/o175.html). Highly recommended, but not all sources are inclusive.

"Pharaoh" (Richard Thompson)—This song is about the modern Pharaoh, and our slavery to money. The recording I have of this is by June Tabor, which is quite menacing. Also see the composer, Richard Thompson (http://www.youtube.com/watch?v=KRtTkBdATS0). Oh, one more version, very Celtic, from The House Band (http://www.youtube.com/watch?v=1ctVMklOGGY&feature=related).

"Goodness Is Stronger Than Evil" (Desmond Tutu / Iona Community)—Words from Archbishop Desmond Tutu. "Victory is ours, victory is ours, through him who loves us." Some congregations change the last line to "Compassion is ours, compassion is ours . . ." It depends on the context in which you sing it, I suppose. Sound sample (http://www.giamusic.com/mp3s/5671.mp3). This could be a good theme song over the next few weeks.

"When Israel Was in Egypt's Land" (African American Spiritual)—Traditional song, quite familiar, and great to sing over the next few weeks.

David Lose

Romans 12; Matthew 16

This is Peter's moment. Jesus is right to declare that this insight is not something he figured out all by himself or had revealed by "flesh and blood" but that it came from God (Matt 16:17 NRSV). Flashes of insight and bursts of intense faith are like that—gifts of grace that come from God for which we can only give thanks. Peter seems to have been both keenly attuned to such movements of the Spirit and bold to declare them. He was by all accounts strong-willed, vocal, even impetuous. Little wonder, then, that when Jesus makes the question about his identity more personal, Peter is the one who boldly gives voice to the great confession of Matthew's Gospel.

Of course, this same depth of emotion and quickness to speak sometimes lands him in trouble. Not only will we see this next week, but time and again—whether on the mountain when Jesus is transfigured or at the Last Supper—Peter will speak with conviction and boldness, and those very qualities will land him in trouble.

But that's Peter. Actually, that's all of us. Our virtues and vices often come from the same source, and so we learn to value the one and compensate for the other; trying to eliminate our shortcomings would also stunt our strengths. Perhaps that's what Paul means by reminding us that we all have distinct gifts, given in different proportions (Rom 12:6). None of us has everything, and we all are a mixture of strengths and weaknesses, virtues and vices. And so we need one another, for while there is no perfect Christian, we can together be the body of Christ in the world, working in complementary harmony for the sake of the gospel and the health of God's beloved world.

John Petty
http://progressiveinvolvement.com

Matthew 16

Who *do* the people say the Son of Man is? John the Baptist, Elijah, and Jeremiah are specifically named. The mention of John the Baptist is quite clear. His name is preceded by the Greek word *men,* which means "truly" or "certainly." This underlines Jesus' continuity with the ministry of John the Baptist. For his part, Elijah was the classic prophet, and, like Jesus, was from northern Israel.

Matthew adds "Jeremiah" (not mentioned in Mark or Luke). The inclusion of the "suffering prophet" makes sense. Jeremiah and Jesus have some important connections. Both opposed the religious and political establishment of their day, and both suffered for it.

Jesus asks, "And what do *you* think?" Peter answers, "You are the Christ, the son of the living God" (v. 15-16 author's translation). In the first use of *makarios* since the Beatitudes, Jesus calls Peter "blessed." (Don't get too excited. He calls him "satan" in just a few verses.) Jesus also identifies him as "Simon, son of Jonah" (v. 17a). Matthew's use of *Jonah* is an image of resurrection. As Jonah was three days in the whale, so Jesus would be three days in the earth. To call Simon Peter the "son of Jonah" was another way of calling him a "son of the resurrection."

With eyes informed by the resurrection, Peter is able to make his confession. Jesus says as much when he says that "flesh and blood" (v. 17b NRSV) has not informed Peter, but rather direct revelation from God.

On this basis, Jesus gives Peter another name and title, that of "Petros" ("Peter" or "rock," v. 18a). This recalls Old Testament figures, such as Abram and Jacob, who were likewise given new names. As God can give new names, so can Jesus. Thus, Matthew affirms again Jesus' equality with God.

The word *ekklesia*—"church" (v. 18b)—literally means "the called-out gathering." It is an eschatological image that recalls the worshiping community at Mount Zion at the end of time. Precisely because it is an end-times image, and because Jesus identifies the church as "*my* church," death has no power over it. "Church" *assumes* resurrection.

Hades was the Greek god of the "underworld" (v. 18c). Jesus asserts that its "gates" will not prevail against the church. We often take this to mean that the assaults of hell cannot doom the church. *Gates,* however, are a stationary image. They do not attack; they defend. In the power of the resurrection, the church does not defend against hell, but rather attacks and defeats it.

Why the so-called "messianic secret" (see v. 20)? As of yet, we know only part of the story. We have heard authoritative teaching from Jesus—the Sermon on the Mount!—and have been told of his miracles and majestic power. We have not yet been through his death and resurrection. Then his authority and ministry will be affirmed and ratified by God in the most powerful way possible. Until then, better not to say anything at all than to tell only half the story.

Peter Woods

Matthew 16

Probably the most famous sculpture by Auguste Rodin (1840–1917) is *The Thinker,* which depicts a seated man, deep in thought or meditation, his chin resting on his right hand. What most people don't know is that this stand-alone piece was first sculpted by Rodin as part of a larger commission titled *The Gates of Hell.* Rodin worked on the project for thirty-seven years until his death. The piece is now part of the Rodin Sculpture Garden at Stanford University.

Critics speculate as to the intended identity of the Thinker who broods over the gates, much as the evil Lord Sauron broods over the gates of Mordor in J. R. R. Tolkien's *Lord of the Rings.* Is the thinker Adam, Danté (on whose "Inferno" Rodin based *The Gates of Hell*), or could it be Rodin himself? We are left to choose our interpretation.

Simon Peter wasn't much of a thinker. He was far too spontaneous and impulsive a person to give considered and thought-through responses. So when Jesus, surrounded by the sculpture and iconography of Roman Caesarea Philippi, asked his disciples who they thought he was, it was Peter who blurted, "You are the Messiah, the Son of the living God" (v. 16 NRSV).

Jesus recognized this spontaneous insight as inspired, and it earned Peter the keys and the commission as "Kingdom Gatekeeper"; secured against even the Gates of Darkness and Shadows.

If the church of modern times has a recurrent failing, it is that we over-think everything. Careful and considerate of public image, market share, orthodox doctrine, and, not to forget, treasury implications, we remain forever frozen like *The Thinker,* puzzling what to do.

That's not the way to open the kingdom gates. They seem to spring their locks at inspired spontaneity.

John Wesley's Notes on the Bible
http://www.ccel.org/ccel/wesley/notes.txt

Matthew 16:18

"Shall not prevail against it"—Not against the Church universal, so as to destroy it. And they never did. There hath been a small remnant in all ages.

Todd Weir
http://bloomingcactus.typepad.com/

Matthew 16

> "You are Peter, and on this rock I will build my church…I will give you the keys of the kingdom of heaven, and whatever you bind on earth will be bound in heaven, and whatever you loose on earth will be loosed in heaven." (vv. 18-19 NRSV)

In hindsight, it is easy to miss that this bold pronouncement would seem ludicrous to an eavesdropper of the moment. Does Jesus really have such authority to give this kind of power, and if so why would he give it to a fisherman? What would make Peter worthy of this trust? As the world looks at people, net-menders are seldom world-changers. He is not a man of wealth, learning, or great intellect. Peter is the first disciple to speak the word *messiah* out loud, but wouldn't they all have been thinking this by now? In just a few verses Peter is going to rebuke the man he just called messiah, and is told, "Get behind me, Satan!" (v. 23 NRSV). Does power so quickly corrupt even fishermen?

I can only speculate on what Jesus saw in Peter. If I were to paste all the scriptures together in one story, Peter's strength is his sense of urgency, his ability to see the importance of the moment and then act boldly. He is often criticized for rash words, such as protesting his courage at the Last Supper. But then what memorable religious leader did not have a few rash moments? Luther, Calvin, or a few Popes? Peter was the first bold enough to speak the word *messiah,* the one who would get out of the boat and try to walk on the water to Jesus; he drew the sword to defend Jesus in Gethsemane, and though he denied Jesus three times that night, there is no record of other disciples trying to follow Jesus to see what happened.

Peter's failings did not stop him from trying again, or rob him of his urgency and boldness. He accepts forgiveness and becomes a great preacher, not fearing authority again. As Gentiles were drawn to Christ, Peter listened to his dream and saw that God showed no partiality between Jew and Gentile. He courageously welcomed the centurion, loosening the gates to the Kingdom of Heaven to one of Caesar's own. This urgency, seeing the import of the moment and acting with boldness and compassion, is what the church is built upon; and the kind of leadership it needs, from pulpit and pew.

August 31
12th Sunday after Pentecost (Proper 17)

Exodus 3:1-15; Psalm 105:1-6, 23-26, 45c; Romans 12:9-21;
Matthew 16:21-28; Jeremiah 15:15-21; Psalm 26:1-8

Peter Woods

Exodus 3; Psalm 26; Matthew 16

In the vicinity of that mystical mountain Horeb that has never been accurately located, Moses encounters the primordial God, who declares his name in a gesture that hints at vulnerability, for to have someone's name is to be able to exercise influence over them. Moses has to turn toward a burning bush that must have been blazing really brightly to get the attention of a shepherd squinting into the desert sun!

Centuries later, the story of our faith tells us, this same God who wants to be known was found walking among us, in Jesus of Nazareth. Over the centuries, the relationship between the primordial presence and people had grown as God revealed more and more of God's relational and vulnerable nature.

This vulnerability, revealed at Horeb, now draws Jesus to the cross, to which Peter objects. "God forbid!" he mutters. "God forbid"? Peter, this is God acting! No wonder Jesus tells Satan to get behind him!

I have never seen Satan in any form, but I do know my shadow. It is that part of me where oppositional energy against any good thing resides. I call it my cockroach self, for it scuttles away from the light. Could this be the "Satan" Jesus wants behind him, the oppositional energy he hears in Peter's words?

I have discovered that the only way I can get my shadow "behind me" is by turning to face the light.

The cross and suffering seemed like darkness to Peter. To Jesus, who could trust beyond the darkness of death and destruction, it was the Holocaust face of God.

"For your steadfast love is before my eyes, / and I walk in faithfulness to you" (Ps 26:3 NRSV).

John Wesley's Notes on the Bible
http://www.ccel.org/ccel/wesley/notes.txt

Exodus 3:2

"And the angel of the Lord appeared to him"—It was an extraordinary manifestation of the divine glory; what was visible was produced by the ministry of an angel, but he heard God in it speaking to him. "In a flame of fire"—To shew that God was about to bring terror and destruction to his enemies, light and heat to his people, and to display his glory before all. "And the bush burned, and yet was not consumed"—An emblem of the church now in bondage in Egypt, burning in the brick-kilns, yet not consumed; cast down, but not destroyed.

Carolyn Winfrey Gillette
http://www.carolynshymns.com/

God, the Mountains Tell Your Glory

God, the mountains tell your glory, lifting praise to you above!
In your Word, each mountain story shows your presence and your love.
Noah built as you commanded; soon the waters swirled around.
Those you saved, Lord, safely landed; you set them on mountain ground.

Lord, when Moses was returning to the mountain that he knew,
There a bush was brightly burning. There it was he heard from you.
Later Moses felt your presence; in the heights he knew your grace.
He brought down the Ten Commandments from your holy mountain place.

Christ, you taught upon a mountain, showing us God's kingdom view.
In the heights when you were praying, God's own glory shone on you.
Climbing to a quiet garden, in your grief and faith you cried.
On a hill for our own pardon, you, O Lord, were crucified.

Thank you now for blue-green mountains, red-brown mesas, high peaks, too.
Here may we enjoy creation, know your presence, learn from you.
Here may we sing out your glory, hear your call and find your grace.
Risen Christ, we'll tell your story, from these heights to every place.

NOTES
Biblical references: Genesis 6–8; Exodus 3; 19–20; Matthew 5–7; 17:1-3; 26:36-46
Tune: AUSTRIAN HYMN 8.7.8.7 D ("Glorious Things of Thee Are Spoken"), Franz Joseph Haydn, 1797
Alternate Tune: ABBOT'S LEIGH 8.7.8.7 D ("God Is Here!") by Cyril Vincent Taylor, 1941

Paul Nuechterlein
http://girardianlectionary.net/

Romans 12

At the heart of Paul's message of grace in Romans 5:8-9, many translators attribute wrath to God by adding "*God's,*" even though it does not appear in the original Greek:

> But God shows his love for us, because while we were still sinners Christ died for us. So, now that we have been made righteous by his blood, we can be even more certain that we will be saved from God's wrath through him.

This action by translators is repeated in all major translations (except KJV) in Romans 12:19 as well: "Leave room for *God's* wrath" (emphasis added). Yet Paul's ethical exhortation throughout Romans 12–13 is rooted in his theology of a God who has loved us even while we were enemies (5:8-10) and not a God of wrath. Romans in its entirety shows the righteousness of God's unconditional love manifested in the lives of both Jesus and his followers. After beginning his letter with a thesis about "God's wrath" (1:18a), I believe that Paul subsequently uses the word *orgè* (*wrath*) alone numerous times to subtly rework "God's wrath" as a function of human idolatry.

In *The Deliverance of God* (Grand Rapids: Eerdmans, 2009), Douglas Campbell adds crucial support to my thesis. He maintains that the words "God's wrath" in 1:18 aren't directly Paul's, but the viewpoint of an opposing Teacher. Using the Greco-Roman rhetorical strategy of Diatribe against the Teacher, Paul must speak his opponent's view into the text in order to speak against it. Campbell contends that Romans 1:18-32 is Paul's *opponent's* voice, appearing without markers because letters were written for oral performance. Paul would have trained the reader to distinguish the opponent's voice from his own voice of rebuttal, which begins at 2:1 (Campbell, 530–47).

Several verses into his rebuttal Paul says, "But by your hard and impenitent heart you are storing up wrath for yourself on the day of [human] wrath, when God's righteous judgment will be revealed" (2:5 NRSV). Paul says "wrath" in his own voice because the most crucial consequence of human idolatry is the wrath we humans inflict in the name of our gods. God's righteous judgment will be revealed as vastly different: a love reaching out in grace as a free gift in faith (3:21-26) even to sinners (5:8-10). Those not living in the faithfulness of Christ—revealing an unconditionally loving and wrath*less* God—will live in faithfulness to the false gods of human wrath. On the day of (human) wrath we will either seek the righteous, forgiving, nonviolent judgment of God in Jesus; or be handed over to our own wrathful, violent judgments upon one another and the wrathful gods we use to justify them.

In the cross, God reveals power as a nonviolent love that suffers—never inflicts—violence, which manifested itself Easter morning as the very power of Life behind Creation. Living by faithfulness to God's nonviolent power of love trusts that the power of wrathful human violence can never ultimately defeat God's power of Life.

Thom Shuman
http://lectionaryliturgies.blogspot.com/

easier

it's a whole lot
   easier
to lose my
    cross,
than to lose my
  life

to leave it propped
   up against the corner
of the closet, dust
   bunnies sleeping
   at its feet;

to ignore it
   standing on the coffee
table, looking out the front
    window, its cow eyes
   brimming with tears,
   as i pull away from
the curb;

to simply reply, 'i can't
remember the last time
   i saw it,' when
   i'm asked, 'whatever
happened to your cross?'

but

each morning, it puts
   Good
  into my hands,
   closing my fingers tight
    over it, whispering,
    'don't let go; don't ever
    let go.'

it tapes a picture of
   evil
    to my bathroom mirror,
so i will know it
   when i see it,
and stand up to
   it;

it spends each lonely day
  at the loom,
   weaving the yarns
labeled hope, love,
   patience, perseverance
    into that community
  which helps me to
  bear what is mine.

David Lose

Matthew 16

We all have, I believe, a picture of God that we carry around with us. These pictures are, by and large, both unconscious and unvoiced. But they're there, shaping our expectations and actions and surfacing only when they are called into question.

This is what happened in "Part 2" of the story of Peter's great confession. For while Peter recognized Jesus as Messiah, he didn't understand what kind of Messiah Jesus must be. Perhaps he was looking for another King David. Perhaps he wanted someone to lead a rebellion. Perhaps he longed for a champion to chase the Romans away. We don't know for sure. All we know is that what he definitely did not expect was a weak, vulnerable Messiah who was going to end up crucified as a criminal. So great was the offense of this, so contrary was it to his expectation—to his picture of God and God's Messiah—that he couldn't even hear the second part of Jesus' predictions, the part about being raised again.

I don't think we can blame Peter. Very often we also want a God of strength and power to make things right in the world and in our lives. Fortunately, neither Peter nor we get the God we *want*. Instead, we get the God we *need*. We get, that is, a God who will not remain in heaven, aloof from our suffering, but rather will abandon all pretext of glory in order to take on our lot and our life. This God favors mercy over strength, forgiveness over judgment, and grace and vulnerability over power and glory. This God not only understands us but also loves us. And, lest we forget, this God also is raised on the third day, promising that at the end of our struggles is peace.

September 7
13th Sunday after Pentecost (Proper 18)

Exodus 12:1-14; Psalm 149; Romans 13:8-14; Matthew 18:15-20; Ezekiel 33:7-11; Psalm 119:33-40

Peter Woods

Exodus 12; Matthew 18

"Okay, Preacher. We have a problem here."
"This is Preacher. Say again, please."
"Uh, Preacher, we've had a problem."
(adapted from Apollo 13 communications, April 13, 1970)

In the dynamic process of communicating our experiences of God we tell stories. These stories explain why things are the way they are: stories of our founders—how they coped with crises, triumphed or failed—stories justifying our present traditions. Stories are our common vernacular.

The Hebrews told stories about their formation as a nation and culture. They told of a dialogue between God and Moses. Did this communication happen as recorded? Did God really want all that blood and mutton?...Preacher, we have a problem.

Storytelling continued for centuries. People close to the significant events relayed and recorded what happened. As the stories passed down, they picked up layers. These accretions were attempts to justify present actions by claiming they originated by instruction of the founders.

The Gospel records Jesus giving instructions on church discipline at a time when there was no church. In the narrative he damns unrepentant members to be treated like "Gentiles and tax-collectors," the very people he ministers to. Furthermore he suggests that coalitions of church leaders can act unilaterally as long as they have a quorum. Did Jesus really say that?...Preacher, we have a problem.

As the story of God in human experience continues to unfold, we will continue to tell one another the stories of God. There are times when we will baulk at the blood and the Jesus Seminar will blackball the text we are telling.

Does that mean we should quit? The Apollo 13 astronauts didn't. They applied their minds, and duct tape! They put square boxes into round holes and survived. Perhaps we "Wordonauts" can do the same?

Dan Clendenin
http://journeywithjesus.net

Exodus 12; Romans 13

I recently read *Dietrich Bonhoeffer's Letters and Papers from Prison* (N.J.: Princeton, 2011) edited by Martin Marty. Bonhoeffer (1906–1945) was a Lutheran pastor who was imprisoned for his resistance to the Nazis, including a plot to assassinate Hitler. After two years in prison, and just three weeks before the war ended, he was hanged at dawn on April 9, 1945.

The original 1951 German edition has the provocative title *Resistance and Submission*. It comes from a question Bonhoeffer asked in prison: "I have often wondered here where we are to draw the line between necessary resistance to 'fate,' and equally necessary submission" (Marty, 4). What does resisting fate and evil powers mean? What does submitting to God's providence look like? Should a Christian will harm to her nation for the sake of the gospel? Can one wish for national victory if it destroys the church or other nations?

Exodus suggests that emancipation for Israel meant subjugation for Egypt. Today we might say that the oppressed became the new oppressor, except that in this narrative revenge was the act of God.

What we should wish for every person and nation comes from this week's epistle. Paul borrows a passage from the Hebrew Old Testament to instruct the earliest followers of Jesus: "Love your neighbor as yourself" (Rom 13:9 = Lev 19:18). The only debt we should carry, he says, is the never-ending debt to love your fellow human being. Loving your neighbor fulfills any and every other divine command, for genuine love does no harm to its neighbor. We are to love not only our neighbor but even our enemy (Matt 5:43-48).

As a matter of practice, though, it's scary to think what our world would be like if brave people like Bonhoeffer didn't risk guilt to resist evil. He never justified his actions. In his *Ethics* he wrote:

> When a man takes guilt upon himself in responsibility, and no responsible man can avoid this, he imputes this guilt to himself and no one else; he answers for it....Before other men [he] is justified by necessity; before himself he is acquitted by his conscience, but before God he hopes only for mercy. (trans. Neville Horton Smith [N.Y.: Touchstone, paperback 1995], 244)

And so Bonhoeffer's question resonates today. How do we resist the evil forces of fate while submitting to the good providence of God?

David Lose

Romans 13; Matthew 18

It's easy to rush to the good stuff in Matthew's passage: whatever we bind on earth is bound in heaven, and whatever we agree upon God will do (18:18-19). But trust me, that's not the most important part of this passage. The most important part is the difficult but essential truth that community—real community in Christ—is hard. Real community demands that we confront one another in love, that we speak the truth to one another in love, that we be willing to accompany one another through difficulty and disagreement . . . all in love.

That's what Paul speaks about, too. All of God's law—the gift of knowing what is right and wrong that we may tend one another's well-being—is summed up in a commandment that is as clear and simple as it is challenging: "Love your neighbor as yourself" (Rom 13:9).

That's why I think that Jesus was not simply laying out a formula by which to resolve conflict. It's rarely that easy. Different conflicts—and different contexts—will invite different methods of resolution. What's clear, however, is the need to regard one another in love so as to keep the well-being of all in the forefront.

Why is that so difficult? The obvious answer is because of our sinfulness. But it's also more than that, as we need to recognize that we have little practice in demonstrating love during times of disagreement. We live in a culture that is far quicker to rush to judgment, preferring polarized positions and the rhetoric of blame and accusation than speaking truth in love. For this reason we will need to practice patience, practice forbearance, and practice love. But if we do . . . what, then, can we not accomplish in the life and love of the Father?

Ann Scull
http://seedstuff.blogspot.com

Listening Song

Keb Mo, ***"Just Like You"*** on *Just Like You* (New York: Epic, 1996). This song goes very well with the Gospel reading.

Call to Worship

Jan Brind and Tessa Wilkinson, *"All God's People,"* in *Crafts for Creative Worship* (Norich: Canturbury Press, 2009), 205–6. This goes well with the Romans reading. The activity is for the northern hemisphere, but I am sure those of us in the southern hemisphere could think of something appropriate: spring petals, for example?

Film Clip

The Day Is Near. This goes really well with the Romans reading—it's from the Work of the People, http://www.theworkofthepeople.com (accessed April 16, 2012). The clips are reasonably priced and they are well worth it.

Drama

"No Thumping Whatsoever," Verena Johnson (ed.), *Mega Drama 2* (Adelaide: Open Book, 2001), 21–22. This drama is based on the Gospel reading and is set out as a puppet play but works just as well using people.

Story

Kevin Johnson, *"Don't Hire a Hit Man,"* in *Could Someone Wake Me up Before I Drool on the Desk?* (Minneapolis, Minn.: Bethany House Publishers, 1995), 49–50. This is based on the Gospel reading and aimed at teens, but it adapts very well for adults as well—just make the story a little more generic.

Discussion

"Romans 13:15-18." After reading Romans and the Gospel, divide into groups to discuss together and make a list together of the means by which a Christian community can live in harmony.

Quotation

"Do It Anyway." Written originally by Dr. Kent M. Keith and adapted by Mother Teresa, these words connect so well to the readings for today. You can find the original and the adapted words at http://prayer foundation.org/mother_teresa_do_it_anyway.htm (accessed April 16, 2012).

Adult Responses

This, of course, will work only for those in the southern hemisphere, but I am sure northern hemispherians can adapt. Give everybody a piece of spring blossom. Tell everyone that the blossom is a sign of spring, new life, and new growth. In the silence, encourage people to think of a broken relationship in their lives and encourage them to ask God to show them how to repair it.

Give everyone a small piece of self-hardening modelling clay (1cm cube is big enough for this) and

1. Ask people to mould their feelings about someone they disagree with in their faith community.
2. Ask them to mould the clay back into a ball.
3. Ask them to mould the clay into a symbol of Jesus' love for them.
4. Encourage them to take home their symbol as an example of relationship.

Suzanne Guthrie
http://www.edgeofenclosure.org

"What You Bind on Earth" (Matthew 18)

I sometimes wonder if heaven, if there is a heaven, is created by our consciousness, our actions, our love, our self-sacrifice. "Whatever you bind on earth will be bound in heaven, and whatever you loose on earth will be loosed in heaven" (v. 18 NRSV). Our polluted, exploited earth begets a barren, poisoned heaven. Our humility and awe and cooperation with nature creates our paradise. Our war-making or peace-making here determines the state of being there. Our exclusion excludes us and our inclusion includes us all. If so, our actions, cooperation, sacrifices, and love bind and loosen consequences more far-reaching and vital than imagined. Even the smallest moral victories and heroics of daily life may link each of us to the unfolding plane of consciousness, unleashing forces of good and evil.

Here, then, is the war in heaven, not played out in some apocalyptic landscape with seven-headed dragons and mighty archangels fixed and bound forever in a static state of judgment. Rather, heaven evolves, co-created in the crucible of daily life with people closest to me. Every moral victory of humility and tenderness, every act of stretching my intellect to understand someone different from me, every effort to love my enemy, every prejudice painfully burned in the purgative fire of the Holy Spirit, lets loose the unfolding reality of universal consciousness. In this, I embrace the terrifying destiny of finding myself made in the image and likeness of God.

John van de Laar
http://www.sacredise.com/

Matthew 18

It is not surprising that Jesus, whose central commandment was to love one another, should offer a process for reconciliation. His teaching is common sense and is not new—it follows the Torah's laws of evidence in court. But, characteristically, Jesus goes much deeper than it appears at first.

This discourse comes immediately after the parable of the shepherd who leaves his flock to search for one lost sheep. Jesus' call to reconciliation, then, is less about "setting the other person straight" and more about seeking and finding one who may become lost. The call is to grace and compassion for anyone who has found a place in our community, no matter what they may do or become. Verse 17 could be taken to indicate that excommunication is sometimes necessary, until we remember that Jesus always sought to include "Gentiles and tax-collectors." So, even when relationships appear to have broken down irrevocably, there is to be no end to our striving for reconciliation.

Furthermore, it is easy to view evil as "out there" and threatening to us, which usually leads us to withdraw from the "evil" world, point judging fingers at the "sinners out there," and retreat into an insulated Christian compound. But Jesus' message reveals that evil also resides "in here"—in our own communities and hearts. We, too, sometimes find ourselves in service of evil and conflict, and we need others who will speak the truth to us and help us to be found by the grace and forgiveness of God and our community.

Finally, we must avoid the twin temptations of either turning to aggression or pretending that everything is fine without ever really addressing that which causes our relationships and communities to break down. We are called to peace and justice, but both require us to learn to do conflict well—refusing to become either violent or passive. Avoidance of conflict is not a Christian value. Doing conflict with concern for the other and in a peaceful, but active, attempt to turn our enemies into our friends—that is the way of Christ.

When we learn true reconciliation, we discover the magic of true community. We experience God's presence as never before, because we recognize that God's image is reflected even through our "enemies." We know that when two or three gather Christ is there, because we have suffered as Christ to create this community, and we have discovered Christ even in "the least." We also discover that prayer has a new power, because it becomes a shared asking for what brings life, healing, peace, and justice to the whole community (which includes the whole world).

If we will embrace Christ's journey into confrontation and reconciliation, and if we will recognize that we are never released from the quest to seek and win the "lost" (which will, at times, include us), then we will find that we are active participants in bringing a new world of truth-telling, justice, and peace into being.

John Wesley's Notes on the Bible
http://www.ccel.org/ccel/wesley/notes.txt

Matthew 18:15

"Tell it to the elders of the Church"—Lay the whole matter open before those who watch over yours and his soul. If all this avail not, have no farther intercourse with him, only such as thou hast with heathens. Can any thing be plainer? Christ does here as expressly command all Christians who see a brother do evil, to take this way, not another, and to take these steps, in this order, as he does to honour their father and mother. But if so, in what land do the Christians live? If we proceed from the private carriage of man to man, to proceedings of a more public nature, in what Christian nation are Church censures conformed to this rule?

Thom Shuman
http://lectionaryliturgies.blogspot.com/

Great Prayer of Thanksgiving

May God be with you!
And also with you!
People of God, open your hearts.
We open them to the One who feeds us with freedom and hope.
Children of God, sing songs of thanksgiving to the One who journeys with you.
We join our voices in praise to our loving God!

You spoke and liberated chaos, Holy God,
time marking the start of creation.
You watered earth with joy's tears,
planting seeds of hope and peace
so we might be fed by your heart.
Asked simply to be your children,
we could not obey, but wandered off to feast
at the table groaning with lies and curses.
Your gracious word was sung
in new ways by the prophets,
but we tuned them out,
so we could listen to temptation's songs.
So, you sent Jesus,
who came to set us free
and bring us home from
our exile in rebellion.

So, with those who longed for your coming,
packed and ready to journey into freedom,
we sing our praises with our sisters and brothers from every time:

Holy! Holy! Holy! Living God of grace!
All creation echoes your praise:
creatures roaming the fields,
dolphins splashing in the seas,
eagles soaring in the bright sky.
Glory to you forever and ever.
God of the captives!

You are righteousness, God our Deliverer,
and blessed is Jesus Christ, your Child, our Brother.
Because we break your heart
with our words and deeds,
he came to shatter the chains
of arrogance and selfishness.
When we became gluttons,
feasting on bitterness and fear,
he became the sweet Bread
of healing and hope.

Because we become drunk
on sin's soured wine,
he came, salvation poured
into our parched souls.
When death smiles at us,
waiting with open arms,
he gathers us up
in the embrace of grace and life,
carrying us out of the empty tomb
into life forever.

You have prepared this Table for us,
your children, so we might remember
the promises fulfilled to us in Christ our Lord:

Eating the Bread,
Christ's life strenghtens us;
drinking from the Cup,
Christ's Spirit nourishes us;
going to serve others,
we proclaim Christ's death
 and resurrection.

Bless the gifts of the Bread and the Cup,
anointing us with your Spirit
which brings us together.
As your grace touches our lips with hope,
may we reach out our hands
to set free those captive to injustice.
As your peace is poured
into the empty corners of our hearts,
may we go forth to love
others as much as we love ourselves,
and to serve them, showing our love for you.

And when time has marked the end of history,
and we gather with our sisters and brothers,
all division done,
all brokenness healed,
all barriers broken,
all your children freed from despair,
we will join our hands and hearts
around your Table of eternity, singing:

Glory to you, Liberating God!
Alleluia to you, Christ our Servant!
Thanks to you, Spirit of Peace! Amen.

September 14
14th Sunday after Pentecost (Proper 19)

Exodus 14:19-31; Psalm 114 or Exodus 15:1b-11, 20-21; Romans 14:1-12; Matthew 18:21-35; Genesis 50:15-21; Psalm 103:(1-7), 8-13

Paul Bellan-Boyer

Have You Been Saved? (Exodus 14)

We hear that so often as a question tossed off by proselytizers. It may just roll past, but I'm really asking—have you been saved?

For an experience of being saved, of being plucked from the fire, is crucial to Christian faith. We're not talking about finding a parking space when you're running late. Perhaps that kind of experience might serve as a pale proxy, a way to imagine salvation.

But well before Jesus' resurrection, God was in the salvation business. The exodus (along with exile) is a central story that shaped Jewish faith as Jesus knew it. The God of Israel, the God of the Bible, the God of Jesus does not make sense without this experience of being delivered from imminent disaster.

The movie version cannot do this scene justice. Imagine yourself in the sandals of those Hebrew slaves. With your back to the sea, you can see the dust of the chariots coming. When they catch you, they will kill you and your family and everyone around you, except for the "fortunate" ones that they will beat, rape, and drag back to slavery. If you have not knowingly been that close to the brink, I guarantee that someone you know has. Listen for those stories.

Just recently I talked with a parent whose house went up in flames in the middle of the night. She's not quite sure how she got out the window to summon help, but she is sure about the firefighters who went in and brought out her child, and about the medical teams who kept the firefighters' lungs working past the smoke damage. To her, salvation is very real.

Liz Crumlish
http://somethingtostandon.blogspot.co.uk/

Genesis 50; Matthew 18

Over these last few weeks, we have wandered in and out of the Old Testament story of Joseph alongside our Gospel readings. And today, we reach the end of Joseph's story as recorded in Genesis.

Joseph's brothers, in spite of all the kindness their brother has shown them, have cause to be worried again. Their father is now dead. And they are worried that Joseph has been kind to them only for the sake of their father. So now they're busy trying to work out how to make sure their brother doesn't decide to exact revenge on them.

The interesting thing is that all through this story, we don't read of the brothers being sorry for what they've done. We read only of them working out ways where they won't be brought to justice—avoiding payback.

And so, after their father's death, when they think the game might finally be up—what do they do? Do they say sorry to their brother? Do they fall on his mercy? No. They blackmail him. They tell him that it was their father's dying wish that he forgive them. And it works.

I like to think that Joseph had already forgiven them anyway. He certainly had opportunity for payback that he chose not to take. I like to think that it wasn't just the presence of his father that stopped him getting even. So all the scheming his brothers indulged in was unnecessary effort on their part.

Forgiveness is the theme of our readings today. Practicing forgiveness because we experience forgiveness from a forgiving God. Isn't it a fact that withholding forgiveness in the long run causes more harm to the person who is withholding than it does to the one who goes unforgiven? If we go on holding a grudge against someone, we are the ones who ultimately suffer. Because bitterness builds up in us, affects our well-being, and prevents us from knowing wholeness.

What, then, are some of the advantages of forgiveness? Aside from forgiveness protecting us from bitterness or resentment, when we forgive others who have wronged us, don't we experience just a little triumph? Don't we, just for a while, hold the upper hand when we are able to forgive?

That last bit in the story of Joseph always makes me think: How good must it have felt for Joseph to be able to say to his weeping brothers—its okay, I forgive you. His brothers, coming to him in fear and trepidation, not actually admitting they were in the wrong all those years ago but surely knowing it deep in their hearts. It must have been quite satisfying for Joseph to take the high moral ground and pronounce his forgiveness.

There's nothing like rubbing salt in the wounds. Of course that's NOT why Jesus teaches us to forgive. But, you have to admit, it could be a spin off!

Julie Craig
http://winsomelearnsome.com

Romans 14

It's about a cake, but it is about more than cake.

I am extraordinarily blessed to have found a group of women clergy and other church women who live out our community on the Internet. These women have become my deeply cherished friends in ways that overcome how we first met. And I've met many of them in person.

Events that brought us closest together were the hurricanes of 2005. One of our online friends lives in Gulfport, Mississippi, in direct line to be hit by the storms, and we all sort of gathered at her website in the hours before the hardest of the storms made landfall. Another of our friends shared a recipe for a Texas chocolate sheet cake, and mentioned that she would be baking one to work off some anxiety while waiting to see what the storm would bring.

Soon messages kept popping up from different online friends saying, "I'm baking one, too." And the next thing you know we were calling it Solidarity Cake, and then later, when our friends were spared from the direct horrors of Katrina and Rita, losing only some property instead of life or loved ones, we called it Grace Cake. When I hear a bad weather forecast, I head out to the store for butter and eggs and cocoa powder and powdered sugar.

It sounds like mindless busy work or a decadent distraction, but it's more than a cake, really. What I like about Grace Cake is that it uses ordinary ingredients that we all can have access to—there's not a gourmet item on the list. If you can't make it to the best supermarket in town, you can get everything at the local convenience store. There is no fancy equipment to use to make this cake—not even a mixer, just a pan, a bowl, and a spoon. You do need to boil some ingredients, and of course need an oven to bake it in. But that's it. When you pour the cake batter into the pan, it seems like such a runny, gloppy mess that the batter almost convinces you that it will never work. And yet every time, if you follow the instructions, it works beautifully.

What I *love* about Grace Cake is the relationships that brought the recipe to me, and the loving way we all take to our kitchens to bake one when we know that one or more of us is facing something that can be truly life-changing, and knowing that if something tragic were to happen in my life, my sisters would run to the store to get butter and eggs and cocoa powder and powdered sugar. In kitchens I've never seen, there would be stirring and measuring and boiling and praying, and they would await the word that I was okay. We may die alone, but we live together.

NOTE

The recipe, courtesy of Jody Harrington, can be found on her blog, Quotidian Grace, at http://quotidiangrace.blogspot.com/2005/07/texas-chocolate-sheet-cake-july-4th.html. Of course, being from Wisconsin, I used butter, not shortening or margarine in my cake. Enjoy!

Carolyn Winfrey Gillette
http://www.carolynshymns.com/

A King Once Told His Servants

A king once told his servants, "Now pay me what is mine!"
One came to him and begged him, "I'll pay! Just give me time!"
And so the king forgave him, though that man's debt was great.
What joy to be unburdened! What cause to celebrate!

Though he had been forgiven, that man was not so kind.
He threatened one who owed him, "Now pay me what is mine!"
He would not show compassion toward one whose debt was small.
What judgment came upon him! How bitter was his fall!

O God, in Christ you freed us; now may we not forget.
Our sin was overwhelming but you once paid the debt.
May we live lives of mercy, forgiving, blessing, too;
And may our grace toward others reflect our thanks to you.

NOTES

Biblical References: Matthew 18:25-35; 6:12, 14-15; 18:21-22
Tune: LLANGLOFFAN 7.6.7.6 D ("Rejoice, Rejoice, Believers"), Welsh Folk Melody; Evans's *Hymnau a Thonau,* 1865 as in *English Hymnal,* 1906
Alternative Tune: AURELIA ("The Church's One Foundation"), by Samuel S. Wesley, 1864

Todd Weir
http://bloomingcactus.typepad.com/

Matthew 18

The story opens with Peter's question about how many times you should forgive a person. He is wondering if there is a time when forgiveness becomes absurd because someone keeps on hurting us. I imagine most of us have someone in our lives who is very difficult to forgive. They just don't get it. They know where all our buttons are, and they just keep on pressing them. We try to be Christian and pray the Lord's Prayer, "Forgive us our debts as we forgive our debtors." After several times of forgiveness, we may feel that we are the doormat on which someone else wipes their feet, and we pray to God and say, "Lord, I have tried to forgive, but I have reached my limit."

Peter reflects on this, and to show that he had a magnanimous spirit, he says, "[Should we forgive] as many as seven times?" (v. 21 NRSV). Seven times seems like quite a bit, doesn't it?! In the Jewish mind, seven is a number that represents completion and finality. Throughout the Bible we find seven days of creation, seven signs in the book of Revelation, and so on. Surely this would be more than enough!

Jesus answers with a word play on the number seven and says that we should forgive seventy times seven. He doesn't mean that we should keep track and forgive someone four hundred ninety times, but rather that we must throw away the calculator and live a lifestyle of continual forgiveness. I imagine the disciples responded much as I would, absolutely dumbfounded at such a notion. Here's the problem. We understand intellectually the notion that we forgive because we have also sinned and been forgiven, but sometimes the sins against us seem out of proportion and unforgivable.

A woman told me that she had been seriously injured in a car accident. She had gone through many hardships during her recovery and had been very bitter toward the driver who hit her. Guilt at the inability to forgive had plagued her, doubling her misery. "Then one day," she said, "I realized that forgiveness is not a duty, it is the answer. When we forgive the grace comes to heal our hearts."

Working out forgiveness in the complexity of life is a subtle art. There are no simple formulas that will take care of the problem for us. Yet we can't walk away from forgiveness. Going through the process of forgiving is painful work, but so is living with the open wounds of unresolved anger and resentment. Forgiveness is not a virtue that comes from within, nor is it a duty we owe to someone else. It is a cry to God that says, "Lord, heal my heart." Forgiveness is not an easy answer to our problems, but it is the most powerful answer.

John Wesley's Notes on the Bible
http://www.ccel.org/ccel/wesley/notes.txt

Matthew 18:24

"One was brought who owed him ten thousand talents"—According to the usual computation, if these were talents of gold, this would amount to seventy-two millions sterling. If they were talents of silver, it must have been four millions, four hundred thousand pounds. Hereby our Lord intimates the vast number and weight of our offenses against God, and our utter incapacity of making him any satisfaction.

Karoline Lewis

Matthew 18

Forgiveness is never easy, but it is especially difficult when the amount to forgive far exceeds the ability to imagine the act. Such is the case in this parable. It explores whether or not certain acts or words are easier to forgive than others. Is that really true for us? Does our forgiveness depend on the circumstances, the context? Are particular acts of transgression, of recalcitrance, of hurt easier than others to forgive or forget? The attention to the amount of forgiveness in this parable seems to imply the absurdity of measuring it. When forgiveness is necessary, called for or asked for, whether small or in great measure, the act is still necessary.

How we define forgiveness is also a place to land for preaching. How do we really explain what it is? How might we imagine inviting conversation around our assumptions of forgiveness and what is at stake for each of us in moments of receiving and offering forgiveness? The nature of forgiveness in this story suggests that what it means depends on when and why it is needed. A blanket statement such as "Forgiveness is letting go of the fact that the past cannot be changed" is a useful definition, but it may not match the particularity of the moment.

This story from Matthew calls us to extravagance in forgiveness. Partial or perfunctory forgiveness will not do; they leave a residue that eats away at the forgiveness seemingly granted. How forgiveness is perceived and experienced certainly depends on that which is being forgiven; but the amount of forgiveness meted out is not in question when it comes to God.

September 21
15th Sunday after Pentecost (Proper 20)

Exodus 16:2-15; Psalm 105:1-6, 37-45; Philippians 1:21-30; Matthew 20:1-16; Jonah 3:10–4:11; Psalm 145:1-8

Paul Bellan-Boyer

"What Is It?" (Exodus 16)

The story is a familiar one. It happens again and again, not just on the Hebrew people's trek through the wilderness, but in our communities today. When times are tough, when we are threatened, when we are afraid, it is hard to remember our blessings, and very easy to focus on what is lacking.

Nor should we underestimate the difficulties of life in the desert. The routines of Egypt—whatever their hardships—were a known quantity. Life as slaves is difficult, but survivable. The wilderness, though, has no known support system. But when the waters of the sea closed over Pharaoh's army, God burned any bridge back to Egypt.

The story of manna in the desert is rightly understood as God's providential care, God's mercy for the people, and God standing with them to see them through—bread from heaven, indeed. What are we to make, though, of the Lord's purpose? The Lord speaks to the peoples' need to "test them to see whether or not they follow my Instruction" (v. 4).

"What is it?" the people exclaim, when they encounter this manna (v. 15). Apparently this is a test indeed. This manna is food (the Egyptian word *mennu* means "food"), but it is strange food (the Arabic *man hu* means "This is insect secretions").

God will faithfully send manna throughout the time in the wilderness. Is the "testing" a part of the Lord's teaching process, reinforcing again and again that God is trustworthy and worth following?

Today it is enough to remember that we are tested like this all the time. More than a thousand years after this story, Jesus will teach that asking for daily bread is enough to pray. We might wish for a lifetime supply of our favorite delicacies, but can we be thankful for what God provides? For the gift of life? For all that God has done and has promised?

Teri Peterson
http://clevertitlehere.blogspot.com

Exodus 16

The Israelites are in the wilderness just six weeks when they start living in the past. Hungry and cranky, realizing they don't know where they're going or how they'll get there or how long it will take, with no established religion or government, no social safety net, and no leftovers—they complain. "If only we had died in Egypt where we sat around and ate as much as we wanted!" (Ah, flawed memories!) But God *again* listens to their cries and provides abundance they could never have imagined.

This is the central wilderness experience, the first of many lessons in the making of a people. God says, "I will be your God," calls them "my people," then has to teach them what that means—they have to work the visioning process and discern a mission statement ("Love the Lord with all your heart, soul, mind, and strength, and love your neighbor as yourself" [see Deut 6:5; Lev 19:18] seems pretty good!). They have to wander in order to discover that God will lead them if they will follow. They have to look back without rose-colored glasses so they can look forward with hope. They have to learn that God is love and discern who God is calling them to be. This first lesson is learning to rely on God's goodness and abundance. It sounds cliché and naïve now, and I suspect then, too—but alone out in the desert, the Israelites literally depended on God for their daily bread, their safety, their lives.

Even as they learn the stark truth that we are all dependent on God despite our perceived independence, they learn of God's faithfulness. They learn that hoarding doesn't get us anywhere. They learn that God's abundance comes along with justice—not whatever I want, but what we, the community, need. They learn to call on God to hold up God's end of the covenant, and that God will. They start to learn what faithfulness looks like from our side. They learn that they are chosen to be a community of God's people, a blessing to the world, not just ragtag wanderers. Most important, they learn that the journey from "if only" to "I AM" goes through a question: "What is it?"

They aren't used to being provided for—it takes time to get slavery out of your system, time to turn from Pharaoh's non-people into God's people, time to figure out that God is not just another Pharaoh, time to learn trust and reliance, time to know providence—God will provide, even if we don't recognize that providence at first.

What is it? (*manna*) turns out to be heavenly, good enough for forty years of nourishment. The journey from "If only" to "my people," from whiner to baker, involves lots of "what is it?" Throughout our whole journey God provides, though we may not see, understand, or have words for it. God kneads us together, a community learning to trust, learning to look around and ahead rather than only back, learning to bake.

Julia Seymour
http://lutheranjulia.blogspot.com

Jonah 3–4; Matthew 20

There are three miracles in Jonah. The least interesting is the big fish. More intriguing is the idea of an entire city repenting, from the king to the smallest child. Was their repentance a demonstration to forestall holy wrath? Perhaps, but it hardly seems like speculation to say the God who cared enough to send Nineveh a prophet also knew their hearts and minds.

The greatest miracle has to be that such a resistant prophet could preach with enough enthusiasm to bring a city to repentance. The work of Jonah in Nineveh should bring confidence to even the most rookie preacher. The Spirit works in you, just as in Brother Jonah, because presumably you care a bit more about your hearers.

Despite his distaste for the Ninevites and his perception that God was a little too free with the grace to non-Israelites, Jonah preached. Then he sat down to wait for the show, promptly having a fit when God did not deliver the fireworks, "God, I knew this would happen. It's not fair! You always forgive. Why did I need to come all the way out here? Couldn't you have done this without me? I'd rather die than watch this."

The whale portion of Jonah's story is the most popular because it bears the least resemblance to anything familiar. The rest of the story is too painful. Are we more likely to run to Nineveh, uncertain of our reception, or flee to Tarshish, pretending our instructions were lost in translation? How frequently do we wallow in frustration at change or innovation, without considering this might be God's way of showing grace to the people we forget? If God is gracious and merciful, slow to anger, and abounding in steadfast love, and ready to relent from punishing—then why do we need to do anything? If the last will be first and the first, last—then why make the effort to be anywhere but the middle?

Because there are still Ninevehs in the world where people long for hope and good news. There are places where people are already wearing sackcloth and ashes and yearn for a word of resurrection for this life and the next. There are workers waiting to be invited into the harvest, and they do not even care about the wages.

Jonah's anger sets the scene for one of the best verses in the Bible. God says,

> You are concerned about the bush, for which you did not labor and which you did not grow; it came into being in a night and perished in a night. And should I not be concerned about Nineveh, that great city, in which there are more than a hundred and twenty thousand persons who do not know their right hand from their left, and also many animals?" (4:10-11 NRSV)

That sentence reveals the heart of a God who knows and loves all creation, who welcomes all to the feast, and whose vineyard has a welcoming task for everyone, regardless of when they come.

Natalie Sims
http://lectionarysong.blogspot.com

Psalm 105

A song of thanks, including references to the Israelites coming out of Egypt and God providing food and water.

"O Sing to the Lord / Cantai ao Senhor / Cantad al Señor" (Traditional Brazilian)—A good, fun, and simple song that is easy to learn in Portuguese or Spanish.

"Hear the Message We Now Are Proclaiming / El Mensaje Que Hoy Proclamamos" (Eleazar Torreglosa)—This jubilant Colombian song of liberty and new life for the poor and suffering would fit well with God's care for the Israelites. Free sheet music (http://www.oikoumene.org/fileadmin/files/wcc-main/2007pdfs/WoPCUsongs/El_men saje_que_hoy_proclamamostorreglosa.pdf).

"Let the Hearts of Those Who Seek God Rejoice!" (Elaine Kirkland)—Good joyous refrain, which could be used with the sung or read psalm.

"Bless the Lord" (Traditional Kenyan)—A good call-and-response chant—would make a good processional. Lyrics (http://www.oremus.org/hymnal/b/b112.html).

"Know That God Is Good (Mungu Ni Mwema)" (Traditional Congo)—A simple joyous chant from Congo. Sheet music and melody line sample (https://www.riteseries.org/song/mhso/1224/).

"Alleluia" (Sylvia Duncan)—A simple Alleluia. Gaither version has a descant cantor part. Here are some nice notes on how to teach it to your congregation (http://www.leaderonline.org/Archives/pentecost05/Duncan%20Alleluia%20notes.pdf). Sound sample (http://www.amazon.com/There-Among-Goose-Worship-Group/dp/B00004SAYQ).

"Alleluia" (South Africa, transcribed from the singing of George Mxadana)—Beautiful and peaceful, especially if you can work all the harmonies in.

"We Give Our Thanks / Reamo Leboga" (Traditional Botswana)—A joyous song to sing for the offering.

"You Shall Go Out with Joy" (Steffi G. Rubin / Stuart Dauerman)—This is a good hand-clappy foot-stomping song. Fun. Can't get enough of this song, really. Chords and lyrics (http://www.higherpraise.com/Lyrics4/YouShallGoOut WithJoy1.htm).

John Wesley's Notes on the Bible
http://www.ccel.org/ccel/wesley/notes.txt

Philippians 1:23

"To depart"—Out of bonds, flesh, the world. "And to be with Christ"—In a nearer and fuller union. It is better to depart; it is far better to be with Christ.

Paul Nuechterlein
http://girardianlectionary.net/

Matthew 20

In the parable of the Workers in the Vineyard, the owner *seems* to represent God. He displays a generosity that goes beyond conventional human economics—potentially overturning our usual sense of fairness. He models a generosity that *might* move our human sense of fairness to include those most often left out.

But is "might" good enough? Doesn't God send Jesus in order to rescue us from our human kingdoms for living in God's kingdom? I believe that if—as a general rule for interpreting Matthew's "parables of judgment"—the interpreter refrains from placing God somewhere in the parable, then it yields a deeper meaning. (This is especially true of the parable of the King's Banquet, Matthew 22:1-14; see my website for an alternate reading.)

I use as an example of this practice, to help with the parable of the Vineyard, Matthew's previous parable of the Unforgiving Servant (Matt 18:23-35), where the master invites the servant into *a whole new world* in which even massive debts are completely forgiven. But when given the chance to live debt-free, the servant effectively declines the invitation by insisting on keeping the tiny debt that he is owed by a fellow servant. The master's generosity challenges the conventional debt-keeping world where everything is tallied in order to keep track of who *deserves* what.

It points to the anthropological fact that a perceived *scarcity* of resources rules in our conventional human world, such that our economics involve objects of desire being "fairly" distributed according to those who are most deserving. Having become rivals for the same objects of desires, those objects *appear* scarce to us, even if they are in fact plentiful. Think of children fighting over the same toy, even when there are duplicate toys available. (For more on the "mimetic" nature of desire, see my essay in March 9). Our everyday worldview of *scarcity* is a breeding ground for resentment arising from any transgressions against what we think we deserve.

In the two parables we are examining together, the master of the Unforgiving Servant and the vineyard owner seem to be operating out of a worldview of *abundance,* presenting a stiff challenge to our worldview of *scarcity,* and thereby modeling a generosity that we might imitate. But if we allow ourselves to *not* see these two as representing God, we can go even deeper to what we actually receive in the sending of Jesus Christ into our vineyard. With the parable of the Unforgiving Servant in mind, we are offered to step into a brave new world where debts are not kept against us. But like that Unforgiving Servant, we ordinarily turn down the invitation to instead live in our worlds where we *think* we get what we deserve—that is, to keep living in the self-made worlds of debt-keeping. But the God of Jesus Christ transcends both representatives of human power in these two parables by *not* continuing to hold us to our decisions. The God of Jesus Christ sends the Son to do the hardest work of all—the work of the cross, the work of God's self-emptying out of abundance (Phil 2:6-8)—precisely so that we do *not* get what our ordinary decisions deserve.

John Petty
http://progressiveinvolvement.com

Matthew 20

This parable appears only in Matthew. It follows Peter's question to Jesus about what the disciples will get for having left everything to follow him. Jesus tells him that "at the renewal of all things," the disciples will sit on twelve thrones to judge the twelve tribes of Israel. Not only that, they will receive "a hundredfold," and eternal life to boot (19:28-29 NRSV).

Nevertheless, reward for the in-crowd is not quite the whole story because "many who are first will be last, and the last will be first" (v. 30 NRSV). Then follows the parable of the laborers in the vineyard in which the last hired receive the same reward as those—the disciples?—who were first.

The vineyard is an oft-used symbol for Israel. The owner of the vineyard, the "house-ruler"—*oikodespotace*—is God. The "house-ruler" makes five trips into town to hire day-laborers to work in the vineyard. He pays a denarius, "the usual daily wage."

The contrast is clearly between the "first" and the "last." The last are paid first so that the first hired will see what they have been paid. Otherwise, what difference would it make? When the first see that the last get a full denarius, as do they, they begin grumbling. Who wouldn't?

The "house-ruler" hears the grumbling and responds to one of the grumblers whom he calls *etairos*—"friend." Matthew uses *etairos* in only three places—here, in 22:12, and in 26:50 where it refers to Judas. None would be considered a positive example. Here it should be considered sarcastic; substitute "buster" or "fella."

The "house-ruler" denies doing wrong. The contract he had made with the "first" is fulfilled. Moreover, the "house-ruler" asserts his freedom to pay the rest "whatever is right."

Then, the "house-ruler" asks, "Or is your eye evil because I am good?" (20:15b author's translation). The word "good"—*agathos*—is framed by the words *ego* and *eimi*. *Ego eimi* is the Greek translation of the tetragrammaton, YHWH, the name of God revealed to Moses. In other words, *ego eimi* is the name of the God of Israel.

That the word *agathos*—"good"—is placed "inside" of the *ego eimi* is to confirm what Matthew had just written in 19:17 (NRSV): "There is only one [God] who is good."

In the context of this parable, the "goodness" of God is revealed not as justice—the "first" have a strong case for protest, after all, according to generally recognized moral standards. But no, God's "goodness" is revealed not as justice, but rather as mercy.

Themes of justice abound throughout the parable, but the fullness of that justice comes to expression as equal treatment for all. The overflowing generosity of God's love ignores all human merit. "The last will be first, and the first will be last" (v. 16). God's mercy reigns supreme, and precisely there is God's "goodness."

Karoline Lewis

Matthew 20

Generosity is perhaps one of the hardest characteristics of being human. We want to receive generosity, and yet we begrudge its blessings on others. Why is that? What is so difficult about generosity? Generosity rubs against our sensibilities because, in the end, it cannot be tied to the measures that we want to assign it. There can be no quantifiers for generosity because such computations would negate its very nature. The enumerations and calculations that we think should flow from or match up with how generosity is reckoned continually disappoint and disturb.

Calling attention to these very true and honest human reactions to generosity in a sermon on this text, should not only get at that which makes this parable uncomfortable but also invite people to sense its profound claim about God. We try so hard to gauge and estimate God's favor, to assess God's grace by our evaluations, to determine God's delight by our regulations. The root word translated "generous" in the NRSV is "good" and we simply do not know what to do with God's goodness and beneficence. In the midst of our maneuverings, we miss the extraordinary good news of this parable and of God's love. When will we be forced to put ourselves in the place of receiving God's generosity? When will we need it the most, when will we believe that we are the least worthy or deem ourselves underserving? If we are truthful, perhaps it is more often than we care to admit. At those times, we sense that we are the last, that being the first will feel like the grace that it is.

September 28
16th Sunday after Pentecost (Proper 21)

Exodus 17:1-7; Psalm 78:1-4, 12-16; Philippians 2:1-13; Matthew 21:23-32; Ezekiel 18:1-4, 25-32; Psalm 25:1-9

Paul Bellan-Boyer

"Why Do You Test the Lord?" (Exodus 17)

You can hear Moses' frustration. Two weeks ago (in the lectionary) God delivered the people from Pharaoh's army. Last week, God delivered them from starvation. And yet, this week they are thirsty, and doubt yet again that God will see them through.

"Why are you testing the Lord?" (v. 2). It's a foolish question. Why do we doubt God's power or God's favor? Because we are human and fearful; we have seen before when our hopes did not work out, when things or people we needed were not there for us. And, truthfully, we know how frail our lives really are.

Lack of water in the desert seems an occasion more appropriate for panic than for trust.

And notice Moses. He, like the people, is in danger from thirst, and he fears their anger: "They are getting ready to stone me" (v. 4). In fact, while the people complain to Moses, Moses complains about them to the Lord. One begins to wonder if Moses is more concerned that the people doubt the Lord or that they're on his case.

Yet the Lord does not seem very concerned about the people's testing, not in this passage or throughout the wilderness journey. What is God's response to the people's need, their doubt, their fear? Water. Not more commandments, not punishment, not a new teaching. Just water.

We see a difference between God and Moses, between a man of God and God's self. Moses, perhaps due to fear, questions the people's faith and memorializes their quarreling. So often we get sidetracked with our own baggage. God goes straight to the point of need: "You're thirsty? Here's water."

You doubt God's care, God's steadfast faithfulness? That's okay. God's graceful providence is not frustrated by our weakness. Have some cool water, straight from the rock.

Beth Quick
http://bethquick.blogspot.com

Psalm 78

- "I will open my mouth in a parable" (v. 2 NRSV). I hadn't realized that the word *parable* appeared in the Old Testament. It reminds us that in Jesus' day, the people would have related to Jesus' style, more, perhaps, than we are able to relate today.

- "We will not hide them from their children; / we will tell to the coming generation" (v. 4 NRSV). I like these verses that convey a sense of the necessity to tell the story of a people, to make sure the history is known through time and generations. We have a tendency to forget whole chunks of our history until we are repeating it!

• Verses 12-16 refer to the Israelites being led through the Red Sea, traveling into the wilderness, and receiving water to drink from the rock, which tie in with our Old Testament reading.

Philippians 2

• "If then there is any [*fill in the blank*] in Christ…be of the same mind, having the same love" (vv. 1-2, NRSV). Paul says that whatever exists in Christ, we should be like-minded, a good strategy!

• "Did not regard equality with God / as something to be exploited" (v. 6 NRSV). I find this such a unique statement. Imagine if Christ had used his equality to exploit? What would that look like? Perhaps this is what Satan tempted Christ to do—to exploit his equality.

• "Work out your own salvation" (v. 12 NRSV). I find this a very Wesleyan sentiment. Obviously, Paul does not mean that we save ourselves, but he means to remind us that we are active participants in the justifying and sanctifying grace that should mark our lives as people of faith.

Matthew 21

• "By what authority" (v. 23 NRSV). The priests and elders want to know why Jesus thinks he has the right to teach as he's teaching. Who is he? Who is backing him?

• I love this, this trick Jesus sets them up for. Jesus himself knows the answer to his own question, doesn't he? But he traps them in a way that makes it impossible to answer. I think Jesus was having a good time here.

• Jesus says that it is more important what you *do* than what your *lips claim* you believe. Did you hear that?

Lowell Grisham
http://lowellsblog.blogspot.com/

Prayers of the People (Exodus 17; Psalm 78)

Presider: Gracious God, you exercise your authority chiefly in showing love through your Son Jesus Christ: Enable us both to will and to work for your good pleasure, that we may pray and serve faithfully, as we say: We will recount to generations to come your praiseworthy deeds and your power, O God.

Litanist: You have called the members of Christ's body to work out our own salvation with fear and trembling: Encourage us in Christ with the consolation of your love, that we may share in your Spirit of compassion. We will recount to generations to come

your praiseworthy deeds and your power, O God.

Inspire our leaders and all who hold authority in the nations to do nothing from selfish ambition or conceit, but to serve God's people with humility and grace. We will recount to generations to come

your praiseworthy deeds and your power, O God.

Be with our community that our actions and words may be consistent as we look generously to the interests of our neighbors. We will recount to generations to come

your praiseworthy deeds and your power, O God.

Fill the world with your Spirit that all people may serve one another with humble faithfulness. We will recount to generations to come

your praiseworthy deeds and your power, O God.

Make our joy complete by bringing your healing love to all for whom we pray, especially _____. Accept our gratitude and thanksgiving for all that we enjoy, especially for _____. Hear our prayers for those who have followed our savior Jesus through death into exaltation, especially _____. We will recount to generations to come

your praiseworthy deeds and your power, O God.

Presider: Through the death and triumphant resurrection of your Son Jesus, O God, you have raised all humanity into your divine presence: Be at work in us that we may do your will on earth with joyful and obedient hearts, and share in the consolation of your Spirit, through Jesus Christ our Savior. **Amen.**

Melissa Bane Sevier
http://melissabanesevier.wordpress.com

Limited (Philippians 2)

For centuries the church has talked—and argued—about the character of Jesus. After all, we say that he was the fullest expression of what God is like. And yet we also say that he was human in every way, just like us. Just like God? Just like us? Which is it?

Here's Paul's take on it, probably quoting an early Christian hymn, as you can see from the poetic motion of the text:

> Let the same mind be in you that was in Christ Jesus, / who, though he was in the form of God, / did not regard equality with God / as something to be exploited, / but emptied himself . . . . (vv. 5-7a NRSV)

The essence of this faith is that the divine took on the human in order to gain us, and to teach us how to live. The self-limiting of Jesus.

It's seen throughout the Gospels, isn't it? One minute, we see Jesus performing great miracles. The next, we see him almost fumbling with his humanity, the way the rest of us do. Changing his mind about people, getting worn out, stressed by so much to do. Tired of those disciples he had to hang with all the time. The holy takes on the ordinary. Jesus was often limited by the ordinary, choosing limitation over strength and power.

This ordinariness is at the same time scandalous and appealing. The very Son of God limited by the things that limit all the rest of us: time and space, living and dying, illness and health, the actions and expectations of others, good and bad relationships. Every day Jesus had to figure out how to get food, where they were going to sleep. Someone needed to be in charge of the money. They had to figure out what road they were going to take to the next town, and sometimes they were running late.

God chose not just to view the messiness that we call humanity from some other plane, but to enter this messiness and to be at home in it. The spiritual and the physical are so intertwined that they cannot be separated, not even in the Christ. Neither is holier than the other. Each is made holier by the other. Wouldn't it be something if we could see the intertwining of spirit and physicality today? We do, but in an even messier way than Jesus lived it: it is called the Church.

The church is the body of Christ. We worry sometimes that we are not spiritual enough. And we're probably right. But it's also likely that we are not mundane enough. One without the other is not the body of Christ. The mundane must be infused with the spiritual, and the spiritual with the mundane. This gets messy, and we make lots of mistakes trying to get it right. We're limited by our location, our resources, our personalities. Jesus, too, chose to be limited. That puts us in good company.

Martha Spong
http://marthaspong.com/

Philippians 2; Matthew 21

In the Gospel lesson, Jesus is parrying a rhetorical attack by the chief priests and elders of the temple. Since we saw him last week, he has entered Jerusalem, and over the next eight Sundays, we'll be hearing the stories that happened in the first Holy Week, the things he taught in the days before his arrest and crucifixion. It is still early in the week. In this chapter, he turns over the tables of the moneychangers and sellers of sacrificial animals, and then he curses a fig tree that fails to give him fruit, and in the midst of that display of the most human emotion we see from him in Matthew's Gospel, the leaders challenge him. Who said you can do these things? He is upsetting the status quo, and they want to hear the reason why from his own mouth.

He answers a question with a question, which they don't dare answer, and then he tells them a story about two brothers. Both are sent by their father to work in the vineyard. One says no, but later thinks better of it and goes to work. The other says yes, but doesn't go. Which one obeyed his father? This time they answer, and it's the right answer. It's the one who went to do the work who did the will of his father, not the one who gave the right answer without any actions to back it up.

I preached these texts on the day my youngest child was confirmed. Now I want to be clear. It's possible to live a life of faith without ever saying the words she said in affirming her baptism. It's also possible to make the promises very sweetly and never live into them. That was Jesus' indictment of the religious leaders. They knew the right words to say; they just didn't bother to work in the vineyard. But there are more choices than just those two! We can say the words and strive to live them.

It's important to remember that whether we're being baptized or confirmed or becoming members of a local church or simply conversing with God about where we are in our lives, we make the promises about how we will live with the understanding that doing so requires God's help. The qualities we are urged to express in Paul's letter to the Philippians do not come easily. He tells us clearly, "work out your own salvation with fear and trembling" (Phil 2:12b NRSV). I put my emphasis on the trembling. The work of faith shakes us. Even Jesus, who took on our form and lived a human life, lost his temper, and while his indignation in the temple was surely righteous, his anger at a fig tree proves his humanity.

If it could happen to Jesus, surely we all need help to live a life that pleases God.

Marci Auld Glass
www.marciglass.com

Matthew 21

Before this parable, Jesus did some things you might want to know about. *Minor little things*. A triumphal entry into Jerusalem on a colt. A little moment when he entered the temple and turned over some tables and called people names.

So, when the temple leadership, the chief priests and the elders, come up and ask him the questions, "By what authority are you doing these things, and who gave you this authority?" (v. 23 NRSV), we can understand their point of view. They just spent the night picking up the temple, sweeping up the turtle dove "offerings" that were left after their cages were broken open and they nested in the rafters. We understand their frustration. If someone did that here, the Building Committee would want to know who gave them permission to walk in here, move the pews, and leave a big mess!

But their questions are bigger. They consider themselves to be the authority. And they certainly didn't invite this itinerant rabbi from Nazareth into their midst. "Just who do you think you are, mister?" Their questions remind us of the questions Jesus asks his disciples: "Who do you say that I am?" (16:15 NRSV).

Identity. Authority. Kingdom. The questions of the religious leaders are dangerous. If Jesus answers, "God has given me all authority," they can get him on blasphemy charges. If he says, "I am my own authority," they can dismiss him. Both of those answers would be true, of course, but they wouldn't see that. Because they continue to order their world, their understanding of authority, power, and God differently than Jesus does.

And his continuing conflict with the temple leadership will lead him straight to the cross. *They will kill him before they will change their minds.* Because that is what he's asking them to do. Change their minds, reconsider what they thought to be true, and believe that God is working for the repentance, the renewal, of the world, in new ways.

Jesus criticizes the religious leaders for not changing their minds when presented with the message of John the Baptist and when presented with the person of Jesus. And, looking back on it with the advantage of history, we realize they were wrong. But they thought they were being faithful Jews. They thought they were upholding tradition.

They knew that not all change is good. We aren't called to follow every new thing that is out there. But we are called to change our minds when God sends prophets to lead us on the path of righteousness. We are called to change our minds when God sends God's own Son to live among us and teach us what true, sacrificial love looks like.

So this week, as your life unfolds, ask if there are places where you are being called to change your mind. Is God asking you to see the world differently?

NOTE: Adapted from "Mind Changing: Jesus, Neutrinos, and New Coke," a sermon preached by Marci Auld Glass (http://marciglass.com/2011/09/25/mind-changing-jesus-neutrinos-and-new-coke/).

John Wesley's Notes on the Bible
http://www.ccel.org/ccel/wesley/notes.txt

Matthew 21:32

The most notorious sinners were reformed, though at first they said, I will not. "And ye seeing the amazing change which was wrought in them, though at first ye said, I go, sir, repented not afterward"—Were no more convinced than before. O how is this scripture fulfilled at this day!

Karoline Lewis

Matthew 21

"We do not know," is the question of faith, isn't it? This is especially true when we are called to adjudicate questions of belief. The question to Jesus from the chief priests and the elders, "By what authority...who gave you this authority?" (v. 23 NRSV), gets at the heart of our resistance to change, our struggle for control, and our disbelief that someone else could be in charge. When we find ourselves uncertain of forces that seem beyond our capacity to direct, we move quickly to matters of authority, its origins, and where to locate it. As soon as we do, we realize that authority is not so easily determined.

This is the very human dynamic in the text from Matthew, and as it turns out, our questions are all wrong. "By what authority?" and "Who gave it to you?" take the issue of authority down the wrong path. When we assume that questions of authority can be answered by resolving origins, we have framed authority as a solvable problem. If we can get to the source of a perceived authority, then maybe we can better handle, define, or even eliminate, its manifestations. But power and authority are never that easy to explain. When the chief priests and the elders go this direction, Jesus counters with, "Okay, you want to go that route?" (see vv. 24-27). Jesus refers to both heavenly and human authority, and names the implied dichotomy of their question. The worldview of the chief priests and the elders embraces only the great chasm between that which is from God and that which is humanly derived. Jesus, as Immanuel, has obliterated this divide. God's power is now inseparable from perceived weakness; and questions of authority will thus demand a whole new way of thinking.

October 5

17th Sunday after Pentecost (Proper 22)

Exodus 20:1-4, 7-9, 12-20; Psalm 19; Philippians 3:4b-14; Matthew 21:33-46; Isaiah 5:1-7; Psalm 80:7-15

John Wesley's Notes on the Bible

http://www.ccel.org/ccel/wesley/notes.txt

Exodus 20:1

"God spake all these words"—The law of the ten commandments is a law of God's making; a law of his own speaking. God has many ways of speaking to the children of men by his spirit, conscience, providences; his voice in all which we ought carefully to attend to: but he never spake at any time upon any occasion so as he spake the ten commandments, which therefore we ought to hear with the more earnest heed. This law God had given to man before, it was written in his heart by nature; but sin had so defaced that writing, that it was necessary to revive the knowledge of it.

Eric D. Barreto

Exodus 20; Isaiah 5; Matthew 21

Somehow, the Ten Commandments have become a political lightning rod in our culture and politics. Debates about their public display profoundly miss the importance of this well-known text. If we were to ask most Christians what the first words of the Ten Commandments are, most would point to the first commandment: You shall have no other Gods before me. It is vital to help remind Christians that God begins this passage not with a commandment but with a story, with a memory. The Ten Commandments begin not with a rule but with the recalling of a promise. They begin not with a regulation but with a declaration of God's character as reflected by God's actions on behalf of Israel. They begin by recalling God's deliverance of God's people from the bondage of slavery. So the commandments are not arbitrary rules by a detached being who cares little for God's people. Instead, the commandments are a proper and grateful response for God's deliverance. Our identity as a people is dictated not by the whims of God but by the character of God as a life-giving companion in the midst of our many struggles and chains. The commandments are not burdens but a joyful response to who God is: a deliverer and a liberator.

Of course, the story of God's involvement with God's people has had moments of faithfulness and moments of failure. The strange parable in Matthew 21:33-46 evokes the image of Israel as God's vineyard found in Isaiah 5:1-7. In both cases, a dedicated God plants a vineyard only to find its produce or its stewards falling short. The story of God's faithfulness being met by our faithlessness is not new in the story of Israel or in our faith lives. Nonetheless, in God's grace, God is always faithful.

Sharron Blezard

Philippians 3

Sometimes you have to lose to win. Of course, this runs counter to everything our culture tells us. Winners get the prize; losers get nothing. First place is best; anything less is a loss. It is no surprise that the upside-down, inside-out Savior of the world has other ideas about the relationship between winning and losing.

Paul told the church at Philippi about the joy of losing, saying,

> Yet whatever gains I had, these I have come to regard as loss because of Christ. More than that, I regard every-thing as loss because of the surpassing value of knowing Christ Jesus my Lord. For his sake I have suffered the loss of all things, and I regard them as rubbish, in order that I may gain Christ. (vv. 7-8 NRSV)

What a loser! Paul, a Roman citizen and respected Jew, gave it all up for Jesus. His present loss led to eternal gain. By losing the identity he had claimed since birth, Paul was claimed as an heir to the kingdom of God and gained an identity beyond measure in earthly accounting. The win/loss equation Paul preached will never make sense by the world's way of keeping score. So why do we keep trying?

The twenty-first-century church faces new challenges in a post-Christian, pluralistic, global culture. To "win" we must lose. We must lose old, tired ways of being church. We must lose preconceived notions about who is welcome at the table. And we must lose our grip on the center and go to the margins because that's where Jesus is always found. By losing ourselves and the way things "used to be," we are free to press on unencumbered, winners in the eyes of the only One who really matters in the end.

Julie Craig
http://winsomelearnsome.com

Philippians 3

The images of clean-up after a disaster are haunting and heartbreaking. Once, after an outbreak of tornadoes in the Midwest, I watched as a woman, ignoring the television news camera pointed at her, found something she recognized in the rubble. She exclaimed out loud that she had found her chair, and I watched as she ran to the object, dug her hands into the debris, and pulled out what could only be described as a fragment of what could have once been a chair. She clutched it to her in shock as if it had been made of gold. She seemed so glad to have found something she thought she had lost in the storm.

In this place of loss and grief, even a part of a chair that is recovered seemed like a treasure, for it may have sym-bolized for the woman a truth she had known but could not prove: "Once upon a time I lived here. I had a normal life, I had a job, I had a car, I had a chair on which I used to sit. This is a piece of that chair."

Paul's message to the church comes in a time of turmoil and chaos; suddenly everything the followers of Jesus thought to be true about the fellowship of believers has been turned upside down, and Paul reminds the church to take stock, to count every earthly gain as loss, and to count any suffering that has to be endured for Christ's sake as ultimate gain.

What are the remnants of our earthly selves that we search for, in an effort to hold on to something that reminds us that we exist, that we count for something in this world? What scraps would we hold dear to our chest as if they were gold? For Paul the answer is this: "Christ Jesus has made me his own" (v. 12 NRSV). That's it. That's the bot-tom line.

After taking stock of his conversion on the road to Damascus, after accounting for all the church plants he created, after being arrested and thrown in prison for the sake of the gospel, it all boils down to this one truth, and the symbol for it all is the cross.

The cross is the piece of chair, you see. In every church that ever has burned to the ground, or has blown away, the cross—or even the *idea* of the cross if we couldn't find a physical, tangible one—is the evidence that once a upon a time, God loved the world, came to earth and dwelt among us and died for us, and we have life because of it.

Thom Shuman
http://lectionaryliturgies.blogspot.com/

Call to Worship

From north and south,
from east and west, we come:
God's people called to the Table
where simple grace nourishes us.
From down the street to across town,
from single households to apartment dwellers:
God's people are called to community,
where we live and serve one another.
From every class, every race, every status;
from little ones with sippy cups to elders with overflowing hearts:
God's people are called to witness to God's hope,
to offer peace to a shattered world.

Prayer of the Day

Seeing your children
in bondage and despair,
you brought them to freedom
by your compassion and hope.
Longing to create a people
who would care for one another,
you spoke simple truths
about integrity and justice.
Fill our worship
with sighs more precious than
all we value, Word Speaker.

You came,
not to build a grand scheme,
but to be our foundation of faith.
You came,
not to choose sides like we do,
but to be that peace
that brings us together.
You came,
not worrying about what
lay ahead for you,
so we could see
your kingdom prepared for us.

Fill our worship
with your grace more precious
than our deepest fears, Word Bearer.

When we cling
to all that holds us back,
you empty our arms,
putting our past in a rummage sale.
When we hesitate
to stand with the lost,
you nudge us forward
with the wind of justice.
Fill our worship
with your peace more precious
than the brokenness we grasp,
    Word of Wisdom.

God in Community, Holy in One,
hear the words of our hearts
as we pray as Jesus has taught us, saying,
Our Father . . .

Call to Reconciliation

We are good at rules: making them and then breaking them. Paul reminds us that, when we gain Christ Jesus as our Lord and Savior, we receive exactly what we need—forgiveness, grace, hope. Let us confess our sins to God, so we might know God's healing love for us!

Unison Prayer of Confession

If we were to name all the gods we have before you, Rock of Redemption, we would be here a very long time. We elevate politicians into saviors, though they are as broken as we are. We misuse your name so much during

the day, we have trouble speaking to you in prayer at night. We are so busy, we do not notice how creation witnesses to your goodness and grace.

Forgive us, God our Hope. Help us to let go of what we value most, so we may open our emptiness, our hearts, our lives to the healing and loving presence of Jesus Christ, our Lord and Savior.

Silence is kept.

Assurance of Pardon

Persistently, patiently, lovingly, God pours out grace and joy into our lives, healing our brokenness, forgiving our sin.

Loved, we are sent to love;
forgiven, we are freed to forgive;
graced, we can offer our gifts to everyone we meet.
Thanks be to God. Amen.

Liz Crumlish
http://somethingtostandon.blogspot.co.uk/

Philippians 3

Establishing credentials is something we like to do in church circles. Until recently, I might have tagged credential bagging as a predominantly male sport. However, recently I was with a group of women clergy and each of us, in introducing ourselves, stated how long we'd been ordained or had served in the church, until it began to sound like a competition. There is something about credentials—be it educational qualifications, length of service, or the number of battle scars we carry—that brings an imagined status and confidence in stressful situations. In such a competitive world, how can we simply rely on the greatest credentials of all—being called beloved children of God? How can we appreciate and realize the magnificence of that gift that God, in grace, freely presents to us, endowing us with a status beyond our imagining? God created us and calls us wonderful. There are all sorts of ways to live into that reality. Some of those might involve study, service, determination, maybe even perseverance; but none of it involves competition, because God has already decreed our acceptability and, in Christ, our freedom is bought. So, in the knowledge of all that Christ endured for us, how can we claim any credence other than that bought with Christ's life?

On the contrary, God declaring us beloved children brings us a confidence that, whatever we do, we can do it well because we are already equipped and already approved—that's a lot to live up to. We strive to fulfill the confidence that God places in us, knowing that God spurs us on, having already declared us winners.

Todd Weir
http://bloomingcactus.typepad.com/

Matthew 21

It is helpful to place yourself as one of the characters in the Gospel to see what Christ has to say to you in that role. In the parable of the Wicked Tenants, it feels absurd at first to imagine identifying with a heinous crime. My first take would see the passage applying to demagogues who steal elections and persecute their citizens, or clergy who distort the Gospel to justify war and oppression. It is they who seize Heaven by force and take it for their own purposes.

Yet Jesus' parables have a way of penetrating the soul. As a young pastor I wanted to be a disturber of the status quo and change the world. I was in seminary when Liberation theology was exposing the bias toward power and challenging the church to be on the side of the poor and oppressed. Ministry was "comforting the afflicted and afflicting the comfortable," and I much preferred the latter. In my first solo pastorate, I preached that new wine must go into new skins, and that the seven last words of a dying church were "we've never done it that way before." Either the congregation was tolerant or I wasn't too overbearing, because I had twelve good years there.

I have noticed a shift as I move into middle age and more authority as an institutional leader. Changes that I had nurtured in the church in my early days were suddenly challenged by newer members as being part of the old status quo. I had stayed in the church long enough to see my own best ideas outlive their usefulness. Defensiveness crept into my heart: "This is my church and my flock. I worked hard to build it, and I know best." Isn't this in essence the same mind-set of the wicked tenants? Because they had worked the ground, they felt the right to keep it for themselves. Afflicting the comfortable began to mean dealing with myself.

Jesus judged few sinners harshly, but most of his exchanges with religious leaders were confrontational. Clergy are not worse than anyone else, but we have a unique temptation to believe we are owners of the church rather than tenants. This is a twofold danger. First, we are tempted by selfishness and ego to defend our status, authority, and ideas. We think we must be the finest Christian in the room in order to lead. The second temptation comes from the congregation, who often don't want to hear the challenging aspect of the Gospel. They wish us to seize the vineyard for them and protect their bias and comfortable way of life. The pastor who only comforts the afflicted will be much loved, but Christ is still murdered just like the landlord's son in the parable.

Christ is the sole head of the church, the cornerstone. The parable cautions us to avoid usurping the church for ourselves.

October 12
18th Sunday after Pentecost (Proper 23)

Exodus 32:1-14; Psalm 106:1-6, 19-23; Philippians 4:1-9; Matthew 22:1-14; Isaiah 25:1-9; Psalm 23

Sharron Blezard

Exodus 32

Everybody loves a party, right? Wherever there is food and fun, folks will follow. The words "You're invited" have a welcome ring to them. This Sunday's lessons abound with images of celebrations, feasting, food, and of course, humankind's uncanny ability to make a mess of things.

In Exodus 32, the people of Israel are tired of waiting for Moses and start their own "party" with a god of their own creation—a golden calf. "They rose early the next day, and offered burnt offerings and brought sacrifices of well-being; and the people sat down to eat and drink, and rose up to revel," says the writer (v. 6 NRSV). But things don't go so well for the impatient partygoers, and they end up drinking the dust of their own idol. In the Gospel lesson from Matthew, Jesus speaks of a wedding banquet and unwilling and unprepared guests. Again, things don't go so well for those who fail to follow proper party etiquette.

Fortunately, outer darkness, weeping, and gnashing are not the last word. The Lord of Hosts is much bigger than our messes and will not permit us to spoil the divine banquet. God has other plans and, as the consummate host, continually invites us to the divine party. The alternate Old Testament lessons (Isaiah 25:1-9; Psalm 23) speak of feasting, of bountiful tables spread, of overflowing cups, of well-aged wines and rich food. There are no tears and no fear when God is the host, only goodness and mercy.

Why not make the invitation explicit? Use these lessons to proclaim God's desire to include us in the never ending salvation celebration. Come with rejoicing and thanksgiving to the table for Communion, for a potluck and fellowship, and for eternity. Celebrate the goodness and mercy of God!

Teri Peterson
http://clevertitlehere.blogspot.com

Exodus 32

It's comforting to be reminded that our instant-gratification culture is not a byproduct of the digital age, nor a particular failing of "young people these days." Unwillingness to wait, desire for immediate tangible results, and impatience with the mysterious slowness of spiritual life seem to go back millennia, rather than being a hallmark of the Millennial generation.

Couple that inability to wait with a leader willing to give in to the anxiety, and you have the perfect storm. How many congregations have faced this problem? The people are anxious and uncertain, and they demand a solution. The leader, even while knowing better, gives in to the demands, and soon we are worshiping something that is decidedly not God.

213

Part of the difficulty is that, at least initially, the idea seems to make sense. People desire a deeper relationship with God—how can we resist giving it to them? Resist we must, because no preacher, teacher, pastor, or parent has ever been able to simply hand spiritual depth over on a golden platter.

Building a relationship with our God takes time. Even face to face, it took many days for Moses and God to get to know each other well enough to reach the point where the commandments could be delivered, let alone where they spoke to each other "as one speaks to a friend" (33:11 NRSV). Desire for relationship is the first step, and the Israelites certainly had that. But a spiritual life, whether that of an individual or a community, also requires effort, energy, honesty, perseverance, endurance, and trust. We have to be willing to wait, to "trust in the slow work of God" (as Pierre Teilhard de Chardin said in a letter to his cousin Margeurite in October 1915), to sit in silence, to put in the same amount of time both listening and speaking as we would with a human friend.

But it is so much easier to work with something we can see and touch. As a leader it is so much easier to offer the cheap facsimile than to nurture true spiritual relationship. We know how this story ends: Moses ends up in the strange position of *convincing God* to reclaim the people as God insists they belong to Moses. (God having apparently forgotten how much work it was to convince Moses to go back to Egypt in the first place!) Yet even knowing this story, the temptation is great. It takes a long time, and "we don't have a clue" (32:1) what is happening during the time when nothing appears to be happening, and suddenly we are sacrificing and dancing and giving our hearts to something hard, cold, and unforgiving.

As preachers we may tire of wondering what the golden calf looks like in our community. It is important that our own spiritual lives are strong, so we don't fall into Aaron's trap of believing we can provide people with anything more than tools and space to seek, no matter how uncomfortable or anxious they (or we) might be.

John Wesley's Notes on the Bible
http://www.ccel.org/ccel/wesley/notes.txt

Exodus 32:1

"Up, make us gods which shall go before us." They were weary of waiting for the promised land. They thought themselves detained too long at mount Sinai. They had a God that stayed with them, but they must have a God to go before them to the land flowing with milk and honey. They were weary of waiting for the return of Moses: "As for this Moses, the man that brought us up out of Egypt, we know not what is become of him"—Observe how slightly they speak of his person, this Moses: And how suspiciously of his delay, we know not what is become of him. And they were weary of waiting for a divine institution of religious worship among them, so they would have a worship of their own invention, probably such as they had seen among the Egyptians. They say, make us gods which shall go before us. Gods! How many would they have? Is not one sufficient? And what good would gods of their own making do them? They must have such Gods to go before them as could not go themselves farther than they were carried!

Eric D. Barreto

Exodus 32; Psalm 23

Psalm 23 is one of the most well-known passages of Scripture. Why is that? Perhaps because the psalm speaks about our deepest hopes and longings, fears and anxieties. When I spent a summer as a chaplain intern in a hospital, the King James version of Psalm 23 was a profound comfort to all kinds of patients. Whether they were church-goers or had long ago left the faith, this psalm was a comfort in the midst of despair. The psalm expresses trust in the promise that God will not desert us, even when pain and death seem to engulf us. It does not promise an easy or comfortable life. Instead, when life gets most difficult, God is with us in our own shadowed valleys.

The trust in God confessed in Psalm 23 is not naïve. The psalmist knows that God's faithfulness does not rest on the absolute fealty of a people. Exodus 32:1-14 brings us to a moment of great failure on the part of God's people.

While Moses is carving the tablets that would contain God's holy writ, the people are frightened and worried back at camp. Concerned that Moses will not return from the holy mountain, they, together with Aaron, craft a golden calf to be an object of worship. At the very moment that God invites God's people to have no other gods, Israel is melting gold and creating a god in its own image. It is certainly easy to point fingers at these Israelites. But such blame might miss an extraordinarily important point: we also fall easily into patterns of idolatry. We also will face the temptation to satiate our fear with something tangible when God calls only for our trust.

Carolyn Winfrey Gillette
http://www.carolynshymns.com/

Lord, You Are My Shepherd

Lord, you are my shepherd and so I am blessed;
You make me lie down in green pastures to rest.
You lead me beside the still waters, O Lord;
In you I find peace and my soul is restored.

Refrain
In this world, there is much that can tempt me away,
Yet in you, I'm content, as you guide me each day.
O Lord, I don't need to feel lost or alone;
For you are my Shepherd and I am your own.

You lead me to do what is just, in your name;
You guide me through valleys of death and deep pain.
I'll fear nothing evil with you by my side;
Your rod and your staff, Lord, will comfort and guide. *Refrain*

You set me a table right here by my foes;
You bless me with joy till my cup overflows.
Your goodness and mercy will follow me through;
I'll live in your presence, forever with you. *Refrain*

NOTES
Biblical Reference: Psalm 23
Tune: TO GOD BE THE GLORY 11.11.11.11 with refrain, William Howard Doane, 1875
Text: Copyright © 2012 by Carolyn Winfrey Gillette. All rights reserved.

John Petty
http://progressiveinvolvement.com

Matthew 22

It is Holy Week. Jesus has entered Jerusalem, driven the profiteers out of the temple, and told two parables, the parable of the two sons, and the parable of the wicked tenants.

Then, he tells this story, the parable of the wedding banquet. The king is holding a wedding banquet in honor of his son. He sends his servants to call those invited, but they hold the king's invitation in low regard. This symbolizes Israel's resistance to the first servants sent by the king, the Old Testament prophets.

The king then sends out "other" servants. They represent the followers of "the way"—the early Christians, in other words. They announce the arrival of the Great Banquet: "Behold! I have made ready my dinner. . . . Come into the marriage feast" (v. 4 author's translation).

"All is ready" is clear eschatological language. How is it that "all is ready"? Note that "the son" does not actually appear in this parable. This "son" had been killed in the parable of the wicked tenants. Yet, in *this* parable, the son is obviously alive. The story assumes that the son has been raised from the dead. It is in his death and resurrection that "all is ready."

This time, the invitees are called neglectful. They did not care about the king's dinner. One went to his farm, the other went to his business. They went back to preserving and expanding their economic interests, in other words.

The "other servants" are seized, mistreated, and killed. The king retaliates by sending soldiers who destroy the murderers and burn the city. (Any connection with a real event is hereby sundered. You don't get angry, start a war, and conquer a city all before the pot roast gets cold.)

The king then tells his servants to "go therefore into the main streets, and invite everyone you find" (v. 9 NRSV). The servants gather all, "both good and bad" (v. 10a NRSV). This is a pointed rejection of morality as a basis for determining who goes to the banquet. The servants are to gather up all they find without regard to whether anyone deserves it or not. Accordingly, the wedding banquet is "filled with guests" (v. 10b NRSV).

The king, however, zeroes in on one person who is not dressed right. This person is called "friend" (*etairos*). The word carries a certain chill—think: "hey, pal."

The host of the banquet must have supplied the wedding garments. Otherwise, how could you expect people rounded up off the streets to have the proper clothes? You don't leave for work in the morning by packing a tux in your lunch box on the off-chance that someone might drag you to a wedding party.

The wedding garment is the death and resurrection of Jesus. The Great Banquet has been made possible and ushered in by that and that alone. One person has apparently thought the banquet is based in something other than that. He wears some other garment. Whether rags or a tux, it matters not. Anything other than the wedding garment of Christ's death and resurrection is irrelevant.

Natalie Sims
http://lectionarysong.blogspot.com

Matthew 22

Who will come to the wedding banquet? God invites everyone!

"Draw the Circle Wide" (Gordon Light)—A great song about welcoming all people. Lyrics (http://www.unityvictoria.ca/lyrics.doc; downloads a Word document).

"Among Us and Before Us Lord You Stand" (Iona Community)—Good if you are celebrating Communion this week. The tune is simple, and the words provide a fully inclusive welcome: "Who dares say No, when such is your request that each around your table should be guest?"

"Gather Us In" (Marty Haugen)—Excellent words, very well known. "Nourish us well and teach us to fashion / lives that are holy and hearts that are true."

"Gather Your People" (Bob Hurd)—Excellent words and eucharistic theology. Good if you are celebrating Communion this week.

"I Cannot Come to the Banquet" (Medical Mission Sisters)—This song from the Medical Mission Sisters lists all the excuses (I have married a wife! I have bought me a cow!). Lyrics and CD (http://store.augsburgfortress.org/store/product/7334/Kingdom-Stories-Parable-Tunes-Music).

"Come to the Banquet There's a Place for You" (Fay White)—An excellent song by Melbourne singer and songwriter Faye White; one of those that can work well as an energetic or laid-back song.

"Come to the Feast / Ven al Banquete" (Bob Hurd)—Simple song with English and Spanish words, including a bilingual refrain. You could just use the chorus on its own, too. Sample and sheet music (http://www.ocp.org/compositions/16049#tab:sheetmusic).

"God's Table" (Iona Community)—I wish this song wasn't exclusively masculine for God; perhaps someone has updated it? "God has a table, and one day we'll meet him there." The tune is great, though, and the images are excellent, so I just sing it as it is, and try to balance it out elsewhere in the service. It's very awkward to change it. Book and CD (http://www.wgrg.co.uk/product_info.php?cPath=21_27&products_id=75).

"God Has Laid a Feasting Table / Invitation" (Shawn Whelan)—Feminine imagery of God gathering her guests to a feasting table. Fun Cuban rhythm. Sample and songbook (http://www.wholenote.com.au/songs/invitation.html).

Julia Seymour
http://lutheranjulia.blogspot.com

Matthew 22

Sometimes the pastor needs a sermon. Not the one to write, but the soul needs to hear a sermon, a good word, some guidance. When the written word seems to yield no inspiration, we appeal to the Living Word as our pastor and shepherd.

Pastor, speak to me with clarity. I need understanding and I need the faith that comes without understanding. Let me trust that revelation follows your faithfulness and not my own. This is the gospel I need today.

Pastor, in this long, green ordinary season, life and death come and go. I do not want riddles. I can handle the truth. I long for the truth. I remain hopeful, but cynicism and frustration curl the edges of my hope. Is this a parable of open doors or closed ones? Come, Holy Spirit, and reveal the meaning of this parable. I would prefer that it point to inclusion, especially of me. And the people I like. Maybe I cannot handle the truth. This is the gospel I need today.

Pastor, speak to me of sin and of release. Speak the hard truth about sin—about its power to separate us from our neighbors and to make us feel separated from God. Look me in the eye and tell me that sin is action and intention, both concrete and nebulous. Use words that are familiar, but help me understand in a new way that sin is that which I have done and left undone, said and remained quiet about, things I have given too freely and things I have withheld. This is the gospel I need today.

Pastor, now preach to me about release. I don't want to hear about forgiveness only, about a formula or words that make things right. I want a powerful, truthful, toe-curling honesty about release—release from the fear of death, release from the captivity of sin, release from the mistakes of the past, release into the freedom of a new future in God. Speak to me of the release that is offered through Jesus, every day, every minute. Tell me that the love of Christ is the clothing for the banquet. Pastor, speak to me of amazing grace and do not stop. This is the gospel I need today.

Pastor, speak to me of invitation. Tell me that I have not missed the angel, the mail, the train. Speak to me of repeated calling, the ongoing work of the Spirit, of God beating the bushes so that the table seating is full and complete. Speak to me as a co-inviter, as a witness to the summons. Tell me of the need and longing people have to hear Jesus' invitation. With the help of the Spirit, compel me into new understanding of table, washing, and body. Tell me how hard this parable is for you. Then speak to me with certainty about what is true, whether or not this story reveals it. This is the gospel I need today.

October 19
19th Sunday after Pentecost (Proper 24)

Exodus 33:12-23; Psalm 99; 1 Thessalonians 1:1-10; Matthew 22:15-22; Isaiah 45:1-7; Psalm 96:1-9, (10-13)

Beth Quick
http://bethquick.blogspot.com

Exodus 33

• "My presence will go with you, and I will give you rest" (v. 14 NRSV). This is the promise that God makes to Moses. Moses makes God repeat it, because he knows that God's presence means good things for the Israelites. Does Moses expect a different kind of protection and presence than God has planned? I think Moses sees God's presence as a safety net instead of a foundation. Do we ever see and treat God's presence that way?

• "You cannot see my face" (v. 20 NRSV). Meeting "face to face" usually is something we want so that we can be on equal footing with another. God reminds us that we are not exactly on equal footing with God! But still, that we see God, that Moses can be so close with and to God shows that God has a unique relationship with humanity. We can talk to God! Compared with characteristics of other deities worshiped in Moses' day, this God of Israel is a different kind of God.

Psalm 99

• "Lover of justice, you have established equity" (v. 4 NRSV). God *loves* justice. We don't need to wonder what is meant by justice in this case. This is not God-lover-of-justice who loves to punish and condemn. The justice that God loves is the justice that brings equity, fairness for everyone.

• "You were a forgiving God to them, but an avenger of their wrongdoings" (v. 8 NRSV). God who is both forgiving and avenging. Can God forgive us and punish us? Parents can, right? I worry because we like to point out how God is punishing others who are not like us, or we believe that everything that happens to us that we don't like is due to God's punishment. Does God punish? What do you think?

1 Thessalonians 1

• "We always give thanks to God for all of you and mention you in our prayers, constantly" (v. 2 NRSV). It's nice to know that someone is praying for you, isn't it? Do we remember to pray for one another in our ministry?

• "And you became imitators of us and of the Lord" (v. 6 NRSV). If someone were to imitate you, could they also say they were imitating Christ? What would it look like for someone to imitate you?

• "In every place your faith in God has become known, so that we have no need to speak about it" (v. 8 NRSV). Could someone say this of *your* faith?

Matthew 22

• The Pharisees and Herodians patronize Jesus in their question, but they've at least noticed correctly: Jesus shows no deference and no partiality to people. Clearly, though, this drives them crazy. They want his deference!

• Jesus says, give "to God the things that are God's" (v. 21 NRSV). What is God's? Do we not believe that it all belongs to God? What is ours, or the emperor's?

Melissa Bane Sevier
http://melissabanesevier.wordpress.com

Presence (Exodus 33)

"[God] said, 'My presence will go with you, and I will give you rest.' And [Moses] said to [God], 'If your presence will not go, do not carry us up from here'" (vv. 14-15 NRSV).

A recovery room, a blur of voices, then a ride on a gurney down hallways and onto an elevator. All the voices were kind and friendly, but not one of them was familiar. Consciousness was elusive.

Out of the elevator and down another hallway, then into a room and transferred onto a bed. All these hands moving me, adjusting the bedding, checking my IV. I felt them, but they seemed distant. Then someone touched my hand, and for the first time I opened my eyes. Through the haze of anesthesia and myopia (I didn't have my glasses), I immediately recognized my husband's face and voice. His touch was different from the others, because his presence meant something to my deepest self, even though that self was shrouded in fog. How had I recognized him through just a touch? Disorientation gave way to a sense of place. Not a specific location. But I knew who I was with, and that was enough.

Even though that surgery was twenty years ago, and I don't remember much about it, the memory of relief in that one moment is strong. Someone who loved me was there. I knew I wasn't alone.

In the story of the exodus, *presence* is a constant theme. The wilderness was disorienting. The goal was so far away, even after years of being nomads. In the cloud and fire they somehow found strength and presence. They could sense the connection between them and God, and they could also see that God never left, day or night, whether they were traveling or staying still.

Sometimes God's absence is more palpable to us than God's presence. We look for God but find…nothing. We long for God but feel nothing. We pray to God and hear nothing.

But then there are moments. Moments when in the midst of a horrendous day we have the sense that we are surrounded by a warm cloud of God's love. Moments when in a sleepless night we think we might see the flame of God's peace that has not been extinguished. When these moments come, we latch onto them, so we can remember them when neither fire nor cloud is visible.

For me, the moments of cloud and fire usually come through the love and actions of someone else. A kind word. A look of understanding. The touch of my husband's hand in a hospital room. May you know the presence of God in those around you, and may you offer God's presence to those who need it. You are not alone.

Lowell Grisham
http://lowellsblog.blogspot.com/

Prayers of the People (Exodus 33, Psalm 99)

Presider: Holy God, lover of justice, you have promised that your presence will go with us to guide and protect your people: Show us your glory, we pray, that we may know you and find favor in your sight, as we pray: Proclaim the greatness of our God, for our God is the Holy One.

Litanist: Holy God, you have chosen your Church for your work of faith and labor of love and steadfastness of hope in our Lord Jesus Christ: Grant that we may be true to you, not in word only, but also in power and in the Holy Spirit, with full conviction. Proclaim the greatness of our God,

for our God is the Holy One.

Mighty God, you urge this nation and all in authority into your ways of peace and equality: Save our leaders from showing partiality and grant them vision and courage to give only that which is appropriate to the claims of politics and state, and to give to God the things that are God's. Proclaim the greatness of our God,

for our God is the Holy One.

Loving and gracious God, your presence inspires us and our neighbors in this community to continue to work in faith, to labor in love, and to be steadfast in hope: Let our welcome go forth in grace and peace. Proclaim the greatness of our God,

for our God is the Holy One.

Immanent God, your presence is everywhere and your glory touches all the earth: Show your gracious goodness to people throughout the world, so that all may know you and find favor in your sight. Proclaim the greatness of our God,

for our God is the Holy One.

Merciful God, your grace and peace fill our community and connect us with ties of loving regard: Hear our prayers for those whom we remember in intercession, especially _____. Accept our grateful thanksgiving for the goodness of life, especially for _____. Receive into the full vision of your goodness and glory those who have died, especially _____. Proclaim the greatness of our God,

for our God is the Holy One.

Presider: Living and true God, your strong arm is extended to bring justice and truth to the earth: Guide the powerful into your ways and keep us ever faithful to your will, that everyone in heaven and earth may work to bring about your intention of reconciliation and peace; through Jesus Christ our Savior, who lives and reigns with you and the Holy Spirit, one God, forever and ever. **Amen.**

Martha Spong
http://marthaspong.com/

Exodus 33

Here's something I love about Moses. No matter how many times he saw or heard from God, he wanted more. Not content to rest on the burning bush, or the magic powers, or the pillars of smoke and fire or the receiving of the tablets bearing THE LAW, Moses says to the Lord: "Show me your glory, I pray" (v. 18 NRSV).

I understand this. I am one of those people who cannot hear enough times that she is loved. I appreciate displays of affection. I get Moses. And I love the way God responds. "Okay, honey, I'll show you my glory, to the extent you can take it in, and I'll even protect you from looking at me too directly, sort of like one of those pinhole things people use to keep from blinding themselves during an eclipse."

If you have ever needed to reassure a child who did not want to go to school or to daycare, you probably know why I am picturing God as an Awesome Mama here. "Sweet potato, go stand over there where it's safe, and just to be extra sure, Mama will cover your eyes for you with her Big Giant Hand." Much of the time, this is what we need.

My own children, two of them, are far away, and I want to do this for them, and not being supernatural, I cannot. I have to pray for them instead, pray that they will find their way in the adult world as creative artists and not starve to death. Frankly, I could use a dose of proof right about now, and I'm guessing many of us, worried about the general state of the world, could use it, too.

But Moses! Why did he need it? Hadn't he gotten more than enough? Can you get enough of God? Perhaps not. Perhaps they had a relationship so intimate that one appearance could not suffice. Because apparently God enjoyed their little talks, too.

Another thing I love about Moses is that he talked to God the way I do when I am driving the car. "Oh, Lord. What can I do to guide my sons?" "How can I best help the people at church?" "Why can't that person see things the way I do when the answer is so clear?" Moses came to God over and over with his doubts and his frustrations, and by doing just that, he found favor in God's sight. It doesn't matter that he was impulsive. It doesn't matter that he was initially doubtful and frankly resistant. He gave God his all, his flawed and human all, and he found favor with God. Maybe that I can do.

Sharron Blezard

1 Thessalonians 1

"You have been chosen…" the letter or phone call begins. Even though most of us assume a marketing ploy will follow, these words nonetheless pique our interest. After all, we humans like to be noticed and called out from the teeming masses in the vast sea of ordinariness. In a world that constantly tells us we are "less than" or not good enough, attractive enough, rich enough, or clever enough, being chosen and deemed "special" has a right fine ring to it.

Do you think of yourself as being "chosen" or set apart? Those of us who are called to vocational ministry understand ourselves as called by God for particular service in the church and world. I seriously doubt, however, that the average Christian warming the pew on Sunday morning feels "chosen" by God. In the midst of work, family, and community responsibilities, the concept of being set apart and called out to make a difference in the world is not marked on the daily calendar.

We must be reminded that we are chosen and called by God. In his first letter to the Christians in Thessalonica, Paul says "For we know, brothers and sisters beloved by God, that he has chosen you" (v. 4 NRSV). God even works through people without their direct knowledge. The ruler Cyrus is one such example in today's alternate reading from Isaiah. In short, we may not realize the difference, the impact we are making in the world as people of God.

How wonderful it would be if the congregation could leave worship with a renewed sense of Christian vocational identity. Consider sending the congregation out with a special blessing to go and be God's beloved in the world—chosen, claimed, redeemed, and sent—in the name of Jesus.

Paul Nuechterlein
http://girardianlectionary.net/

1 Thessalonians 1; Matthew 22

In the first century, Paul wrote,

> You became imitators of us and of the Lord when you accepted the message that came from the Holy Spirit with joy in spite of great suffering. As a result you became an example to all the believers in Macedonia and Achaia. (1 Thess 1:6-7)

In this twenty-first-century age of individualism, if Paul praised *us* for being good imitators, we would probably be insulted. We hate the thought of being perceived as copying anyone, so we eschew imitation in favor of "being a unique individual" (although we love it when others imitate us—imitation being "the sincerest form of flattery").

No matter how much we believe our identities have been formed without imitation, we must be honest. As babies we learn the basics of body language (e.g., returning smiles), walking, and talking, all through imitation. For something as complex as learning to be a doctor, we require apprenticeships, learning by imitation. According to the biblical anthropology known as Mimetic Theory (see my essays in January 19, February 16, and March 9), our modern efforts to be absolutely unique are founded on illusion. Science is proving that we are hard-wired for imitation—a significant portion of our cortex being devoted to "mirror neurons." Imitation is also confirmed in our consumerist culture: advertisers count on the fact that we will catch the desires of those in the ads whose desiring behaviors are on display precisely for us to imitate. For, above all, the desires that animate us and move us through each day are "mimetic"—a term borrowed from the Greek word *imitators* in 1 Thess. 1:6 (*mimētēs*). Mimetic Theory hypothesizes that it is not a matter of *whether* we imitate the desires of others; it is simply a matter of *whose* desires we imitate.

With a fresh understanding that humans are hard-wired for Mimetic Desire, the biblical interpretation of human desire becomes clear. Paul shows his understanding in this Epistle—"You became imitators of us and of the Lord.…As a result you became an example" (vv. 6-7). Matthew's Gospel of the day is yet another instance. Jesus avoids the trap set for him by the Pharisees with a veiled reference to our need to imitate God. Confronted with an imperial coin, he inquires about the "image" on it, using a word that would recall for most Jews a central tenet of their faith: human beings are made in the image of God. His clever quip—"Give to Caesar what belongs to Caesar and to God

221

what belongs to God" (Matt 22:21)—is really saying, "That coin has Caesar's image on it, so you can give it back to Caesar. *You* are made in God's image, so give your entire self to God." Made in God's image, we are created with the ability to imitate God's desiring, *agape* Love. Love has shown itself on the cross, and the Holy Spirit has been unleashed; we are called to imitate God's "complete" love (Matt 5:48) and live it as examples to others.

Eric D. Barreto

Matthew 22

The Pharisees and Herodians approach Jesus with a rhetorical question. They are not seeking answers but hatching a plot that would trap Jesus. In Jesus, they see a political threat. Why? He is a threat because of his radical teachings and actions. He is a threat because if the crowds following Jesus get a little too feisty the oppressive hand of Rome will surely fall on them all. Thus, with mixed motives, they approach Jesus with what they imagine is a perfect trap: should we pay taxes to Caesar? If Jesus answers yes, then he will lose the support of the adoring crowds. They know the oppression of Roman rule too well and will see in Jesus' affirmative response that he is no different from any number of powerful individuals who accommodate Roman rule. If Jesus answers no, then he would be seen by the Roman state not merely as a conscientious objector, but as a rank insurrectionist. Paying taxes is not just a civic duty in the Roman Empire but a sign of allegiance. Not paying your taxes is tantamount to taking up a sword against Rome. A negative response is a one-way ticket to execution. So, how will Jesus escape this certain trap? As Jesus often does, he answers a question with yet another question. When his opponents identify that they are carrying Caesar's graven image, Jesus famously concludes to give to Caesar what is Caesar's and to God what belongs to God. We err when we see Jesus here dividing the secular and religious. What belongs to God if not everything in the world? What then is left to give to Caesar? To Jesus, there was only one kingdom, only one king. What would it cost for us to view the reign of God in the same way?

John Wesley's Notes on the Bible
http://www.ccel.org/ccel/wesley/notes.txt

Matthew 22:21

"They say to him, Caesar's"—Plainly acknowledging, by their having received his coin, that they were under his government. And indeed this is a standing rule. The current coin of every nation shows who is the supreme governor of it. Render therefore, ye Pharisees, to Caesar the things which ye yourselves acknowledge to be Caesar's: and, ye Herodians, while ye are zealous for Caesar, see that ye render to God the things that are God's.

October 26
20th Sunday after Pentecost (Proper 25)

Deuteronomy 34:1-12; Psalm 90:1-6, 13-17; 1 Thessalonians 2:1-8; Matthew 22:34-46; Leviticus 19:1-2, 15-18; Psalm 1

Amy Persons Parkes

Deuteronomy 34

"Would you like for me to pray for you?" I asked the elderly man I was visiting.

Without hesitation, "Yes, I would like that."

"Is it okay if I hold your hand as we pray?"

"Please," he smiled.

I have no idea what I actually said in my prayer. However, after my "Amen" he softly offered, "I felt the Spirit through your hands as we prayed." And as hesitant as I am to acknowledge it (being a mainline intellectual Protestant and all), he was right. I had felt something, too.

The Spirit of God has expression in and through our touch. How we touch one another, when we touch, who we touch evidences our relationship, or lack thereof, to the Spirit of the Living God. In the Pentateuch, the Law—with its ordering of boundaries and social structures and the governance prescribing what is holy and profane—for all practical purposes, is defining "good" and "bad" touch. Though Moses and Joshua had been called by the Lord to the tent of meeting for the transfer of leadership (Deut 31:14), our text from Deuteronomy states, "Joshua son of Nun was full of the spirit of wisdom, *because* Moses had laid his hands on him" (Deut 34:9a NRSV, emphasis added). We baptize with touch. We offer the gifts of bread and wine with our touch. We anoint for healing, confirm, and ordain with our touch. Though we must, with preference and compassion, tend with great sensitivity those among us abused by unholy touch and those at risk of being hurt, the Church cannot deny the gift of the Spirit that can be revealed through our touch. God's breath gives our bodies life, and Christ embraced our flesh. Let our touch testify to the Spirit of Truth at work in us and in the world.

Marci Auld Glass
www.marciglass.com

Deuteronomy 34

The Rev. Dr. Martin Luther King, Jr., preached on this text the night before he was assassinated in 1968. He told the crowd that he had seen the Promised Land. For him, it wasn't about standing on Mt. Nebo and looking across the Jordan River Valley into the Promised Land as Moses did before he died. For King, it was about standing with people in the midst of Civil Rights struggles, fighting to be treated as human beings. The fight had not been won on April 3, 1968, when he said those words. But he had seen the Promised Land by watching people come together to work together for change, even when that change seemed too far away. It was about having hope for the future, despite the reality on the ground.

Moses knew that. He knew the forty-year-long road to the Promised Land was not easy. It wasn't a walk through the park. It was people complaining in the wilderness that he had brought them there to die. It was disobedience. It was being bitten by snakes. It was knowing that you were wandering and not moving forward. It was eating manna, manna, more manna, and quails.

And God took Moses and showed him the Promised Land, a panoramic sweep of the land for each of the tribes. What is it like, do you think? To be so close that you can see what you've wanted for your whole life? And to know that you aren't going to make the rest of the journey?

Because of the Hebrew people's disobedience, and Moses' failure as a leader to obey, the original generation of Hebrew people who left Israel died before they reached the Promised Land. It was only the next generation who made it across the river. The first generation, other than Caleb and Joshua, died in the wilderness. But they didn't stop when they knew that justice was out of reach for them. They kept on the journey to make a better future for their children.

It can be hard to seek the Promised Land when the milk and honey will be flowing for someone else. But Moses kept on leading the people toward a goal he knew he would never reach.

I keep thinking of Martin Luther King's final sermon. He, of course, did not know that an assassin's bullets would claim his life the next day. But I would suspect that had he known, his final words would not have been much different.

Moses knew the end of his life was approaching. And chapter 33 of Deuteronomy is his final sermon to the Israelites, giving each of the tribes instruction and encouragement.

What would you say to people if you knew you were at the end, if you knew the Promised Land was in reach? How would you want to be remembered? What would you want people to know about your faith?

NOTE: Adapted from "Writing Your Obituary," a sermon preached by Marci Auld Glass (http://marciglass.com/2011/10/23/writing-your-obituary/).

Dan Clendenin
http://journeywithjesus.net

Leviticus 19; Matthew 22

The "holiness code" in Leviticus specifies in minute detail clean and unclean foods, purity rituals after childbirth or a menstrual cycle, regulations for skin infections and contaminated clothing or furniture, prohibitions against contact with a human corpse or dead animal, instructions about nocturnal emissions, laws regarding bodily discharges, guidelines about planting seeds and mating animals, keeping the sabbath, forsaking idols, tattoos, and extensive decrees about sex. Leviticus 18 codifies about twenty types of (un)lawful sexual relations.

Some of these ancient commands seem self-evident. We gladly follow them today and neglect them at our peril. Honor your parents. Take special care of the poor, the blind, the deaf, and the alien. Don't steal or lie. Don't have sex with your parent, your child, or an animal. Don't cheat your employee or your customers.

But side by side with these timeless truths are other commands that are lost to a different time and place, and we feel no compunction in ignoring them today—don't mate different kinds of animals, plant your field with two kinds of seeds, cut the hair at the sides of your head, or wear garments made of two kinds of materials. Similarly, we rightly ignore some of the punishments for breaking these laws, such as the death penalty for cursing your parents or for adultery.

Scholars debate how much or how little ordinary first-century Jews concerned themselves with maintaining "ritual purity" by obeying the holiness code in Leviticus, but the Pharisees about whom we read so much in the Gospels certainly did. And so in the Gospel text for this week, a Pharisee who is described as an "expert" in the law "tested [Jesus] with this question: 'Teacher, which is the greatest commandment in the Law?' " (Matt 22:35-36 NIV 1984).

Maybe this was a trick question designed to trap Jesus. If he privileged a single commandment, didn't that mean he neglected others? How dare he imply that we can wink at some of God's laws! Or if he suggested that all the commandments were equally weighty, didn't that contradict common sense? Surely a tattoo (Lev 19:28) wasn't as morally weighty as child sacrifice (Lev 18:21)! Or maybe the expert was posing an honest inquiry: "Lord, so many commands! How should we understand them all? Are some more important than others?"

Buried deep in that holiness code was one, single command, Leviticus 19:18, that Jesus said was more important than the six hundred eleven other commands. Jesus responded that the most important commandment is this: " 'You shall love the Lord your God with all your heart, and with all your soul, and with all your mind.' This is the greatest and first commandment. And a second is like it: 'You shall love your neighbor as yourself.' On these two commandments hang all the law and the prophets" (Matt 22:37-40 NRSV; see Deut 6:4; Lev 19:18).

With that deft response Jesus linked our love of God with our love of neighbor. You cannot separate the two. To have one is to have the other, and to neglect one is to lose them both.

John Wesley's Notes on the Bible
http://www.ccel.org/ccel/wesley/notes.txt

1 Thessalonians 2:3

"For our exhortation"—That is, our preaching. A part is put for the whole. "Is not, at any time, of deceit"—We preach not a lie, but the truth of God. "Nor of uncleanness"—With any unholy or selfish view. This expression is not always appropriated to lust, although it is sometimes emphatically applied thereto. "Nor in guile"—But with great plainness of speech.

Ann Scull
http://seedstuff.blogspot.com

A Useful Image

This is my photo I took from the summit of Mt. Nebo (biblical Moab, present-day Jordan) with the biblical text from Deuteronomy 34:4. You can find this image at http://seedstuff.blogspot.com.au/2011/10/proper-25-ordinary-30-october-23.html (accessed April 16, 2012).

Listening Song

Point of Grace, *"Gather at the River"* on *The Whole Truth* (New York: Epic, 1995). This song is about loving one another.

Prayer of Confession

This prayer, based on Psalm 90, by Rachel C. Hackenburg and found in Marin C. and Maria I. Tirabassi (eds.), *Before the Amen: Creative Resources for Worship* (Cleveland: Pilgrim Press, 2007), 200–1.

Film Clip

Liar Liar (Universal Pictures, 1997). Show the film clip where Max and Fletcher talk about why adults might need to lie. The clip can be found at "Grown Ups Lie" at http://www.wingclips.com/movieclips/liar-liar/grown-ups-lie#.TqJZW1X51W4.blogger (accessed April 16, 2012)—there is a charge but it is very reasonable. Discussion:

1. Do you agree that adults have to lie sometimes to be kind?
2. How transparent should we be to those around us?
3. Where does God fit into this discussion?

Drama

"We Are a Family," in Verena Johnson (ed.), *Let's Make a Scene Too* (Adelaide: Lutheran Publishing House, 1991), 31–32. A drama about not being at home with God.

Quotation: Robert Frost

"Home is where when you go there they have to take you in." Found at http://www.brainyquote.com/quotes/quotes/r/robertfros101059.html (accessed April 16, 2012).

Sermon: DIY

Have three stations for people to visit in any order—each with input and response activities:

Station 1: Give each person a small folded card (three fit on an A4 for me; 8.5x11 in the USA) with two empty frames printed on the inside. Have the poem by Adrian Plass, *Clear Away the Rubbish* (Great Britain: Minstral, 1988), 142–44—a poem about not being at home with one another—printed on the other side. Ask people to read the poem first and then to write or draw their public image in the left-hand frame, and their real person in the right-hand frame. Reassure everybody that this is an activity between them and God—that no one will see what they write or draw. Provide pens or pencils.

Station 2: Have a poster of the story, *Witnessing,* found at http://www.preaching.com/resources/articles/11545578/ (accessed April 16, 2012), pinned up and in large print—it is a small story so it will be easy to do this. Ask people to read the story and then respond.

Station 3: Have pens or pencils and a pile of A5 sheets (basically, 5x8 in the USA). Print:

> Side One: "Write a list, in order of priority, of those you wish to please the most. When you have finished, read side two."

> Side Two: The text of 1 Thessalonians 2:1-8, with the question "How does your list compare with Paul's?" underneath.

Suzanne Guthrie
http://www.edgeofenclosure.org

"Love by Loving" (Matthew 22)

Without love I am nothing, says Saint Paul: "If I speak in the tongues of men and of angels, but have not love, I am a noisy gong or a clanging cymbal" (1 Cor 13:1 RSV). He goes on to say that prophetic powers, the power to move mountains, giving away all we have, and even delivering our bodies to be burned—all amount to nothing without love.

Love begets love. It seems the more love you give, the more love you have to give. Love by loving. The way of loving God and neighbor is by loving God *in* neighbor and loving neighbor in the love of God. And loving the most difficult neighbor at that. "For if you love those who love you, what reward have you?" (Matt 5:46a RSV).

> If any one says, "I love God," and hates his brother, he is a liar; for he who does not love his brother whom he has seen, cannot love God whom he has not seen. And this commandment we have from him, that he who loves God should love his brother also. (1 John 4:20-21 RSV)

And if that isn't enough practice for you, and you desire a true filial relationship with God, "Love your enemies and pray for those who persecute you" (Matt 5:44 RSV).

In Matthew 25, Jesus tells a story of the righteous backing into this knowledge accidentally in his account of judgment of the sheep and the goats. John of the Cross says that in the end we shall be judged by love alone. Unfortunately, or fortunately, the world offers plenty of opportunity for the challenges of love. But here is "the kingdom prepared for you from the foundation of the world" (v. 34 RSV). The very foundation is love. And every step toward loving builds up the foundation of the kingdom of love. Without grounding in that love I am nothing. But with it . . .

John van de Laar
http://www.sacredise.com/

Matthew 22

In the Gospels of Matthew and Mark, when Jesus is questioned about the greatest commandment, his answer is decisive and simple: *"You must love the Lord your God with all your heart, with all your being,* and with all your mind....[And] *love your neighbor as you love yourself*. All the Law and the Prophets depend on these two commands" (vv. 37-39). If we remember what was happening when Jesus said these words, the impact of his message is even more startling.

Both of these Gospels place this conversation directly after Jesus' triumphal entry into Jerusalem. There were probably two processions riding into town that day. The first, with the central figure on a warhorse surrounded by a demonstration of military might, was that of Pontius Pilate. This procession was intended to remind the Jews of Rome's power, and warn them to behave during the volatile Passover season, lest it be used against them.

The second procession was that of Jesus. The warhorse was replaced by a donkey's foal. The military display was replaced by a ragtag group of celebrants. The peace-making, empire-defying message was clear, and it ultimately got Jesus killed. Soon after, Jesus went into the temple and overturned the tables of the moneychangers and animal sellers. This act of defiance against the corruption of the sacrificial system caught the attention of the religious leaders, and a debate ensued covering the three central human questions—authority (Matt 21:23-27), money (22:16-22), and sexuality (22:23-32).

It is in this context that the question of the greatest commandment was raised. Jesus' response, then, must be taken as a guide for how all of life is to be approached. In the face of oppression and military dominance, of power struggles and abuses, of economic struggles and disparities, of questions of sexuality and gender equality, we are called to one task—to love. This one commandment, Jesus taught, summarizes the entire Bible.

The other two Gospels follow different routes to the same goal. In Luke an antagonistic lawyer asks how to inherit eternal life, and Jesus' answer—quoting the commandment—includes the parable of the Good Samaritan. The Fourth Gospel never quotes the great commandment, but does something just as significant. The pivotal moment comes just after Jesus washes his disciples' feet in John 13:34: "I give you a new commandment: Love each other. Just as I have loved you, so you also must love each other."

There can be no question that for Jesus the doorway to life is love. The essential guiding principle as we face all of life's big questions is love. If we are serious about following Jesus, then we will have no choice but to learn to open our hearts and make love the primary focus of our lives—as tough and messy as that may be. If we call ourselves by Christ's name then the truth we will have to live with is this: love can be our only law.

NOTE: Adapted from my book *The Hour That Changes Everything* (Cape Town, South Africa: Sacredise Publishing, 2010), 117–19.

November 2
All Saints Sunday

Revelation 7:9-17; Psalm 34:1-10, 22; 1 John 3:1-3; Matthew 5:1-12

Amy Persons Parkes

Revelation 7

Sometimes the book of Revelation feels like the Patmos version of the Disney World attraction "It's a Small World," and I am floating along the river of the water of life (Rev 22:1), catching mechanized glimpses of the summation of all that was, is, and ever shall be. Much like I experience the ride, I am enthralled by the creativity, passion, attention to detail, and surreal depiction of various scenes. And yet, I am saddened by the caricature of people, places, ideas, and events that allows the inattentive and less prayerful reader an opportunity to oversimplify the complex and rich traditions at work in this book.

The book of Revelation reveals the constraints (and sometimes failure) of one person's (or one culture's) idealistic portrayal of reality. Though Revelation can manifest what is most offensive about an individualized understanding of reality, the book also highlights the ability of a uniquely personal experience to transform perceptions in the wider culture of the Church. From the writer of Revelation, we receive the hope springing forth from this one saint's encounter with God. From this one saint, we have a vision meticulously described and offered to us, a vision of all the faithful gathered from every tribe and place worshiping before the throne of God. From this one saint, we receive a vision that calls the Church forward to a day when all needs will be met and God will personally guide and comfort those "who have come out of the great ordeal" (v. 14b NRSV). For this reason, we celebrate All Saints Day. We celebrate the ability of God's relationship with one person, one saint, to affect and effect the Christian vision of all that has been, all that is, and all that is to come.

John Wesley's Notes on the Bible
http://www.ccel.org/ccel/wesley/notes.txt

Revelation 7:9

"A great multitude"—Of those who had happily finished their course. Such multitudes are afterwards described, and still higher degrees of glory which they attain after a sharp fight and magnificent victory, chap. xiv, 1; xv, 2; xix, 1; xx, 4. There is an inconceivable variety in the degrees of reward in the other world. Let not any slothful one say, "If I get to heaven at all, I will be content:" such an one may let heaven go altogether. In worldly things, men are ambitious to get as high as they can. Christians have a far more noble ambition. The difference between the very highest and the lowest state in the world is nothing to the smallest difference between the degrees of glory. But who has time to think of this? Who is at all concerned about it?

Thom Shuman
http://lectionaryliturgies.blogspot.com/

Call to Worship

At all times we are called to bless God's name.
Our lips drench with praises, exalting God.

The proud will bend knees in worship,
the humble will lift glad songs.
Set free from our fears, we search for God and are found.
Our faces glow with thanksgiving,
our spirits overflow with grace.
God has wiped away our tears, feeding us from the storehouses of hope.

Prayer of the Day

They are gathered around you,
God of forever and ever.
Some are well known,
Like Martin Luther, Mother Teresa,
C. S. Lewis, Helen Keller.
Some have been forgotten,
like Agnes and Cadoc,
Tuda, Mary of Egypt, and Ebba.

But many are ordinary folk,
the teacher from kindergarten
guiding our fingers under the words;
the nurse in the hospital holding
our hand while blood was taken;
the coach trusting us with the ball,
not the end of the bench.

There's an old man who left retirement behind,
the barren woman who laughed at promises;
there are popes, princes, power-brokers,
who are taught heaven's hymns
by paupers and pretenders;
there are those who moved mountains
and those who murmured in wildernesses;
there are those who build churches,
and those who flounder on Galilee's waves.

All saints, just like us, and we join them
in praying as Jesus has taught us, **Our Father...**

Call to Reconciliation

When God sets the table of the Lamb, all will be welcome—young and old; those who were faithful, and those who failed; those who followed Jesus, and those who lost their way. Let us confess to God our unsaintly ways, knowing how quick God is to forgive.

Unison Prayer of Confession

We did not listen, when the Teacher spoke, God of Sinners.
Rich in pride and arrogance,
**   our spirits have no need for a kingdom;**
taught not to let anyone see us cry,
**   we refuse your comfort;**
seeing the powerful have their way,
**   we yearn to inherit their hardened hearts;**
noticing the hungry by the side of the road,
**   we make sure we get more than our share;**
taking note of how the merciful are pushed aside,
**   we develop calluses on our souls.**
Forgive us, Saint Maker, that we follow the wrong examples and listen to false teachings. It is the peace-makers who live into your hope; it is those whose hearts are shaped by yours who are able to see you in the poor and broken; it is those who serve others who are your saints, following the example of Jesus Christ, our Shepherd, guiding us to the wellsprings of life.

Silence is kept.

Assurance of Pardon

When we seek God, we are found;
when we cry out, we are heard;

when we confess, we are forgiven and made new.
We can taste the yeasty flavor of grace,
we can drink the deep wine of hope,
we can find our home in God's heart receiving mercy and new life.
Thanks be to God. Amen.

Teri Peterson
http://clevertitlehere.blogspot.com

1 John 3; Matthew 5

Our culture seems to have a strange fascination with the afterlife. We make every effort to avoid death, yet the images of heaven and hell are too intriguing for us to turn away our eyes. Sometimes the church has played into that fascination by offering the carrot/stick method of evangelism, in which we entice people with promises of eternal bliss or threats of eternal torture. In this worldview, how we live in the now is sort of irrelevant—as long as we ask Jesus to love us and we're basically good people, we're through the pearly gates, and we can get even better seats by coming to church and volunteering sometimes.

Unfortunately, Scripture is lamentably vague on this topic. None of the handful of people raised from the dead offer any description or insight. All Jesus will say on the matter is that we don't know anything and that our expectations are woefully inadequate. Yet still we wonder. What happens? How do we ensure the best outcome for ourselves and those we love, and a lesser outcome for those we don't love?

First John 3:2 reminds us "we are God's children now; what we will be has not yet been revealed" (NRSV). Even now, we are already chosen, already loved, already called. What we will be...well, no one knows about that yet, and it isn't the point anyway. "Some people are so heavenly minded they're no earthly good" (attributed to both D. L. Moody and Oliver Wendell Holmes, but a great line, no matter who said it). First John reminds us to live as God's children now, and wait (not obsess about!) for whatever will be revealed later.

Most of the Bible seems more intent on the here and now, on learning to love those we don't love naturally, on facing the issues of hunger, injustice, heartache, mourning. When Jesus says, "blessed are those" and follows that up with words like "weep" and "hunger," we can't just push that blessing off to the afterlife and let the suffering continue now. This is present-tense blessing, present-tense honor to go along with the present-tense suffering. How would the children of God respond to these situations? How would the children of God live as though love is just as present as weeping?

On All Saints/Souls, we have a tendency to focus only on the great cloud of witnesses, to remember those who have gone before and wonder where they are now. We tend to think that they have entered the kingdom of God, while we wait to join them. Yet John writes to us that we are God's children now. Can we adjust our perspective, so we live in the kingdom of God now and don't worry about what is yet to be revealed? Can we participate in the blessing of the world, rather than waiting to escape it?

Julia Seymour
http://lutheranjulia.blogspot.com

1 John 3; Matthew 5

Who among us has ever read the Beatitudes, the list of blessings in Matthew 5, and not felt more than a little inadequate? On a day when we rejoice in the saints we have known and loved and who now rest in light, we read a list of behaviors that makes even the most saintly shudder. For, in truth, each of us knows the thoughts of our hearts. We remember when we have resentfully offered words of mercy, while not yet feeling forgiving (v. 7). We recall the times we have remained silent rather than face persecution (v. 11). We consider the cynicism with which we have received the stories of other saints, ancient and contemporary. What was their motivation (v. 6)?

As meekness is hardly prized in our day and age, we cling to the idea of sinning boldly, rather than the milquetoast vision that the Beatitudes offer...at least in our perception. When we ponder the lives of the saints we have known, we do not think of them as weak. We marvel at their courage, their creativity, their humility, their frankness, and their subtlety. We despair of living up to their example, even though they would likely be surprised at being seen in that light. On the same day that we express gratitude for and hope in their rest and resurrection, we often privately doubt that we will be worthy of the same thing.

All Saints Day requires a great deal of faith, more than we are able to muster from within ourselves. Rather than beat ourselves up about how we fall short of perfectionism, on this day let us be grateful for how God's love in Jesus brings us to perfection. Let us remember and cling to this grace: none of us is defined in the eyes of God by either the worst thing we have done *or* the best thing we have done. The eyes of Love do not view us as the sum of our virtues, minus our grievous errors. Instead, we are defined by the Living Word of love, which is Jesus Christ.

"See what love the Father has given us, that we should be called children of God; and that is what we are" (1 John 3:1 NRSV). This is the grace that carries us into love in this life and into perfected love in the next. The blessing we receive through fulfilling any of the actions in the Beatitudes is not because we were able to do the thing we did. The blessing comes from the aid and consolation of the Holy Spirit being with us, guiding us, and bridging the gap that is simply part of being created.

On this day, let us remember those saints who have gone before us and who cheer us on in our pilgrimage. Yet, let us rejoice in that we are made saints, not by what we have done or left undone, but through what God has done for all people in Christ.

Natalie Sims
http://lectionarysong.blogspot.com

Matthew 5

Oh, the Beatitudes…my favourite…

"Amen Amen It Shall Be So!" (John Bell)—A beautiful chant from John Bell. Works well with a cantor or small choir leading the verses and the congregation joining in on the "Amen, amen…." You could do this song instead of reading the passage.

"We Are the Light of the World" (Jean Anthony Greif)—Would be best with a cantor or small choir, and the congregation can respond with the chorus. You could do this instead of the reading too. Sheet music and lyrics (http://c1824532.cdn.cloudfiles.rackspacecloud.com/GC2_515-1.jpg); sound sample (http://c1824532.cdn.cloud files.rackspacecloud.com/GC2_515-1.mp3).

"Blessed Are the Poor in Spirit" (Anon.)—A simple response to the Beatitudes that can be read responsively with this refrain. Find it in the *Chalice Hymnal* (#185).

"All the Sleepy Should Have a Place to Sleep" (Rusty Edwards)—Great chorus: "Make love happen by God's grace and by God's power. / Let God move you on this day and in this hour."

"Hey My Love" (John Bell / Graham Maule)—A lovely lilting tune (Lady Maisy). This gentle song would be good for a reflection. Sound sample (http://www.ionabooks.com/1105-190155791X-I-Will-Not-Sing-Alone-songbook.html).

John Petty
http://progressiveinvolvement.com

Matthew 5

There are nine beatitudes—two groups of four, followed by a final one. The first four speak to the victims of injustice, those in poverty, grief, the meek, and those with a deep desire for justice.

Greek has two words for "poor," *penes* (working poor) and *ptochos* (destitute). Matthew uses *ptochos*. In the time of Jesus, perhaps as many as 15–20% of the population were *ptochoi*. Moreover, another 60–70% of the people stood in real danger of being forced to join that already large core of the homeless and destitute.

The second *makarism*—"blessed are those who mourn" (v. 4 NRSV)—follows from the first. One way to become destitute in the first century was to lose one's family through the death of one's parents.

Loss of land and loss of family would make a person "meek" (v. 5 NRSV). Either one represented loss of status. This was especially important in a society where status revolved around honor and shame. Loss of land or family could move a person from an honored place in society to a shameful one—from high social standing within the context of one's village to social ostracism.

Blessed are the poor in spirit, those who mourn, and those who are meek. Blessed are those, in other words, who are down-and-out, rejected, destitute, without a home. They have honor with God. They are not despised and rejected. They are lifted up, held in high esteem, blessed by God. This is called "preferential option for the poor."

These first three *makarisms* are underlined by the fourth: "Blessed are those who hunger and thirst for justice" (*dikaiosune*, v. 6; "righteousness" NRSV). Matthew chose the words *hunger* and *thirst* with a purpose—they recall those who genuinely did hunger and thirst—and then turned these words in the direction not only of food and drink, but also of justice. Blessed are those who yearn—who hunger—for a world where all are honored and none are shamed.

If the first four *makarisms* are for those who lack justice, the next four are for those who work for justice. They promise reward at the end of time for those who live into the reign of God now—the merciful, the pure in heart, the peacemakers, and (again) the persecuted.

In the final blessing (v. 11), Jesus shifts from the third person to the second person—not "blessed are they" this time, but "blessed are *you*." Those who suffer for the cause of Jesus are to "rejoice and be exceedingly glad" for their reward is great in heaven. They are victims of persecution, yes, but they are in a line with the great prophets of the past as well as John the Baptist and Jesus himself. They are in good company.

It appears that Jesus was primarily instructing the disciples, but doing so within earshot of the crowds (5:1, 7:28). This means that the crowd heard the same teaching the disciples did and were in a good position to hold the disciples accountable for it.

November 9

22nd Sunday after Pentecost (Proper 27)

Joshua 24:1-3a, 14-25; Psalm 78:1-7; 1 Thessalonians 4:13-18; Matthew 25:1-13; Wisdom of Solomon 6:12-16 or Amos 5:18-24; Wisdom of Solomon 6:17-20 or Psalm 70

Lowell Grisham
http://lowellsblog.blogspot.com/

Prayers of the People (Joshua 24; Psalm 78)

Presider: Gracious and Holy One, you have made us children of God and heirs of eternal life: Enliven us to be alert and responsive to your awakening word, that we may participate in the work of healing and reconciliation that you intend for all, as we pray: Awaken us, O God, that we may always be alert for your coming among us.

Litanist: Arouse your church with such mindfulness and hope, O Christ, that we will be ready and prepared to welcome you as you visit us with your ministry of healing and reconciliation, peace, and justice. Awaken us, O God,

that we may always be alert for you coming among us.

Visit our leaders and all who have authority in the nations and the world, that they might put their trust in you and not forget your deeds, but keep your commandments. Awaken us, O God,

that we may always be alert for you coming among us.

Let your love be manifest in this community and fill us with such hope that we may live in constant wisdom, so that when Christ comes again with power and great glory, all may be made like him in his eternal and glorious kingdom. Awaken us, O God,

that we may always be alert for you coming among us.

Come to the aid of your children throughout the world to bring out all who live in the house of slavery, to protect them along their way, and to bring them into safe communities of peace and prosperity. Awaken us, O God,

that we may always be alert for you coming among us.

We put our trust in you; hear our prayers for all for whom we intercede, especially for _____. Hear our prayers of thanksgiving and praise, especially for _____. We do not grieve as others do who have no hope, for we believe that Jesus died and rose again. We remember especially _____. May God bring to Jesus all who have died, where they will be with the Lord forever. Awaken us, O God,

that we may always be alert for you coming among us.

Presider: Let your church offer to you our sincere worship and prayer, O God, that we may be wise and responsible stewards of your earth and inheritors of the glorious kingdom you have promised through Jesus Christ, who with the Father and the Holy Spirit we worship, one God, forever and ever. **Amen.**

Beth Quick
http://bethquick.blogspot.com

Joshua 24

• This passage is sort of an inauguration scene for leadership in the community.

• "Choose this day whom you will serve...but as for me and my household, we will serve the LORD" (v. 15 NRSV). Joshua puts it in their hands—serving is a choice. We can serve lots of people/things/gods these days. What choice have you made? How can others see your choice by your actions?

• Joshua spends the rest of the passage trying to convince the people not to follow God because of how costly it will be and how demanding it will be. In a great reverse-psychology sort of way, this only gets the people begging, pleading to serve God. Isn't that a great tool of evangelism? Telling people not to be Christians because it is too hard? Jesus, of course, sometimes uses these (truth-based) strategies in the Gospels.

Psalm 78

• "I will open my mouth in a parable" (v. 2 NRSV). I hadn't realized that the word *parable* appeared in the Old Testament. It reminds us that in Jesus' day, the people would have related to Jesus' style, more, perhaps, than we are able to relate today.

• "We will not hide them from their children; we will tell to the coming generation" (v. 4 NRSV). I like these verses that convey a sense of the necessity to tell the story of a people, to make sure the history is known through time and generations. We have a tendency to forget whole chunks of our history until we are repeating it!

Matthew 25

• Jesus reminds us that we have to make our own decisions about discipleship. It seems to me that the foolish maids were almost, in a sense, waiting to see how things would play out for the wise maids before they would want to go to the party.

• Preparation. Jesus wants us to always live like this is it—our last day to live in discipleship. Our society prizes living as if we are immortal, doesn't it? How do you live? How would you have to change your normal patterns if today was your last day to be a disciple?

Amy Persons Parkes

1 Thessalonians 4

Paul is responding to someone's concern, "What happens to believers who have died?" However, like many of the "I have a friend who..." scenarios, the real question here is more personal. These infant Christians are asking, "What happens if I die?"

For a moment, let's put aside the specific Thessalonian context of those who believe Jesus will return for them before they die. For this moment, we will lay to rest questions about the *parousia* and whether or not Jesus will be on a white horse, come after or before the trumpets blow, during which the moon may or may not turn to blood. Let's table the specifics of whether we can track the indicators of Christ's return.

Just for this moment, can we lie quietly alongside the grave question, "What happens when I die?" If we haven't allowed ourselves to ponder any vision from Daniel or Revelation, chances are we have landed square in the middle of another distraction, "How will I die?" Old age? Car wreck? Heart attack? We fantasize about these options (and more) on mental screens. We follow one possibility and another down to the terrible moment, only to find more questions, "Will it hurt? Will I know what is happening? How long will it take?"; pursued closely by, "Where will I be? Will I be able to see those I love, those alive and dead? Will I be at peace?" I don't know *what* happens when we die, but I know *who* has us. Though the context changes from age to age, the eternal affirmation is that faith in Christ renders us a people whose hope is in a loving and constant God. Whether we live or whether we die, we can affirm with Paul, "we will be with the Lord forever" (v. 17 NRSV).

Paul Nuechterlein
http://girardianlectionary.net/

Matthew 25

In 2008, this Gospel Reading fell the weekend following Barack Obama's election to the presidency. President-elect Obama began his election night speech with "This is our moment. This is our time." He continued with a list of challenges that lay ahead. I believe that this is what the parable of the Ten Bridesmaids is about as well—having the wisdom to say, "This is our moment. This is our time." It is about the challenge of taking up discipleship with Jesus before dire consequences begin to pile up, and not risking once again being left out in the cold as the marriage of heaven and earth comes one step closer to the time of fulfillment.

For a number of generations, interpretation of this Scripture passage has equated being locked out of the wedding with missing out on heaven, and, therefore, one must have some *urgency* in deciding for Jesus before dying, or it will be too late. N. T. Wright has been correcting our Christian eschatology such that we hear the warnings of the Gospels as warnings for consequences for this world, not for missing heaven (see esp. *The Resurrection of the Son of God* [Minneapolis: Fortress Press, 2003] and *Surprised by Hope* [New York: HarperOne, 2008]). The world needs disciples of Jesus to follow his lead into the Way of God's New Creation, or we may once again be left out of our dreams for peace. The next great apocalypse of violence (think World War II, not the *Left Behind* series) may come upon us at any time, so our sense of urgency must be for this world.

Matthew illuminates God's Way for us supremely in the Sermon on the Mount. Its conclusion has echoes in both the parable of the Ten Bridesmaids (e.g., the "Lord, Lord" of Matt 7:21, and the response "I've never known you" in 7:23); as well as the same kind of warning against foolishness:

> But everybody who hears these words of mine and doesn't put them into practice will be like a fool who built a house on sand. The rain fell, the floods came, and the wind blew and beat against that house. It fell and was completely destroyed. (7:26-27)

Jesus is talking, not about God punishing us after we die, but rather about the real-life consequences in this world of not following in his Way of peace and life.

With our discipleship of Jesus at the forefront of our minds and hearts, we need to learn to say, "This is our moment. This is our time." This is our chance to repent and get on board with God's agenda, God's kingdom, God's will for this creation. For the problems we now face are our opportunity to follow Jesus and be part of God's defeating the powers of sin and death for good. We need to learn to say, "Yes, Lord Jesus, we will get on board with what you started in this world so long ago. We will answer your call. This is our moment. This is our time—to reclaim God's Dream of a creation that lives in harmony, grace, peace, and love."

John Wesley's Notes on the Bible
http://www.ccel.org/ccel/wesley/notes.txt

Matthew 25:13

"Watch therefore"—He that watches has not only a burning lamp, but likewise oil in his vessel. And even when he sleepeth, his heart waketh. He is quiet; but not secure.

Melissa Bane Sevier
http://melissabanesevier.wordpress.com

Too Late (Matthew 25)

Jesus told a story about missing out. "Then the kingdom of heaven will be like this. Ten bridesmaids took their lamps and went to meet the bridegroom . . ." (Matt 25:1 NRSV). It's an awful story. The metaphor is pretty grim. The door is closed. The ones who used up their oil have been shut out of the kingdom. But I don't think Jesus' parable is one of exclusion.

My modern ears believe we're hearing a warning about regret. We have so many opportunities to do things right, and to undo things we've done wrong. You have heard it said that no one on his or her deathbed wishes to have spent more time at the office, or regrets not having done more laundry. The things we regret are estrangement from family, friends, and God. We regret not having taken more moments for pure joy, more time for prayer and reflection. We regret moving too fast through life and not savoring the time we've been given, not appreciating the people we love, not exploring the deeper places in our souls. We burn up all our oil on things that don't matter and then don't have anything left for the things that do.

I hate it when Jesus is so right. About me. How many times do I eat lunch at my desk instead of enjoying an hour laughing with a friend? How often do I make one more phone call for work, when I could be calling to hear my parents' voices? How many evenings do I spend at my desk trying to catch up (is that ever really possible) when I would be renewed catching up with my husband while we cook together? How much have I missed because I was doing something else that *seemed* important at the time?

When a tragedy occurs, or when we get sick, or when the children are grown, we often look back and wonder where the time went. And we have regrets about missed opportunities, conversations that never happened, life that went by when we were doing something else.

Be ready and watchful, says Jesus. You'll want to be paying attention when the moment presents itself, when a friend needs an ear, when a family member needs your time, when God needs your heart, when the important (not just the urgent) is waiting. Don't be left outside because you were too preoccupied. Life is happening on the other side of the door.

Martha Spong
http://marthaspong.com/

Matthew 25

My mother's best friend, who was a bridesmaid more than once, collected wedding disaster stories. Remember when, she would say, the bride fell down the stairs? Remember the groomsman so inebriated he stood in the wrong place? I tell couples, "Don't worry if something goes wrong, it will just give people a funny story to tell someday." Weddings do not run like clockwork. In the story Jesus tells, the bridegroom is *so* late that the bridesmaids, whose job it is to keep the light on for him, fall asleep. When they hear him coming, they get up and trim their lamps, which is to say they trim the wicks and refill their lamps with oil, to keep them burning. Unless, of course, they have no oil left.

We are left with a troubling set of possibilities. Could they really go out to the oil dealers at midnight? Why wouldn't the wise bridesmaids share? Was Jesus really warning that people would be shut out of the kingdom of heaven? He kept talking this way in the next two parables in Matthew 25. He intended to give a shake of the shoulders to the complacent and the easy-going, I have no doubt. He intended to remind the people around him that the future might be unexpected, that delays and exhaustion might well be part of it. He warned them to be ready, whatever might happen. Be ready, no matter the chaos and confusion of everyday life. Be ready, and know what you need to stay that way.

Sometimes it feels like a long, long time. Sometimes the waiting seems unbearable. When will things be set right? When will we really see the kingdom of God? And how will we keep ourselves ready?

Not long before my wedding, sleeping in my childhood bed, I woke to realize the power had gone out in my parents' home. I thought immediately of my grandmother, who had a first-floor bedroom. I didn't know the time; my electric clock gave no help. But I knew my night-owl grandmother might still be awake. In the dark, I felt my way across the upstairs hall, carefully down the stairs, took a left into our family room, right hand waving in front of me to identify the chair, the TV, the corner of the big, brick fireplace and finally...aha...the wide mantelpiece. I felt along until my hand touched the familiar textures of cardboard, brass, and wax. I struck a match and lit a candle.

By the light of the candle I made my way to my grandmother's bedroom, where I found her still sitting up in the armchair in front of a now-darkened TV screen, relieved to see me, rejoicing to see a light. Her daughter, my mother, was the one who prepared—although she slept through the storm—leaving the matches and the candle in the plain sight of my memory, ready for a dark night.

November 16

23rd Sunday after Pentecost (Proper 28)

2014

Judges 4:1-7; Psalm 123; 1 Thessalonians 5:1-11; Matthew 25:14-30; Zephaniah 1:7, 12-18; Psalm 90:1-8, (9-11), 12

Mark Stamm

Zephaniah 1; 1 Thessalonians 5; Matthew 25

Aspects within the Sundays following All Saints Day reflect the eschatological focus characteristic of Advent. Following this insight, some scholars have suggested the possibility of a seven-week Advent (see http://theadventproject. org, accessed April 22, 2012). The reading from Judges, the last in the semi-continuous reading of the *Hexateuch* (and Judges) in Revised Common Lectionary Year A, does not fit this pattern. Following the eschatological focus requires using the Zephaniah reading, which exhorts, "Be silent…for the day of the LORD is at hand" (v. 7 NRSV).

The 1 Thessalonians 5:1-11 text also references "the day of the Lord," which will come in a surprising way, "like a thief" (v. 2 NRSV). Eschatological themes have been badly misused to encourage otherworldly "rapture" religion, and sometimes as justification for violent crusades. How does one hear such eschatological themes in a way relevant to one's work on Monday morning? The challenge is to live as those who are "awake and sober" (v. 6 NRSV), that is, to look for God's activity that leads to justice and compassion, and then to join it.

In like manner, Matthew 25:14-30, the parable of the talents (large sums of money), is about eschatology and accountability. The Master entrusts, he goes away, and he returns for an accounting, asking what his servants did with the money while he was away. There is threat here, and the language about giving more to those who already have may bother us, especially if we hear it individualistically. It is important that we hear this parable in the context of an entire Gospel that addresses a community. Has God suddenly become harsh? As community, we might also hear this parable as a challenge to live boldly with all God has given us, to be increasingly bold in our mission. Will God take our boldness and increase it?

Suzanne Guthrie
http://www.edgeofenclosure.org

"Adventurous Loving" (Matthew 25)

St. John of the Cross wrote that "in the evening of life we will be judged on love alone." The two servants, probably more experienced in loving, fearlessly invest their portions of love. Heedless of the sheer fool-hardiness of the project, they risk ego, rejection, derision, even death, adventurously increasing the master's wealth of love in the world.

The last servant misses the point, and as with sin against the Holy Spirit (Matt 12:32), the poor clueless man finds himself in the outer darkness for clinging to the supposed safety of burying his love in the ground. John Wesley comments, "So mere harmlessness, on which many build their hope of salvation, was the cause of his damnation!"

Love begets love. The more you give the more you get, exponentially. But investing love can seem counterintuitive, because true love can be mundane, ordinary, passionless, plodding. And love shape-shifts to fit circumstances of tragedy and necessity, loss and age and death, for better, for worse, in sickness and in health. True love is anything but shallow. But it is not gorgeous and glamorous and perpetually young.

The last servant, fearing the shape-shifting dirtiness of love, paradoxically buries it in the ground to preserve it as it is. By protecting love from change and tragedy, adventure, wildness, and the sheer awe of engaging in life, this servant loses the very gift he had, through simple lack of imagination.

May the Master of the house find you and me adventurous in our loving.

Carolyn Winfrey Gillette
http://www.carolynshymns.com/

O God, We Yearn for Safety

O God, we yearn for safety; We long to be secure.
Yet faithful, loving service Is what you value more.
You give us what is needed; You love, forgive, and save.
Then, sending us to serve you, You call us to be brave.

You give to some ten talents—to others, two or three;
To some you give one blessing To manage faithfully.
For you, O Lord, are loving And don't demand success;
You daily call your people To lives of faithfulness.

You give your church the gospel—Good news for us to share.
You give us great compassion For neighbors everywhere.
You give us skills to serve you And loving work to do.
We're blest to be a blessing, And called to risk for you.

O God, it seems much safer To live from day to day,
Protecting what you lend us And hiding it away.
Yet all these gifts can't flourish When hidden in the ground;
When we are brave to share them Your blessings will abound.

NOTES
Biblical Texts: Matthew 25:14-30 and Luke 19:12-27
Tune: ANGEL'S STORY 7.6.7.6 D ("O Jesus, I Have Promised"), Arthur Henry Mann, 1881
Alternative Tune: AURELIA 7.6.7.6 D ("The Church's One Foundation")

Paul Escamilla

Matthew 25

"I was afraid." Too many times those words have been a door closing against an invitation to grow. I was afraid to love. I was afraid to let another love me. I was afraid to reach beyond the familiar, to share my faith, to raise my voice, to stand apart, to move beyond a stereotype. In the terrain of the heart, "I was afraid" is buried in a place both deep and yet highly accessible.

You have to give this third servant credit. He was only following what was, in his day, a sensible and responsible course of action. A talent was one of the largest values of currency in the Hellenistic world, a silver coinage you'd want to get help carrying home—it weighed between fifty-seven and seventy-four pounds. This is fifteen years' wages for a day laborer, about a quarter of a million dollars when adjusted for inflation. In ancient times, the safest place on earth for something of such great worth was underground. Josephus, first-century historian, said that it was not unusual for people to bury their treasure during times of military conflict. Further, unexpectedly discovering underground treasure, a scenario we stumble upon in one of Jesus' parables, was not uncommon. "If you want to secure your money," advised a rabbi from antiquity, "bury it."

In telling a story in which such a prudent and proven protective practice is challenged, Jesus subverts conventional wisdom toward a more faithful end. This is something he does repeatedly in Matthew, where "You have heard that it was said . . . but I say to you . . ." has such currency. Here the sensible thing is the wrong thing because God's reign manifests itself not in safety, but in surrender; not in guardedness, but in growth.

John Wesley's Notes on the Bible
http://www.ccel.org/ccel/wesley/notes.txt

Matthew 25:30

"Cast ye the unprofitable servant into the outer darkness"—For what? what had he done? It is true he had not done good. But neither is he charged with doing any harm. Why, for this reason, for barely doing no harm, he is consigned to outer darkness. He is pronounced a wicked, because he was a slothful, an unprofitable servant. So mere harmlessness, on which many build their hope of salvation, was the cause of his damnation!

Ann Scull
http://seedstuff.blogspot.com

A Useful Image

A photo of a small daisy flowering in the Simpson Desert in Central Australia together with the words, "We are all meant to shine." Find this image at http://seedstuff.blogspot.com.au/2011/11/proper-28-ordinary-november-13-risk.html (accessed April 16, 2012).

Call to Worship

Talk about taking risks (to link with the parable of the talents, where one man took no risk at all). Then ask for people who have never taken an up-front part in a service before to volunteer to participate in a part of the service. Make sure they have plenty of clear instructions and help. Emphasize to everyone that these people are taking a risk, that understanding is needed, and that they are not "performing" but worshiping.

Listening Song

DC Talk, *"Fearless"* on *Supernatural* (Brentwood, Tenn.: Forefront, 1998). This is a song about trusting God in our ministries.

Film Clips

Dead Poets Society (Touchstone, 1989). Show the clip where Robin Williams's character encourages his students to seize the day.

Lord of the Rings: The Fellowship of the Ring (New Line Cinema, 2001). Show the clip where Sam stops walking. When Frodo asks Sam what he is doing, Sam replies that he has gone as far as he has ever been and that his next step will take him into the unknown. Frodo has to encourage Sam to keep going. Discussion:

1. Why do you think people are afraid to take risks?

2. How can we be like Frodo encouraging Sam, and encourage one another to go further in our walk with God?

Dramas

"The Ringmaster's Gift," in Verena Johnson (ed.), *Mega Drama 2* (Adelaide: Open Book, 2001), 48–50. This is based on the Gospel reading.

Prue Taylor, *"Using Our Gifts."* Find this drama at http://seedstuff.blogspot.com.au/2011/11/proper-28-ordinary-november-13-risk.html (accessed April 16, 2012).

Story

"The Survey for the over 95s." Found at http://www.cvillechurch.com/BibleClasses/DanielLesson4Rebuild SoYourEffortsWillLast.pdf, page 6 (accessed April 16, 2012). Discussion:

1. What are some of the things that stop us doing what the surveyed elderly think are important?

2. What are some of our excuses?

3. What do we need to know or do so that we do grab the opportunities that God gives us?

4. What can we do for one another?

Meditation/Poem

Marianne Williamson, *"Our Deepest Fear,"* in Susan A. Blain, Sharon Iverson Gouwens, Catherine O'Callagan, and Grant Spradling (eds.), *Imaging the Word Volume 3* (Cleveland: United Church Press, 1996), 72. I put images with these words and the following music: *"End Titles,"* on the soundtrack for the TV Miniseries *Queen Kat, Carmel & St Jude* (Australia: Trout Films, 1999).

Adult Response

Before the service, I laid out small cards depicting different gifts and abilities that people may have. I made roughly four per person and asked people as they arrived to take three that best described their gifts. During my sermon on the parable of the talents, I asked people to consider the cards they had chosen, and then at the end I asked people to get into groups and share why they had chosen the cards they had. Then they discussed if and how their gifts could be used in the church, in the community, and/or in the world.

John van de Laar
http://www.sacredise.com/

Matthew 25

When I was a little boy, my parents bought me my first toy lawn mower. I loved it and eagerly joined my father as he cut the grass. Keeping lawns tidy was important work, I had come to learn, and I wanted to share in it.

This is essentially what the parable of the talents is about. It flows out of a series of parables and discourses in Matthew 21–23 in which Jesus challenges the religious leaders for their failure to be faithful caretakers of God's Reign. Then, in chapter 24, Jesus warns his disciples about the traumatic events that are coming, exhorting them to be prepared. It's a powerful sermon about the difference between God's Reign and the systems of empire that oppose it, and why those who follow Christ must always suffer.

Jesus then offers a parable to teach his followers how they should live, even when he is no longer with them. The foolish servant shirks duty when the Master is away, but the wise one continues to work faithfully and honestly (24:45-51). Faithfulness requires three characteristics that are the themes of the parables in Matthew 25—readiness (the bridesmaids), active participation (the talents), and the willingness to recognize Jesus in the "least" (the sheep and the goats).

The parable of the talents sits at the center of this long discourse and calls followers of Christ to participate in bringing God's Reign into the world. The amounts given to the three servants are massive, but, for Jesus, this is not about money. It's about the Reign of God that is a priceless pearl worth more than an entire merchant's fortune (13:45-6). This gift of inestimable value is entrusted by the Master to his servants. Two of them use it wisely and help it to grow. But one servant, having completely misjudged his master as a fearful and hard man, buries the gift.

The leaders of God's people have been entrusted with a kingdom of awesome value, but instead of growing it they have buried it, keeping its liberating value to themselves and, in so doing, keeping the least from inclusion in God's realm. Followers of Christ, however, are to be faithful servants who strive to grow God's Reign, bringing life and abundance to others. The time when the kingdoms of the world oppose God's Reign is not a time for caution. It is a time for dangerous investments in the lives of people—especially the "least."

Christ-followers are supposed to be the ones who have entered the Reign of God, who "get" Jesus' mission. But the true measure of our commitment to Christ is whether we invest the priceless treasure of God's Reign, helping it grow to welcome those who need its life, or bury the gift and keep it hidden for ourselves. If we have honestly, authentically received the Kingdom of God, then we have no choice but to be participants in its life-giving, grace-bringing, abundance-sharing growth.

November 23
Reign of Christ/Christ the King

Ezekiel 34:11-16, 20-24; Psalm 100 or Psalm 95:1-7a; Ephesians 1:15-23; Matthew 25:31-46

Paul Escamilla

Ephesians 1

We find in the Ephesians reading a remarkable image: eyes in the heart. It's a rare phrase; in the form in which it is found, it is unique to this verse. In a reference that sounds more like *The Little Prince* than the Bible, the writer shares the following prayer:

> I pray that the God of our Lord Jesus Christ, the Father of glory, may give you a spirit of wisdom and revelation as you come to know him, so that, with the eyes of your heart enlightened, you may know what is the hope to which he has called you, what are the riches of his glorious inheritance among the saints, and what is the immeasurable greatness of his power for us who believe, according to the working of his great power. (vv. 17-19 NRSV)

With such an image, we are introduced to the idea that to come to know God is to begin to see the world differently. That is to say, the knowledge of God is the beginning of the opening of those metaphorical eyes of the heart. And with those opened eyes, one can see life in hopeful ways (v. 18b), perceive the community of faith as richly endowed (v. 18c), and understand something of the immeasurable greatness of God's dynamic presence and purpose through the faith of the community (v. 19).

What is suggested here is that our lives of faith and discipleship consist in seeking to see higher things from lower perspectives; to expand our locus of sight to include the heart as well as the head. Behold the church, challenged and challenging; fatigued and fatiguing, troubled and troubling. Now, close your eyes, and open your *other* eyes, and behold the church a second time, this time as a community summoned by hope, endowed with great treasure, immeasurably empowered for its sacred task.

Mark Stamm

Ephesians 1; Matthew 25

"King" remains a problematic metaphor for God, and especially if the spiritual and political traffic moves in both directions. That is, if God is king, then the king is God. Much sorrow results from such readings. Suspicion of this and other biblical metaphors, such as *Father* and *Lord,* is well placed; but that does not mean that we should avoid them. We cannot do so if we plan to read the Bible in worship. Preachers can help congregants hear the hermeneutic of suspicion operating within the texts themselves, texts that take these images and break them, reforming them according to a vision of God's justice and love (see Gordon Lathrop, *Holy Things* [Minneapolis: Fortress Press, 1998], 27–31).

The Ephesians text speaks of Christ raised from the dead and seated in the place of authority, God's "right hand" (v. 20 NRSV), with great power and riches to be shared with the saints, should their eyes be enlightened to see it. Is this the prosperity gospel? Or is it, rather, the idea of inheritance itself broken to the shape of the gospel? As Christians, our privilege is to participate in Christ's mission, neither more nor less.

Matthew's judgment scene, with the separation of the sheep and the goats, continues a pre-Advent eschatological focus. Can we receive this scene somewhere beyond that round of tedious questions about who is saved and who not? While it is a parable pointing to Christ's coming, readers must challenge themselves to hear this text as a message of judgment and promise to the assembly gathered, and not to someone else. There is a harsh word of judgment here, but also a call to a new way of life focused on "the least of these," whom the Son of Man regards as family (v. 40 NRSV).

Julie Craig
http://winsomelearnsome.com

Matthew 25

It turns out that Mom was right—we are known by the company we keep. When I was growing up in rural Indiana, where our closest living neighbors were quite literally livestock, it wasn't hard to keep company that my parents would approve of, because I spent most of my days around my family. Even at school, the rules were pretty easy to figure out. The boys played with the other boys and the girls played with the girls, and the only bleeding over of those two groups was that the very athletic girls sometimes played games with the boys, if the boys were feeling conciliatory on the playground that day.

It got a little more complicated, of course, in junior high school when seventh graders from four of those country schools came together as one class, and suddenly there was a little variety—just a little, though, maybe one hundred twenty students total in each grade. Suddenly I could hang with the smart kids, or the arty kids, or the sporty kids, or the burn-outs. And to my wonder and amazement, it was suddenly okay to pal around with boys, although if I'm being honest, I'll admit right here that the only boys who wanted to hang with awkward, twelve-year-old me were—across the board—attracted to my ability to help with homework, and nothing else.

Junior High is an exciting but sometimes excruciating time to figure out who we are, much less who our friends are supposed to be. And we haven't quite figured out yet that the choices we make when we are adolescents need not rule the rest of our lives. Everything feels so weighty, as if our making one wrong choice would disrupt the course of our whole life. At least that is what I thought I understood when I was twelve or thirteen years old.

At first blush, our text for today seems to be about how to earn a place in heaven with Jesus, how to be judged favorably by the Shepherd King: be a sheep, not a goat. The original hearers of this sermon would have understood "sheep" and "goat" to be very specifically coded words with deeply ingrained cultural meaning. Matthew reinforces this with the use of "left" and "right." The right hand was the socially acceptable hand, used for eating and greeting. The left hand was used for unmentionable, private tasks, and was never used for public greeting. For all intents and purposes, everybody was a righty, whether they wanted to be or not. To be on the left was a very bad thing, and everybody hearing this story would have understood that.

So really, it seems as if Jesus is simply saying, "Do the right thing." The problem is that the sheep don't really understand why they are sheep, and the goats don't know what goat-like behavior has left them in the predicament they are in. Since, in reality, sheep and goats grazed together and traveled together and acted as one herd until it was shearing time or sacrifice time; it is almost as though everybody ended up surprised when the sorting happened. It can't really be as simple as that, can it? The secret here to being favorably judged can't be just "Don't do anything stupid." Don't we wish.

Liz Crumlish
http://somethingtostandon.blogspot.co.uk/

Matthew 25

Matthew's Gospel is very concerned with how we practice faith—the practicalities of living out our faith. Early on, in the Beatitudes (chap. 5), Jesus teaches of those who are blessed —the poor, the bereaved, the hungry, the thirsty—those marginalized and expelled to the fringes of society. Here, toward the end of the Gospel, Matthew points us to the notion that, not only are those on the fringes blessed but Christ lives in them!

The way Matthew's Gospel is arranged, this passage about the sheep and the goats comes just before we get into the passion narratives and start to read about Jesus' suffering and death. So, almost immediately before we read of Jesus in the upper room, stooping to wash the disciples' feet (see John 13), we find this major focus on Christ as king—

But what kind of king? A king who hangs out with the outcasts, a king who serves others, a king who gets down and dirty with the people. A king whom we can glimpse as we look at one another.

And that is the challenge—to see Jesus. It wasn't just the goats who couldn't see Jesus in those who needed help—in the hungry, the thirsty, the stranger, the naked, the prisoner. But the sheep, those whom Jesus calls blessed—also failed to recognize Jesus.

It seems a shame that, if we are going to show compassion, if we are going to reach out to others—even though we're doing the right thing, even though we're serving God in others—we don't recognize Jesus. It's possible to go through the motions and not feel the blessing. It's possible to serve others but not be aware of Christ present in their lives and in ours.

There is no avoiding the fact that this passage contains words of judgment—the sheep are separated from the goats, and the goats are cast out. Of course we'd like to count ourselves among the sheep—the blessed. We might even have an idea of who would come into the goat category. If we're honest we might even be prepared to admit that sometimes we act like the sheep who are blessed and at other times we act like the goats who are cursed.

But judgment is not ours to make. What we are called to is service. Serving Christ by serving one another. Looking for—and finding—Christ in the least of these.

As we come to the end of the church's year and prepare to embark on another Advent, prepare to welcome again the Christ child, may our eyes be open to Christ fully grown in those around us, and may we reach out to the least of these with the compassion of Christ the servant king.

John Wesley's Notes on the Bible
http://www.ccel.org/ccel/wesley/notes.txt

Matthew 25:35

"I was hungry, and ye gave me meat; I was thirsty, and ye gave me Drink"—All these works of outward mercy suppose faith and love, and must needs be accompanied with works of spiritual mercy. But works of this kind the Judge could not mention in the same manner. He could not say, I was in error, and ye recalled me to the truth; I was in sin, and ye brought me to repentance. "In prison"—Prisoners need to be visited above all others, as they are commonly solitary and forsaken by the rest of the world.

Todd Weir
http://bloomingcactus.typepad.com/

Matthew 25

I feel edgy when someone starts dividing people into categories, like sheep and goats. Maybe it is a leftover from getting picked last once in third grade kickball, but I am skeptical about the human tendency of saying who is in and who is out. In fairness to Jesus, I like the idea that the insiders are those who have cared for the "least of these." Since I have managed a homeless shelter for eight years, I should be on the inside track, right? Big points! I am tempted to go with the flow about the chosen sheep being the ones that help the poor, and the nasty goats are those who ignore the poor.

The one theological argument of my seminary days that almost turned into a fist fight was a debate over giving money to homeless people who begged at the subway station. The strong consensus of the class was that this was enabling people. The poor wretches would probably take your money and get hammered on a bottle of Wild Irish Rose. Besides, there were so many con artists who were good at telling some terrible story and walking away with a tidy profit at the end of the day. There was great concern about accountability, responsibility, and not having someone take advantage of you. Someone suggested that we all carry cards with directions to the city's soup kitchens instead. (As if the homeless didn't already have the schedules memorized!)

My best friend pointed out Jesus' words "If you have two coats and someone else has none, give it to them" (Luke 3:11, paraphrased). That winter he had seen a man on the street rubbing his hands together, and he took his own gloves off and stuffed his hands into his pockets for the day. Isn't that what Jesus would want us to do? Well, that is a very touching story, but hardly a model for social transformation. What we need is public policy to deal with affordable housing, not more band-aids for the homeless. I was shocked by how quickly my friend and I were labeled as disempowering, naïve band-aid throwers, who were not on the cutting edge of social justice, because we felt that sometimes you should look a person in the eye and give them something they needed. We were the goats, who were just as big a problem as those who were heartless because we were "doing justice."

I was tempted to defend my honor and my extensive lobbying for social change. I refrained because that would just be joining the silly game of "who is more righteous." The real issue is that we not lose sight of the humanity of people who are suffering. We must certainly work for justice, while realizing that the poor will always be with us. We also need to see people face-to-face and freely offer them what they need for that day. We must know their names, and not just see them as objects of our good work and intentions.

November 27
Thanksgiving Day

Deuteronomy 8:7-18; Psalm 65; 2 Corinthians 9:6-15; Luke 17:11-19

John Wesley's Notes on the Bible
http://www.ccel.org/ccel/wesley/notes.txt

Deuteronomy 8:2

It is good for us likewise to remember all the ways both of God's providence and grace, by which he has led us hitherto through the wilderness, that we may trust him, and cheerfully serve him.

Mark Stamm

Deuteronomy 8; 2 Corinthians 9

Thanksgiving is always appropriate, but it must remain firmly grounded in the biblical narrative. Otherwise, it can become an exercise in self-congratulation and nationalism.

Deuteronomy was compiled for exiles returning to the Promised Land, and thus verses 7-18 address a group whose ancestors had once before forgotten God's generosity and their covenantal responsibilities as beneficiaries of God's blessing. Such caution can speak well to contemporary listeners. In what ways are we forgetting God's generosity?

Second Corinthians 9:6-15 occurs as part of Paul's appeal for contributions to the Jerusalem Church, a discussion that extends over chapters 8 and 9. Some preachers have exploited this discussion about the relationship between the amount of seed sown and the size of the subsequent harvest (v. 9) to a self-centered end, but that is not the intent of the text. It may be that many who first heard it were themselves little better off than persons they were asked to assist. The exhortation seems to suggest, rather, that in Christ we always have something to give, and that those who give have opportunity to participate in God's generosity. The harvest they receive is not always measured in material terms. What if we lived as if this were true? Sometimes people of the least means understand this secret best.

How prosperous are we, and how shall we understand it? Many who hear these texts will be under significant financial strain. Others have become financially successful according to most measures, and especially according to what they may have imagined for themselves. We might ask why so many then remain discontented and anxious. Is it because we are not thankful, that we are always protecting ourselves against bad things that might happen? What might God do if we lived according to a different perspective?

Paul Nuechterlein
http://girardianlectionary.net/

Deuteronomy 8; Luke 17

In recent years, traditional Thanksgiving Day worship and celebrations have become nuanced as the romanticized version of history painted by dominant culture slowly falls away. The stories painting a rosy picture lie in stark contrast to the sober reality of the European invasion, colonialism, and the eventual genocide of ten to thirty million people indigenous to this land. The traditional U.S. Thanksgiving for prosperity came at a terrible price.

The appropriate reminder for giving thanks to God in Deuteronomy 8 brings a similarly sober awareness of the cost paid by others, when we look at its wider context. Deuteronomy 6 rings out a very similar admonition for Israel to remember their dependence on God—but with a difference: we are made explicitly aware that people already occupied the land and were about to be displaced.

> Now once the LORD your God has brought you into the land that he swore . . . to give to you—a land that will be full of large and wonderful towns that you didn't build, houses stocked with all kinds of goods that you didn't stock, cisterns that you didn't make, vineyards and olive trees that you didn't plant—and you eat and get stuffed, watch yourself! Don't forget the LORD. . . . (Deut 6:10-12)

A dozen verses later we read the terrible cost of forgetting:

> Now once the LORD your God brings you into the land you are entering to take possession of, and he drives out numerous nations before you—the Hittites, the Girgashites, the Amorites, the Canaanites, the Perizzites, the Hivites, and the Jebusites: seven nations that are larger and stronger than you—once the LORD your God lays them before you, you must strike them down. . . . Don't make any covenants with them, and don't be merciful to them. (Deut 7:1-2)

It is striking how remarkably similar the context of Deuteronomy's message of thanksgiving is to our contemporary celebration of the traditional Thanksgiving—they are both set within the horror of genocide.

Luke's Jesus shows us a different way to Thanksgiving. The seven nations of Deuteronomy 7 were not completely wiped out—the Jews of Jesus' era saw them as "pagans" behind the syncretism of their contemporary enemies, the Samaritans. But Luke's Jesus has three encounters involving Samaritans, which paint them in a favorable light: rebuking his disciples' wishes to have fire rained down on a Samaritan village (9:54-55), the famous parable of the "Good Samaritan" (10:30-37), and applauding the Samaritan leper, the only one of ten to return and give thanks to his healer (17:11-19).

As followers of Christ, we give thanks that he forgives our past imperialisms of robbing other peoples' lands and sacrificing them in the process. We give thanks he redeems the prosperity we have gained at the expense of others—that we might generously share with the least of Jesus' family. We give thanks that Jesus has opened us to those we have formerly labeled as pagans to be our teachers of true spirituality. At our parish we now use the "Prayer of Chief Seattle" within our Thanksgiving liturgy (see one version at http://www.thesacredpaths.com/village/2006/02/07/chief-seattles-prayer/, accessed June 2012).

Paul Escamilla

2 Corinthians 9

The literary shift in tone and texture of the 2 Corinthians pericope from "The point is this" (v. 6 NRSV) to "his indescribable gift" (v. 15 NRSV) reflects its internal philosophical movement. What begins acutely, pointedly, matter-of-factly, ends generatively, expansively, even lyrically. The gradual warming and widening of the subject matter—financial giving—is emblematic of what occurs in the life of the disciple who finally makes the discovery Paul articulates in such a variety of ways within this text: to sow bountifully is to reap bountifully; that the gift be given freely is finally the only prerequisite for our giving; in response to our giving we are amply provided for; generosity enriches the giver. Had verse 7 ("Each of you must give as you have made up your mind . . ." NRSV) appeared toward the wider end of this section, it might have afforded a translation of *kardia* as "heart" instead of "mind." A mind's decisions are a dime a dozen; dedicated *hearts* are more precious than gold. We have all known those saints among us who need little and offer much, their hearts having been made up early or late that the truest happiness in life, the "indescribable gift," is the joy of a self-emptying way of being that is nonetheless ever filled by this One who loves, provides, scatters, gives, supplies, multiplies, increases, enriches, and gives the more (vv. 7, 8, 9, 10, 11, 14 NRSV). The munificent nature of God is our own truest nature, and we discover spiritual resonance, joy, even hilarity (v. 7, Greek: God loves a *hilaron* giver) when we find our hearts and hands handling treasure as God handles grace.

Thom Shuman
http://lectionaryliturgies.blogspot.com/

Call to Worship

Our help is in the name of the Lord who made heaven and earth.
We glorify God with songs of thanksgiving.
We will not forget all that God has done,
feeding our grandparents with manna,
quenching our thirst with streams of living water.
We will not forget to say "Thank You!" to our God.
We will sing and shout of God's amazing love.

Prayer of the Day

Hot showers in the morning
and cool breezes in the evening;
work that provides for our families
and abundance that makes us generous;
silly jokes told by third graders,
and silent tears of a grandmother lost
in her childhood forever.
What blessings are ours, Creation's Joy!

Teachers who patiently help us with our math,
and mentors who keep us on the right paths;
friends who shovel snow off sidewalks before we waken,
and employers with hearts greater than profits;
piano teachers who smile at repeated mistakes,
and coaches who teach us (again)
how to curl the ball into the goal.
What blessings are ours, Servant of Joy!

Dogs who bounce us awake early in the day
and cats who lullaby us to sleep;
grandfathers who teach us how to whittle
and sisters who give up a date to babysit;
little boys who always forget to wipe their mouths,
and folks who always say, "thank you."
What blessings are ours, Joyous Spirit!

God in Community, Holy in One,
thanksgiving is in every word we speak,
even as we pray as Jesus taught us, saying, **Our Father...**

Call to Reconciliation

How easily we think it is our power, our skills, our selves that have given us what we have. In our feasts of self-exaltation, we no longer remember the One who is giver of all we need. Let us confess our sins as we pray, saying,

Unison Prayer of Confession

In this modern, tech-savvy, instant-message world, we forget how much we need you, Blessing God. We exalt our skills in surfing the Internet, yet forget the One who hears our prayers before we open our hearts. Because grocery stores have more than we could ever eat, we forget your waters that nurtured the food in our baskets. Because our closets spill over with unworn clothes, we cannot see the meadows garbed in your radiant joy.

Forgive us, Generous Creator. Enrich us with blessings to make us generous spenders of your grace on others. With our hands full of treasures beyond imaging, may we think of new ways to share. Feasting on your constant grace, may we love others more than ourselves, even as Jesus loved us more than he loved his own life.

Silence is kept.

Assurance of Pardon

This is the good news for you: God provides every blessing; God forgives every sin; God delivers every one of us.

So simple, yet so hard to say, "Thank you"
for grace,
for hope,
for new life,
for new ways to serve.
Thank you, Holy God, for forgiving us! Amen.

John Petty

http://progressiveinvolvement.com

Luke 17

Jesus was on the boundary between Galilee and Samaria (v. 11). Jews of the time considered Samaritans to be a half-breeds and heretics. We don't know much about Samaritans' attitude toward Jews. The woman at the well in John 4 seems wary and self-protective, a not unusual posture for religious minorities.

Jesus always portrays Samaritans in a positive way. Previously in Luke, Jesus' initial foray into Samaria had been rebuffed (9:51-56), yet, a short while later (10:25-37), Jesus tells the story of the "good Samaritan."

Galilean Jews and Samaritans actually had much in common. They were both poor and oppressed by a corrupt religion and a brutal government. One suspects that the Galileans, after their initial shock at the idea of Samaritans as positive examples, began to see that the reason they thought the Samaritans were "outsiders" in the first place was because the Jerusalem elite had named them so, a Jerusalem elite that also considered the Galileans themselves to be "outsiders," albeit in a different way.

The Galileans were not ethnic or religious outsiders like the Samaritans. The Galileans were economic and cultural outsiders, looked down upon by cosmopolitan Jerusalem as hicks and rubes from the sticks. The Galileans, instructed by Jesus, began to think, "Say, maybe we have more in common with Samaritans than we thought."

When Jesus enters a certain village, ten lepers meet him. They stand at a distance, and shout out, "Jesus, Master, have mercy on us!" (v. 13 NRSV). Jesus tells them, "Go and show yourselves to the priests" (v. 14 NRSV). The priests could certify whether or not a person was healed. If so, they could then be reintegrated into common everyday life.

As they are going, they are "cleansed" (v. 17, *katharizo*, "purified"). One of the now-cleansed lepers sees that he has been healed and returns to Jesus. Luke portrays his actions as effusive. He praises God in a loud voice, falls with his face to Jesus' feet, and gives thanks *(eucharistone)* to him.

So far, so good. Then in verse 16, ". . . and he was a Samaritan," a shocking disclosure. As he did in the story of the "good Samaritan" in chapter 10, the one Jesus lifts up as a positive example is a foreigner. As he always seems to do whenever he gets the chance, Jesus subverts a racist stereotype. Luke uses the specific word "foreigner" (*allogenes*), which is the only use of this word in the entire New Testament.

Jesus says "your faith has saved you" four times in Luke's Gospel: to the woman who anointed his feet (7:50), the woman with the twelve-year hemorrhage (8:48), this leper who is identified as a Samaritan (17:19), and the blind man who calls Jesus "Son of David," who is obviously a Jew (18:42).

In other words, Jesus says "your faith has saved you" to two men, two women—one specifically identified as a Jew and one specifically identified as a Samaritan. Luke likes this kind of egalitarian balance.

Carolyn Winfrey Gillette

http://www.carolynshymns.com/

All of Life Is Filled with Wonder

All of life is filled with wonder, so we thank you, God of love—
For the crash of evening thunder, clearing clouds, then stars above;
For the night that turns to glowing as we feel the morning mist,
God, we praise and thank you, knowing every day we're truly blessed.

For the joy of daily waking, for the gift of each new day,
For the smell of fresh bread baking, for the sound of children's play,
For the ways we seek to serve you as we work and volunteer,
God we humbly praise and thank you for your presence with us here.

For the ways we're blessed with plenty—love and laughter, neighbors, friends,
Nature's wonders, seasons' bounty, life in you that never ends,
For the ones who've gone before us, giving witness to your way—
We rejoice in all you give us every moment, every day.

For your love in times of trouble, for your peace when things are tough,
For your help when hardships double, for your grace that is enough,
For a stranger's gentle kindness, for a doctor's healing skill—
God, we thank you that you bless us, and you bless your world as well.

For the baby in the manger, for the cross and empty tomb,
For each time a searching stranger finds at church a welcome home,
For your kingdom's great surprises—poor ones lifted, lost ones found—
God, we thank you! Hope still rises, for your gifts of grace abound.

NOTES
Biblical references: Deuteronomy 8:7-18; Psalm 65
Tune: HYMN TO JOY 8.7.8.7 D ("Joyful, Joyful, We Adore Thee"), Ludwig van Beethoven, 1824
Alternate Tune: IN BABILONE 8.7.8.7.D ("There's a Wideness in God's Mercy")
Text: Copyright © 2010 by Carolyn Winfrey Gillette. All rights reserved.

November 30
1st Sunday of Advent (Year B)

Isaiah 64:1-9; Psalm 80:1-7, 17-19; 1 Corinthians 1:3-9; Mark 13:24-37

Dan R. Dick

Isaiah 64

"O that you would tear open the heavens and come down, / so that the mountains would quake at your presence—" (Isaiah 64:1 NRSV). A quick scan of a news website or a few minutes watching the evening news on television can instill a sense of foreboding and despair. Our world is in such terrible shape, and people seem incapable of treating one another with civility and decency. Our news media choose to highlight the very worst in human behavior, and they seem to glory in the devastation of natural and unnatural disaster. Even among the most peace-loving and kind, a murmur may be heard, "Why doesn't God *do* something about all of this?"

Indeed, God has done something! In the gift of God's Son, Jesus the Christ, God set in motion an active and visible response to the terrors and tragedies of earthly existence. Jesus came, teaching and healing, creating a covenant community of those who love God to stand against the forces of death, decay, and despair. After his resurrection, God's own Spirit was reborn into the hearts and lives of those who accepted the gift of Christ. Birth after birth, revelation after revelation, until today we are born and reborn as the church to be Christ for the world.

There is suffering, but Christ is with us. There is tragedy, but the Spirit of God prevails. There is death, but only as prelude to new life. What we may not see with our eyes, we must know in our hearts—once more salvation is near, and once more God will send a Savior that all may know God's grace. Advent—the time of anticipation and the time of waiting—is a test of faith. We may not know the hour or the day (Mark 13:32), but we know and trust our God!

Mike Lowry

Living Between What Is and What We Hope Will Be (Isaiah 64)

We come to Christmas to behold the birth of the Savior and to travel the dusty road to Bethlehem. We traverse the rocky outcropping between what is and what we hope will be. We wait and prepare. Christmas is about the birth just not of a baby but of eternity. I look back on the births of our children with delighted joy, but I also remember the anxious worry that was part of their coming and the seemingly endless wait in the days preceding their births. In the holy story of the Savior's birth, we also come to the time of joy through an anxious time of preparation.

This gap between what is and what is hoped for is the result of the fall of creation. Like a mother in the early stages of childbirth, all of creation has been groaning and longing for the salvation of the world. Isaiah speaks a painful truth. "All of us wither like a leaf; / our sins, like the wind, carry us away" (v. 6b). This is neither complaint nor punishment; it is a statement of reality. Creation is broken, and as part of God's great creation, we are broken as well. The text can be read as a confession, a prayer for deliverance, and a plea for mercy. "Don't rage so fiercely, LORD; / don't hold our sins against us forever, / but gaze now on your people" (v. 9).

How are we to respond? Why, like any good parents to be. First, trust the truth of this time. God is coming to redeem creation and offer salvation. Second, live in the not yet and the present struggle. Between the now and the not yet we live in hope. Third, wait with wonder. The biblical concept of waiting is not about sitting back in passive pleasure; it is about great anticipation and expectation.

Our dog Molly is a beagle mix, and you can see the hunting dog in her genes. She believes her mission is to keep our backyard free of squirrels and birds. She crouches on the patio in intense anticipation, ready to spring into action. That is what the apostle Paul is after when he calls on Christians to "wait for it with patience" (Romans 8:25). Trust the truth, hold to the hope, wait with wonder; God is in action!

Marci Auld Glass
www.marciglass.com

Isaiah 64; Mark 13

Christians have the somewhat regrettable habit of pulling Isaiah out for the holidays—much as we dig the Christmas decorations out of the attic. We read Isaiah as if he's a fortune teller or Nostradamus, making predictions about Jesus. But we should fight that tendency. Because Isaiah wasn't writing about Jesus, *per se*. He was passing on the messages he received from God, intended to provide specific comfort to specific people in the midst of a specific crisis. These people are in exile. The temple in Jerusalem had been destroyed. The very home of God had been destroyed. Isaiah wasn't writing to predict the future. He was writing to give courage to his people so they could endure.

How do you hear Isaiah's words when exile is your reality? You are little Israel. You don't have military might. And you are beginning to wonder if your God has also been defeated—where is God when he's not in the temple?

I invite you this week to spend some time with Isaiah. Listen to his words in their own context. Let them speak to you in your context. What is going on in your life such that heaven being torn apart and mountains quaking would be a sign of hope?

We, I think, have a hard time reading Isaiah without immediately thinking of Jesus. Because while we are preparing for Jesus' birth in four weeks, we know what happened two thousand years ago. God did tear open the heavens. And good, observant Jews, who had been hearing Isaiah's writings all of their lives, recognized a connection between Jesus and the words of Isaiah. The Gospel accounts of Jesus were written down by people who often framed their understanding of who Jesus was through the lens of Isaiah's writing.

"Oh that you would tear open the heavens and come down" (v. 1 NRSV). And God did come down. God heard the cries of God's people and changed the way we relate to the Divine. A baby was born in Bethlehem. In a manger. Away from the halls of power and privilege. And the world was turned upside down by this man, fully human, fully divine.

Once the Divine enters the world, even the heavens themselves will be shaken. By making reference to sun, moon, and stars, Mark is cluing us in to the truth that God's reign is a cosmic reign, it isn't just a change of administration. It isn't just new people taking over. It is an entirely new creation.

So, as we enter Advent, we begin it with a revelation that a change is coming. And we are told to wait for it. To watch for it. In the coming weeks, as we light the candles and prepare for Christ's return and for Christ's birth, watch, wait, and keep awake. The Good News is at hand.

NOTE: Adapted from "Heaven Torn Open," a sermon preached by Marci Auld Glass (http://marciglass.com/2008/11/30/heaven-torn-open/).

Dan Clendenin
http://journeywithjesus.net

Isaiah 64; 1 Corinthians 1; Mark 13

Sometimes there's a painful disconnect between what we fervently pray for and what we actually experience. Praying to God for mighty acts of deliverance is an entirely human and genuinely Christian response to the suffering of the world. I intend never to stop praying for God's miraculous intervention; those prayers remain a staple of my morning walks. Who would not beg God to rescue Congo and Zimbabwe from the dark forces ravaging those lands? What parent doesn't lie awake at night praying that their kid makes it home safely from a party? Who wouldn't beseech God when they see a police car pull into their neighbor's driveway? Lord, wake up! God, come down!

The season of Advent adds an important nuance to our prayers. God is not our Cosmic Concierge. Human experience belies the delusion and pious happy talk, so deeply embedded in the American sense of entitlement, that the Gospel solves every problem and answers every question. Rather, God offers us a way to live without answers to questions and with problems that don't disappear. Advent reminds us that sometimes we must wait, and that God acts in God's own time, in God's own ways, and for God's own reasons.

At Advent, we wait. Even though Costco displayed their seasonal merchandise in October, Christmas is still a long way off. The winter solstice will envelop us in the longest night and the shortest day of the year. Leaves will fall, and grass will fade to brown. So we enter a season of waiting, and God, writes Isaiah, "acts on behalf of those who wait for him" (64:4 NIV 1984). Paul sounds the same note, commending the Corinthians who "eagerly wait for our Lord Jesus Christ to be revealed" (1 Cor 1:7 NIV 1984).

But "no one knows," says Jesus, the day or hour when God will act, "not even the angels in heaven, nor the Son" (Mark 13:32 NIV 1984). He compares our situation to servants who wait for their master who has gone on a long journey without saying when he'll return. Our task is to remain vigilant and to "watch!" (13:37 NIV 1984). Patient waiting is not an excuse to avoid helping those whom we can help; but there will always be plenty of unresolved heartaches this side of heaven that require us to cultivate endurance, confidence, and hope through waiting.

We wait in patience, knowing that not every act of God resounds like a pounding sledgehammer. In Isaiah's metaphor, God does not always split open the heavens. Whereas even his closest disciples longed to call down fire from heaven and to brandish swords, Jesus compared his coming kingdom to tiny mustard seeds and to the imperceptible but certain fermentation of yeast. In his classic Advent hymn, "O Little Town of Bethlehem" (1868), Phillip Brooks, a university preacher at Harvard where today a house is named for him, described the discipline of patient waiting for the invisible kingdom that emerges bit by bit:

> How silently, how silently, the wondrous gift is given!
> So God imparts to human hearts the blessings of his heaven.
> No ear may hear his coming, but in this world of sin,
> Where meek souls will receive him, still the dear Christ enters in.
> (*The United Methodist Hymnal* [Nashville: The United Methodist Publishing House, 1989], 230, stanza 3).

Mary J. Scifres

The Ever-Expanding Promise of Advent: God's Steadfast Love: Introduction

One of the greatest gifts that Jesus' message brings to an increasingly diverse world is the message of full inclusion for all people. During the Advent and Christmas seasons, preachers are able to offer a full-throated Yes! to the question of whether the gospel and God's kingdom truly include everyone and everything. Jesus proclaimed God's steadfast love, not just for his Jewish sisters and brothers, but for all creation. In these Advent lections, we see an ever-expanding understanding of God's steadfast love as Scripture moves us toward Christmas, when Scripture and Christ's birth reveal the promise of God's steadfast love for all of creation. Using this theme, our sermon starters will help you to celebrate the gift of God's love for all of humanity and all of creation, even as you proclaim the promise of Christ's presence and love in the world.

Steadfast Love: A Christmas Gift to God's People (Isaiah 64; Psalm 80; 1 Corinthians 1; Mark 13)

Even God's people grow weary and neglect the signs of God's love in our lives. Even God's people fall short and wander away from the path to which Christ calls us. Even God's people can be stubborn and unyielding, refusing the gift of new creation God offers as God's Spirit seeks to shape and mold us. And yet, God loves. And yet, Christ calls. And yet, God creates and breathes the Spirit into our lives, seeking to shape and mold us—that we might be co-creators with God, bringing forth the promised wholeness that God intends for this world.

And so, this Advent season begins with a lively message to counter our turkey-laden fatigue and our shopping-worn weariness. Wake up! Pay attention! God is ready to do an awesome thing, even in the weariest of God's followers. God has blessed us with every spiritual gift we need. The Spirit will strengthen us for the journey, but it's up to us to pay attention and see how blessed and capable we are. God's love is ours, which is the best Christmas gift of all—a gift given to us despite our shortcomings and our fatigue. God is still molding and shaping us, trusting and guiding our steps, and calling and partnering with us to bring about the kingdom. Wake up, people of God. The Christmas gift is already ours! No shopping needed! God's steadfast love is already here, and this love is here to stay!

Melissa Bane Sevier
http://melissabanesevier.wordpress.com

One Candle (Mark 13)

This Sunday is the first of Advent, and many churches will light one candle in the Advent wreath, with readings about hope and peace. As an additional candle is lit on each of the successive three Sundays, the figurative light in the darkness grows.

One candle won't make much of a difference in a well-lit room. Even if the room were darkened, a single flame, though more visible, wouldn't do much good. The candle serves, though, as a strong symbol of watching and waiting in expectation and hope through the dark times.

Advent is about waiting. We talk to our children about waiting to open gifts. There are heavier kinds of waiting. I don't know about you, but I'm honestly pretty tired of waiting—waiting for war to be over, so we don't have to send any more people into harm's way; waiting for the end to terrorism, so no one anywhere has to be afraid to get on an airplane; waiting for an end to abuse, so that children and adults don't have to be afraid in their own homes; waiting for the hungry to be fed and the jobless to find work; waiting for people to sit at the negotiating table to end violence in all the hot spots around the world; waiting for our own leaders to come to some helpful compromise.

Waiting is tiresome. It seems as though nothing will ever be resolved in our lifetime. Waiting is scary. What if things don't turn out in a good way? Waiting is difficult. We want answers and we want them *now*.

Jesus said, "What I say to you I say to all: Keep awake" (v. 37 NRSV). We are waiting, yes, but it is an active waiting. We have to stay awake, be alert and on the lookout for the movement of God. It can be in the large things: peace talks, good news from the oncologist, a job. It can be in the small things: an unexpected phone call that makes a tough day easier to manage, some sense of a lightening of depression, a visit that brings joy.

And so together we light one candle, we stay awake, and we watch. We are watching for any signs of God, we are listening for the stirrings of the Spirit, we are participating in the life of justice. We are ready to catch the flame of this one candle and gently carry it wherever we go, taking hope with us to share. This is the season of waiting. This is the season of Advent.

John Wesley's Notes on the Bible
http://www.ccel.org/ccel/wesley/notes.txt

Mark 13:34

"The Son of man is as a man taking a far journey"—Being about to leave this world and go to the Father, he appoints the services that are to be performed by all his servants, in their several stations. This seems chiefly to respect ministers at the day of judgment: but it may be applied to all men, and to the time of death. Matt. xxv, 14; Luke xix, 12.

December 7

2nd Sunday of Advent

Isaiah 40:1-11; Psalm 85:1-2, 8-13; 2 Peter 3:8-15a; Mark 1:1-8

Mary J. Scifres

Steadfast Love: A Christmas Gift to Ungodly People (2 Peter 3; Mark 1)

Advent is not an easy season, with its harried pace and busy schedule. Even non-Christians are surrounded by the holiday patterns of shopping, partying, decorating, and hurrying. Many people are haunted by grief: lamenting broken family relationships, deceased loved ones, and failed friendships. Even non-believers may find themselves yearning for connections with God and community that they seldom notice at other times of the year.

And so, God offers the gift of steadfast love to the godly and ungodly alike. The sinful Israelites are offered hopeful words of comfort. Peter reminds us that God does not want any person to perish. And John comes preaching not just repentance, but forgiveness. God's gift of love is not just for perfect people, not just for loving people, not just for Christians or Jews or Muslims or Buddhists. God's Christmas gift of love is for all people, so that "all people shall see it together" (Isa 40:5 NRSV).

We are given this season of waiting as a gift. For in the waiting, we are all invited to hear God's glorious promise of love. In the waiting, we are all allowed to grieve absent loved ones and lament unfulfilled hopes. All the while, God is waiting with us—waiting for the godly and ungodly alike to hear God's tender voice, to perceive God's constant presence, and to accept God's steadfast love. In this season of hurriedness and impatience, Peter's words fall like the water of a soothing fountain: "Regard the patience of our Lord as salvation" (2 Pet 3:15 NRSV). God is in no hurry to force us into a realm of love and peace that we are not prepared to accept and embrace. God awaits the day when we will hear and believe: "The glory of the LORD shall be revealed, / and all people shall see it together."

Paul Nuechterlein
http://girardianlectionary.net/

2 Peter 3; Mark 1

"The Lord isn't slow to keep his promise, as some think of slowness, but he is patient toward you, not wanting anyone to perish but all to change their hearts and lives" (2 Peter 3:9). What an incredible declaration of grace! The later books of the New Testament canon (like 2 Peter) were tasked with answering disappointed hopes for a speedier return of Christ. And 2 Peter answers it with grace: Christ is patiently giving us more time to repent.

From the perspective of evangelical anthropology,* God's patience is a dominant theme undergirding all of Scripture. Stanford scholar René Girard's Mimetic Theory hypothesizes that religion of sacred violence, which arises out of the ritual repetition of collectively murdering scapegoats (i.e., ritual blood sacrifice), is what founds human culture and saves *homo sapiens* (thus far, anyway!) from self-destruction in its own interspecies violence. The gods that evolved over many eons of human evolution always include gods of wrath who demand sacrifice. So when Yahweh, the God of Israel and Israel's Messiah, began the task of trying to break through the human evolution of religion, it would always require colossal patience. For if the true God is Love (as attested to most clearly in 1 John), then the question has always been: how can a God of Love, who never uses force by the very nature of that Love, break through to human beings, who have only had eyes and ears for gods of wrath? The answer, I believe, is what we have in the Judeo-Christian Scriptures: a God who makes a *covenant* to abide with a people over many centuries and millennia, because that's how long it will take for us to finally listen and understand.

It begins with the hugely important near-sacrifice of Isaac, the first step in moving away from sacrifice (see June 29 essay). It continues with Moses and the Decalogue, the move to Torah as the heart of religion. (Was it supposed to leave behind sacrifice altogether, but the incident with the Golden Calf showed unreadiness for that?) The prophets began to speak with one voice that God wants compassionate justice, not sacrifice (see, for example, Isa 1:11-17; Jer 7:22-23; Hos 6:6; Amos 5:21-24; Micah 6:6-8). It comes to a climax with the Lamb of God who takes away the sin of the world**, attested to by the letter to the Hebrews as the end of sacrifice.

Even after two thousand years of following Israel's Messiah, do we hear and understand yet? How often have Christians relied on a god of wrath to justify their violence? How long will we continue with doctrines of a God whose wrath demands atonement by killing God's Son? How much longer will we fight wars as carrying out God's punishment against evil-doers? Will not God's seemingly infinite patience with us begin the most amazing Christmas gift to us again this Christmas: God's forgiveness for a repentance that may yet change our hearts and lives?

NOTES
* The perspective of my website, which has been interwoven into the previous 12 essays in this volume.
** See January 19, essay on John 1. It is different that John the Baptist proclaims this insight in John's Gospel, since the John the Baptist of the Synoptics seems to still be at least partially bound to a god of wrath.

Carolyn Winfrey Gillette
http://www.carolynshymns.com/

When John the Baptist Preached

When John the Baptist preached for all to hear,
He said, "Repent! The kingdom has come near!"
His rough, prophetic manner caused surprise,
But people heard his words and were baptized.
Prepare the Lord's own way! Make his paths straight!
It's time to change! We can no longer wait!

Among the crowds that day were mighty men
Who proudly traced their line to Abraham.
But John proclaimed that they should change their ways—
For trees that don't bear fruit are set ablaze.
Prepare the Lord's own way! Make his paths straight!
It's time to change! We can no longer wait!

O God, we harm creation by our greed;
We overlook our neighbors in their need.
We let our lives be ruled by hate and fear;
Your call to change is one we need to hear:
Prepare the Lord's own way! Make his paths straight!
It's time to change! We can no longer wait!

And Lord, you call for change in your church, too,
For even here we've wandered far from you.
Renew in us a vision of your Way,
And give us strength and courage to obey.
Prepare the Lord's own way! Make his paths straight!
It's time to change! We can no longer wait!

NOTES
Biblical Text: Matthew 3:1-12 and Mark 1:1-8
Tune: VENITE ADOREMUS 10.10.10.10. with refrain ("The Snow Lay on the Ground"), English melody.
Adapt. C. Winfred Douglas (1867–1944)
Text: Copyright © 2010 by Carolyn Winfrey Gillette. All rights reserved.

John Wesley's Notes on the Bible
http://www.ccel.org/ccel/wesley/notes.txt

2 Peter 3:8

In a word, with God time passes neither slower nor swifter than is suitable to him and his economy; nor can there be any reason why it should be necessary for him either to delay or hasten the end of all things. How can we comprehend this? If we could comprehend it, St. Peter needed not to have added, with the Lord.

Thom Shuman
http://lectionaryliturgies.blogspot.com/

Call to Worship

You come to us, alive and present
in that Word clothed in human flesh,
so we might hear those songs about
forgiveness, echoing with joy.
You come to us, Shepherd of God's people,
feeding us with your peace,
so we might go out and offer
the bread of hope to all the lost.
You come to us, Spirit of comfort,
welcoming us into the kingdom,
where righteousness is our best friend,
where justice lives right next door.

Prayer of the Day

While others are making lists
of things we have enough of,
you come:
   to offer us salvation,
   the one gift we cannot purchase.
As the world prepares
to entice us with more and more,
you come:
   to fill our hearts with all the hopes
   you have dreamed about us forever.
When skepticism and fear
callous our hearts,
you come:
   to bathe us in the soothing
   lotion of compassion.
When stress scoops out potholes
for every step we take,
you come:
   filling the emptiness with serenity
   as tough as your grace.

As the clock turns
faster and faster each day,
you come:
   to swaddle us in a shawl
   woven with patience.
When others push past us
to get to the front of worry's line,
you come,
   so we can clasp them
   so close to our hopes
they can hear your heartbeat.

So come to us, come to us,
God in Community, Holy in One,
even as we pray, saying, **Our Father...**

Call to Reconciliation

We can no longer play dumb. We not only know the lives we are called to lead; we are well aware of how we fail—through our words as well as our silence, by our deeds and our unwillingness to act. Let us confess to the God who comes to us,

Unison Prayer of Confession

You call us home to live with you, Comfort of the lost, but we are too busy right now to listen. We flock to the stores run by temptation and seduction, seeking the best prices. We rush to judge everyone around us, but ask you to be more patient with our repeated errors. We feast at the table piled high with broken promises and drink from the cup of fading dreams.

Yet you continue to cry out to us, Broken Heart, speaking to us of your love. Forgiveness is the gift for every moment, not just one day; hope is our constant companion as we journey with Jesus Christ, our Lord and Savior, who is your Messenger of mercy.

Silence is kept.

Assurance of Pardon

At the beginning, at the end, and in every time between, the good news speaks to us of God's tender mercy and love for us.

Our God comes! Not to punish, but to gift us with peace, not to judge, but to save us. Thanks be to God. Amen.

Dan R. Dick

Mark 1

In our "church world" today we take the concept of a gospel for granted. We have heard the "good news" throughout our lives. Even outside the church, scriptures are quoted and biblical principles are espoused so that it is impossible to escape some level of "gospelization." What would it be like to hear the good news for the very first time? What might the stories of Jesus elicit in our hearts and minds had we not heard them over and over since childhood?

In the opinion of most scholars, the gospel ascribed to Mark is the "beginning," at least of the written form. Truly, it was a "new thing." Imagine yourself in a life of poverty, locked into a spiral of hard work for little gain, tied to one place for all time, under the sovereignty of a foreign power, denied basic rights and freedoms, and lacking any real hope of change or advance. It is easy to frame such an existence as futile and desperate. But into such a reality comes a message of possibility, a story of a redeemer and savior. This is a story of a champion rising from the common herd, someone just like us, but in very significant ways nothing like us at all—a man who possesses the very power and wisdom of God.

Could the stories be true? Could the prophesies and promises of the ages come to fulfillment? Was there hope for the oppressed and the downtrodden? In our modern world, it is difficult to imagine what first-century Jewish people heard when they first received the "good news." Yet, in our modern world, we can reflect on what we hear as, again and again, we hear the gospel message. Do we hear promise? Do we receive hope? Does the gospel still contain power to transform lives?

December 14
3rd Sunday of Advent

Isaiah 61:1-4, 8-11; Psalm 126 or Luke 1:47-55; 1 Thessalonians 5:16-24; John 1:6-8, 19-28

Julie Craig
http://winsomelearnsome.com

Isaiah 61

When something as extraordinary as a new baby comes into your life, time takes on new meaning. The change is instantaneous, and before you know it, you cannot imagine what it was to live life any other way. Hours, days, weeks, months, take on new meaning. One thing for sure, you cannot predict the fullness of time any more than you can predict what God will do in any given moment, or exactly when a baby will be born.

Of course, the idea of the fullness of time also means that we believe that there is a general trajectory to the world and that God is the one with the finger on the pulse of that trajectory. Time and time again, we are given clues in Scripture about what that path looks like:

> The spirit of the Lord GOD is upon me, / because the LORD has anointed me; / he has sent me to bring good news to the oppressed, / to bind up the brokenhearted, / to proclaim liberty to the captives, / and release to the prisoners; / to proclaim the year of the LORD's favor, / and the day of vengeance of our God; / to comfort all who mourn; / to provide for those who mourn in Zion— / to give them a garland instead of ashes, / the oil of gladness instead of mourning, / the mantle of praise instead of a faint spirit. (vv. 1-3 NRSV)

This is no promise of business-as-usual. This is the doors of the prison flung open. This is Guantanamo Bay shut down. This is the atrocities of Darfur completely reversed forever. This is flood-ravaged plains dried up and restored and hurricane destruction rebuilt. This is AIDS eradicated and foreclosures cancelled. This is a promise so radical, a trajectory so extraordinary, a world so upside down that it prompts only one question: "When, Lord?"

We do not know where we are on the arc of God's plan, any more than we know when a baby will come or when the fullness of time will be revealed once again or God's great reversal will play out or our world will be turned upside down in the most remarkable, unpredictable, and spectacular of ways. We know only that those who mourn will wear garlands of roses and orchids and lilies as they dance with delight, and will splash one another with the oil of celebration instead of wallowing in the stink of death. We know that those who hunger and thirst and long to be filled with something other than regret shall be filled, and those who have lavished in plenty and luxury and satisfied self-confidence will have to wait their turn.

Those promises make the struggle worth it. In a stable surrounded by farm animals, with the cold reality and the stink of life all around her, a young girl gave herself over to the fullness of time and leaned her body and her spirit fully into that long arc, and the world was turned upside down forever. Thanks be to God.

Mary J. Scifres

Steadfast Love: A Christmas Gift to Unloved People (Isaiah 61)

You are a Christmas gift to the world! You, members of the body of Christ, are the hands and feet of Jesus; you are children of the Spirit; you are a Christmas gift to the world! Listen to the gift you are given: "The spirit of the Lord

GOD is upon [you], / ... to bring good news to the oppressed, / to bind up the brokenhearted, / to proclaim liberty to the captives, / and release to the prisoners" (v. 1 NRSV).

Being God's Christmas gift to the world is a huge calling. We are God's gift, not just to the pretty parts of the world, but to the ugly, dirty, uncomfortable parts, so that we can bring hope to the hopeless, justice to the downtrodden, and freedom to the enslaved. John the Baptist could say he was only a witness, sent to testify to the light. But we are more than witnesses; we are children of the light. Jesus, Light of the World (John 8:12), told his followers that we were to be the light of the world with him (Matthew 5:14). Yes, following Christ means walking in some very large footsteps—but Christ walks with us, and God's Spirit empowers us to fulfill this calling.

Rejoice, dear friends! We are here to show God's love to the unloved, to transform cries into laughter, and to partner with God to turn tears of sorrow into shouts of joy. God's steadfast love is with us always, and that is a marvelous Christmas gift indeed. But the greatest Christmas miracle is this: God's steadfast love is with the least and the lost, the poorest and the saddest. How? Through us. We help the Christmas miracle of God's steadfast love transform the world when we live this calling and proclaim this message. Rejoice! You are a Christmas gift to the world!

John Wesley's Notes on the Bible
http://www.ccel.org/ccel/wesley/notes.txt

Luke 1:47

"My spirit hath rejoiced in God my savior"—She seems to turn her thoughts here to Christ himself, who was to be born of her, as the angel had told her, he should be the Son of the Highest, whose name should be Jesus, the saviour. And she rejoiced in hope of salvation through faith in him, which is a blessing common to all true believers, more than in being his mother after the flesh, which was an honour peculiar to her. And certainly she had the same reason to rejoice in God her saviour that we have: because he had regarded the low estate of his handmaid, in like manner as he regarded our low estate; and vouchsafed to come and save her and us, when we were reduced to the lowest estate of sin and misery.

Teri Peterson
http://clevertitlehere.blogspot.com

Isaiah 61; Luke 1

I wonder how much Christmas cheer Mary and Joseph had that first Advent. Mary, an unmarried teenager suddenly pregnant; Joseph, a man who'll be supporting a family before he even pays for a wedding; both of them in a small village where everyone will know their scandal before lunch, in a culture where Mary's choice to say yes to God could easily have gotten her killed. Yet in the midst of that, she sings! "My spirit rejoices in God my Savior, for the Mighty One has done great things for me. He has fed the hungry and lifted up the lowly, and holy is his name" (see Luke 1:46-55).

Or the prophet Isaiah, looking around at the ruined city his people were hoping to rebuild, trying to preach to people of fair-weather-faith, proclaiming that God has promised to plant them in fertile ground so they can grow into oaks of righteousness that glorify the Lord, offering a vision of justice and joy.

If anyone had reason to mask their fear with cheerfulness, it was these three, yet they sing joyfully instead! Joy is an act of faithful subversion in a world that tells us to hide our true selves behind the shallow sad-mad-glad. Joy is well beyond anything our culture, our possessions, our country, our media, or even our relationships can give us. Joy comes from one place: seeking God. And, in Isaiah 61, it seems that God has even shown us the way to joy.

Could it be that the way to know the joyful fruit of the Spirit is to practice? Not to gaze heavenward, anticipating something better; not to turn away from suffering because it's depressing and ugly; but instead to get more grounded, reach to our roots, push down into the earth and let God grow in us like a seed...to live fully into our calling as anointed ones, the body of Christ, made to bring grace to a world in need, to shine light into a world of darkness.

Is it possible that the way to joy—to real Christmas Spirit—is through being more fully who God has called us to be, in the place God has called us? Is it possible that Christmas Joy comes from being the site of God's incarnation? Maybe when we bear Christ into the world, the way Mary bore Christ in her body, when we don't just speak good news but *are* good news; when we are creators of justice, then we will also find joy—joy beyond mere cheer, joy that is grounded and growing, joy that is subversive and holy.

Dan R. Dick

1 Thessalonians 5

We live in a world of "hurry up and wait." Long lines in coffee shops, slow-moving elevators, heavily congested highways, and slow download speeds contribute to the mounting frustration that we waste an awful lot of time—waiting. Much of our day is spent waiting upon small and insignificant nuisances and inconveniences; however, occasionally we are forced to wait for truly important things. The results of a test or biopsy, news about a job, or about the safe passage of a family member. Such instances heighten our anxiety, making waiting especially challenging.

So how do we fill our time while we wait? What tools and techniques do we employ to "kill" time? This is the essence of the epistle writer's advice to the congregation in Thessalonica as they anticipate the return of the Christ. Don't just sit there! Do something. But do something worthy of our faith. As we wait, rejoice—celebrate and sing, offer praise and thanksgiving. Pray without ceasing—invoke God's will and wisdom to address the multitude of joys and concerns of the community. Don't quench the Spirit—stop talking about all the things we shouldn't do, and focus instead on all the good we should do. Pay attention to the prophets among us (and test the wisdom of what they say)—talk about God's will and a vision for what God has promised. Think about God and the things that please God. Abstain from evil—we all know the things we shouldn't do, but if we fill our time doing the good things, we won't have any time left over to do the bad things! Time is a gift. Let us delight God by being excellent stewards of this precious gift, filling our time with praise, hope, and joy.

Todd Weir
http://bloomingcactus.typepad.com/

John 1

Baptism in our context is a right of passage. We don't treat this as an especially radical act. Infant baptism has a warm, cozy feel. Beaming parents hand me their little bundle of joy, nervously hoping that she will be as quiet as Baby Jesus in the manger and not spit up on the pastor. The congregation cranes their necks to see new life just starting out on the journey, "oohs and aahs" join the liturgy. It is a joyous and wonderful welcome into the life of the community, but certainly nothing like what John was up to by the River Jordan.

I had a different experience growing up Baptist. When you were baptized, it was made clear that you were dying with Christ, dying for your sins and having them washed away, and then being raised to new life. It was important that you felt a moment of panic, a panic that if you didn't follow Jesus, it was like drowning. When I was baptized, I wondered if Pastor Roy was still a little upset about catching me throwing a Frisbee from the balcony. It's what I think of when I try to imagine what "water-boarding" feels like. It was abundantly clear that baptism required a new way of life.

John's practice was transforming the religious observances of his day. The Greek word for *baptize* literally means "immersion," and was often used for the Hebrew practice of *Tivlah,* ceremonial washings especially important to the religious practices of the Pharisees. In Luke 11:37-38, a Pharisee criticizes Jesus for not engaging in ritual *Tivlah* washings before joining them for dinner. This is a serious charge in the mind of a Pharisee; purity is everything. Their plan for transforming the world was to be a pure example, and if they stayed pure, then God would protect and save Israel. Jesus, in the spirit of his baptism from John, firmly denounced this practice as trivial without real spiritual reform. Rituals alone did not bring about the needed human transformation.

The location of John's baptizing practice is laden with meaning. The Jordan River was of great importance to Israel. It was the place where Hebrew people left the wilderness and started their campaign to take the Promised Land.

Caesar had to decide to cross the Rubicon, Joshua had to cross the Jordan. They crossed the Jordan near Jericho and then fought the famed battle that brought down the city walls. The symbolism in John's baptism was more than just the personal spiritual transformation and a call to be holy. It was also launching a campaign to transform the social order, a retaking of the Promised Land. John saw Jesus as the messiah, and expected that Jesus would bring about this great reordering, throwing off Rome, the temple aristocracy, the Pharisees, and anyone aligned with the current power structure. This helps us understand the symbolic power of John's Baptism in the Jordan for first-century Israel. *It was a spiritual, moral, and political renewal campaign.*

Liz Crumlish
http://somethingtostandon.blogspot.co.uk/

John 1

John the Baptist, in all his strangeness and austerity, was the one sent by God to preach the good news. And the people flocked, not only to hear him but also to repent and be baptized. John the Baptist took the good news of God's love back where it belongs—on the margins of society, to those who are tired, defeated, and ground down by the rigors of daily life. John took the good news to those who had lost almost everything—except hope. It was hope that propelled folk out of their usual surroundings to the wilderness where John was preaching. It was hope that kept them there, hanging on to his every word and making a response in baptism.

How often have we rejected what we need to hear because of who it comes from or where we hear it? Or because it wasn't quite what we wanted to hear. We're all good at filtering news so that we take in—and pass on—only those bits that we deem to be useful. And, in doing that, we often dilute the message or miss the point altogether. Maybe we're not prepared to hear the gospel in a different way or in a different place. And even less prepared to take the good news to the margins of our society.

The good news proclaims for us a way forward in the uncertainty of the world and of the church. A way forward in our changed landscape. Gone are the familiar things we cherished, the old ways and traditions, packed churches and faith respected, if not embraced. How is it possible to follow Jesus, to proclaim good news in this changed landscape? How about looking for God in unexpected places? Hearing the good news from unexpected people? Being prepared to undergo change so that God can transform us? Waking up to the fact that God lives at the margins of life?

This is nothing new. It has always been so. That is why, in Advent, our texts call us back to reality. A reality that enables us to welcome the baby born in Bethlehem from a changed perspective. A reality that takes us out of our cozy sentimental preparation into a more challenging, life-changing preparation. The kind of preparation that belongs not in our church buildings, but out at the margins of our society. And, in this changed landscape, a reality that invites us to discover anew that the life-changing word of God is still good news.

December 21
4th Sunday of Advent

2 Samuel 7:1-11, 16; Luke 1:47-55 or Psalm 89:1-4, 19-26; Romans 16:25-27; Luke 1:26-38

Dan R. Dick

2 Samuel 7

Second Samuel provides us with a beautiful metaphor for the significance of the birth of Jesus, the Christ. Jewish history recounts the dispossessed and marginalized nature of God's chosen people—always moving or being moved, in many ways rootless and nomadic, enjoying the possession of their own lands in freedom for only very brief periods of time. In the time of David, the king desired to establish a "house" for God to live in—a permanent residence that would honor God and recognize the fulfillment of God's promises. While building such a dwelling did not end the cycle of "moving about," it did give the Chosen People a vision upon which to hope and dream.

In the time of Jesus' birth, the Hebrew people were essentially servants and squatters in their own homeland. Their "place" wasn't truly theirs. In the physical realm, the people of God were mere visitors, never destined to stay in one place very long. But in the spiritual realm, a new hope appeared. Through the birth of a Messiah, all the rules changed. Through belief in the Christ, those who had no "place" suddenly belonged to something greater. The "church" was to be built around the grace of God through the body of Christ; not an earthly dwelling place, but a spiritual and eternal home.

No matter who you were, no matter where you lived, all could become one in Christ Jesus. The physical dwelling place proclaimed by the prophet Nathan to king David was transformed, becoming the spiritual promise of God for all time. In Christ, we have the hope of becoming the house of God, an eternal dwelling place where we are made one with Christ, one with each other, and one in ministry to all the world.

Mary J. Scifres

Steadfast Love: A Christmas Present with All the People (2 Samuel 7)

God did not want David to build a temple. God liked moving among the people and being in the center of things (vv. 5-11). God likes being with us! *Emmanuel,* a central message of Advent and Christmas, is an echo of Gabriel's words to Mary: "The Lord is with you" (Luke 1:28). God is with us! God is always among the people, not stuck inside four walls. Even when we focus our festive activities inside ornately decorated sanctuaries, God refuses to be contained—challenging us to share the Christmas gift of God's steadfast love with everyone.

Mary proclaimed God's steadfast love and bore the Christ child. Despite her fears and confusion, she celebrated that first Christmas miracle: "My soul magnifies the Lord . . . / for the Mighty One has done great things" (Luke 1:46, 49a NRSV). God's love came to earth, to a poor Jewish couple, to dirty shepherds and pagan kings, as a gift for all people. We are now called to proclaim and carry forth this gift for all to see, sharing Jesus' message of love and grace everywhere we go.

God's steadfast love has come, yearning to dwell among us in caves and stables, in tents and tabernacles, in gutters and fortresses. God's steadfast love is here, for God is with us. God is dwelling in our very midst, a Christmas present of divine presence amongst the people. God's steadfast love is present amongst us in temples and mosques, in churches and synagogues, in factories and fields. God is with us all—even with those who would reject the gift offered them. This Christmas miracle is mystery and blessing for all. Shout it from the rooftops! Take the message to the streets: God is living among us. God's love is with us. God's mercy is a gift for all!

John Wesley's Notes on the Bible
http://www.ccel.org/ccel/wesley/notes.txt

Romans 16:25

"Now to him who is able"—The last words of this epistle exactly answer the first, chap. 1, 1-5, in particular, concerning the power of God, the gospel, Jesus Christ, the scriptures, the obedience of faith, all nations.

Dan Clendenin
http://journeywithjesus.net

Luke 1

Luke recounts the birth of John the Baptist from the viewpoint of John's father. Zechariah was a married man, "too old" for sex, and his wife was barren. He was a member of the religious establishment in the holy city of Jerusalem, a priest of the professional class. His vision of the angel Gabriel occurred in the inner sanctuary of the temple. When Gabriel foretold the birth of his son, John, Zechariah responded in disbelief and consequently was struck silent so that he could not speak.

The birth narrative of Jesus is told from the viewpoint of his mother. Mary was a single, teenage girl, "too young" for sex. Given the strongly patriarchal nature of society in her time and place, Joseph, to whom she was betrothed, is notable for his invisibility in this story. Mary was a peasant girl from a working-class neighborhood of carpenters in Nazareth, a village so insignificant that it is not mentioned in the Old Testament, in the historian Josephus (c. 37–100), or in the Jewish Talmud. "Can anything from Nazareth be good?" (John 1:46). Her encounter took place in an unknown, ordinary house. When the angel Gabriel foretold the birth of her son, Jesus, Mary responded in words of faith that have echoed through the centuries: "I am the Lord's servant . . . may it be to me as you have said" (Luke 1:38 NIV 1984). Her bold belief startled her pregnant cousin Elizabeth, who "in a loud voice . . . exclaimed: 'Blessed are you among women, and blessed is the child you will bear! . . . Blessed is she who has believed that what the Lord has said to her will be accomplished!" (Luke 1:42, 45 NIV 1984). Whereas Zechariah was struck silent for his unbelief, Mary praised God in her majestic "Magnificat" (vv. 46-55).

For their part, and to their loss, Protestants have tiptoed around Mary, fearing that such exalted language about her veers too close to making her a coredeemer of humanity. Anything that elevates Mary to that degree is cause for concern. In more syncretistic and popular forms of Christian folk religion among uneducated people, it is not difficult to find such abuses. We have also taken exception to dogmatic formulations about Mary that were made much later and that do not enjoy clear biblical support, such as her freedom from both actual and even original sin (Immaculate Conception), and the idea that after her death she was taken directly to heaven (Bodily Assumption). So Protestants rightly press a caution that both Catholics and Orthodox believers themselves acknowledge, that we honor or venerate (*duleia*) Mary as the Mother of God, but we do not offer her our worship (*latreia*), which is due to God alone. Genuine veneration of the Mother of God should lead to unambiguous exaltation of the Son of God.

Mary played a unique role in the mystery of salvation whereby God humbled Himself to be born as the baby of a peasant teenager in order to reconcile the world to Himself. We can only stand in awe of this woman who was faithful to God's call to such an improbable role in redemption.

Suzanne Guthrie
http://www.edgeofenclosure.org

"Find in Us a Mansion" (Luke 1)

> Oh, then, soul, most beautiful among all the creatures, so anxious to know the dwelling place of your Beloved that you may go in quest of Him and be united with Him, now we are telling you that you yourself are His dwelling and His secret chamber and hiding place. This is something of immense gladness for you, to see that all your good and hope is so close to you as to be within you, or better, that you cannot be without Him. Behold, exclaims the Bridegroom, the kingdom of God is within you. Luke 17:21. And His servant, the apostle St. Paul, declares: You are the temple of God. 2 Corinthians 6:16. (John of the Cross, The Spiritual Canticle, 1:7, *The Collected Works of John of the Cross,* Kieran Kavanaugh, O.C.D., and Otilio Rodriguez, O.C.D., trans. [Washington, D.C.: ICS Publications,1973], 418.)

Mary! Answer quickly! (The angels hold their breath.... Will she say yes?) Once the urgency is perceived, how can anything be more important? And finally, Mary says, "Let it be it with me according to your word" (v. 38 NRSV). But it is not only Mary who must respond to the angel's *Ave.* You and I are asked to receive the Spirit's indwelling. The soul is the dwelling place, the secret, hidden room of growing compassion, justice, peace, Emmanuel/God-with-Us. Your own heart and mine are the womb, the inn, the resting place for the Christ being born.

And the Beloved's journey continues in us. In love and in suffering, through Jesus' death and resurrection, we are transformed through the Paschal mystery by the Christ event, hidden within our very being and manifested by our loving actions.

Here's the very heart of it: "...that your Son at His coming, may find in us a mansion prepared for himself." This phrase comes from the collect for the fourth Sunday of Advent in *The American Prayer Book,* which in turn comes from the eighth-century *Gelasian Sacramentary*.

As humble as this dwelling might be, we're asked to prepare a mansion for the one who prepares a mansion for us.

> In my Father's house are many [mansions]; if it were not so, would I have told you that I go to prepare a place for you? And when I go and prepare a place for you, I will come again and will take you to myself, that where I am you may be also. (John 14:2-3 RSV)

"Dwell in my love," said Jesus (John 15:9 NEB). And so we sing at Christmastide, "Let every heart prepare him room!" (Isaac Watts, "Joy to the World").

Ann Scull
http://seedstuff.blogspot.com

A Useful Image

This image of a sunset with text from Romans 16:27 is found on my site, Mustard Seeds: http://seedstuff.blogspot.com.au/2011/12/advent-4-b-december-18-lovesaying-yes.html (accessed March 22, 2012). The photo was taken about ten minutes by slow boat from my place on the Gippsland Lakes in Australia.

Dramas

Wild Goose Worship Group, ***"The Village Gossips,"*** in *Cloth for the Cradle* (Glasgow: Wild Goose Publications, 1997), 58–60. This is a comical little drama that endeavors to get into the mind of the community in which Mary and Joseph lived.

Wild Goose Worship Group, ***"Mary and the Angel,"*** in *Cloth for the Cradle* (Glasgow: Wild Goose Publications, 1997), 42–43. Another comical little drama that rewrites the conversation between Mary and Gabriel in a way that not only brings a smile to the faces of those watching but also makes them think about the implications of such a conversation.

Reading

Wild Goose Worship Group, *"Mary Pondering,"* in *Cloth for the Cradle* (Glasgow: Wild Goose Publications, 1997), 47. This makes a lovely handout for people to take home and is particularly good if you can find a pregnant Mum to read or recite it.

Discussion: On Luke Readings

1. When is it hardest for us to say yes to God?

2. What makes Mary able to say it?

3. How can we follow her example?

4. What is one way we can show God's love this Christmas?

Stories

Max Lucado, *"Gabriel's Questions,"* in *When God Whispers Your Name* (Dallas: Word Publishing, 1996), 55–59. Max Lucado has a way of bringing the biblical story into present reality almost without us noticing.

Walter Wangerin, *"The Hornbill,"* in *The Manger Is Empty: Stories in Time* (New York: Hodder and Stoughton, 1989), 21–24. This evocative story from nature explains the Christmas story and its implications for God and people with depth and sensitivity. Response Activity: Print some of the questions from the last part of the story onto cards for people to take home and think about.

Poem

Pro Hart and Norman Habel, *"Mary's Fear,"* in *Outback Christmas* (Adelaide: Lutheran Publishing House, 1990), 14–15. This puts the Gospel story into an Australian context.

Meditation

"Sightings" by Kathy Galloway in Jan Sutch Pickard (ed.), *Dandelions and Thistles: Biblical Meditations from the Iona Community* (Glasgow: Wild Goose Publications, 1999), 44–45. This encompasses more of the Christmas story than just Mary and therefore can be used selectively or as a whole.

Response Activity

Give everyone the following prayer, a pen or pencil, and a silent space to write their responses:

Lord, help me to marvel at Gabriel's message when I am _____.

Lord, give me courage like Mary to tell you about _____, to ask questions when I feel _____, and to confidently give you my _____.

Help me to see the Christmas story with new eyes and to thank you for _____. Amen.

John van de Laar

http://www.sacredise.com/

Luke 1

The incarnation is the greatest of all love stories.

The story of Mary's call to give birth to the incarnate One leads her—and us—into a radical encounter with God's love and its impact on the world. The angel's message begins with an affirmation of God's love—"Greetings, favored woman!" (v. 28 NLT)—and as Mary's journey unfolds, this love sustains her through a painful, and potentially dangerous, time. She could have become a lonely outcast, but she finds that her relative Elizabeth is also, miraculously, pregnant, providing Mary with a support network to help her face what is to come. She could have been rejected by her betrothed, but she finds him gracious and committed because of God's loving activity. Beyond her personal experience, however, Mary comes to recognize the way God's love can, and will, impact the world and its systems. Her "Magnificat" is a challenging proclamation of God's care for the least, and God's opposition to oppressive and exploitative powers. Because of this moment of love's birth in human flesh, the world is forever different.

Only Luke's Gospel includes the account of the annunciation. As he writes to a persecuted church, he reminds them that God has broken into human history in a unique way in this specific moment. As he writes to a diverse church, including both Jew and Gentile, he reminds them of God's incarnate love that unites them. Luke connects the birth of Christ with Bethlehem, the city of David, and with God's promise of an eternal Davidic dynasty. But, by highlighting Mary's role, he shows that this moment is dramatically different from anything that has come before. This time, instead of a triumphalist realm won through violence, the God-promised dynasty is peaceful, just, and loving—subversively impacting the world one radically changed heart at a time.

Mary cannot understand this new work of God or see how it will work out in her life. She knows only that it has something to do with God's liberating purposes. In an immense step of faith and hope, she accepts her call, somehow makes peace with not knowing, and willingly gambles on love.

Luke's story is not about this one young woman alone. He invites his readers to make the same step of faith—to jump blindly into God's newly arrived Reign by gambling on love. There is no requirement that we understand God's vision. There is simply the invitation to allow incarnation to happen with us, for love to be born in us, and for God's Reign to come through us. It is not because we are significant or because we have answers that love seeks to be born in and through us. It is because God makes what seems impossible completely attainable. God simply waits for our yes, and once we have given it, God goes to work to bring the incarnated love to birth in us and, through us, in the world. The incarnation really is the ultimate love story

December 24/25
Christmas Eve/Day (Proper 3)

Isaiah 52:7-10; Psalm 98; Hebrews 1:1-4, (5-12); John 1:1-14

Beth Quick
http://bethquick.blogspot.com

Isaiah 52

• "How beautiful…are the feet" (v. 7). What a great image! Are your feet beautiful? What message do your feet carry from place to place? Do you bring peace with your feet? Salvation?

• Isaiah speaks of the joy of Israel returning back home after exile in Babylon. When have you experienced your most joyful homecoming? When have you been away from home and not wanted to be away from home? Homesick? Without a home?

• God's arm (see v. 10)—I can't help but imagine a God-flexing-muscles picture.

Psalm 98

• There's God's arm again in verse 1, twice on one Sunday!

• "Let the floods clap their hands; / let the hills sing together for joy" (v. 8 NRSV). How would you create this image in your worship space?

• This is a psalm of joy and thankfulness for God's action in someone's life, in the life of a whole people. How do you celebrate as an individual? As a community? Do we celebrate as nations? A world? How do we express our joy in God? Through worship? Action?

Hebrews 1

• Hebrews talks of Jesus as the reflection of God's glory. I think we are also reflections of God's glory, if we let ourselves be, if we let God make us into these reflections. This is what it means to be created in God's image, isn't it?

• "Exact imprint of God's very being" (v. 3 NRSV). This brings fingerprints to my mind, or plaster casts of babies' feet.

• The argument here seems to be: Jesus is better than angels. This was apparently a question to debate in the early church!

John 1

• This is John's take on a birth narrative. No shepherds, no angels, no Mary and Joseph, no manger. This is how John describes Jesus' coming into the world. The language is rich in metaphor, and though it lacks the characters of the traditional nativity, the point is still communicated without a doubt: "And the Word became flesh and lived among us" (v. 14 NRSV). Passages like this from John provide the strongest base for our trinitarian Christian creeds. Jesus was "in the beginning with God" (v. 2 NRSV).

• I think we are all, like John the Baptist, meant to *testify*, or witness, to the light. How do you do it? Witnessing means telling what you know about something, like at a trial. What do you know about the light that is Christ?

Martha Spong
http://marthaspong.com/

Hebrews 1

A motley nativity decorates our mantelpiece, the figures acquired over the course of fifty years. Some I first saw in my grandmother's apartment. The olive-wood wise men set out from the left edge with their camels. The shepherds came from the right. Grandma Galli had background artwork, long since lost when she moved to assisted living, bounced to my parents' house, and ended her life in a nursing home.

We will all wear out like clothing.

Widowed in her fifties, my grandmother set out to see the world. She was a Laubach Literacy volunteer in Japan, did mission work in India, and visited the Holy Land. She collected more than one nativity set on her travels. When my oldest was a toddler, my mother packed up the soft set, wire figures with fabric faces and actual clothes, the animals not as bendable as my second child's fondness for them required. The "doh-doh" was his special friend, carried around the house and hidden and rediscovered until finally one leg fell limply from his soft, grey body.

The olive-wood figures came to me after my parents died. We set them up each year, Grandma Galli–style: wise men on the left, shepherds on the right, an empty manger at the middle waiting for the baby. But I felt wistful for the by-now hard-used textile set, and I scrounged through the box looking for pieces I could add. Two shepherd boys; why, they were only a little out of scale! And I could add the lambs, because their dear little legs remained intact.

Somewhere among the Christmas things were other little wooden camels, smaller than the handsome set belonging to my grandmother. If I put them far to the left, maybe they would look like the camel train stretching into the distance. Yes?

And that Italian angel, the only piece of a set an elderly cousin meant to start for us, she could stand by the manger, surely, to worship the baby Jesus.

A dear, faraway friend has what she calls a "grotto" in her house. It's full of other people's leftovers, found in thrift stores and at yard sales. One day I looked up and gasped with recognition. A flamboyantly posed and painted plaster Wise Man gazed at me, just like the one in a set my mother had discarded long ago. He came home in my suitcase and joined the eclectic nativity.

We will all wear out like clothing. Even if the world sees the church as worn out, or as old-fashioned and eccentric as a cloak they would just as soon roll up and put away, the truth of the Incarnation goes on forever, finding new forms of expression. So if that wooden baby Jesus hits the hearth again and the break is beyond the power of Super Glue, I won't feel I have to replace the whole set. Olive-wood Mary can beam just as easily at the leftover textile baby. God will still be among us.

Lowell Grisham
http://lowellsblog.blogspot.com/

Prayers of the People

Presider: In Christ God's Word has become flesh dwelling among us, full of grace and truth. Let us pray to the true light that enlightens the world, that from the fullness of God all creation may receive grace upon grace, saying: What has come into being in Christ was life, and the life was the light of all people.

Litanist: Let your Church bring good news and announce salvation to comfort all your people, O God, that we may be your witnesses to testify to the light. What has come into being in Christ was life,
and the life was the light of all people.

Judge the world with your justice and the peoples with equity; bare your holy arm in the eyes of all the nations, O Holy One, that all the ends of the earth may see the salvation of our God. What has come into being in Christ was life,
and the life was the light of all people.

Be our light in the darkness for all the earth, O God, that the fullness of your heart may be made known for the healing of all the people. What has come into being in Christ was life,

and the life was the light of all people.

Live among us, O Word made flesh, and reconcile this community to your light. What has come into being in Christ was life,

and the life was the light of all people.

You have comforted your people, O God: Hear us as we pray in faith for _____. Let the rivers clap their hands and let the hills ring out with joy before God as we bring our prayers of thanksgiving and gratitude, especially for _____. Receive those who have died as heirs of eternal life, especially _____. What has come into being in Christ was life,

and the life was the light of all people.

Presider: Loving and gracious Creator, from the beginning you have brightened our darkness with the light of your life, and in these days you have spoken to us by a son, who is the reflection of your glory and the exact imprint of your divine being: Let your light shine forth, that your Word made flesh may bring grace upon grace to all the earth, in the power of your Holy Spirit, through Jesus Christ our Savior. **Amen.**

Dan R. Dick

John 1

Scholars throughout the ages debate the question: "When did Jesus 'become' divine?" Our scriptures actually fuel the debate rather than answer it. In Paul's writings, it is evident that Paul believes Jesus became divine at his resurrection—that he suffered all as a human before God resurrected him and imbued him with power. Mark, the earliest of the Gospel writers, indicates that Jesus "received the Spirit" at his baptism, being adopted as God's Son. Matthew and Luke trace different genealogies, but both concur that Jesus was divine at birth. John takes it a step further. Jesus did not "become" divine. No, from before the foundation of the world, from the very beginning, Jesus the Christ was the Word, and the Word is eternal—without beginning or end. The Word is the essence and Spirit of God, from which all things come into being. And at the appropriate time, the Word became flesh and dwelt among us.

For John, only God is worthy to be praised, and the man Jesus was a manifestation of the one, true, eternal God. The gift that God gave was that we would be blessed to know, to talk to, and to walk with divinity in human form. The very idea that God would become present to humanity was the incredible fact that John wanted to emphasize. Worthiness had nothing to do with it, nor did our desire or piety. No, "God so loved the world that he gave his only Son, so that everyone who believes in him may not perish but may have eternal life" (3:16 NRSV). Our celebration of Christmas is in fact a celebration of God's unconditional love, and the gift that God gave us is the gift we now have to share with others. Thanks be to God!

Melissa Bane Sevier
http://melissabanesevier.wordpress.com

Every Day (John 1)

Each year on Christmas Day, I have the privilege of witnessing our church and other volunteers do a great but simple thing in our community. It is as simple as providing a meal and as profound as making Christmas a better day for many.

Some people bring casseroles to the church. Others give their time and energy to organize, set up, and clean up. Still others show up to assemble boxes full of great food or deliver meals to shut-ins or to workers at the hospital, the fire and police departments. It is always quite a spectacle.

As we end one year and get ready to start another, I appreciate that less spectacular events are played out every day of every year in every community. Every day, people work at hospitals, doing everything from treating injury and illness to cleaning patient rooms to filing insurance forms. Every day, our public safety workers patrol or answer emergency calls, at great personal risk. Every day, there are many others who make our communities good and safe places to live. They collect our trash, grow our food, deliver our mail, make or sell what we need. They teach our children, supply our power, offer their labor, operate government and courts, conduct research, and provide a myriad of other services.

Every day, volunteers give uncountable hours by offering their time, money, and gifts and skills in education, religious communities, and healthcare. They feed the hungry, provide clothing, build and repair homes, care for the weak, bring clean water, and lift spirits. Every day, the need continues. People get sick, they lose their jobs, go hungry, suffer a loss, lose their way, lack the basic necessities of life.

This year past has been all these things: need and response. Sometimes we are on one side of that equation; sometimes on the other. All the years to come will be the same. There's a passage in Deuteronomy that addresses this: "Since there will never cease to be some in need on the earth, I therefore command you, 'Open your hand to the poor and needy neighbor in your land'" (15:11 NRSV). Every day there is need. Every day we are called to open our hands.

May Christmas be a time when the need is lessened because more hands are opened. May it be a time when our eyes and hearts are opened as well. "And the Word became flesh and lived among us, and we have seen his glory, the glory as of a father's only son, full of grace and truth" (John 1:14 NRSV).

On this Christmas Eve, I give thanks to God that, though the need will never cease, there will also never cease to be people who respond to that need with their work, their prayers, their faith, and the love they show through their actions. Every day.

Mary J. Scifres

Steadfast Love: A Christmas Gift of Joy (John 1)

There is a dramatic series of scenes in J. R. R. Tolkien's novel *The Two Towers* when trees begin walking and talking, and eventually march upon an evil wizard and his tower of destruction. They take down the wizard's fortress and begin to restore the earth's rhythm so that future trees can live and grow in their forest. When I read Psalm 96, I always think of the trees in that book and their cousins of the earth, dancing around and celebrating their new-found freedom: "let the earth rejoice; /...Let the field exult.../ all the trees of the forest sing for joy" (Ps 96:11-12 NRSV). On this night, angels sing, a star shines, a maiden gives birth, and shepherds rejoice. Surely, the fields and forests sing and dance with us on this night of celebration and joy.

Celebrating and singing for joy is an important part of our Christmas experience each year. Christmas caroling to the homebound, humming along with Frosty at school programs, and singing carols on Christmas Eve are all echoes of this joyous season. When we sing and rejoice on this darkest week of the year, in the midst of this crazy-mixed up commercialized holiday, it is as if we are the angel speaking to those shepherds: "Do not be afraid; for see—I am bringing you good news of great joy for all the people" (Luke 2:10 NRSV). We sing with the angels, and we sing for the angels, as we rejoice on this night. We proclaim with the angel in the field: Christmas joy is a gift for all people; rejoice with heaven and earth; give glory to God in the highest; and offer peace upon the earth!

John Wesley's Notes on the Bible
http://www.ccel.org/ccel/wesley/notes.txt

Luke 2:14

"Glory be to God in the highest; on earth peace; good will toward Men"—The shouts of the multitude are generally broken into short sentences. This rejoicing acclamation strongly represents the piety and benevolence of these heavenly spirits: as if they had said, Glory be to God in the highest heavens: let all the angelic legions resound his praises. For with the Redeemer's birth, peace, and all kind of happiness, come down to dwell on earth: yea, the overflowings of Divine good will and favour are now exercised toward men.

December 28
1st Sunday after Christmas

Isaiah 61:10–62:3; Psalm 148; Galatians 4:4-7; Luke 2:22-40

Dan R. Dick

Galatians 4

What comes to mind when you hear the word *rules*? Is your initial reaction positive or negative? Do rules make you feel happy or sad? Do rules give you a sense of freedom or restriction? Do rules inspire you or stifle you? Both? Neither? Generally, almost everyone sees the need and value for rules, but they don't necessarily make us feel happy or free or inspired. Paul, writing to the members of the Christian community in Galatia, offers a middle ground. For centuries, the people of God followed the constraints of rules and commandments, known by all as the Law. Every Jewish person was born under the Law, even Jesus himself was born under the Law. But through Jesus an amazing thing happened: the yoke of Law that governed citizens became the rules of a loving parent for a beloved child. Through Jesus, the Law-giver God became Abba—a loving, familiar name for a parent. The rules still apply, not as rigid Laws, but as helpful guidance to allow us all to grow to full maturity as children of God.

Parents do not impose rules to control or limit or constrain their children. They do not impose the same level of restraint on a grown child as they do on an adolescent, or the same expectations on an eight-year-old that they do on an infant. Rules shift and adapt to help the child grow and mature and function capably in the world. Rules truly are given for our own good, and as we evolve in our understanding of what is right and wrong, the need for rules to be enforced by an outside authority lessens. Christ came that we might be in new relationship with God; a relationship bound not by the heavy hand of Law, but by the loving hand of a parent.

Marci Auld Glass
www.marciglass.com

Luke 2

When Jesus was only forty days old, his family, like all observant Jewish families of the day, presented themselves at the temple for purification, and they offered a sacrifice of two turtledoves. I read this story in Luke and wonder if the two turtledoves in the "Twelve Days of Christmas" come from this passage. Surely they must. But Luke's original audience would have wondered something else. *"Turtle doves? Why didn't they sacrifice a lamb?"*

Here are the directions in Leviticus 12:6-8 (NRSV):

> When the days of her purification are completed,...she shall bring to the priest at the entrance of the tent of meeting a lamb in its first year for a burnt offering, and a pigeon or a turtledove for a sin offering. He shall offer it before the LORD, and make atonement on her behalf....If she cannot afford a sheep, she shall take two turtledoves or two pigeons, one for a burnt offering and the other for a sin offering..."

So without saying, "Mary and Joseph were very poor," Luke lets the reader know that Mary and Joseph were very poor.

There are preachers who will tell you that if you have faith, you will be financially prosperous. They have found a few verses in Scripture that support this "prosperity gospel" and it appears to be making these preachers prosperous, at least.

Our culture wants this prosperity gospel to be true, because the American dream is not built on finding the blessings in poverty. But if Joseph and Mary had faith enough to listen to the angel, to bring God's own son into the world, and to be obedient enough to take him to the temple to obey the Laws of Moses, then they should have been prosperous beyond measure. Yet this couple couldn't even afford to buy a lamb for the sacrifice. If God's own family was struggling to get by, then we need to reconsider the connection between being blessed and being prosperous.

Simeon, about whom we know only what Luke tells us, was led by the Spirit to the temple. He has been waiting for the "consolation of Israel" (v. 25 NRSV). When Mary and Joseph walk in the doors of the temple, the Spirit helps Simeon know he has found the right family, and Simeon takes the baby Jesus and blesses him.

But here's what I want to know. What did Simeon do after he spoke the blessing? After he realized that the family of God's own son was in financial need. Did he do something more for the family than *speak* a blessing? Did he do anything to *be* a blessing for them? Did he take them to a Subway restaurant to make sure they had dinner before they headed back to Nazareth?

I trust that anyone who was led by the Spirit as Simeon was would have done something to alleviate their immediate hardship. But Luke doesn't give us those details. So we have to figure out how to be blessings on our own.

NOTE: Adapted from "Be a Blessing," a sermon preached by Marci Auld Glass (http://marciglass.com/2008/12/28/be-a-blessing/).

Natalie Sims
http://lectionarysong.blogspot.com

Some New Christmas Carols for the Season:

"Sing Alleluia" (Francis Patrick O'Brien)—Excellent Christmas song that reflects the Magnificat and the happiness of Jesus' parents. The chorus would also work nicely on its own. Lyrics and sheet music sample (http://c1824532.cdn.cloudfiles.rackspacecloud.com/GC2_362-1.jpg); sound sample (http://c1824532.cdn.cloudfiles.rackspacecloud.com/GC2_362-1.mp3).

"Her Baby Newly Breathing" (Brian Wren)—Realistic words of Mary's motherhood of a real-life type of infant, to the familiar MERLE'S TUNE. The final verse sings of creating Wisdom "constricted into maleness, and of a woman born." Lyrics (http://campus.udayton.edu/mary/resources/music/mus_words/christma.htm; scroll down the page).

"Dream a Dream" (Shirley Murray)—Broad words of hope for the future of creation and the world's people. There are a number of possible tunes available. Sheet music sample (http://c1824532.cdn.cloudfiles.rackspacecloud.com/G6653rebox.jpg); sound sample (http://www.giamusic.com/product_search.cfm?criteria=6653&loc=hymnprint).

"He Came Down That We May Have Love" (Traditional Cameroon)—A simple, repetitive song. You can also use "joy, peace, hope" instead of only "love." Great for kids and for drumming; some translations have "Jesus came bringing us love." Sound and sheet music samples (http://hymnprint.net; search for Gather Comp. 2, #364).

"No Wind at the Window" (John Bell)—Wonderful words to the familiar Celtic tune COLUMCILLE that focus on Mary's decision to say yes to God. Very easy to sing. Lyrics (http://www.kristykarensmith.com/wind_window.htm); sound sample (http://c1824532.cdn.cloudfiles.rackspacecloud.com/GC2_768-1.mp3).

"Star-Child" (Shirley Murray)—This song is easy to sing and has beautiful lyrics, especially for Christmas Eve as it still has a sense of anticipation about it. Also available in Spanish. Lyrics (English and Spanish) and sheet music (http://c1824532.cdn.cloudfiles.rackspacecloud.com/OC_035-1.jpg).

Jesus Presented to Anna and Simeon (Luke 2:22-40)

"Now Let Your Servant Go" (Ruth Duck)—Excellent words from Ruth Duck present the *Nunc Dimittis* to a familiar chant tune (CONDITOR ALME SIDERUM). If you have a non-chanting congregation, just use the tune for "Creator of the Stars of Night," which is an adapted chant, and no-one will ever suspect that they were chanting. Sound sample (http://www.hymnprint.net; search Gather Comp. 2, #767).

"Now Bid Your Servant Go in Peace" (*Nunc Dimittis* translated by James Quinn, S.J.)—Familiar American folk tune (LAND OF REST). It could also be sung to the tune MORNING SONG ("Awake, awake to love and work")—just the first four lines of the tune.

"Let Your Servant Now Go in Peace / Nunc Dimittis" (Jacques Berthier)—Very simple and straightforward. Listen (http://www.youtube.com/watch?v=4vlaORJXLo8).

"Lord God You Now Have Set Your Servant Free" (Rae E. Whitney)—A very straightforward and traditional blessing. Sound sample (http://www.oremus.org/hymnal/1/1285.html).

"Holy One Now Let Your Servants" (Richard Bruxvoort-Colligan)—A nice sending out that picks up the song of Simeon. Lyrics and sound sample (http://www.worldmaking.net/holy-one-now-let-your.php).

John Wesley's Notes on the Bible
http://www.ccel.org/ccel/wesley/notes.txt

Luke 2:38

And the revival of the spirit of prophecy, together with the memorable occurrences relating to the birth of John the Baptist, and of Jesus, could not but encourage and quicken the expectation of pious persons at this time. Let the example of these aged saints animate those, whose hoary heads, like theirs, are a crown of glory, being found in the way of righteousness. Let those venerable lips, so soon to be silent in the grave, be now employed in the praises of their Redeemer. Let them labour to leave those behind, to whom Christ will be as precious as he has been to them; and who will be waiting for God's salvation, when they are gone to enjoy it.

John Petty
http://progressiveinvolvement.com

Luke 2

Joseph and Mary are presented as religiously devout. Joseph is taking Mary and the baby Jesus to the temple for "their purification" (v. 22 NRSV). Strictly speaking, the purification ritual was for Mary only. The purification of the new mother occurred forty days after the birth of a male child, and eighty days after the birth of a female child. The firstborn male didn't need to be purified. He was to be dedicated to the Lord, which could be had for the price of five shekels.

Thus, Luke is either wrong about a ritual of Israel, or he is making a point. Let's pick the latter. The phrase "their purification" is a reference to Jesus' solidarity with humanity. The Christ Child doesn't need to be "purified," but he's "purified" anyway, a sign that he stands with the people.

Readers will note the combination of temple, religious ritual, the power of the Spirit, and the "law of the Lord" (v. 23 NRSV). The Spirit is mentioned three times, and "the law" five. The text is palpably Judaic, yet notice that for Luke, Spirit and temple are not opposed. The religion of Israel is still vital and capable of bringing renewal and inspiring devotion.

Luke is careful, however, to avoid priests. Simeon is not identified as a priest. He may, in fact, be a layperson, while Anna is identified as a prophet. The people and traditions of Israel are seen positively by Luke, but priests and scribes are not.

Both Simeon and Anna are "looking forward with confidence" (*prosdexomai*). Simeon is "looking forward" for the "comfort" or "consolation" of Israel (v. 25 NRSV). Anna is also "looking forward," but she is looking for something slightly different. She's looking for *lutrosin* ("ransom, redemption, the end of obligation") (v. 38). These two concepts—related, but slightly different—are found together in Isaiah 52:9 (NRSV): "for the LORD has comforted his people, / he has redeemed Jerusalem."

The clear message of Luke, then, is that the "comfort" and "redemption" of Jerusalem—the prophetic tradition of Isaiah—is fulfilled in the Christ Child.

Luke goes on to note the opposition that Jesus will meet. The rest of Simeon's oracle has had many interpretations. This much can be said: The reference to "sword" strikes a note of violence, as later events will prove. The "sword" appears directed, however, to the inner life—"the thoughts of many hearts" (v. 35 NLT). Luke indicates inner turmoil. Everything will be revealed. It will be painful, though not fatal. Human resistance will not thwart God's saving purpose.

All the characters represent parts of the tradition. Elizabeth represents Hannah, the mother of the prophet Samuel. (Zechariah represents clueless priests, also part of the tradition.) Anna represents not only the prophetic tradition but also its capacity for renewal and ability to do, as Isaiah said, "a new thing"—for the "prophet Anna" is a woman. Simeon represents Israel's long wait for the Messiah. Having seen the Messiah, Simeon may now die in peace. His song brings to a climax the infancy narrative of Luke.

Mary J. Scifres

Rejoicing in the Christmas Gift of God's Presence and Steadfast Love (Luke 2)

Simeon leads us in the celebration of Christmas, rejoicing that he has finally seen the world's salvation, the presence of God in our very midst. This is a Sunday to celebrate God's presence, for we are children of God's light—a light that shines on all people and all nations. Rejoice greatly, for we are clothed in salvation and love. All the earth rejoices with us, for Christ's presence upon this earth and God's gift of steadfast love is for all of creation.

Simeon is the personification of the Advent promise fulfilled. For years and decades for God's Messiah to appear: he waited; he trusted; he hoped; he prayed; he believed. And when the promise was revealed in the child Jesus, Simeon rejoiced.

Over these past weeks, we too have been invited to wait with trust, hope, love, and faith. Today, we celebrate with joy, for God's promised salvation has come. Christ is born. Christ is alive. Christ lives in the hearts and love of every person who celebrates this glorious season of light and life. Rejoice greatly, for the child is growing in stature and wisdom in all who walk with Christ.

Mike Lowry

Pause or Prelude? (Luke 2)

Welcome to "low Sunday." Historically the Sunday after Christmas is the lowest attended worship service of the year. It is a time to pause after the celebrations of Christmas are done. Or is it? Luke thinks this is a prelude of things to come.

Mary and Joseph do what good Jewish parents do. They present their newborn child in the temple for circumcision and the ritual of purification in accordance with the Mosaic Law (Luke mentions no less than five times that they kept the Law)—no shortcut, only faithful obedience. They are both model and map for raising our own children.

In the temple, a "righteous and devout" (v. 25) man named Simeon accosts them. To understand the passage best, the exegete needs to step into the scene. Young, nervous, and maybe scared parents interact with a crazy old man. Holding the child, Simeon completes Mary's Magnificat (Luke 1:46-55): "Now, master, let your servant go in peace according to your word, / because my eyes have seen your salvation. / . . . a light for revelation to the Gentiles. . . . This boy is assigned to be the cause of the falling and rising of many in Israel" (vv. 29-30, 32, 34).

The blessing comes from the leading of the Holy Spirit, and praise is the only appropriate response. On this Sunday after the Savior's birth, praise in awe is our best response as well.

Only one other person sees the drama of God at work. An old prophetess named Anna gives thanks to God and offers her witness, speaking "about Jesus to everyone who was looking forward to the redemption of Jerusalem" (v. 38). Just as this time after Christmas demands that we pause, it also gives us a prelude to what will come. There is a new Master in town! This is the one we have been looking for!

Pause to reflect. Embrace Mary and Joseph as models of faithfulness. Offer praise; the Christmas story is not over. This is the prelude. Give witness to the Lord! Share Jesus' name, will, and way with all.

Julia Seymour
http://lutheranjulia.blogspot.com

Luke 2

How long shall I wait, O Lord, for your return?
I am not certain that I have the patience of Anna,
That I can continue in prayer through pain for eighty-four years.
Test me not in that way, for I will certainly fail.
You are coming, but when?

How long shall I wait, O Lord, for the fulfillment of prophecy?
I worry that I do not have the faith of Simeon,
A constant vigil keeping eyes open for your work,
A lifted hand ready to point to your grace.
You are coming, but

How long shall I wait, O Lord, for a judgment?
I may not have the heart of Mary, to act while pondering.
I wrestle with your word, while your Spirit breathes on my neck
Trying to move me, but I swat away the stream and look for another verse.
You are coming,

How long shall I wait, O God, for an established kingdom?
I might lack the courage of Joseph, who dared
to take up the fatherhood of the Son with grace.
Intimidated by your call, I wait for a second sign that
You are

How long shall I wait, O God, for you to keep promises?
This story of patient people's joy in Jesus is uplifting, but
Would You do it over? Would You do it again?
Entering into the created world as a child is so hopeful. It is just so
You.

Online Media and Other Helpful Resources

(Please check at each site for copyright restrictions)

Activity Sheets for Children

http://www.ucc.org/children/fun-page/activity-sheets-for-children.html—Weekly activity sheets from the United Church of Christ.

Activity Sheets for Younger Children and Older Children

http://homiliesbyemail.com/activity-sheets.html—Free weekly activity sheets from Homilies by E-mail.

Agnus Day

http://www.agnusday.org/—The weekly lectionary cartoon by Pastor James Wetzstein, with archives and indexes.

Art in the Christian Tradition, Vanderbilt's Jean and Alexander Heard Divinity Library

http://diglib.library.vanderbilt.edu/act-search.pl—Classical and contemporary images with attributions.

Bulletin Covers

http://www.scholia.net/bulletins.htm—.doc file bulletin covers using line drawings and scripture readings from Our Redeemer Lutheran Church in Emmett, Idaho.

Christian Reflection from Baylor University, The Center for Christian Ethics

http://www.baylor.edu/christianethics/index.php?id=14715—A site that includes excellent adult study resources, articles, and media resources based on theme. Issues are indexed into the lectionary cycle at www.textweek.com.

Faith Element

http://www.faithelement.com/—A Bible study curriculum for youth and adults which includes images and movie clips.

Faith Lens

http://blogs.elca.org/faithlens/—From the Evangelical Lutheran Church in America, Faith Lens contains weekly conversations with youth about contemporary issues, including videos and images. Available from September to May.

Hermanoleon Clipart

http://www.cruzblanca.org/hermanoleon/—Free clipart for church bulletins, etc.

Hymnary.org

http://www.hymnary.org/—A comprehensive index of 1,181,339 hymns from 5,465 hymnals. Includes scores, media, and information.

ON Scripture, Odyssey Networks

http://odysseynetworks.org/on-scripture—Weekly commentaries by various authors relate contemporary issues and scriptural themes. These articles include videos of contemporary events.

Oremus Hymnal

http://oremus.org/hymnal/—Traditional and original hymns based on the weekly lectionary texts. Includes sound files.

Pitts Theological Library Digital Image Archive Lectionary Index

http://pitts.emory.edu/dia/elca_lectionary.html—Many images from the Kessler Reformation Collection.

Scripture Pics

http://www.scripturepics.org/—Free PowerPoint backgrounds.

Sermon Brainwave

http://www.workingpreacher.org/brainwave.aspx—Excellent podcast discussion of weekly scriptures by faculty at Luther Seminary. Found at WorkingPreacher.org, an excellent resource for preaching.

Sermons 4 Kids

http://www.sermons4kids.com/—Weekly coloring pages, puzzles, games, songs, and children's ideas in English and Spanish by Charles Kirkpatrick.

Sing for Joy

http://www.stolaf.edu/singforjoy/—Radio broadcasts of lectionary-related music from St. Olaf College in Northfield, Minnesota.

Together to Celebrate

http://www.togethertocelebrate.com.au/—A resource for contemporary worship music by David MacGregor. Here you'll find original material plus information for finding contemporary music resources for each lectionary week.

Visual Theology by Dave Perry

http://visualtheology.blogspot.com/—Lectionary-themed photography.

Commercial Sites

Church Galleries

http://www.churchgalleries.com/—PowerPoint backgrounds and other images by/from Dorothy Okray. Images are for purchase along with free weekly samples.

Jan Richardson Images

http://www.janrichardsonimages.com/—My favorite contemporary art site. Jan creates new images each week. Images and subscriptions available for purchase.

Ministry Matters

http://www.ministrymatters.com/—An excellent resource for preaching, teaching, worship, evangelism, and leadership in the church. Available by subscription, with free weekly samples of worship resources.

The Work of the People

http://www.theworkofthepeople.com/index.php?ct=site.home—Excellent scripture-based videos, available for purchase individually or by subscription.

Conversation Partners Index

Chuck Aaron

Charles Aaron serves as pastor of Whaley UMC in Gainesville, Texas. He tries to balance parish ministry with scholarship, writing, and participating actively in the Society of Biblical Literature. He has pastored churches in Texas, Tennessee, North Carolina, and Virginia. He has written or edited four books, and published several articles and sermons. He has taught courses in Bible and preaching at Duke, SMU, Austin Seminary, and Union Presbyterian Seminary.

Find Chuck's contributions in March 5, March 9, March 16, March 23, March 30, April 6.

Eric D. Barreto

Eric D. Barreto is Assistant Professor of New Testament at Luther Seminary in St. Paul, Minnesota, and an ordained Baptist minister. The author of *Ethnic Negotiations: The Function of Race and Ethnicity in Acts 16* (Mohr Siebeck, 2010), he is also a regular contributor to ONScripture.org, the Huffington Post, Working Preacher.org, and EntertheBible.org.

Find Eric's contributions in April 13, April 17, April 18, October 5, October 12, October 19.

Paul Bellan-Boyer

Paul Bellan-Boyer is a member of St. Matthew's Lutheran Church (ELCA) in Jersey City, N. J., where he runs a special needs housing program for Garden State Episcopal CDC. Paul is actively involved in community organizing locally and statewide, leading successful campaigns in housing reform and community health care. He continues to be involved in 9/11-related ministry, where he served as a chaplain. Paul blogs at citycalledheaven.org.

Find Paul's contributions in April 20, April 27, May 4, September 14, September 21, September 28.

Sharron Blezard

The Rev. Sharron Blezard is an ELCA pastor who serves Trinity Evangelical Lutheran Church in Rouzerville, Pennsylvania. Also a freelance writer, editor, and college writing instructor, Sharron is married to the Rev. Robert Blezard. Between them they have four children ages 13-24. Sharron's interests include film, fiction, poetry, and the interplay of spirituality and the arts. She blogs at www.adventuresinthanksliving.com and writes a weekly lectionary reflection for stewardshipoflife.org.

Find Sharron's contributions in June 1, June 8, June 15, October 5, October 12, October 19.

Daniel B. Clendenin

http://journeywithjesus.net

Daniel B. Clendenin (PhD) was a professor of theological studies in Michigan and Moscow (Russia) for ten years, then a campus minister at Stanford University for eight years. In 2004 he founded a weekly webzine for the global church called Journey with Jesus. He was raised in the Presbyterian Church (USA) and today worships in an Episcopal Church near his home in Palo Alto, California.

Find Dan's contributions in January 19, February 9, March 2, April 27, May 11, May 18, June 8, July 20, August 10, September 7, October 26, November 30, December 21.

Julie Craig

http://winsomelearnsome.com

Julie Craig is a writer, speaker, and pastor living in Wisconsin. She is an ordained minister in the Presbyterian Church (USA) and has served in the local and synod level. She currently lives in the suburbs with her spouse while their adult children manage just fine without them in far-flung places. A reluctant dog walker, failed knitter, and capricious reader, she is fueled by strong coffee, deep laughter, and really cute shoes.

Find Julie's contributions in January 26, February 16, March 5, April 18, May 18, June 15, July 27, August 17, September 14, October 5, November 23, December 14.

Liz Crumlish

http://somethingtostandon.blogspot.co.uk/

Liz Crumlish is a Church of Scotland minister, working in Ayr, on the west coast of Scotland. She LOVES *The Vicar of Dibley* (BBC) and aspires to be like her, teaching the gospel while having fun—that presents challenges for a Scottish Presbyterian! Liz's passion in life is to discern the presence of God in everything and, along the way, to reveal that presence for others.

Find Liz's contributions in January 26, February 16, March 5, April 18, May 18, June 15, July 27, August 17, September 14, October 5, November 23, December 14.

Barbara Dick

Barbara works as a freelance editor for Abingdon Press and other religious publishers. Her editing projects include *The Wesley Study Bible* (project coordinator) and *Newscope* (managing editor), along with a wide variety of preaching, leadership, and worship resources. Barbara serves as facilitator of the Spiritual Formation Resource Team for the Wisconsin Annual Conference (of The United Methodist Church).

Find Barbara's contributions in March 9 and April 27.

Dan R. Dick

Dan Dick is a pastor serving as the Director of Connectional Ministries in the Wisconsin Annual Conference (of The United Methodist Church). Dan has a passion and love for the church, working for over thirty years in spiritual formation, leadership development, spiritual giftedness, stewardship, planning, evangelism, and outreach. He has authored (or co-authored) fifteen books and hundreds of articles. Dan's thoughts on the church and other topics are reflected in his blog, United Methodeviations (http://doroteos2.wordpress.com).

Find Dan's contributions in November 30, December 7, December 14, December 21, December 24-25, December 28.

Paul Escamilla

The Rev. Dr. Paul L. Escamilla is pastor of St. John's United Methodist Church in Austin, Texas (www.stjohnsaustin.org). He has served six congregations in Texas and taught preaching, worship, and administrative leadership at Perkins School of Theology, SMU. His writings include *Seasons of Communion, Longing for Enough in a Culture of More,* and *True When Whispered*. He has contributed to *The Wesley Study Bible, At Home with God,* and numerous other publications.

Find Paul's contributions in May 11, May 18, May 25, November 16, November 23, November 27.

Safiyah Fosua

Dr. Safiyah Fosua is the assistant professor of Congregational Worship at Wesley Seminary of Indiana Wesleyan University. She is a former director of transformational preaching at the General Board of Discipleship (The United Methodist Church). Safiyah has written several Bible study and devotional books, served as associate editor for Discipleship Resources' *Africana Worship Book* series, contributed to several commentaries and preaching anthologies, and is a columnist for WorkingPreacher.org. Safiyah is married to Kwasi Kena, who also teaches at Wesley Seminary at IWU.

Find Safiyah's contributions in July 13, July 20, July 27, August 3, August 10, August 17.

Carolyn Winfrey Gillette

http://www.carolynshymns.com/

Carolyn Winfrey Gillette is the author of *Songs of Grace: New Hymns for God and Neighbor* (Upper Room Books) and *Gifts of Love: New Hymns for Today's Worship* (Geneva Press). She and her husband, Bruce, are the co-pastors of Limestone Presbyterian Church in Wilmington, Delaware. She is the mother of John, Catherine, and Sarah.

Find Carolyn's contributions in January 12, February 9, March 9, April 20, April 27, June 8, June 29, July 20, August 31, September 14, October 12, November 16, November 27, December 7.

Marci Auld Glass

http://www.marciglass.com

The Rev. Marci Auld Glass is the pastor of Southminster Presbyterian Church in Boise, Idaho. She and her husband, Justin, have two sons, Alden and Elliott. She is soon to be the shortest person in her family. Marci is a professional espresso drinker, labyrinth walker, lapsed cellist, and probably a future "cat lady," and voluntarily listens to opera.

Find Marci's contributions in January 26, February 23, March 16, April 20, May 25, June 29, July 27, August 24, September 28, October 26, November 30, December 28.

Lowell E. Grisham

http://lowellsblog.blogspot.com/

The Rev. Lowell Grisham is Rector of St. Paul's Episcopal Church in Fayetteville, Arkansas. He is working to complete a three-year cycle of Prayers of the People. Lowell is involved in several social justice ministries and writes a local newspaper column. He has special interests in congregational development and contemplative prayer. Lowell's blog is also picked up four days a week by EpiscopalCafe.com on their Speaking to the Soul blog.

He's a native of Mississippi. He and his wife, Kathy, have two children and two grandchildren.

Find Lowell's contributions in January 12, February 2, March 23, April 13, May 4, June 1, July 13, August 3, September 28, October 19, November 9, December 24.

Suzanne Guthrie

http:www.edgeofenclosure.org

Suzanne Guthrie is an Episcopal priest, writer, and retreat leader. She and her husband, Bill, live with the sisters of The Community of the Holy Spirit, a women's religious order in the Episcopal Church on their organic farm in Brewster, New York. Suzanne has served the church as a pastor, children's priest, college and university chaplain. She creates Soulwork Toward Sunday: self-guided retreats based upon the coming Sunday's Gospel at http://www.EdgeOfEnclosure.org.

Find Suzanne's contributions in January 19, February 9, March 2, March 16, April 17, May 11, June 8, July 20, August 10, September 7, October 26, November 16, December 21.

Cameron Howard

Cameron B. R. Howard is assistant professor of Old Testament at Luther Seminary in St. Paul, Minnesota, and a member of the Presbyterian Church (U.S.A.). Among her publications are contributions to *The New Interpreter's*

Bible One-Volume Commentary, published by Abingdon Press, and the twentieth-anniversary edition of the *Women's Bible Commentary,* published by Westminster John Knox Press.

Find Cameron's contributions in July 13, July 20, July 27, August 3, August 10, August 17.

Karoline Lewis

Karoline M. Lewis (www.karolinelewis.com) is the Alvin N. Rogness Chair of Homiletics at Luther Seminary in St. Paul, MN and is an ordained pastor in the Evangelical Lutheran Church of America. She holds degrees from Northwestern University, Luther Seminary, and a Ph.D. in New Testament Studies from Emory University, Atlanta. A contributing writer for www.workingpreacher.org, she is also co-host of the site's weekly podcast, Sermon Brainwave.

Find Karoline's contributions in January 5, January 12, January 19, September 14, September 21, September 28.

David Lose

David Lose is the author of the popular books *Making Sense of Scripture, Making Sense of the Christian Faith,* and *Making Sense of the Cross.* You can find his writing on faith and life at his blog "…In the Meantime" (www.davidlose.net). David is the Director of the Center for Biblical Preaching at Luther Seminary, where he led the creative team that developed WorkingPreacher.org.

Find David's contributions in May 11, May 18, May 25, August 24, August 31, September 7.

J. Michael Lowry

J. Michael (Mike) Lowry was elected to the episcopacy in July of 2008 and assigned to the Fort Worth Episcopal Area, and has served as the president of the South Central Jurisdiction College of Bishops, chair of the Board of Ordained Ministry, chair of the Board of Global Ministries' Committee on Church Extension, and chair of the Council on Church Revitalization and Church Extension. Bishop Lowry serves the larger connection of The United Methodist Church as a member of the Texas Methodist Foundation Board, The United Methodist Publishing House Board of Directors, Trustee for Southwestern University and Texas Wesleyan University, the Methodist Children's Home, and Harris Methodist Hospital Board among others.

Find Mike's contributions in April 6, November 30, December 28.

Rick Morley

Rick Morley is a priest in the Episcopal Church and serves as rector of St. Mark's Episcopal Church in Basking Ridge, New Jersey. Rick has been married to Karen for over 11 years, and they have two daughters, Zoe and Mattie. They live in downtown Basking Ridge, and love the small-town, tight-knit feel of the community, and the proximity to the Big City. Rick's personal website and blog,s http://www.rickmorley.com/, features some of his writing, thoughts, and photography.

Find Rick's contributions in January 5, January 12, January 19, June 22, June 29, July 6.

Paul Nuechterlein

http://girardianlectionary.net/

Paul is the senior pastor of Prince of Peace Lutheran Church in Portage, Michigan. "My take on the Bible thus begins with this question: If there is a creative, nonviolent God trying to break through our idolatry, what would that true God have to do?… (1) Make a covenant with someone with whom to interact as a covenant people over many centuries…. (2) …send a faithful Messiah to embody the identity of the loving God as one whose truth would necessarily need to suffer our untruth as death, as a victim of sacred violence. (3) …intervene with Resurrection, raising the Victim as forgiveness, in order for a beach-head of Truth to be established in history forever."

Find Paul's contributions in January 19, February 16, March 9, April 20, June 15, June 29, July 13, August 31, September 21, October 19, November 9, November 27, December 7.

Amy Persons Parkes

Amy Persons Parkes, an ordained elder in The United Methodist Church, serves as a minister in the United Church of Canada. As transplanted Southerners, Amy and her family live in the Toronto area. Her passion is in the area of faith development and spiritual formation; and with some bits of intentionality and much grace, Amy tries to grow beautiful flowers, to keep clean clothes in the closets, and to be open to God's Spirit.

Find Amy's contributions in April 13, April 17, April 18, October 26, November 2, November 9.

Teri Peterson

http://clevertitlehere.blogspot.com

Teri Peterson is a Presbyterian pastor in the suburbs. She holds a degree in clarinet performance from DePaul University and an MDiv from Columbia Theological Seminary. She enjoys exploring new cities, being a bit of a music snob, writing, and coming up with creative ideas for worship. Teri co-authored *And Then We Just Got Really Busy: Spirituality for a New Generation* (Chalice, 2013) and founded and contributes to www.liturgylink.net as well as her own blog, clevertitlehere.blogspot.com. Teri is a great lover of farmer's markets, reading, snuggling with kitties, and any TV show made by Joss Whedon.

Find Teri's contributions in January 5, February 23, March 5, April 6, May 25, June 22, July 6, August 24, September 21, October 12, November 2, December 14.

John Petty

http://progressiveinvolvement.com

John Petty has been a Lutheran pastor for twenty-five years. He is a graduate of Wartburg Theological Seminary in Dubuque, Iowa, and serves as pastor of All Saints Lutheran Church in Aurora, Colorado. John has been active in Habitat for Humanity since the early 1980s and currently serves on the board of Habitat Metro Denver. He serves as ecumenical representative for the Rocky Mountain Synod of the Evangelical Lutheran Church in America, and chair of the Unity Commission of the Colorado Council of Churches.

Find John's contributions in January 5, February 23, March 16, April 6, May 25, June 22, July 6, August 24, September 21, October 12, November 2, November 27, December 28.

Beth Quick

http://bethquick.blogspot.com

Beth is a United Methodist pastor serving Liverpool First United Methodist Church, near Syracuse, New York. She is currently working on a Doctor of Ministry at Methodist Theological School in Ohio, focusing on Leadership for Transformational Change. Beth is passionate about social justice issues, particularly in the areas of environmental, economic, and racial justice.

Find Beth's contributions in January 12, February 2, March 23, April 13, May 4, June 1, July 13, August 3, September 28, October 19, November 9, December 24.

Kathryn Schifferdecker

Kathryn Schifferdecker is Associate Professor of Old Testament at Luther Seminary in St. Paul, Minnesota. She is an ordained pastor in the Evangelical Lutheran Church in America, having served rural parishes in Iowa and Wisconsin. She is the author of *Out of the Whirlwind: Creation Theology in the Book of Job* (Harvard, 2008), and she is currently working on a commentary on the book of Esther. Kathryn is a regular contributor to workingpreacher.org and enter thebible.org.

Find Kathryn's contributions in January 26, February 2, February 9, June 22, June 29, July 6.

Mary J. Scifres

A graduate of Boston University and the University of Indianapolis, Mary is a United Methodist pastor in Laguna Beach, California. The Rev. Scifres's writings include *The Abingdon Worship Annual, The United Methodist Music and Worship Planner, Prepare, Searching for Seekers,* and *Just in Time! Special Services.* As a consultant and teacher in leadership and worship, Mary hosts workshops at her Top of the World Retreat, with her UCC clergy-spouse B. J. Beu. Learn more at www.maryscifres.com.

Find Mary's contributions in November 30, December 7, December 14, December 21, December 24/25, December 28.

Ann Scull

http://seedstuff.blogspot.com

Ann is married to Joe and they have two great kids—Jared and Kate. Ann is an ordained Minister of the Word in parish ministry in the Uniting Church in Australia. She has a passion for contemporary worship (whatever that means) and has set up her blog in order to share resources that she finds interesting and exciting.

Find Ann's contributions in January 19, February 9, March 2, April 17, May 11, June 8, July 20, August 10, September 7, October 26, November 16, December 21.

Melissa Bane Sevier

http://melissabanesevier.wordpress.com

Melissa Bane Sevier is a pastor, writer, and photographer in Kentucky. In addition to her blog, check out her writing services business at http://www.mbswriting.com/. When not working at Versaille Presbyterian Church or writing, or leading the occasional retreat, she may be cooking, gardening, hiking, canoeing, or jogging. Eating supper with her husband on the porch as the sun goes down is one of her favorite ways to let go of the day.

Find Melissa's contributions in January 12, February 2, March 23, April 27, May 4, June 1, July 13, August 3, September 28, October 19, November 9, November 30, December 24/25.

Julia Seymour

http://lutheranjulia.blogspot.com

Julia Seymour currently serves as pastor of the Lutheran Church of Hope in Anchorage, Alaska. Ordained in the Evangelical Lutheran Church in America (ELCA), Seymour enjoys reading, gardening, and fishing in the oodles of spare time that comes with being solo clergy. Regarding living in and loving Alaska, Seymour says winter is never as bad as you expect and summer is never as long as you hope.

Find Julia's contributions in January 5, February 23, March 16, April 6, April 20, May 25, June 22, July 6, August 24, September 21, October 12, November 2, December 28.

Thom M. Shuman

http://lectionaryliturgies.blogspot.com/

Thom M. Shuman is a Presbyterian Church (USA) pastor and poet whose lectionary-based liturgies are used throughout the world. These include the Advent devotionals, *The Jesse Tree* and *Gobsmacked* (Wild Goose Publications) and his contributions to worship resources of the Iona Community. Thom is currently involved in transitional (interim) ministry and always on the lookout for new challenges and positions, especially in or near Columbus, Ohio.

Find Thom's contributions in January 5, February 2, March 9, March 30, April 20, June 1, June 29, July 6, August 31, September 7, October 5, November 2, November 27, December 7.

Natalie Ann Sims

http://lectionarysong.blogspot.com

Natalie Sims is a laywoman, and one of a number of volunteer musicians and liturgists at Brunswick Uniting Church in Melbourne, Australia. Reading, playing, and singing church music provide respite from her work as a medical research scientist. Her blog began as a weekly e-mail to three Uniting Church ministers who wanted help choosing songs for their congregations.

Find Natalie's contributions in January 5, February 23, March 16, March 30, April 6, May 25, June 22, July 6, August 24, September 21, October 12, November 2, December 28.

Matthew L. Skinner

Matt Skinner is Associate Professor of New Testament at Luther Seminary (Saint Paul, Minnesota). Ordained as a teaching elder in the Presbyterian Church (USA), he co-hosts the weekly *Sermon Brainwave* podcasts on Working Preacher.org, is a contributing editor of the resource *ON Scripture—The Bible* published online each Wednesday by Odyssey Networks, and blogs occasionally for the Huffington Post's religion page. For more of his writings about biblical texts and preaching, visit MatthewSkinner.org.

Find Matt's contributions in February 16, February 23, March 2, June 1, June 8, June 15.

Martha Spong

http://marthaspong.com/

I'm a United Church of Christ pastor, a longtime blogger, a practicing poet, and an incessant knitter. I'm a proud founder of RevGalBlogPals (http://revgalblogpals.blogspot.com/), created to provide support to women in ordained ministry. I've raised three children in a house full of books, music, cats, and dogs. My next adventure promises more of the same, now with my Beloved and her 8-year-old.

Find Martha's contributions in January 12, February 2, March 23, March 30, April 13, May 4, June 1, July 13, August 3, September 28, October 19, November 9, December 24/25.

Mark Stamm

Mark W. Stamm is Professor of Christian Worship at Perkins School of Theology, Southern Methodist University in Dallas, Texas. He came to Perkins in July 2000 after serving seventeen years as a pastor of United Methodist congregations in Pennsylvania and Kentucky. As Director of Community Worship for Perkins, he gives oversight to the school's chapel program. He is also known for organizing trips to baseball games.

Find Mark's contributions in April 20, April 27, May 4, November 16, November 23, November 27.

John van de Laar

http://www.sacredise.com/

John van de Laar is a Methodist minister and the founding director of Sacredise.com, a liturgical training and publishing ministry. He holds a Masters degree in Theology and is the author of *The Hour That Changes Everything: How Worship Forms Us into the People God Wants Us to Be.* John lives in Cape Town, South Africa, with his wife, Debbie (also a minister); they have two sons.

Find John's contributions in January 19, February 9, March 2, March 30, April 17, May 11, June 8, July 20, August 10, September 7, October 26, November 16, December 21.

Todd Weir

http://bloomingcactus.typepad.com/

Todd Weir is the pastor at First Churches (UCC/ABC) in Northampton, Massachusetts; where Jonathan Edwards preached during the Great Awakening (see www.firstchurches.org). Todd operated an emergency shelter and transitional housing for homeless people for eight years in Poughkeepsie, New York. He has a Master's degree in psychology, focusing on mindfulness-based therapies. Todd is interested in spiritual practices, socially responsible investing, and ballroom and Latin dancing.

Find Todd's contributions in January 26, February 16, March 5, March 30, April 18, May 18, July 27, August 17, August 24, September 14, October 5, November 23, December 14.

John Wesley

An Anglican priest and theologian (1703–1791), John Wesley was one of the founders of the Methodist movement. His *Explanatory Notes on the Bible, Journals,* and published *Sermons* all offer rich insights into his evolving theology of grace. Wesley drew from a broad array of theological sources and thinking, encouraging an active life of intentional faith development through both devotion and action for individuals and communities.

Find John's contributions throughout the Annual.

Jenee Woodard (editor)

http://www.textweek.com/

Jenee is the creator and curator of the major lectionary study website "The Text This Week." She is a 1984 graduate of Saint Paul School of Theology in Kansas City; and a 1980 graduate of Augustana College (ELCA) in Sioux Falls, South Dakota. Jenee is Mama to two children. Jaie is a PhD student in biophysics at Harvard. Phil, diagnosed with severe autism when he was two years old, works part-time at Michigan Public Schools and the Geek Squad at Best Buy. The financial, physical, and emotional energy required for Phil's care precluded further career plans for Jenee. She started The Text This Week in 1998 as a means of observing diverse and informed voices in conversation about the lectionary, linking scholars and storytellers from across the theological and ecumenical spectrum.

Peter Woods

Peter Woods is a Methodist minister recently retired after thirty years of pastoral preaching ministry in mainly urban congregations. He is passionate about making the gospel understandable to people inside and outside the church. Peter pursues this as a Lectionary blogger at The Listening Hermit (http://thelisteninghermit.wordpress.com/), and as Spirituality columnist for the *Weekend Post*. He lives in the Eastern Cape Province of South Africa.

Find Peter's contributions in January 26, February 2, February 9, August 24, August 31, September 7.